International Technical S

**IBM @server Certificatic
pSeries AIX System Adm** ..ɔn

December 2001

SG24-6191-00

First Edition (December 2001)

This edition applies to AIX 5L for POWER Version 5.1, program number 5765-E61 and subsequent releases running on an RS/6000 or pSeries server and is based on information available in October 2001.

Comments may be addressed to:
IBM Corporation, International Technical Support Organization
Dept. JN9B Building 003 Internal Zip 2834
11400 Burnet Road
Austin, Texas 78758-3493

Contents

Figures

Tables

Preface

The AIX and IBM pSeries @server Certifications offered through the Professional Certification Program from IBM, are designed to validate the skills required of technical professionals who work in the powerful and often complex environments of AIX and IBM @server pSeries. A complete set of professional certifications are available. They include:

- ► IBM Certified AIX User
- ► IBM Certified Specialist - AIX System Administration
- ► IBM Certified Specialist - AIX System Support
- ► IBM Certified Specialist - Business Intelligence for RS/6000
- ► IBM Certified Specialist - Domino for RS/6000
- ► IBM @server Certified Specialist - pSeries AIX System Administration
- ► IBM @server Certified Specialist - pSeries AIX System Support
- ► IBM @server Certified Specialist - pSeries Solution Sales
- ► IBM Certified Specialist - RS/6000 Solution Sales
- ► IBM Certified Specialist - RS/6000 SP and PSSP V3
- ► RS/6000 SP - Sales Qualification
- ► IBM Certified Specialist - Web Server for RS/6000
- ► IBM @server Certified Specialist - pSeries HACMP for AIX
- ► IBM Certified Advanced Technical Expert - RS/6000 AIX

Each certification is developed by following a thorough and rigorous process to ensure the exam is applicable to the job role, and is a meaningful and appropriate assessment of skill. Subject Matter Experts who successfully perform the job, participate throughout the entire development process. These job incumbents bring a wealth of experience into the development process, thus, making the exams much more meaningful than the typical test, which only captures classroom knowledge. These experienced Subject Matter Experts ensure the exams are relevant to the real world and that the test content is both useful and valid. The result is a certification of value, which appropriately measures the skills required to perform the job role.

This redbook is designed as a study guide for professionals wishing to prepare for the certification exam to achieve: IBM @server Certified Specialist - pSeries AIX System Administration.

The system administration certification validates a broad scope of AIX administration skills and the ability to perform general AIX software system maintenance. The certification is applicable to AIX administration professionals who conduct the AIX problem determination and resolution activities needed to successfully support customers, or clients, in an AIX environment, to maintain system reliability.

This redbook helps AIX administrators seeking a comprehensive and task-oriented guide for developing the knowledge and skills required for the certification. It is designed to provide a combination of theory and practical experience needed for a general understanding of the subject matter. It also provides sample questions that will help in the evaluation of personal progress and provide familiarity with the types of questions that will be encountered in the exam.

This redbook does not replace practical experience you should have, but is an effective tool that, when combined with education activities and experience, should prove to be a very useful preparation guide for the exam. Due to the practical nature of the certification content, this publication can also be used as a desk-side reference. So, whether you are planning to take the pSeries AIX System Administration certification exam, or if you just want to validate your AIX system administration skills, this redbook is for you.

For additional information about certification and instructions on How to Register for an exam, visit our Web site at:

```
http://www.ibm.com/certify
```

The team that wrote this redbook

This redbook was produced by a team of specialists from around the world working at the International Technical Support Organization, Austin Center.

Christian Pruett is an RS/6000 and IBM @server pSeries IT Specialist at IBM Global Services in Boulder, Colorado. He has been working for IBM since July 1999. He has a Bachelor's degree in History from Colorado State University. He is an IBM @server Certified Specialist in pSeries AIX System Administration and pSeries AIX System Support. His areas of expertise include RS/6000 and IBM @server pSeries systems, RS/6000 and IBM @server pSeries hardware, and AIX installation and system recovery. Currently, he is an account lead for the AIX Standalone Support team at the IGS NA West GeoPlex Center.

Kristian Strickland is a System Support Specialist in Moncton, New Brunswick, for Co-op Atlantic, a dynamic Atlantic Canadian co-operative wholesaler. He has been involved professionally in system administration and support since 1995. He holds a Bachelor of Science degree in Math and Computer Science from St. Francis Xavier University, and is an IBM @server Certified Specialist in pSeries AIX System Administration and pSeries AIX System Support. His areas of expertise include AIX and Compaq's OpenVMS operating systems.

Thanks to the following people for their contributions to this project:

International Technical Support Organization, Austin Center
Wade Wallace

IBM Texas and Atlanta
Darin Hartman and Shannan L. DeBrule

IBM Germany
Volker Haug

Special notice

This publication is intended to help IBM business partners, technical professionals, and customers of IBM prepare for the pSeries AIX System Administration exam as part of the IBM @server Certified Specialist program. The information in this publication is not intended as the specification of any programming interfaces that are provided by AIX 5L Version 5.1. See the PUBLICATIONS section of the IBM Programming Announcement for AIX 5L Version 5.1 for more information about what publications are considered to be product documentation.

IBM trademarks

The following terms are trademarks of the International Business Machines Corporation in the United States and/or other countries:

AFP™	AIX®
AIX 5L™	AIXwindows®
DFS™	Domino™
e (logo)® @	HACMP/6000™
IBM.COM™	IBM ®
Language Environment®	Micro Channel®
Perform™	PowerPC®
PowerPC Reference Platform®	pSeries™
PTX®	Redbooks™
Redbooks Logo	RISC System/6000®
RS/6000®	Sequent®
SP™	Versatile Storage Server™

Comments welcome

Your comments are important to us!

We want our IBM Redbooks to be as helpful as possible. Send us your comments about this or other Redbooks in one of the following ways:

► Use the online **Contact us** review redbook form found at:

  ibm.com/redbooks

► Send your comments in an Internet note to:

  redbook@us.ibm.com

► Mail your comments to the address on page ii.

Certification overview

This chapter provides an overview of the skill requirements for obtaining an IBM @server Certified Specialist - pSeries AIX System Administration certification. The following chapters are designed to provide a comprehensive review of specific topics that are essential for obtaining the certification.

1.1 pSeries AIX System Administration (Test 191)

This certification validates the ability to install, configure, and perform a broad range of AIX system administrative activities. The certification is applicable to AIX system administrators who are responsible for supporting end-users and the day-to-day operation of an pSeries AIX environment.

To attain the IBM @server Certified Specialist - pSeries AIX System Administration certification, candidates must pass one test: Test 191: pSeries AIX System Administration.

1.1.1 Recommended prerequisites

The following are the recommended prerequisites for this certification.

► A minimum of six months experience administering in an AIX Version 4 and Version 5 environments. Note: Exam 191 contains AIX content up to and including AIX 5L Version 5.1.

► One year of AIX or UNIX user experience.

► Training in AIX system administration or equivalent experience.

1.1.2 Registration for the certification exam

For information about how to register for the certification exam, visit the following Web site:

http://www.ibm.com/certify

1.1.3 Certification exam objectives

The following objectives were used as a basis when the certification exam was developed. Some of these topics have been regrouped to provide better organization when discussed in this publication.

Installation and configuration

The following are the installation and configuration topics.

► Identify customer's needs (for example, architecture, scalability, physical requirements, and so on).

► Establish strategy for crisis recovery.

► Install base operating system.

► Perform initial configurations (for example, networks, paging space, date/time, root password, and so on).

- ► Install LPPs.
- ► Install and configure other software systems (for example, Netscape).
- ► Apply software updates.
- ► Remove software.
- ► Upgrade operating system (for example, preservation and migration upgrades).
- ► Create and install a `mksysb`
- ► Upgrade hardware.
- ► Configure printers and queues (for example, add, change, show, or delete printers and queues).
- ► Configure and manage resources (for example, manage `cron`, configure skulkers, configure power management).
- ► Configure devices (for example, `cfgmgr`, TTY, parallel and manual devices).
- ► Configure subsystems and subservers (for example, start/stop system resource manager).

Problem determination

The following are the problem determination topics.

- ► Troubleshoot problems with hardware installation (for example, cable connections).
- ► Troubleshoot problems with software installation (LED hang, system hang).
- ► Troubleshoot problems with software (disk space, prerequisites, `lslpp`, and so on).
- ► Troubleshoot hardware (for example, hardware parameters, `cfgmgr`, prerequisites, ODM tools).
- ► Evaluate performance and resource problems (for example, check log files, skulkers, `ps -ef`).

System and user maintenance

The following are the system and user maintenance topics.

- ► Identify suspect hardware components before hard failure by monitoring error logs.
- ► Install necessary patches to prevent known problems.
- ► Reboot servers (gracefully).
- ► Add, delete, and modify users.

- ► Modify user environment (for example, modify initialization files, edit .profile, edit dtwmrc, and so on).
- ► Modify system environment.
- ► Work with Volume Groups (add, import, remove, export, modify, list, and so on).
- ► Work with physical volumes (add, list).
- ► Work with logical volumes (add, remove modify, list, and so on).
- ► Work with file systems (for example, create, remove, modify, list, and so on).
- ► Modify paging space (increase size, add, remove, activate, list, and so on).
- ► Troubleshoot file system problems (for example, mount/unmount problems, file system full, and so on).
- ► Troubleshoot paging space problems (for example, low paging space conditions).
- ► Troubleshoot device related problems (for example, file system not available at IPL, volume group not varying on IPL, SCSI device problems, and so on).
- ► Back up the system.
- ► Back up the applications.
- ► Back up the application data files.
- ► Restore files from tape.
- ► Establish a backup and recovery process based upon customer requirements.
- ► Recover the system.

Communications

The following are the communications topics.

- ► Install device driver.
- ► Work with TCP/IP daemons (for example, start and stop TCP/IP daemons).
- ► Create interface (set IP address, set subnet mask, configure DNS).
- ► Configure interface (define node, gateway).
- ► Modify interface (change IP parameters).
- ► Configure TCP/IP services.
- ► Work with NFS (for example, start and stop NFS).
- ► Export directory (**exportfs**).
- ► Mount remote file system.

- Troubleshoot hardware communications problems (for example device unavailable, device not functioning and so on).

- Perform TCP/IP troubleshooting (for example, daemons will not start/stop, cannot create a `telnet` session on a server, user cannot log on to server, and so on).

- Perform NFS troubleshooting (for example NFS daemon will not start/stop, host server is not responding, permission denied error messages).

System performance

The following are the system performance topics.

- Manage CPU and memory resources (for example, display CPU/memory usage, start/stop a processor, and so on).

- Manage I/O performance resources.

- Manage network performance resources (show network, I/O counts, connections and queues).

- Manage workloads (for example, scheduling, setting up job queue, and so on).

- Manage disk/data (partitions, RAID, mirroring, defragmenting file systems, and so on).

Security

The following is the security topic.

- Modify default password attributes for system users (for example, maxage, maxlength, maxexpire, minrepeat, and so on)

1.2 Certification education courses

Courses are offered to help you prepare for the certification tests. These courses are recommended, but not required, before taking a certification test. The following tables show the courses that were available at the time of the publication of this guide. For a current list, visit the following Web site:

`http://www.ibm.com/certify`

AIX Version 4 System Administration	
Course Number	Q1214 (USA), AU14 (Worldwide)
Course Duration	Five days
Course Abstract	Learn the basic system administration skills to support AIX RS/6000 running the AIX Version 4 operating system. Build your skills in configuring and monitoring a single CPU environment. Administrators who manage systems in a networked environment should attend additional LAN courses.
Course Content	•Install the AIX Version 4 operating system, software bundles, and filesets. •Perform a system startup and shutdown. •Understand and use AIX system management tools. •Configure ASCII terminals and printer devices. •Manage physical and logical volumes. •Perform file systems management. •Create and manage user and group accounts. •Use backup and restore commands. •Use administrative subsystems, including cron, to schedule system tasks and security to implement customized access of files and directories.

AIX Version 4 Advanced System Administration	
Course Number	Q1216 (USA), AU16 (Worldwide)
Course Duration	Five days
Course Abstract	Learn how to identify possible sources of problems on stand-alone configurations of the RS/6000 and perform advanced system administration tasks.
Course Content	•Identify the different RS/6000 models and architects. •Explain the ODM purpose for device configuration. •Interpret system initialization and problems during the boot process. •Customize authentication and set up ACLs. •Identify the TCB components, commands, and their use. •Obtain a system dump and define saved data. •Identify the error logging facility components and reports. •List ways to invoke diagnostic programs. •Customize a logical volume for optimal performance and availability. •Manage a disk and the data under any circumstance. •Use the standard AIX commands to identify potential I/O, disk, CPU, or other bottlenecks on the system. •Customize SMIT menus and define how SMIT interacts with the ODM. •Define the virtual printer database and potential problems. •List the terminal attributes and create new terminfo entries. •Define the NIM installation procedure.

AIX Version 4 Configuring TCP/IP and Accessing the Internet	
Course Number	Q1107 (USA), AU07 or AU05 (Worldwide)
Course Duration	Five days
Course Abstract	•Learn how to perform TCP/IP network configuration and administration on AIX Version 4 RS/6000 systems. •Learn the skills necessary to begin implementing and using NFS, NIS, DNS, network printing, static and dynamic routing, SLIP and SLIPLOGIN, Xstations, and the Internet.
Course Contents	•Describe the basic concepts of TCP/IP protocols and addressing. •Explain TCP/IP broadcasting and multicasting. •Configure, implement, and support TCP/IP on an IBM RS/6000 system. •Use networking commands for remote logon, remote execution, and file transfer. •Configure SLIP and SLIPLOGIN. •Use SMIT to configure network printing. •Connect multiple TCP/IP networks using static and dynamic routing. •Implement DNS, NFS, and NIS. •Perform basic troubleshooting of network problems. •Configure an Xstation in the AIX environment. •Explain how to access Internet services. •Understand and support TCP/IP. •Plan implementation of NFS. •Support LAN-attached printers. •Support AIX networking. •Determine network problems. •Implement network file systems.

1.3 Education on CD-ROM: IBM AIX Essentials

The new IBM AIX Essentials series offers a dynamic training experience for those who need convenient and cost-effective AIX education. The series consists of five new, content rich, computer-based multimedia training courses based on highly acclaimed, instructor-led AIX classes that have been successfully taught by IBM Education and Training for years.

To order, and for more information and answers to your questions you can do one of the following:

► In the U.S., use the online form at the following URL:

    http://www.ibm.com/services/learning/spotlight/pseries/cdrom.html

► Outside the U.S., contact your IBM sales representative, or contact an IBM Business Partner.

System startup problem handling

This chapter discusses the boot process and the common problems that you might encounter while the system is in the initialization phase. It also covers the common commands that are used to manipulate the elements associated with the boot process.

Upon completing this chapter, you should be able to:

► Understand the basics of the boot process and be able to perform an orderly system shutdown.

► Determine and control the devices involved in the boot process.

► Access the AIX error log.

► Troubleshoot boot problems.

► Understand and have memorized basic LED error codes.

2.1 Key commands used throughout the chapter

The following is a list of the important commands that are used throughout this chapter.

alog   Used to maintain and manage log files. Refer to Section 2.4.1, "Using the alog command" on page 14 for further details.

cfgmgr   Configures devices and optionally installs device software into the system. Refer to Section 2.4.2, "Using the cfgmgr command" on page 18 for further details.

last   Displays all the previous logins and logoffs that still have entries in /var/adm/wtmp file. Refer to Section 2.4.3, "Using the last command" on page 20 for further details.

bootlist Displays and alters the list of boot devices available to the system. Refer to Section 2.4.4, "Using the bootlist command" on page 22 for further details.

uptime   Shows how long the system has been up. Refer to Section 2.4.5, "Using the uptime command" on page 23 for further details.

mpcfg   Enables a user with root authority to manage service information. Refer to Section 2.4.6, "Using the mpcfg command" on page 24 for further details.

shutdown Used to shut down the system. Refer to Section 2.4.7, "Using the shutdown command" on page 26 for further details.

2.2 Boot process

During the boot process, the system tests the hardware, loads and runs the operating system, and configures devices. To boot the operating system, the following resources are required:

► A boot image that can be loaded after the machine is turned on or reset.

► Access to the root and /usr file systems.

There are three types of system boots:

► Hard Disk Boot

A machine is started for normal operations with the key in the normal position. On PCI-based systems with no key locking, this is the default startup mode.

► Diskless Network Boot

A diskless or dataless workstation is started remotely over a network. A machine is started for normal operations with the key in the normal position. One or more remote file servers provide the files and programs that diskless or dataless workstations need to boot.

► Service Boot

A machine is started from a hard disk, network, tape, or CD-ROM with the key set in the service position. This condition is also called maintenance mode. In maintenance mode, a system administrator can perform tasks, such as installing new or updated software and running diagnostic checks.

During a hard disk boot, the boot image is found on a local disk created when the operating system was installed. During the boot process, the system configures all devices found in the machine and initializes other basic software required for the system to operate (such as the Logical Volume Manager). At the end of this process, the file systems are mounted and ready for use.

The same general requirements apply to diskless network clients. They also require a boot image and access to the operating system file tree. Diskless network clients have no local file systems and get all their information by way of remote access.

The system finds all necessary information for the boot process on its disk drive. When the system is started by turning on the power switch (a cold boot) or restarted with the reboot or shutdown commands (a warm boot), a number of events must occur before the system is ready for use. These events can be divided into the following phases:

1. Read Only Storage (ROS) Kernel Init Phase

   During this phase, problems with the motherboard are checked, and the ROS initial program load searches for the bootlist. Once the bootlist is found, the boot image is read into memory and system initialization starts.

2. Base Device Configuration Phase

   All devices are configured in this phase, with the help of the **cfgmgr** command.

3. System Boot Phase

   In this phase of the boot process, all the logical volumes are varied on, paging is started, and the /etc/inittab file is processed.

2.3 Power on sequence, LEDs, and audio signals

Several MCA based RS/6000 systems have LED displays to show what phase of the boot process the system is going through. If something goes wrong, you can interpret the LED codes and take the appropriate action to rectify the problem.

> **Tip:** As a specialist, memorizing the error codes enables you to quickly get to the heart of critical system problems. Therefore, it is one of the sections of the exam that requires memorization.

PCI RS/6000 systems use sounds and graphics to show the different phases of the boot process. For example, as soon as you power on the system, an audio beep is produced when the processor is found to be active, the PowerPC logo is shown (or text is presented) when the system memory checking is completed, and device logos are shown for all devices that have a valid address. At the end of the device logo display, if the system ROS is not damaged, an audio beep is again produced.

System administrators solve the problems that they might encounter during the startup process using these indicators.

2.4 Useful commands

The commands that are used to manage system startup, shutdown, and the related tasks are discussed in the following sections.

2.4.1 Using the alog command

There may be instances when you must trace the boot process and find out if something went wrong with the system during the boot process. AIX provides you with an excellent tool to monitor these problems through the help of the `alog` command.

The `alog` command can maintain and manage logs. It reads standard input, writes to standard output, and copies the output into a fixed-size file. This file is treated as a circular log. If the file is full, new entries are written over the oldest existing entries.

The rc.boot script explicitly redirects boot information through the **alog** command to the file /var/adm/ras/bootlog. If something goes wrong with the system, you can boot the system in single-user mode (maintenance mode) and access these logs through the **alog** command to see at what stage the system is failing. A part of the rc.boot script is shown below to illustrate how the logging mechanism has been incorporated.

```
# Error Recovery if customized data is zero

[ -f /no_sbase ] && {
    echo "rc.boot: executing savebase recovery procedures" \
>>/tmp/boot_log
X=`ODMDIR=/mnt/etc/objrepos odmshow CuDv |\
    fgrep population`
count=`echo $X | cut -f2 -d' '`
[ $count -ne 0 ] && {
    /usr/sbin/savebase -o /mnt/etc/objrepos
    [ $? -ne 0 ] && loopled 0x546
    mount /var# so that reboot can log
    echo "savebase recovery reboot" \
        >>/tmp/boot_log
    cat /tmp/boot_log | alog -q -t boot
    reboot
    }
}
```

The **alog** command works with log files that are specified on the command line or with logs that are defined in the **alog** configuration database.

The most common flags used with the **alog** command and their description are given in Table 2-1.

Table 2-1   Command flags for alog

Flag	Description
-f *LogFile*	Specifies the name of a log file. If the specified LogFile does not exist, one is created. If the **alog** command is unable to write to LogFile, it writes to /dev/null.
-L	Lists the log types currently defined in the **alog** configuration database. If you use the -L flag with the -t LogType flag, the attributes for a specified LogType are listed.
-o	Lists the contents of LogFile; writes the contents of LogFile to standard output in sequential order.
-q	Copies standard input to LogFile, but does not write to standard output.

Flag	Description
-t LogType	Identifies a log defined in the **alog** configuration database. The **alog** command gets the log's file name and size from the **alog** configuration database.

AIX logs can be maintained by using either SMIT or by using the **alog** command directly. The general uses of the **alog** command are as follows:

Showing the contents of a log file

To list the contents of a log file, use the command:

```
alog -f LogFile [ -o ]
```

Logging data to a specified log file

You can change the default file that is used to log the activities by using the following command:

```
alog -f LogFile | [ [ -q ] [ -s Size ] ]
```

Displaying the verbosity value of a specified log type

The verbosity value specifies the depth of information that is written to a log. In order to display the verbosity value of a log, use the following command:

```
alog -t LogType -V
```

Changing the attributes of a specified log type

You can use the different attributes of a log type by using the following command:

```
alog -C -t LogType [ -f LogFile ] [ -s Size ] [ -w Verbosity ]
```

Displaying the current attributes of a specified log type

Before you can change the attributes of a log it is recommended to view what the current attributes are. Use the following command to display the current attributes of a log type:

```
alog -L [ -t LogType ]
```

To view the boot log, you can either use SMIT or use the **alog** command directly. Follow the sequence in "Viewing the boot log" on page 17 to view the contents of the boot log.

Viewing the boot log

You can view the boot log by either using the SMIT fast path `smitty alog_show` and giving the name of the log you want to view, or you can use the `alog` command. To view a log using the `alog` command, determine what predefined logs are available to you.

Use the `alog -L` command to view the logs defined in the `alog` database. On the command line enter:

```
# alog -L
boot
bosinst
nim
dumpsymp
```

To view the boot log (the log that holds boot information) enter:

```
# alog -o -t boot
---------
attempting to configure device 'fda0'
invoking /usr/lib/methods/cfgfda_isa -2 -1 fda0
return code = 0
***************** stdout **********
fd0

***************** no stderr **********
------------------------------------------------------------------------
invoking top level program -- "/etc/methods/startty"
return code = 0
***************** no stdout **********
***************** no stderr **********
------------------------------------------------------------------------
invoking top level program -- "/etc/methods/startsmt"
return code = 0
***************** no stdout **********
***************** no stderr **********
------------------------------------------------------------------------
invoking top level program -- "/etc/methods/load_blockset_ext"
return code = 0
***************** no stdout **********
***************** no stderr **********
------------------------------------------------------------------------
invoking top level program -- "/usr/lib/methods/defaio"
return code = 0
***************** no stdout **********
***************** no stderr **********
------------------------------------------------------------------------
calling savebase
return code = 0
```

```
***************** no stdout **********
***************** no stderr **********
Starting AIX Windows Desktop.....
Saving Base Customize Data to boot disk
Starting the sync daemon
Starting the error daemon
System initialization completed.
Starting Multi-user Initialization
 Performing auto-varyon of Volume Groups
 Activating all paging spaces
swapon: Paging device /dev/hd6 activated.
/dev/rhd1 (/home): ** Unmounted cleanly - Check suppressed
 Performing all automatic mounts
Multi-user initialization completed
```

Any errors that are encountered will be logged into this file. However, the **alog** file has no concurrency control; therefore, if multiple processes try to write to the same file at the same time, the contents of the log file might not be as anticipated. Additionally, it is a cyclic file; so, when its size reaches the maximum, it is overwritten.

2.4.2 Using the cfgmgr command

During the boot process, the system has to determine what resources are available to it. For example, the system has to determine what kind of bus the system is using, what type of devices are attached to the system, where the rootvg resides, and so on. The configuration of these devices is handled by the BOS command **cfgmgr**. The **cfgmgr** command configures devices and optionally installs device software into the system.

The general syntax of the **cfgmgr** command is as follows:

cfgmgr [-f | -s | -p *Phase*] [-i *Device*] [-l *Name*] [-v]

The most commonly used flags and their description are given in Table 2-2:

Table 2-2   Command flags for cfgmgr

Flag	Description
-f	Specifies that the **cfgmgr** command runs the phase 1 configuration rules. This flag is not valid at run time (after system start).
-i *Device*	Specifies the location of the installation medium.
-l *Name*	Specifies the named device to configure along with its children.
-p *Phase*	Specifies the phase that the **cfgmgr** command runs.

Flag	Description
-s	Specifies that the **cfgmgr** command follows the phase 2 configuration rules.
-v	Specifies verbose output. The **cfgmgr** command writes information about what it is doing to standard output.

The devices to be configured are controlled by the Configuration Rules object class, which is part of the Device Configuration database. Each configuration rule specifies three items:

► The full path name of an executable program to run.

► When to run the program (in relation to the other rules).

► In which phase to run the program.

During system boot, the **cfgmgr** command configures all the devices that are necessary to use the system. System boot consists of two phases.

► Phase 1

Phase 1 begins when the kernel is brought into the system, and the boot file system is initialized. During this phase, the **cfgmgr** command is invoked, specifying this as phase 1 by using the -f flag. The **cfgmgr** command runs all of the phase 1 configuration rules, which results in the base devices being configured.

► Phase 2

In this phase, the **cfgmgr** command is called with the -s flag.

The **cfgmgr** command recognizes three phases of configuration rules:

► Phase 1

► Phase 2 (second boot phase for normal boot)

► Phase 3 (second boot phase for service boot)

Normally, the **cfgmgr** command runs all the rules for the phase specified during invocation (for example, phase 1 rules for the -f flag). However, if the -l flag is issued, the **cfgmgr** command configures only the named device and its children.

If the **cfgmgr** command is invoked without a phase option (for example, without the -f,-s, or -p flags), then the command runs the phase 2 rules. The only way to run the phase 3 rules is with the -p flag.

If you invoke the `cfgmgr` command with the -i flag, the command attempts to install device software automatically for each new detected device. The device variable of the -i flag specifies where to find the installation medium. The installation medium can be a hardware device (such as a tape or diskette drive), a directory that contains installation images, or the installation image file itself.

> **Important:** To protect the configuration database, the `cfgmgr` command is not interruptible. Stopping this command before execution is complete could result in a corrupted database.

The `cfgmgr` command configures only those devices at the system startup that are powered on and are self configurable, such as SCSI drives or TTYs that have been defined in the inittab file. If you have some devices that were not powered on when the system started, the system will not make them available until you explicitly tell it to configure them. The syntax of the command is:

```
cfgmgr -v
```

It will produce an output similar to the `alog -o -t boot` command. See Section 3.2, "Configuring system devices" on page 45 for additional configuration information.

2.4.3 Using the last command

The `last` command is generally used to display, in reverse chronological order, all previous logins and logoffs recorded in the /var/adm/wtmp file. The /var/adm/wtmp file collects login and logout records as these events occur and retains them until the records are processed by the `acctcon1` and `acctcon2` commands as part of the daily reporting procedures. When the time daemon, timed, changes the system time, it logs entries in wtmp under the pseudo-user *date*. An entry starting with *date* / is logged before the change, and an entry starting with *date* { is logged after the change. This allows for accurate accounting of logins that span a time change. The general syntax of the command is as follows:

```
last [ -f FileName ] [ -Number ] [ Name ... ] [ Terminal ... ]
```

The common flags used with the `last` command are provided in Table 2-3.

Table 2-3   Command flags for last

Flag	Description
-Number	The number of lines to display in the output.
Name	Logins and logouts of the users specified by the name parameter.

Flag	Description
Terminal	Login and logoffs from the terminals specified by the terminal parameter.

For example, if you want to find out when the user root logged on and off from the console, enter the command:

```
# last root console
root      pts/3 dummy Oct 23 12:27    still logged in.
root      lft0                        Oct 22 11:45    still logged in.
root      lft0                        Oct 22 09:46 - 11:27  (01:40)
root      pts/0       dummy           Oct 21 11:36 - System is halted by
system administrator.  (00:24)
root      pts/1       dummy.xyz.abc   Aug 08 13:05 - System is halted by
system administrator.  (02:17)
root      pts/0       dummy.xyz.abc   Aug 08 12:43 - System is halted by
system administrator.  (02:39)
root      lft0                        Sep 18 15:41 - System halted
abnormally.  (14203+20:56)
root      pts/1       dummy.xyz.abc   Sep 18 15:00 - System halted
abnormally.  (00:31)
root      pts/3       dummy.xyz.abc   Sep 18 12:05 - System halted
abnormally.  (14245+02:51)
root      pts/3       dummy.xyz.abc   Sep 18 12:04 - 12:05  (00:00)
root      pts/1       dummy.xyz.abc   Sep 18 11:50 - 12:04  (00:14)
root      pts/1       dummy.xyz.abc   Sep 16 13:32 - 11:11 (1+21:38)
root      pts/2       dummy.xyz.abc   Sep 16 11:35 - System is halted by
system administrator.  (00:04)
root      pts/0       dummy.xyz.abc   Sep 04 15:27 - System is halted by
system administrator.  (00:15)
root      lft0                        Sep 04 15:27 - 15:40  (00:13)
wtmp begins     Sep 04 15:11
```

The **last** command can also be used to determine when the system was last shut down. The syntax of the command follows:

```
# last shutdown
shutdown  pts/0                       Oct 22 09:23
shutdown  lft0                        Oct 21 16:39
shutdown  pts/0                       Oct 21 13:41
shutdown  lft0                        Sep 25 14:43
shutdown  pts/1                       Aug 08 15:22
shutdown  lft0                        Sep 16 11:40
shutdown  ~                           Sep 08 14:47
```

2.4.4 Using the bootlist command

The **bootlist** command allows you to display and alter the list of boot devices from which the system may be booted. When the system is booted, it will scan the devices in the list and attempt to boot from the first device it finds containing a boot image. This command supports updating of the following:

Normal boot list   The normal list designates possible boot devices for when the system is booted in normal mode.

Service boot list   The service list designates possible boot devices for when the system is booted in service mode.

Previous boot device This entry designates the last device from which the system booted. Some hardware platforms may attempt to boot from the previous boot device before looking for a boot device in one of the other lists.

Support of these boot lists varies from platform to platform. Some platforms do not have boot lists. When searching for a boot device, the system selects the first device in the list and determines if it is bootable. If no boot file system is detected on the first device, the system moves on to the next device in the list. As a result, the ordering of devices in the device list is extremely important.

The general syntax of the command is as follows:

```
bootlist [ { -m Mode } [ -r ] [  -o  ] [ [ -i ] |
[ [ -f File ] [ Device [ Attr=Value ... ] ... ] ] ]
```

The most common flags used with the **bootlist** command are provided in Table 2-4.

Table 2-4   Command flags for bootlist

Flag	Description
-m *mode*	Specifies which boot list to display or alter. Possible values for the mode variable are normal, service, both, or prevboot.
-f *File*	Indicates that the device information is to be read from the specified file name.
-i	Indicates that the device list specified by the -m flag should be invalidated.
-o	Displays bootlist with the -m flag. Applies only to AIX Version 4.2 or later.
-r	Indicates whether to display the specified bootlist after any specified alteration is performed.

To display a boot list (AIX Version 4.2 or later) use the command:

```
# bootlist -m normal -o
fd0
cd0
hdisk0
```

If you want to make changes to your normal boot list, use the command:

```
bootlist -m normal hdisk0 cd0
```

This will change the normal bootlist to indicate that when the system is booted, it will first attempt to boot from the floppy disk. If it cannot find a boot image in hdisk0 it will search the CD-ROM. Otherwise, it will instruct the system to provide an LED error code and wait for user intervention.

Boot device choices

The naming conventions that can be used in your boot list are provided in Table 2-5. Each device that you add to your bootlist must be in the AVAILABLE state. Otherwise, the **bootlist** command will fail, and you will encounter an error similar to:

```
0514-210 bootlist: Device xxxxx is not in the AVAILABLE state
```

Table 2-5   Valid device names for the bootlist command

Device	Description
fd*xx*	Diskette drive device logical names
hdisk*xx*	Physical volume device logical names
cd*xx*	SCSI CD-ROM device logical names
rmt*xx*	Magnetic tape device logical names
ent*xx*	Ethernet adapter logical names
tok*xx*	Token ring adapters logical names

2.4.5 Using the uptime command

If you suspect that your system was shutdown and restarted, you can use the **uptime** command to find this out. The **uptime** command shows how long the system has been up. The general syntax of the command is as follows:

```
# uptime
05:10PM up 6 days, 21:45, 13 users, load average 4.00, 3.00, 0.00
```

The **uptime** command prints the current time, the length of time the system has been up, the number of users online, and the load average. The load average is the number of runnable processes over the preceding 5, 10, or 15 minute intervals. The output of the **uptime** command is, essentially, the heading line provided by the **w** command.

2.4.6 Using the mpcfg command

The **mpcfg** command enables a user with root authority to manage service information consisting of the service support and diagnostic flags (-S and -f flags), the modem and site configuration (-m flag), and the remote support phone numbers (-p flag).

The **mpcfg** command works only on multiprocessor systems with Micro Channel I/O. For IBM systems, this includes the IBM 7012 Model G Series, the IBM 7013 Model J Series, and the IBM 7015 Model R Series.

> **Tip:** The discussion about Micro Channel I/O may seem out of date now that PCI is used in every RS/6000 product, but many of the older Micro Channel machines are still in use and require specific skills. A specialist should know how to configure new and old hardware.

The general syntax of the command and the meaning of the flags are as follows:

Display service information

To display service information, you can use:

```
mpcfg -d { -f -m -p -S}
```

For example, To find out what the status is of your diagnostic flags, use the **mpcfg** command as shown in Figure 2-1 on page 25.

```
# mpcfg -df
Index   Name                                          Value
1       Remote Authorization                          0
2       Autoservice IPL                               0
3       BUMP Console                                  1
4       Dial-Out Authorization                        0
5       Set Mode to Normal When Booting               0
6       Electronic Mode Switch from Service Line      1
7       Boot Multi-user AIX in Service                0
8       Extended Tests                                0
9       Power On Tests in Trace Mode                  0
10      Power On Tests in Loop Mode                   0
11      Fast IPL                                      0
#
```

Figure 2-1   Displaying diagnostic flags

Change service information

To change the service information, use the **mpcfg** command with the following combination of flags:

```
mpcfg -c { -f | -m | -p -S -w} Index Value...
```

For example, if you want to fast IPL the system, you can change the value of the diagnostic flag as follows:

```
mpcfg -cf 11 1
```

This command will search the index (see Figure 2-1 on page 25) and change the value of the eleventh item (Fast IPL) to 1. The next time the system is booted, the system will skip the extensive hardware testing and take less time to boot than normal.

Save or restore service information

To store information about the flags, use the **mpcfg** command with the following syntax:

```
mpcfg { -r | -s }
```

The most commonly used command flags for the **mpcfg** command are listed in Table 2-6.

Table 2-6   Command flags for mpcfg

Flag	Description
-c	Changes the values of service information. The values that you want to modify are identified first by the flag -f, -m, -p, or -S, and then by their index (Index parameter) within this category.
-d	Displays the values of service information according to the -f, -m, -p, and -S flags set in the command. These values are displayed associated with their corresponding indexes and names.
-s	Saves the service information in the /etc/lpp/diagnostics/data/bump file.
-f	Indicates that the action (display or change) will be applied to the diagnostic flags.
-m	Indicates that the action (display or change) will be applied to the modem and site configuration.
-p	Indicates that the action (display or change) will be applied to the remote support phone numbers.
-S	Indicates that the action (display or change) will be applied to the service support flags.
-w	Indicates that the change will be applied to a password.

2.4.7 Using the shutdown command

A system shutdown is controlled by a shell script that properly prepares a system with multiple users to be turned off or rebooted. An improper shutdown can have undesirable results on the system's integrity.

The general syntax of the **shutdown** command is as follows:

```
shutdown [ -d ] [ -F ] [ -h ] [ -i ] [ -k ] [ -m ] [ -p ] [ -r ]
[ -t mmddHHMM [ yy ] ] [ -v ] [ +Time [ Message ] ]
```

The common flags used with the **shutdown** command are provided in Table 2-7.

Table 2-7   Command flags for shutdown

Flag	Description
-d	Brings the system down from a distributed mode to a multiuser mode.

Flag	Description
-F	Does a fast shutdown, bypassing the messages to other users, and brings the system down as quickly as possible.
-h	Halts the operating system completely; it is the same as the -v flag.
-i	Specifies interactive mode. Displays interactive messages to guide the user through the shutdown.
-k	Avoids shutting down the system.
-m	Brings the system down to maintenance (single user) mode.
-r	Restarts the system after being shutdown with the reboot command.
-v	Halts the operating system completely.

To perform a fast shutdown and restart the system, enter:

```
shutdown -Fr
```

You will see the message

```
shutdown completed.
```

at the end of this process before the reboot.

Adding applications to the shutdown process

At times, it may be necessary to properly close down all the applications and other user processes without issuing a **kill** command to end the processes. You can achieve this by adding your desired commands and actions to a file named /etc/rc.shutdown. The /etc/rc.shutdown file is checked each time a **shutdown** command is issued. If the file exists, it will be run; otherwise, the system will perform a regular shutdown depending on the flags that are used to bring the system down.

Tip: /etc/rc.shutdown must be set as executable before it can called by the /usr/sbin/shutdown script.

Beginning with AIX Version 4.2.0, the /usr/sbin/shutdown script is changed to incorporate this file. A part of the /usr/sbin/shutdown script executing the rc.shutdown file is shown below:

```
if [ $nohalt = off ]
    then
        # /etc/rc.shutdown is for administrators to create for their
        # own local needs. If it is not successful, shutdown will
```

```
# abort.
if [ -x /etc/rc.shutdown ]
then
     sh /etc/rc.shutdown
     if [ $? -ne 0 ] ; then
     dspmsg -s 1 shutdown.cat 60 \
     "/etc/rc.shutdown failed.  Shutdown aborting.\n"
     exit 1
     fi
fi
```

2.5 Troubleshooting boot problems

There are many contributing factors towards a system failure.

► Due to mishandling, for example, if someone intentionally accesses and ends up corrupting it.

► When conditions, such as a power failure, corrupt the Boot Logical Volume (BLV).

► When a disk encounters many bad blocks under which the system becomes un-usable.

Any of these conditions may prevent the system from restarting.

The sections that follow contain a discussion of the situations where the system will not boot and how to correct the problems.

> **Tip:** You must have root authority to perform all of these functions.

2.5.1 Accessing a system that will not boot

If you are unable to boot your system, the first step is to access the system and see what is the probable cause of the failure. This procedure enables you to get a system prompt so that you may attempt to recover data from the system or perform corrective action that will enable the system to boot from the hard disk.

The following steps summarize the procedure for accessing a system that will not boot. For detailed information, see the *AIX Installation Guide*.

To access the system:

1. Turn on all attached external devices, such as terminals, CD-ROM drives, tape drives, monitors, and external disk drives before turning on the system unit. Turn on the system unit to allow the installation media to be loaded.

2. Insert Volume 1 of the installation media into the tape or CD-ROM drive and power the system unit off.

3. Turn the system key (if present) to the service position or alternatively press F5 (or 5) on PCI-based systems to boot from the tape or CD-ROM drive (during step 4).

4. Turn the system unit power switch to the on position. When booting from alternate media, a screen will appear (before the one in Figure 2-2) asking you to press a function key (such as F1) to select the proper display as the system console. Each display attached to the system will receive a function key number to identify it as the system console. The system begins booting from the installation media. After several minutes, C31 is displayed in the LED (if your system has an LED; otherwise, a screen similar to the one in Figure 2-2 is shown).

```
                    Welcome to Base Operating System
                      Installation and Maintenance


   Type the number of your choice and press Enter.

   >>> 1 Start Installation Now with Default Settings

        2 Change/Show Installation Settings and Install

        3 Start Maintenance Mode for System Recovery



   88 Help ?
   99 Previous Menu

   Choice [1]:
```

Figure 2-2   Welcome to BOS Installation and Maintenance menu

5. Select option 3, Start Maintenance Mode for System Recovery, and press Enter. A screen similar to Figure 2-3 on page 30 is shown.

```
                        Maintenance

    Type the number of your choice and press Enter.

    >>> 1 Access a Root Volume Group

         2 Copy a System Dump to Removable Media

         3 Access Advanced Maintenance Functions

         4 Install from a System Backup



         88 Help ?

         99 Previous Menu

    >>> Choice [1]:
```

Figure 2-3   Maintenance menu

6. Choose 1, Access a Root Volume Group. A screen similar to Figure 2-4 is
   shown.

```
         Warning

    If you choose to access a root volume group, you will not be able to return

    to the Base Operating System Installation menus without rebooting.

    Type the number of your choice and press Enter



              0 Continue



         88 Help ?

    >>> 99 Previous Menu

    >>> Choice [99]:
```

Figure 2-4   Warning message window

7. Enter a 0 (zero), and press Enter. A screen similar to Figure 2-5 on page 31 is
   shown.

```
                    Access a Root Volume Group

Type the number for a volume group to display logical volume
information and press Enter.

1)      Volume Group 00615147b27f2b40 contains these disks:
           hdisk0 958 04-B0-00-2,0
2)      Volume Group 00615247b27c2b41 contains these disks:
           hdisk1 2063 04-B0-00-6,0



Choice:
```

Figure 2-5   Access a Root Volume Group menu

8. Select the volume group whose logical volume information you want to
   display. This is important because rootvg will contain hd5 (the boot logical
   volume). Enter the number of the volume group and press Enter. A screen
   similar to Figure 2-6 is shown.

```
                     Volume Group Information

Volume Group ID 00615147b27f2b40 includes following logical volumes:

   hd5      hd6         hd8        hd4       hd2        hd9var

   hd3      hd1         lv00       lv01

Type the number of your choice and press Enter.
   1) Access this Volume Group and start a shell
   2) Access this Volume Group and start a shell before mounting file systems


99) Previous Menu
   Choice [99]:
```

Figure 2-6   Volume Group Information menu

9. Select one of the options from the Volume Group Information screen and press Enter. Each option does the following:

Choice 1   Access this volume group and start a shell.

Selecting this choice imports and activates the volume group and mounts the file systems for this root volume group before providing you with a shell and a system prompt.

Choice 2   Access this volume group and start a shell before mounting file systems.

Selecting this choice imports and activates the volume group and provides you with a shell and system prompt before mounting the file systems for this root volume group.

Choice 99   Entering 99 returns you to the Access a Root Volume Group screen.

After either choice 1 or 2 is selected and processed, a shell is started and a system prompt is displayed.

10. Take the appropriate measures to recover data or take additional action (such as using the **bosboot** command) to enable the system to boot normally.

2.5.2 Problems with installation media

If you are installing a new system or performing a migration installation to a newer version of AIX, you may run into problems with the installation media. Some symptoms of installation media problems include unexpected halts during installation, failure to read information from the media, or unexpected system reboots. The following steps summarize the procedure for determining installation media problems:

1. Confirm that all attached external devices, such as terminals, CD-ROM drives, tape drives, monitors, and external disk drives, are powered on before turning on the system unit. Turning external units on after turning on the system unit can prevent external units from operating or sending information to the system unit. For example, turning on a SCSI CD-ROM for system installation after the system unit has been turned on may make the CD-ROM inoperative.

2. Visually inspect the media for physical damage. For example, a CD-ROM with scratches on it may not be read properly by the CD-ROM drive. Or, a tape drive with ribbon hanging out the front of the cartridge may not function properly in the tape drive. Installation media that has physical damage should not be used for installation and should be set aside or thrown away.

3. Confirm that all installation options are properly set before installation. If you are attempting an installation and choose options that provide the system with incorrect commands or configuration, the system may not perform the installation as it should. For example, if you tell the system to install the BOS to a disk that is too small to hold the BOS, your installation may not complete.

4. Attempt the installation using another set of media, if the installation process is not working. Your media may be defective due to wear and tear, manufacturing defect, or environmental factors. Obtain another copy of the installation media and repeat the installation process.

5. Confirm that all hardware is functioning properly. If the installation media is functioning properly on another system, but your installation fails on your system, there may be a hardware problem. Check all external cables and ensure that hardware is properly configured. For example, two devices on your system may be sharing the same SCSI address, which could halt an installation. If problems persist, use a diagnostics disk for analysis or contact your local customer engineer for hardware support.

2.5.3 Common boot time LED error codes and recovery actions

The most common boot problems and methods to get your system up and running again are given in Table 2-8.

Table 2-8 Common startup LEDs and recovery actions

LED 201 - Damaged boot image
1. Access your rootvg following the procedure described in Section 2.5.1, "Accessing a system that will not boot" on page 28.
2. Check the / and /tmp file systems. If they are almost full, create more space.
3. Determine the boot disk by using the command: `lslv -m hd5`
4. Re-create boot image using: `bosboot -a -d /dev/hdiskn`
5. Check for CHECKSTOP errors in the error log. If such errors are found, it is probably failing hardware.
6. Shutdown and restart the system.

LED 223-229 - Invalid boot list

1. Set the key mode switch to service (F5 for systems without a keylock) and power up the machine.

2. If the display continues normally, change the key mode switch to Normal and continue with step 3. If you do not get the prompt, go to step 4.

3. When you get the login prompt, log in and follow the procedure described in Section 2.4.4, "Using the bootlist command" on page 22 to change your bootlist. Continue with step 7.

4. Follow the procedure in Section 2.5.1, "Accessing a system that will not boot" on page 28 to access your rootvg and continue with step 5.

5. Determine the boot disk by using the command: **lslv -m hd5**

6. Change the bootlist following the procedure given in Section 2.4.4, "Using the bootlist command" on page 22.

7. Shutdown and restart your system.

LED 551, 555, and 557 - Errors including corrupted file system and corrupted JFS log

1. Follow the procedure described in Section 2.5.1, "Accessing a system that will not boot" on page 28, to access the rootvg before mounting any file systems (Option 2 on the Maintenance screen).

2. Verify and correct the file systems as follows:

   ```
   fsck -y /dev/hd1
   fsck -y /dev/hd2
   fsck -y /dev/hd3
   fsck -y /dev/hd4
   fsck -y /dev/hd9var
   ```

3. Format the JFS log again by using the command:

   ```
   /usr/sbin/logform /dev/hd8
   ```

4. Use **lslv -m hd5** to determine the boot disk.

5. Recreate boot image by using the command:

   bosboot -a -d /dev/hdisk*n*

   Where *n* is the disk number of the disk containing the boot logical volume.

**Led 552, 554, and 556 - Super block corrupted
or corrupted customized ODM database**

1. Repeat steps 1 and 2 for LEDs 551, 555, and 557.

2. If **fsck** indicates that block 8 is corrupted, the super block for the file system is corrupted and needs to be repaired. Enter the command:

   ```
   dd count=1 bs=4k skip=31 seek=1 if=/dev/hdn of=/dev/hdn
   ```

   where *n* is the number of the file system.

3. Rebuild your JFS log by using the command:

   ```
   /usr/sbin/logform /dev/hd8
   ```

4. If this solves the problem, stop here; otherwise, continue with step 5.

5. Your ODM database is corrupted. Restart your system and follow the procedure given in Section 2.5.1, "Accessing a system that will not boot" on page 28 to access rootvg with Choice 2.

6. Mount the root and usr file system as follows:

   ```
   mount /dev/hd4 /mnt
   mount /usr
   ```

7. Copy system configuration to a backup directory:

   ```
   mkdir /mnt/etc/objrepos/backup
   cp /mnt/etc/objrepos/Cu* /mnt/etc/objrepos/backup
   ```

8. Copy configuration from RAM file system as follows:

   ```
   cp /etc/objrepos/Cu* /mnt/etc/objrepos
   ```

9. Unmount all file systems by using the **umount all** command.

10. Determine boot disk by using the **lslv -m hd5** command.

11. Save the clean ODM to the boot logical volume by using the command:

    ```
    savebase -d/dev/hdiskn
    ```

12. Reboot the system. If system does not come up, reinstall BOS.

LED 553 - Corrupted /etc/inittab file

1. Access the rootvg with all file systems mounted by following the procedure described in Section 2.5.1, "Accessing a system that will not boot" on page 28.
 	
2. Check for free space in /, /var, and /tmp by using the **df** command.
 	
3. Check the /etc/inittab file and correct the inittab problems, such as an empty inittab file, a missing inittab file, or a wrong entry in the inittab file.
 	
4. Check for execution problems with:
`/etc/environment`
`/bin/sh`
`/bin/bsh`
`/etc/fsck`
`/etc/profile`
`/.profile`
 	
5. Shutdown the system and reboot.

2.6 Quiz

The following are questions created by the authors to further test your understanding of the topics.

1. A system administrator suspects that a colleague rebooted their server the previous evening. Which of the following commands will confirm this suspicion?

    A. `uptime`

    B. `lastboot`

    C. `reboot -l`

    D. `bootinfo -t`

2. Once the machine has been powered on, which of the following is the correct way to reach the Systems Management Services menu on a PCI machine?

    A. Press the space-bar when the LED displays 262.

    B. Turn the key to Service mode when the LED displays 200.

    C. Choose SMS when the boot option menu appears on screen.

    D. Press the appropriate function key once the keyboard has been enabled.

3. While attempting a preservation install, all of the hardware connections appear to be correct. However, when trying to boot from CD-ROM, the machine ends up in diagnostics. Which of the following is the most likely cause of this problem?

   A. The battery on the machine is bad.

   B. The root volume group is corrupt.

   C. The low-level debugger is not enabled.

   D. There is a hardware problem with the CD-ROM.

2.6.1 Answers

The following answers are for the quiz questions.

1. A

2. D

3. D

2.7 Exercises

The following exercises provide sample topics for self study. They will help ensure comprehension of this chapter.

1. Change your bootlist to boot over the network over your token ring adapter on the next system boot up.

2. Use the `alog` command to find out what events took place during your startup process.

3. Shutdown and restart your system using the `shutdown` command.

4. You have just powered on an external tape drive. Use `cfgmgr` to bring that tape drive into an available state and ensure that you see all the messages with the `cfgmgr` command.

5. Add an application to your shutdown process that gracefully brings down your running databases.

6. Find out the amount of time your system has been online.

7. Find out when root last logged onto the system and from which terminal.

8. Use the `mpcfg` command to change your Fast IPL flag to true.

Hardware assistance

This chapter discusses various methods to determine the devices installed on your system, the methods available to you to record the system error messages, and then ways of using these messages to solve system problems. It also discusses using the system log to record any desired messages.

3.1 Listing hardware devices

To learn about the hardware characteristics of your system, you can use the following commands:

lsdev   Displays devices on the system and their characteristics.

lspv   Displays information about a physical volume within a volume group.

lsattr   Displays information about the attributes of a given device or kind of device.

For example:

► To list the tapes on your system, use the **lsdev -C -c tape** command.

► To list the disks on your system, use the **lsdev -C -c disk** command.

3.1.1 Using the lsdev command

You can use the **lsdev** command to display information about devices in the device configuration database. You can use this command to display information from either the Customized Devices object class in ODM using the -C flag or the Predefined Devices object class in ODM using the -P flag. For more information on the ODM, see Chapter 5, "Object Data Manager" on page 117.

The general command syntax of the **lsdev** command is as follows:

```
lsdev -C [ -c Class ] [ -s Subclass ] [ -t Type ] [ -f File ]
[ -F Format | -r ColumnName ] [ -h ] [ -H ] [ -l Name ]
[ -S State ]
lsdev -P [-c Class ] [ -s Subclass ] [ -t Type ] [ -f File ]
[ -F Format | -r ColumnName ] [ -h ] [ -H ]
```

Some of the commonly used flags with the **lsdev** command are provided in Table 3-1.

Table 3-1   lsdev command flags

Flag	Description
-C	Lists information about a device that is in the Customized Devices object class. The default information displayed is name, status, location, and description. This flag cannot be used with the -P flag.
-c Class	Specifies a device class name. This flag can be used to restrict output to devices in a specified class.
-H	Displays headers above the column output.
-h	Displays the command usage message.

Flag	Description
-P	Lists information about a device that is in the Predefined Devices object class. The default information displayed is class, type, subclass, description. This flag cannot be used with the -C, -I, or -S flags.
-S *State*	Lists all devices in a specified state as named by the State parameter.

Following are some examples of using the **lsdev** command to list different device information about a system.

Listing devices in the predefined ODM database

To list all devices in the Predefined Devices object class with column headers, on the command line, enter:

```
lsdev -P -H
```

The system displays an output similar to Figure 3-1.

```
class           type           subclass    description

logical_volume  vgtype         vgsubclass  Volume group
logical_volume  lvtype         lvsubclass  Logical volume
lvm             lvdd           lvm         LVM Device Driver
aio             aio            node        Asynchronous I/O
pty             pty            pty         Asynchronous Pseudo-Terminal
memory          L2cache_rspc   sys         L2 Cache
memory          totmem         sys         Memory
planar          sysplanar_rspc sys         System Planar
processor       proc_rspc      sys         Processor
sys             chrp           node        System Object
bus             pci            sys         PCI Bus
tape            1200mb-c       scsi        1.2 GB 1/4-Inch Tape Drive
tape            150mb          scsi        150 MB 1/4-Inch Tape Drive
tape            3490e          scsi        3490E Autoloading Tape Drive
tape            4mm2gb         scsi        2.0 GB 4mm Tape Drive
tape            4mm4gb         scsi        4.0 GB 4mm Tape Drive
tape            525mb          scsi        525 MB 1/4-Inch Tape Drive
tape            8mm            scsi        2.3 GB 8mm Tape Drive
tape            8mm5gb         scsi        5.0 GB 8mm Tape Drive
tape            8mm7gb         scsi        7.0 GB 8mm Tape Drive
tape            9trk           scsi        1/2-inch 9-Track Tape Drive
:
```

Figure 3-1   Listing devices from a pre-defined ODM database

Listing devices in customized ODM database

To list all the devices in the Customized Devices object class, enter:

lsdev -C -H

An output similar to Figure 3-2 is shown:

```
$ lsdev -C -H | pg
name         status    location    description

sys0         Available 00-00       System Object
sysplanar0   Available 00-00       System Planar
bus0         Available 00-00       PCI Bus
bus1         Available 04-A0       ISA Bus
pmc0         Available 01-A0       Power Management Controller
fda0         Available 01-C0       Standard I/O Diskette Adapter
ide0         Available 01-E0       ATA/IDE Controller Device
ide1         Available 01-F0       ATA/IDE Controller Device
sa0          Available 01-G0       Standard I/O Serial Port 1
sa1          Available 01-H0       Standard I/O Serial Port 2
sioka0       Available 01-I0       Keyboard Adapter
sioma0       Available 01-J0       Mouse Adapter
iga0         Available 04-C0       E15 Graphics Adapter
scsi0        Available 04-B0       Standard SCSI I/O Controller
gga0         Available 04-01       IBM Personal Computer Power Series S15 Graphic
s Adapter
rmt0         Available 04-B0-00-0,0 4.0 GB 4mm Tape Drive
cd0          Available 04-B0-00-3,0 SCSI Multimedia CD-ROM Drive
hdisk0       Available 04-B0-00-5,0 SCSI Disk Drive
hdisk1       Available 04-B0-00-6,0 1.0 GB SCSI Disk Drive
mem0         Available 00-00       Memory
:
```

Figure 3-2   Listing devices in the customized ODM database

Listing available devices

To list the adapters that are in the Available state in the Customized Devices object class, enter:

lsdev -C -c adapter -S a

An output similar to Figure 3-3 is shown:

```
sa0       Available 01-S1    Standard I/O Serial Port
sa1       Available 01-S2    Standard I/O Serial Port
siokma0   Available 01-K1    Keyboard/Mouse Adapter
fda0      Available 01-D1    Standard I/O Diskette Adapter
scsi0     Available 20-60    Wide SCSI I/O Controller
scsi1     Available 40-58    Wide SCSI I/O Controller
sioka0    Available 01-K1-00 Keyboard Adapter
ppa0      Available 01-R1    Standard I/O Parallel Port Adapter
ssa0      Available 20-68    IBM SSA Enhanced RAID Adapter (14104500)
tok0      Available 40-60    IBM PCI Tokenring Adapter (14101800)
sioma0    Available 01-K1-01 Mouse Adapter
#
```

Figure 3-3   Listing available devices

Listing supported devices

To list all the classes of supported devices on your system, on the command line enter:

```
lsdev -P -r class
```

An output similar to Figure 3-4 is shown:

```
adapter
aio
bus
cdrom
container
disk
diskette
dlc
driver
if
logical_volume
lvm
memory
pdisk
planar
printer
processor
pty
pwrmgt
sys
:
```

Figure 3-4   Listing supported devices

3.1.2 Using the lspv command

The **lsdev** command obtains general information about the devices installed on your system; however, you can find out specific information about your physical volumes using the **lspv** command.

If you do not use command flags with the **lspv** command, the default is to provide every known physical volume on the system along with its physical disk name, physical volume identifiers (PVIDs), and which volume group (if any) it belongs to. If you specify the **lspv** command with a physical volume name, it displays information about that physical volume only. The general syntax of the **lspv** command is as follows:

```
lspv [ -l | -p | -M ] [ -n DescriptorPhysicalVolume] [-v VolumeGroupID]
PhysicalVolume
```

Two of the most commonly used flags with the **lspv** command are given in Table 3-2.

Table 3-2 lspv command flags

Flag	Description
-p	Lists range, state, region, LV name, type, and mount point for each physical partition on the physical volume.
-v *VolumeGroupID*	Accesses information based on the VolumeGroupID variable.

For example, to display the physical volumes on your system, enter:

```
#lspv
hdisk0          00615147ce54a7ee      rootvg
hdisk1          00615147a877976a      rootvg
```

To display the status and characteristics of physical volume hdisk0, use the **lspv** command as follows:

```
lspv hdisk0
```

An output similar to Figure 3-5 is shown:

```
PHYSICAL VOLUME:    hdisk0                VOLUME GROUP:      rootvg
PV IDENTIFIER:      000919746edab91f      VG IDENTIFIER      000919742b739e57
PV STATE:           active
STALE PARTITIONS:   0                     ALLOCATABLE:       yes
PP SIZE:            8 megabyte(s)         LOGICAL VOLUMES:   8
TOTAL PPs:          537 (4296 megabytes)  VG DESCRIPTORS:    2
FREE PPs:           155 (1240 megabytes)
USED PPs:           382 (3056 megabytes)
FREE DISTRIBUTION:  47..00..00..00..108
USED DISTRIBUTION:  61..107..107..107..00
# 
```

Figure 3-5 Listing physical volume characteristics

To list the status and characteristics of physical volume hdisk0 by physical partition number, use the **lspv** command as follows:

```
lspv -p hdisk0
```

A screen similar to Figure 3-6 is shown:

```
hdisk0:
PP RANGE  STATE  REGION         LV NAME        TYPE      MOUNT POINT
  1-1     used   outer edge     hd5            boot      N/A
  2-48    free   outer edge
 49-51    used   outer edge     hd9var         jfs       /var
 52-52    used   outer edge     hd2            jfs       /usr
 53-108   used   outer edge     hd6            paging    N/A
109-116   used   outer middle   hd6            paging    N/A
117-215   used   outer middle   hd2            jfs       /usr
216-216   used   center         hd8            jfslog    N/A
217-217   used   center         hd4            jfs       /
218-222   used   center         hd2            jfs       /usr
223-223   used   center         hd9var         jfs       /var
224-225   used   center         hd3            jfs       /tmp
226-226   used   center         hd1            jfs       /home
227-322   used   center         hd2            jfs       /usr
323-409   used   inner middle   hd2            jfs       /usr
410-411   used   inner middle   hd4            jfs       /
412-429   used   inner middle   hd2            jfs       /usr
430-537   free   inner edge
# ▮
```

Figure 3-6   Listing physical volume characteristics by physical partitions

3.2 Configuring system devices

When you add a new device to your system, or you need to configure devices that were not detected as available during the boot process, the system must have a way of configuring these devices. The **cfgmgr** command is used to configure devices and, optionally, install device software into the system. The devices to be configured are controlled by the Configuration Rules object class, which is part of the Device Configuration database. Each configuration rule specifies three items:

▶ The full path name of an executable program to run.

▶ When to run the program (in relation to the other rules).

▶ In which phase to run the program.

During system boot, the **cfgmgr** command configures all the devices that are necessary.

The **cfgmgr** command recognizes three phases of configuration rules:

▶ Phase 1

▶ Phase 2 (second boot phase for normal boot)

▶ Phase 3 (second boot phase for service boot)

During Phase 1, the **cfgmgr** command is invoked specifying this as Phase 1 by using the -f flag. The **cfgmgr** command runs all of the Phase 1 configuration rules, which results in the base devices being configured. After this, Phase 2 execution begins, and the **cfgmgr** command is called with the -s flag.

Normally, the **cfgmgr** command runs all the rules for the phase specified during invocation (Phase 1 rules for the -f flag). However, if the -l flag is used, the **cfgmgr** command configures only the named device and its children.

If the **cfgmgr** command is invoked without a phase option (for example, without the -f,-s, or -p flags), then the command runs the Phase 2 rules. The only way to run the Phase 3 rules is with the -p flag.

The configuration rules for each phase are ordered based on the values specified in the *seq* field. This field is an integer that specifies the priority in which to execute this rule relative to the other rules for this phase. The higher the number specified by the seq field, the lower the priority; for example, a value of 1 specified in the seq field is run before a rule with a value of 10. There is one exception: A seq field value of 0 implies a *don't care* condition, and any seq field value of 0 is executed last.

Therefore, a seq field value of 1 is the highest priority (first to run).

If there are any devices detected that have no device software installed while configuring devices, the **cfgmgr** command returns a warning message with the name or a list of possible names for the device package that must be installed. If the specific name of the device package is determined, it is displayed as the only package name on a line below the warning message. If the specific name cannot be determined, a colon-separated list of possible package names is displayed on a single line. A package name or list of possible package names is displayed for each of the devices if more than one device is detected without its device software.

An example is as follows:

```
cfgmgr: 0514-621 WARNING: The following device packages are
        required for device support but are not currently
        installed.
devices.pci.22100020
devices.pci.14101800
devices.pci.scsi:devices.pci.00100300:devices.pci.NCR.53C825
```

In this example, two devices were found whose software is missing, and the **cfgmgr** command displayed the names of the device packages that must be installed. A third device whose software is missing was also found but in this case, the **cfgmgr** command displays several possible device package names.

When more than one possible package name is identified for a device, typically only one of the names will correspond to a device package on the installation medium. This is the package to install. However, in some cases, more than one of the names will correspond to device packages on the installation medium. In this case, the first package name in the list, for which there is an actual device package on the installation medium, is the package that must be installed. If the **cfgmgr** command is used with the -i flag, then the correct packages will be installed.

If you invoke the **cfgmgr** command with the -i flag, the command attempts to install device software automatically for each newly detected device. The device variable of the -i flag specifies where to find the installation medium. The installation medium can be a hardware device (such as a tape or diskette drive), a directory that contains installation images, or the installation image file itself. Some of the common flags used with the **cfgmgr** command are provided in Table 3-3.

Table 3-3   cfgmgr command flags

Flag	Description
-i *Device*	Specifies the location of the installation medium.
-l *Name*	Instructs the named device to be configured along with its children.
-p *Phase*	Instructs the **cfgmgr** command to run the specified phase.
-s	Instructs the **cfgmgr** command to run the Phase 2 configuration rules.
-v	Specifies the type of details to be written to stdout.

The configuration rules used by the **cfgmgr** command are provided in Table 3-4.

Table 3-4   cfgmgr configuration rules

Rule	Description
phase	Specifies whether this rule belongs to Phase 1, Phase 2, or Phase 3 (second boot phase for the service mode).
seq	Specifies, as an integer, the relative priority of this rule.
rule	A string containing the full path name of a program to run (can also contain any flags, but they must follow the program name, as this whole string is run as though it were typed in on the command line).

The following examples are based on the configuration rules containing the following information:

```
phase   seq        rule

  1     1          /usr/lib/methods/defsys
  1     10         /usr/lib/methods/deflvm
  2     1          /usr/lib/methods/defsys
  2     5          /usr/lib/methods/ptynode
  2     10         /usr/lib/methods/startlft
  2     15         /usr/lib/methods/starttty
  3     1          /usr/lib/methods/defsys
  3     5          /usr/lib/methods/ptynode
  3     10         /usr/lib/methods/startlft
  3     15         /usr/lib/methods/starttty
```

When the **cfgmgr** command is invoked with the -f flag, the command reads all of the configuration rules with phase = 1 and runs them in the following order:

```
/usr/lib/methods/defsys
/usr/lib/methods/deflvm
```

Note: The -f flag cannot be used once the system has booted.

When the **cfgmgr** command is run with the -s flag, the command reads all of the configuration rules with phase = 2 and runs them in the following order:

```
/usr/lib/methods/defsys
/usr/lib/methods/ptynode
/usr/lib/methods/startlft
/usr/lib/methods/starttty
```

When the **cfgmgr** command is run with the -p 3 flag, the command reads all of the configuration rules with phase = 3 and runs them in the following order:

```
/usr/lib/methods/defsys
/usr/lib/methods/ptynode
/usr/lib/methods/startlft
/usr/lib/methods/starttty
```

If the **cfgmgr** command is run without a flag, the command functions the same as when used with the -s flag. To configure detected devices attached to the SCSI0 adapter, use the **cfgmgr** command as follows:

```
cfgmgr -l scsi0
```

To install device software automatically during configuration (with the software contained in a directory), use the **cfgmgr** command as follows:

```
cfgmgr -i /usr/sys/inst.images
```

3.3 System management services

The `cfgmgr` command configures devices at the software level. You can use the System Management Services (SMS) to check and configure the system at a hardware level. With SMS, you can check to see if all available hardware has been detected, or you can test certain hardware for failure.

To access the SMS utility, use the following instructions:

1. Begin with your machine turned off.

2. If your system requires an SMS diskette, insert it into the diskette drive of the client and turn on the machine. If you do not insert an SMS diskette at this time, and one is required, you will be prompted to insert one later.

3. As icons begin to display from left to right on the bottom of your display, press the F1 key for the Graphical SMS menu or the F4 key for an ASCII SMS menu.

> **Note:** If the last icon is displayed prior to pressing the F1 or F4 key, the normal mode boot list is used instead of the System Management Services diskette.

4. The SMS menu is displayed on your screen. You can do your hardware testing or configuration as needed.

You can change the advisory password in the SMS menu so that only authorized people can access the SMS utility. If you forget this password, the only way to recover from this is to remove the on-board system battery.

3.4 Hardware device compatibility

RSPC and RS/6000 Platform Architecture (RPA) systems including may support attachment of devices using the following methods:

► PCI

► ISA

► SCSI

Provided the device support software is installed, PCI and SCSI devices are configured automatically whenever the Configuration Manager program (`cfgmgr`) is run at system boot and when no conflict (for example, the same SCSI ID for two SCSI devices) is found.

Non-native ISA devices will have to be configured manually, and you may need to change some of the device's predefined or customized attribute values especially when configuring two or more ISA devices of the same type.

Even though you can have multiple adapters on one system, you may not always be able to run different devices on the same adapter. There are various different configurations according to the specification of your particular machine. For example, if you have a SCSI Single-Ended (SE) Ultra Controller, only SE SCSI devices can connect to it, not differential devices. Likewise, If you have a 100 Mbps Ethernet LAN, a 10 Mbps Ethernet card will not work.

3.4.1 Device configuration database

Device information is contained in a predefined database or a customized database that makes up the Device Configuration Database managed by the Object Data Manager (ODM).

▶ The predefined database contains configuration data for all possible devices configured to the system.

▶ The customized database contains configuration data for all currently defined and configured devices in the system.

The device information stored in the Device Configuration Database allows the automatic configuration of microchannel devices on RISC System/6000 systems and PCI devices on RSPC and RPA (non Micro Channel) systems whenever the Configuration Manager (**cfgmgr**) program is run at system boot and run time.

As for non-native ISA devices, the information data contained in the predefined part of the configuration database is not sufficient to perform automatic, conflict-free, ISA device configuration. Thus, the user needs to manually customize some values to be used by the ISA device (for example, interrupt level, shared memory address, and so forth) when configuring the device for the first time.

3.5 Using the lsattr command

After configuring all the devices in the system, you can use the **lsattr** command to display information about the attributes of a given device or kind of device. If you do not specify the device's logical name (-l *Name*), you must use a combination of one or all of the -c *Class*, -s *Subclass*, and -t *Type* flags to uniquely identify the predefined device. The general syntax of the **lsattr** command is as follows:

```
lsattr { -D [ -O ] | -E [ -O ] | -F Format } -l Name [ -a Attribute ] ...
[ -f File ] [ -h ] [ -H ]
```

```
lsattr { -D [ -O ] | -F Format } { [ -c Class ] [ -s Subclass ] [ -t Type ] }
[ -a Attribute ] ... [ -f File ] [ -h ] [ -H ]
lsattr -R { -l Name | [ -c Class ] [ -s Subclass ] [ -t Type ] } -a Attribute
[ -f File ] [ -h ] [ -H ]
```

The flags commonly used with the **lsattr** command are given in Table 3-5.

Table 3-5   lsattr command flags

Flag	Description
-D	Displays the attribute names, default values, descriptions, and user-settable flag values for a specific device when not used with the -O flag. The -D flag displays only the attribute name and default value in colon format when used with the -O flag.
-E	Displays the attribute names, current values, descriptions, and user-settable flag values for a specific device when not used with the -O flag. The -E flag only displays the attribute name and current value in colon format when used with the -O flag. This flag cannot be used with the -c, -D, -F, -R, -s, or -t flags.
-F Format	Displays the output in a user-specified format.
-a Attribute	Displays information for the specified attributes of a specific device or kind of device.
-c Class	Specifies a device class name. This flag cannot be used with the -E or -l flags.
-f File	Reads the needed flags from the *File* parameter.
-H	Displays headers above the column output. To use the -H flag with either the -O or the -R flags is meaningless; the -O or -R flag prevails.
-l Name	Specifies the device logical name in the Customized Devices object class whose attribute names or values are to be displayed.
-O	Displays all attribute names separated by colons and, on the second line, displays all the corresponding attribute values separated by colons.

Flag	Description
-R	Displays the legal values for an attribute name. The -R flag cannot be used with the -D, -E, -F and -O flags, but can be used with any combination of the -c, -s, and -t flags that uniquely identifies a device from the Predefined Devices object class or with the -I flag. The -R flag displays the list attribute values in a vertical column as follows: Value1 Value2 . . ValueN The -R flag displays the range attribute values as x...n(+i) where x is the start of the range, n is the end of the range, and i is the increment.
-s *Subclass*	Specifies a device subclass name. This flag can be used to restrict the output to devices of a specified subclass. This flag cannot be used with the -E or -I flags.
-t *Type*	Specifies a device type name. This flag can be used to restrict the output to devices of a specified class. This flag cannot be used with the -E or -I flag.

When displaying the effective values of the attributes for a customized device, the information is obtained from the Configuration database, not the device. Generally, the database values reflect how the device is configured unless it is reconfigured with the **chdev** command using the -P or -T flag. If this has occurred, the information displayed by the **lsattr** command might not correctly indicate the current device configuration until after the next system boot.

If you use the -D or -E flags, the output defaults to the values for the attribute's name, value, description, and user-settable strings unless also used with the -O flag. The -O flag displays the names of all attributes specified separated by colons. On the next line, the -O flag displays all the corresponding attribute values separated by colons. The -H flag can be used with either the -D, -E, or -F flags to display headers above the column names. You can define the format of the output with a user-specified format where the format parameter is a quoted list of column names separated by non-alphanumeric characters or white space using the -F *Format* flag.

You can supply the flags either on the command line or from the specified file parameter. The following are some examples of the usage of the **lsattr** command.

▶ To list the current attribute values for the tape device rmt0, use the **lsattr** command as follows:

```
# lsattr -l rmt0 -E
mode       yes  Use DEVICE BUFFERS during writes        True
block_size 1024 BLOCK size (0=variable length)          True
extfm      no   Use EXTENDED file marks                 True
ret_error  no   RETURN error on tape change or reset True
```

▶ To list the default attribute values for the tape device rmt0, use the **lsattr** command as follows:

```
# lsattr -l rmt0 -D
mode       yes  Use DEVICE BUFFERS during writes        True
block_size 1024 BLOCK size (0=variable length)          True
extfm      no   Use EXTENDED file marks                 True
ret_error  no   RETURN error on tape change or reset True
```

▶ To list the current value of the bus_intr_lvl attribute for the SCSI adapter scsi0, use the **lsattr** command as follows:

```
# lsattr -l scsi0 -a bus_intr_lvl -E
bus_intr_lvl 14 Bus interrupt level False
```

▶ To list the possible values of the login attribute for the TTY device tty0, use the **lsattr** command as follows:

```
# lsattr -l tty0 -a login -R
enable
disable
share
delay
hold
```

▶ To list the current value of the speed attribute for the serial port that tty0 is connected to, use the **lsattr** command as follows:

```
# lsattr -El tty0 -a speed
speed 9600 BAUD rate True
```

Depending on your software configuration, you may see a different command response than the previous one. Try the command with a different device and attribute and experience how it behaves.

3.6 Using SMIT with devices

The SMIT fast path `smitty devices` allows you to use the SMIT menu interface to do the following:

- ▸ Install or configure devices added after IPL.
- ▸ Remove devices.
- ▸ List existing devices.
- ▸ Change or show the characteristics of devices.
- ▸ Perform problem determination on devices.

3.7 The system error log

Once you have all the devices configured in your system and your system is in production, you may encounter errors related to hardware during your normal day-to-day operations. AIX provides the error logging facility for recording hardware and software failures in an error log. This error log can be used for information purposes or for fault detection and corrective actions.

The error logging process begins when an operating system module detects an error. The error-detecting segment of code then sends error information to either the errsave and errlast kernel service or the errlog application subroutine where the information is, in turn, written to the /dev/error special file. This process then adds a time stamp to the collected data. You can use the **errpt** command to retrieve an error record from the error log.

3.7.1 Using the errdemon command

The errdemon process constantly checks the /dev/error file for new entries. When new data matches an item in the Error Record Template Repository, the daemon collects additional information from other system components.

The **errdemon** command is normally started automatically during system start-up, however, if it has been terminated for any reason and you need to restart it, enter:

```
/usr/lib/errdemon
```

To determine the path to your system's error log file, run the following command:

```
# /usr/lib/errdemon -l
Error Log Attributes
------------------------------------------------
Log File                  /var/adm/ras/errlog
Log Size                  1048576 bytes
Memory Buffer Size        8192 bytes
```

To change the maximum size of the error log file, enter:

```
/usr/lib/errdemon -s 2000000
```

To change the size of the error log device driver's internal buffer, enter:

```
/usr/lib/errdemon -B 16384
```

A message similar to the following is displayed:

```
0315-175 The error log memory buffer size you supplied will be rounded up to a
multiple of 4096 bytes.
```

3.7.2 Using the errpt command

To retrieve the entries in the error log, you can use the **errpt** command. The **errpt** command generates an error report from entries in an error log. It includes flags for selecting errors that match specific criteria. By using the default condition, you can display error log entries in the reverse order in which they occurred and were recorded.

> **Note:** The **errpt** command does not perform error log analysis; for analysis, use the **diag** command.

The general syntax of the **errpt** command is as follows:

```
errpt [ -a ] [ -c ] [ -d ErrorClassList ] [ -e EndDate ] [ -g ] [ -i File ]
[ -j ErrorID [ ,ErrorID ] ] | [ -k ErrorID [ ,ErrorID ]] [ -J ErrorLabel
[ ,ErrorLabel ] ] | [ -K ErrorLabel [ ,ErrorLabel ] ] [ -l SequenceNumber ]
[ -m Machine ] [ -n Node ] [-s StartDate ] [ -F FlagList ]
[ -N ResourceNameList ] [ -R ResourceTypeList ] [ -S ResourceClassList ]
[ -T ErrorTypeList ] [ -y File ] [ -z File ]
```

Some of the most commonly used flags used with the **errpt** command are given in Table 3-6.

Table 3-6   errpt command flags

Flag	Description
-a	Displays information about errors in the error log file in a detailed format. If used in conjunction with the - t flag, all the information from the template file is displayed.
-j ErrorID[,ErrorID]	Includes only the error-log entries specified by the ErrorID (error identifier) variable. The ErrorID variables can be separated by commas (,) or enclosed in double quotation marks ("") and separated by commas (,) or space characters. When combined with the -t flag, entries are processed from the error-template repository.
-s StartDate	Specifies all records posted after the StartDate variable, where the StartDate variable has the form *mmddhhmmyy* (month, day, hour, minute, and year).
-t	Processes the error-record template repository instead of the error log. The -t flag can be used to view error-record templates in report form.
-F FlagList	Selects error-record templates according to the value of the Alert, Log, or Report field of the template.
-J ErrorLabel	Includes the error log entries specified by the ErrorLabel variable.

The following sections show a few examples of using the **errpt** command.

Displaying errors in summary

To display a complete summary report of the errors that have been encountered so far, on the command line, use the **errpt** command as follows:

```
# errpt
IDENTIFIER TIMESTAMP  T C RESOURCE_NAME  DESCRIPTION
2BFA76F6   1025181998 T S SYSPROC        SYSTEM SHUTDOWN BY USER
9DBCFDEE   1025182198 T O errdemon       ERROR LOGGING TURNED ON
2BFA76F6   1025175998 T S SYSPROC        SYSTEM SHUTDOWN BY USER
9DBCFDEE   1025180298 T O errdemon       ERROR LOGGING TURNED ON
2BFA76F6   1025174098 T S SYSPROC        SYSTEM SHUTDOWN BY USER
9DBCFDEE   1025174398 T O errdemon       ERROR LOGGING TURNED ON
..........  (Lines Removed)
2BFA76F6   1021134298 T S SYSPROC        SYSTEM SHUTDOWN BY USER
9DBCFDEE   1021135098 T O errdemon       ERROR LOGGING TURNED ON
2BFA76F6   1021120198 T S SYSPROC        SYSTEM SHUTDOWN BY USER
```

Displaying error details

To display a detailed report of all the errors encountered on the system, use the **errpt** command as follows:

```
# errpt -a
-----------------------------------------------------------------------
LABEL:          REBOOT_ID
IDENTIFIER:     2BFA76F6

Date/Time:        Sun Oct 25 18:19:04
Sequence Number:  60
Machine Id:       006151474C00
Node Id:          mynode
Class:            S
Type:             TEMP
Resource Name:    SYSPROC

Description
SYSTEM SHUTDOWN BY USER

Probable Causes
SYSTEM SHUTDOWN

Detail Data
USER ID
         0
0=SOFT IPL 1=HALT 2=TIME REBOOT
         0
TIME TO REBOOT (FOR TIMED REBOOT ONLY)
.......... (Lines Removed)
-----------------------------------------------------------------------
LABEL:          DISK_ERR3
IDENTIFIER:     35BFC499

Date/Time:        Thu Oct 22 08:11:12
Sequence Number:  36
Machine Id:       006151474C00
Node Id:          mynode
Class:            H
Type:             PERM
Resource Name:    hdisk0
Resource Class:   disk
Resource Type:    scsd
Location:         04-B0-00-6,0
VPD:
        Manufacturer................IBM
        Machine Type and Model......DORS-32160    !#
FRU Number.................
        ROS Level and ID............57413345
```

```
                    Serial Number..............5U5W6388
                    EC Level...................85G3685
                    Part Number................07H1132
                    Device Specific.(Z0)........000002028F00001A
                    Device Specific.(Z1)........39H2916
                    Device Specific.(Z2).......0933
                    Device Specific.(Z3).......1296
                    Device Specific.(Z4)........0001
                    Device Specific.(Z5)........16


Description
DISK OPERATION ERROR


Probable Causes
DASD DEVICE
STORAGE DEVICE CABLE


Failure Causes
DISK DRIVE
DISK DRIVE ELECTRONICS
STORAGE DEVICE CABLE


           Recommended Actions
           PERFORM PROBLEM DETERMINATION PROCEDURES


Detail Data
SENSE DATA
0A06 0000 2800 0088 0002 0000 0000 0200 0200 0000 0000 0000 0000 0000
0000 0000 0000 0000 0000 0000 0000 0000 0000 0000 0000 0000 0000 0000 0000 0000
0000 0000 0000 0000 0000 0000 0000 0000 0000 0000 0000 0000 0000 0000 0000 0000
0000 0000 0000 0000 0000 0000 0000 0000 0000 0000 0000 0000 0000 0000 0000 0000
0000 0000 0000 0000 0000 0001 0001 2FC0
.......... (Lines Removed)
----------------------------------------------------------------------
LABEL:         ERRLOG_ON
IDENTIFIER:    9DBCFDEE

Date/Time:     Fri Sep 18 14:56:55
Sequence Number: 14
Machine Id:    006151474C00
Node Id:       mynode
Class:         O
Type:          TEMP
Resource Name: errdemon


Description
ERROR LOGGING TURNED ON


Probable Causes
```

ERRDEMON STARTED AUTOMATICALLY

User Causes
/USR/LIB/ERRDEMON COMMAND

        Recommended Actions
        NONE

Displaying errors by time reference

If you suspect that the errors were encountered during the last day, you can display a detailed report of all errors logged in the past 24 hours, where the string equals the current month, day, hour, minute, and year, minus 24 hours. To do so, use the **errpt** command as follows:

```
# date
Wed Aug 29 09:30:42 CDT 2001
# errpt -a -s 0828093001
---------------------------------------------------------------------------
LABEL:          REBOOT_ID
IDENTIFIER:     2BFA76F6

Date/Time:        Tue Aug 28 15:53:34
Sequence Number: 2
Machine Id:       003826424C00
Node Id:          mynode
Class:            S
Type:             TEMP
Resource Name:    SYSPROC

Description
SYSTEM SHUTDOWN BY USER

Probable Causes
SYSTEM SHUTDOWN

Detail Data
USER ID
        0
0=SOFT IPL 1=HALT 2=TIME REBOOT
        0
TIME TO REBOOT (FOR TIMED REBOOT ONLY)
        0
---------------------------------------------------------------------------
LABEL:          ERRLOG_ON
IDENTIFIER:     9DBCFDEE

Date/Time:        Tue Aug 28 15:56:27
Sequence Number: 1
```

```
Machine Id:        003826424C00
Node Id:           mynode
Class:             0
Type:              TEMP
Resource Name:     errdemon


Description
ERROR LOGGING TURNED ON

Probable Causes
ERRDEMON STARTED AUTOMATICALLY

User Causes
/USR/LIB/ERRDEMON COMMAND

        Recommended Actions
        NONE
```

3.7.3 Using the errlogger command

The **errlogger** command allows you to log operator messages to the system error log. These messages can be up to 1024 bytes in length.

The use of the **errlogger** command and its output are shown in the following example.

```
# errlogger Testing use of errlogger command
# errpt
IDENTIFIER TIMESTAMP  T C RESOURCE_NAME  DESCRIPTION
AA8AB241   0904103401 T O OPERATOR       OPERATOR NOTIFICATION
1581762B   0831110701 T H cd0            DISK OPERATION ERROR
2BFA76F6   0828155301 T S SYSPROC        SYSTEM SHUTDOWN BY USER
# errpt -a -j AA8AB241
--------------------------------------------------------------------
LABEL:          OPMSG
IDENTIFIER:     AA8AB241

Date/Time:      Tue Sep  4 10:34:17
Sequence Number: 6
Machine Id:     003826424C00
Node Id:        mynode
Class:          0
Type:           TEMP
Resource Name:  OPERATOR


Description
OPERATOR NOTIFICATION

User Causes
```

```
ERRLOGGER COMMAND

        Recommended Actions
        REVIEW DETAILED DATA

Detail Data
MESSAGE FROM ERRLOGGER COMMAND
Testing use of errlogger command
#
```

3.7.4 Other error handling commands

In addition to the **errpt** command, the following commands can be used in conjunction with the **errpt** command to find hardware errors and take corrective measures for any problems reported by the error logging facility:

errclear   Deletes entries from the error log.

errinstall   Installs messages in the error logging message sets.

errupdate   Updates the Error Record Template repository.

3.8 Diagnosing hardware problems

The **diag** command is the starting point to run a wide choice of tasks and service aids that are used to perform hardware problem determination. The **diag** command has a menu driven interface, but can also be directed to perform specific tasks using command line flags.

Use the following steps to run diagnostics if you suspect a problem.

1. Run the **diag** command.

2. Press Enter to advance past the information screen.

3. Select Diagnostic Routines.

4. Select Problem Determination.

This instructs the **diag** command to test the system and analyze the error log. Figure 3-7 on page 62 shows the results of running diagnostics on a system with a problem.

```
A PROBLEM WAS DETECTED ON Tue Sep  4 13:26:04 CDT 2001                    801014

The Service Request Number(s)/Probable Cause(s)
(causes are listed in descending order of probability):

  29A00004: Refer to the Error Code to FRU Index in the system service
            guide.
         Error log information:
               Date: Wed Aug 29 08:59:26 CDT 2001
               Sequence number: 23
               Label: SCAN_ERROR_CHRP
     FRU: n/a                    P1-K1

Use Enter to continue.█




F3=Cancel            F10=Exit              Enter
```

Figure 3-7   diag screen showing a problem

Alternatively, you could use the **diag -d sysplanar0 -v -e** command to perform the same diagnostics if you suspect a problem with the sysplanar0 device.

3.9 The system log

To log system messages, AIX uses syslogd. The syslogd daemon reads a datagram socket and sends each message line to a destination described by the /etc/syslog.conf configuration file. The syslogd daemon reads the configuration file when it is activated and when it receives a hang-up signal.

The syslogd daemon creates the /etc/syslog.pid file. This file contains a single line with the command process ID of the syslogd daemon. It is used to end or reconfigure the syslogd daemon.

A terminate signal sent to the syslogd daemon ends the daemon. The syslogd daemon logs the end-signal information and terminates immediately.

Each message is one line. A message can contain a priority code marked by a digit enclosed in angle braces (< >) at the beginning of the line. Messages longer than 900 bytes may be truncated.

The /usr/include/sys/syslog.h include file defines the facility and priority codes used by the configuration file. Locally written applications use the definitions contained in the syslog.h file to log messages using the syslogd daemon.

The general syntax of the `syslogd` command is as follows:

```
syslogd [ -d ] [ -s ] [ -f ConfigurationFile ] [ -m MarkInterval ] [-r]
```

The flags commonly used when starting syslogd are provided in Table 3-7.

Table 3-7 syslogd daemon flags

Flag	Description
-d	Turns on debugging.
-f *Config File*	Specifies an alternate configuration file.
-m *MarkInterval*	Specifies the number of minutes between the `mark` command messages. If you do not use this flag, the `mark` command sends a message with LOG_INFO priority every 20 minutes. This facility is not enabled by a selector field containing an * (asterisk), which selects all other facilities.
-s	Specifies to forward a shortened message to another system (if it is configured to do so) for all the forwarding syslogd messages generated on the local system.
-r	Suppresses logging of messages received from remote hosts.

The syslogd daemon uses a configuration file to determine where to send a system message depending on the message's priority level and the facility that generated it. By default, syslogd reads the default configuration file /etc/syslog.conf, but if you specify the -f flag, you can specify an alternate configuration file.

3.9.1 The syslogd configuration file

The /etc/syslog.conf file controls the behavior of the syslogd daemon. For example, syslogd uses /etc/syslog.conf file to determine where to send the error messages or how to react to different system events. The following is a part of the default /etc/syslog.conf file.

```
/etc/syslog.conf - control output of syslogd
#
# Each line must consist of two parts:-
#
# 1) A selector to determine the message priorities to which the
#    line applies
# 2) An action.
```

```
#
# The two fields must be separated by one or more tabs or spaces.
#
# format:
#
# <msg_src_list>                   <destination>
#
# where <msg_src_list> is a semicolon separated list of <facility>.<priority>
# where:
#
# <facility> is:
#        * - all (except mark)
#        mark - time marks
#        kern,user,mail,daemon, auth,... (see syslogd(AIX Commands Reference))
#
# <priority> is one of (from high to low):
#        emerg/panic,alert,crit,err(or),warn(ing),notice,info,debug
#        (meaning all messages of this priority or higher)
#
# <destination> is:
#        /filename - log to this file
#        username[,username2...] - write to user(s)
#        @hostname - send to syslogd on this machine
#        * - send to all logged in users
#
# example:
# "mail messages, at debug or higher, go to Log file. File must exist."
# "all facilities, at debug and higher, go to console"
# "all facilities, at crit or higher, go to all users"
#  mail.debug               /usr/spool/mqueue/syslog
#  *.debug                  /dev/console
#  *.crit                         *
```

In addition to the /etc/syslog.conf file that contains the settings for the syslogd daemon, the /etc/syslog.pid file contains the process ID of the running syslogd daemon.

3.9.2 The format of the configuration file

This section describes what the format of the /etc/syslog.conf file is and how you can interpret the different entries in this file. Lines in the configuration file for the syslogd daemon contain a selector field and an action field separated by one or more tabs.

The selector field names a facility and a priority level. Separate the facility names with a comma (,) separate the facility and priority-level portions of the selector field with a period (.), and separate multiple entries in the same selector field with a semicolon (;). To select all facilities, use an asterisk (*).

The action field identifies a destination (file, host, or user) to receive the messages. If routed to a remote host, the remote system will handle the message as indicated in its own configuration file. To display messages on a user's terminal, the destination field must contain the name of a valid, logged-in system user.

Facilities

Table 3-8 lists some of the facilities used in the /etc/syslog.conf file. You can use these system facility names in the selector field.

Table 3-8   Facilities used in the /etc/syslog.conf file

Facility	Description
kern	Kernel
user	User level
mail	Mail subsystem
daemon	System daemons
auth	Security or authorization
syslog	syslogd daemon
lpr	Line-printer subsystem
news	News subsystem
uucp	uucp subsystem
*	All facilities

Priority levels

Table 3-9 lists the priority levels used in the /etc/syslog.conf file. You can use the message priority levels in the selector field. Messages of the specified priority level and all levels above it are sent as directed.

Table 3-9   Priority levels for the /etc/syslog.conf file

Priority Level	Description
emerg	Specifies emergency messages (LOG_EMERG). These messages are not distributed to all users. LOG_EMERG priority messages can be logged into a separate file for reviewing.
alert	Specifies important messages (LOG_ALERT), such as a serious hardware error. These messages are distributed to all users.
crit	Specifies critical messages not classified as errors (LOG_CRIT), such as improper login attempts. LOG_CRIT and higher-priority messages are sent to the system console.
err	Specifies messages that represent error conditions (LOG_ERR), such as an unsuccessful disk write.
warning	Specifies messages for abnormal, but recoverable, conditions (LOG_WARNING).
notice	Specifies important informational messages (LOG_NOTICE). Messages without a priority designation are mapped into this priority. These are more important than informational messages, but not warnings.
info	Specifies informational messages (LOG_INFO). These messages can be discarded but are useful in analyzing the system.
debug	Specifies debugging messages (LOG_DEBUG). These messages may be discarded.
none	Excludes the selected facility. This priority level is useful only if preceded by an entry with an * (asterisk) in the same selector field.

Destinations

Table 3-10 lists a few of the destinations that are used in the /etc/syslog.conf file. You can use these message destinations in the action field.

Table 3-10   Destination description for the /etc/syslog.conf file

Destination	Description
File Name	Full path name of a file opened in append mode.
@Host	Host name, preceded by @ (at sign).
User[, User][...]	User names.
*	All users.

3.9.3 Using the system log

To customize the /etc/syslog.conf file so that your required conditions are met, the system log should be updated by editing the /etc/syslog.conf file. After you have edited and added your lines to the /etc/syslog.conf file, you need to restart the syslogd daemon. You can do this by running the following commands:

1. Check to see what the syslogd daemon process ID is. In this case, it is 5426.

```
# ps -ef | grep syslogd
root  5426  4168    0  Nov 01     -  0:00 /usr/sbin/syslogd
root 24938 25854    2 12:04:03  pts/6  0:00 grep syslog
```

2. Use the **stopsrc** command to stop the syslogd daemon as follows:

```
# stopsrc -s syslogd
0513-044 The stop of the syslogd Subsystem was completed successfully.
```

3. Check if the syslogd daemon has been stopped successfully.

```
# ps -ef | grep syslogd
root 26112 25854    2 12:04:16  pts/6  0:00 grep syslog
```

4. Restart the syslogd daemon.

```
# startsrc -s syslogd
0513-059 The syslogd Subsystem has been started. Subsystem PID is 13494.
```

The following are a few examples on the /etc/syslog.conf file usage.

► To log all mail facility messages at the debug level or above to the file /tmp/mailsyslog, enter:

```
mail.debug /tmp/mailsyslog
```

Where:

– *mail* is the Facility as per Table 3-8 on page 65.

- *debug* is the Priority Level as per Table 3-9 on page 66.
- */tmp/mailsyslog* is the Destination as per Table 3-10 on page 67.

▸ To send all system messages except those from the mail facility to a host named rigil, enter:

```
*.debug;mail.none @rigil
```

Where:

- * and *mail* are the Facilities as per Table 3-8 on page 65.
- *debug* and *none* are the Priority Levels as per Table 3-9 on page 66.
- *@rigil* is the Destination as per Table 3-10 on page 67.

▸ To send messages at the emerg priority level from all facilities and messages at the crit priority level and above from the mail and daemon facilities to users nick and jam, enter:

```
*.emerg;mail,daemon.crit nick, jam
```

Where:

- *, *mail* and *daemon* are the Facilities as per Table 3-8 on page 65.
- *emerg* and *crit* are the Priority Levels as per Table 3-9 on page 66.
- *nick* and *jam* are the Destinations as per Table 3-10 on page 67.

▸ To send all mail facility messages to all users' terminal screens, enter:

```
mail.debug *
```

Where:

- *mail* is the Facility as per Table 3-8 on page 65.
- *debug* is the Priority Level as per Table 3-9 on page 66.
- * is the Destination as per Table 3-10 on page 67.

3.10 Setting up an ASCII terminal

The 3151 display can connect directly, or through a modem, to an AIX system. The connection to the AIX system can be made to one of the native serial ports, as shown in Figure 3-8, or to an asynchronous adapter, as shown in Figure 3-9 on page 69. Additionally, a printer can be connected to the 3151 display and is supported by AIX as Terminal Attached Printing, as displayed in Figure 3-8 on page 69.

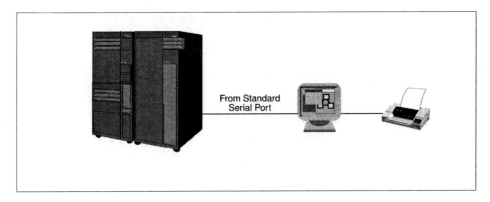

Figure 3-8   Attaching a serial terminal to an RS/6000 system

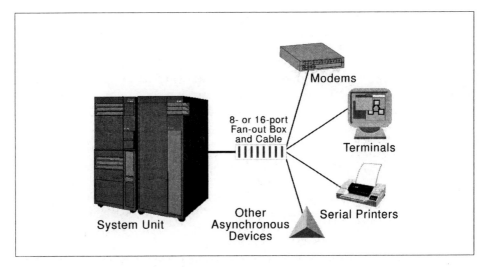

Figure 3-9   Terminal connection to direct-attached asynchronous adapter

To add a TTY, use the following procedure:

1. Issue `smitty tty` and select Add a TTY or issue `smitty maktty`.

2. The system will ask you for the TTY type and the parent adapter. Select the correct values from the list and press Enter.

   A screen similar to Figure 3-10 on page 70 will be shown:

```
                              Add a TTY

Type or select values in entry fields.
Press Enter AFTER making all desired changes.

[TOP]                                              [Entry Fields]
    TTY type                                       tty
    TTY interface                                  rs232
    Description                                    Asynchronous Terminal
    Parent adapter                                 sa0
*   PORT number                                    []                        +
    Enable LOGIN                                   disable                   +
    BAUD rate                                      [9600]                    +
    PARITY                                         [none]                    +
    BITS per character                             [8]                       +
    Number of STOP BITS                            [1]                       +
    TIME before advancing to next port setting     [0]                      +#
    TERMINAL type                                  [dumb]
    FLOW CONTROL to be used                        [xon]                     +
[MORE...31]

F1=Help               F2=Refresh         F3=Cancel          F4=List
F5=Reset              F6=Command         F7=Edit            F8=Image
F9=Shell              F10=Exit           Enter=Do
```

Figure 3-10   Adding a tty

3. Select the port number you want this TTY to be added to in the PORT number
   field. For RANs, follow the location code rules to select the appropriate port
   number.

4. Change the TERMINAL Type field to the type of terminal you are using. This
   field is very important since you might not be able to use all the keys on your
   terminal if this field is set incorrectly. The TERM environment variable stores
   this setting. You can change the terminal emulation setting by using your
   TERM environment variable and using the **export** command to store the
   terminal emulation you want to use. For example, to use ibm3151 terminal
   emulation, use the command:

   TERM=ibm3151; export TERM

5. Set the line speed and the kind of communication (1/8/N or 1/7/E) for your
   terminal and press Enter.

   This will create a device special file in the /dev directory and add an entry to
   the /etc/inittab file to run the getty process on your terminal so that your
   terminal is available at system startup. It also adds another entry to the
   customized ODM (CuDv) database for the terminal you have just added.

You can also add a TTY directly on the command line. To add an ibm3151 RS232
terminal using adapter sa0, and port s1, with login enabled use the following
command:

mkdev -c tty -t tty -s rs232 -p sa0 -w s1 -a login=enable -a term=ibm3151

You can remove a terminal by using the command:

rmdev -l *tty_name* -d

▸ Where *tty_name* can be determined by using the command **tty** or by listing all the TTYs and then selecting the tty you want to remove.

On the ASCII terminal, set the communications options as follows:

```
Line Speed (baud rate) = 9600
Word Length (bits per character) = 8
Parity = no (none)
Number of Stop Bits = 1
Interface = RS-232C (or RS-422A)
Line Control = IPRTS
```

Set the keyboard and display options as follows:

```
Screen = normal
Row and Column = 24x80
Scroll = jump
Auto LF (line feed) = off
Line Wrap = on
Forcing Insert = line (or both)
Tab = field
Operating Mode = echo
Turnaround Character = CR
Enter = return
Return = new line
New Line = CR
Send = page
Insert Character = space
```

Note: If your terminal is an IBM 3151, 3161, or 3164, press the Ctrl+Setup keys to display the Setup Menu and follow the on-screen instructions to set these fields.

If you are using some other ASCII terminal, refer to the appropriate documents for information about how to set these fields.

3.11 Quiz

The following are questions created by the authors to further test your understanding of the topics.

1. The marketing group within the Widget Company plans to implement a new database to house their demographic data. The administrator has requested a tape drive and an additional disk to support the installation of this new database. The IBM hardware engineer has connected the new equipment, and the machine has been rebooted. Which of the following commands should be used to verify the tape device is installed correctly?

   A. `lspv`

   B. `lsdev`

   C. `lstape`

   D. `lsdisk`

2. The marketing group within the Widget Company plans to implement a new database, as in question one. The new tape drive appears to be installed and functioning correctly. However, while attempting to perform a `mksysb` utilizing the new drive, it fails. What would be the first recommended action to take to determine the cause of the failure?

   A. Replace the tape drive.

   B. Run `cfgmgr` to reconfigure the tape device.

   C. Check the error log for tape drive errors.

   D. Use SMIT to change the compression attribute on the tape device.

3. A system administrator has just set up a new machine with two external hard disks in a SCSI chain. One is a 2.2 GB SE (single ended) disk, and the other is a 4.5 GB differential disk. The system administrator reboots the machine and notices that only the SE disk is available. Which of the following is the most likely cause?

   A. The SE disk is most likely experiencing hardware problems.

   B. There is most likely a SCSI conflict between the two drives.

   C. The SE and differential drives are on the same chain.

   D. The differential disk is most likely experiencing hardware problems.

4. Which of the following commands can be used to determine the serial port settings?

   A. `lscfg -vl ttyXX`

   B. `ls -l /dev/ttyXX`

   C. `lsattr -El ttyXX`

   D. `lsdev -C |grep ttyXX`

5. A machine has a bootlist that is set for network booting. In attempting to access SMS menus to change the bootlist to the local disk, it is discovered that someone has set an SMS supervisory password, and the password is not recorded. Which of the following actions will allow the system administrator to gain access to the SMS menus?

   A. Boot from AIX installation media, then reinstall SMS.

   B. Boot from AIX installation media, then reset the supervisory password.

   C. Call IBM and ask for the over-ride password based on the serial number.

   D. Remove the battery from the system for at least one minute. Replace the battery and then reboot.

3.11.1 Answers

The following answers are for the quiz questions.

1. B
2. C
3. C
4. C
5. D

3.12 Exercises

The following exercises provide sample topics for self study. They will help ensure comprehension of this chapter.

1. Check the error log. Are there any problems you should worry about?

2. Check the system log. Determine what information is in the file and add additional information that you want reported on.

3. Configure a new device. Use the cfgmgr command to configure the device.

System and software installation

This chapter describes the installation process, the common commands that are used with the installation process, and the different methods available to you for installing software onto a system. It covers Base Operating System (BOS) installation options, installation of the optional software, and the application of updates to bring your system to the latest maintenance level.

Figure 4-1 shows a flow chart of the steps for installing a system.

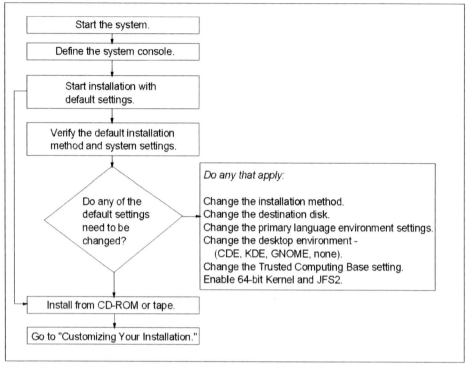

Figure 4-1   Flow chart for AIX 5L Version 5.1 system installation

4.1 Base Operating System installation

To install the Base Operating System, you should first boot the system into maintenance mode. The Welcome to Base Operating System Installation and Maintenance screen is displayed, similar to the one in Figure 4-2 on page 77.

```
                   Welcome to Base Operating System
                      Installation and Maintenance

Type the number of your choice and press Enter.  Choice is indicated by >>>.

>>> 1 Start Install Now with Default Settings

    2 Change/Show Installation Settings and Install

    3 Start Maintenance Mode for System Recovery




    88  Help ?
    99  Previous Menu
>>> Choice [1]:
```

Figure 4-2   Welcome to Base Operating System menu

Select 2 on this screen, and you will be shown a screen similar to Figure 4-3.

```
                      Installation and Settings

Either type 0 and press Enter to install with current settings, or type the
 number of the setting you want to change and press Enter.

     1  System Settings:
           Method of Installation............Preservation
           Disk Where You Want to Install.....hdisk0

     2  Primary Language Environment Settings (AFTER Install):
           Cultural Convention...............English (United States)
           Language .........................English (United States)
           Keyboard .........................English (United States)
           Keyboard Type.....................Default

     3  Advanced Options

>>> 0  Install with the current settings listed above.

                          +----------------------------------------------------
    88  Help ?            ¦   WARNING: Base Operating System Installation will
    99  Previous Menu     ¦   destroy or impair recovery of SOME data on the
                          ¦   destination disk hdisk0.
>>> Choice [0]:
```

Figure 4-3   Installation and Settings menu

Select 3 on this screen, and you will be shown a screen similar to Figure 4-4.

```
                        Advanced Options

Either type 0 and press Enter to install with current settings, or type the
  number of the setting you want to change and press Enter.

    1  Install Configuration.............. Default

    2  Install Trusted Computing Base...... No

    3  Enable 64-bit Kernel and JFS2....... No




>>> 0  Install with the current settings listed above.

    88  Help ?
    99  Previous Menu
>>> Choice [0]:
```

Figure 4-4   Advanced Options menu

In the Installation and Settings screen, you can set the method of installation, the primary language environment settings, and modify advanced options. There are three ways in which you can install AIX on your system. These methods are as follows:

▶ New and Complete Overwrite Installation

▶ Migration Installation

▶ Preservation Installation

4.1.1 New and Complete Overwrite installation

Generally, the New and Complete Overwrite method is used when:

▶ You have a new machine. In this case, the hard disk or disks on which you are installing the BOS are empty. This is the only possible installation method for a new machine.

▶ You want to install onto a hard disk that contains an existing root volume group that you wish to completely overwrite. For example, this might occur if your root volume group has become corrupted.

▶ You want to reassign your hard disks, that is, to make your rootvg smaller and assign less disk space to it.

Note: The New and Complete Overwrite installation overwrites all data on the selected destination disk. This means that, after the installation is complete, you will have to manually configure your system using the Configuration Assistant application, SMIT, or the command line. If you want to preserve your system configuration, and you do not need to completely overwrite your root volume group, do not use the New and Complete Overwrite option.

4.1.2 Migration installation

Use this installation method to upgrade AIX Version 3.2, AIX Version 4.1, AIX Version 4.2, or AIX Version 4.3 to AIX 5L Version 5.1 while preserving the existing root volume group. With the exception of /tmp, this method preserves all file systems, including the root volume group, logical volumes, and system configuration files. Migration is the default installation method for AIX Version 3.2, AIX Version 4.1, and AIX Version 4.2 machines.

In most cases, the user configuration files from the previous version of a product are saved when the new version is installed during a Migration installation.

4.1.3 Preservation installation

Use this installation method when a version of the BOS is installed on your system, and you want to preserve the user data in the root volume group. However, this method overwrites the /usr, /tmp, /var, and / (root) file systems by default; so, any user data in these directories is lost. These file systems are removed and recreated; so, any other LPPs or filesets that you installed on the system will also be lost. System configuration must be done after doing a Preservation installation.

The /etc/preserve.list file contains a list of system files to be copied and saved during a preservation BOS installation. The /etc/filesystems file is listed by default. You can add the full path names of any additional files that you want to save during the Preservation installation to the preserve.list file. For example, you can alter the /etc/preserve.list file to tell your installation process that you want to preserve your /var file system.

For detailed information on installing the BOS, refer to the *AIX Installation Guide*.

4.2 Advanced Options installation

In the AIX 5L Version 5.1 Advanced Options screen, you can modify more settings for system operations parameters. There are three options you can modify:

▶ Installation Package Set or Desktop

▶ Enable Trusted Computing Base

▶ Enable 64-bit Kernel and JFS2

4.2.1 Installation Package Set or Desktop

The Installation Package Set or Desktop screen allows you to configure the type of interface that the system will use at startup. The Installation Package Set is the default and is the only selection for ASCII consoles.

The Desktop selection is for graphical systems. This will allow you to choose the type of graphical interface to use with the system. The types of graphical interfaces are:

▶ CDE

▶ KDE

▶ GNOME

▶ NONE

If you do not choose a desktop by selecting NONE, a minimal configuration is installed including X11, Java, perl, SMIT, and the Web-based System Manager. If you choose CDE, GNOME, or KDE, the desktop and documentation service libraries are also installed. If you choose GNOME or KDE, the interface prompts you for the Toolbox for Linux Applications CD-ROM. If this CD-ROM is not available, you can type *q* to continue the installation without it.

For detailed information on the Installation Package Set or Desktop settings, refer to the *AIX 5L Version 5.1 Installation Guide*, SC23-4374.

4.2.2 Enable Trusted Computing Base (TCB)

The Trusted Computing Base provides an extra level of security and ensures that whatever you are trying to run is actually run. If you set this attribute to YES, the install process installs the bos.rte.security fileset and you can configure TCB. It is important to note that you can enable TCB only at this time. If you decide not to install TCB now, you will have to reinstall the operating system to enable TCB at a later stage. TCB can be removed by removing the bos.rte.security fileset from the system.

4.2.3 Enable 64-bit Kernel and JFS2

AIX 5L Version 5.1 allows you to install a 64-bit kernel as well as the previously available 32-bit kernel during installation. If your system has 64-bit processors, the 64-bit kernel is automatically loaded with the base operating system. However, the 64-bit kernel is only enabled if you set the Enable 64-bit Kernel and JFS2 option to yes during the initial AIX installation.

You can also install this kernel later by installing the bos.mp64 fileset.

The `bootinfo -y` command will identify the type of system hardware you have, either 32-bit or 64-bit. If the command returns a 32, you cannot use the 64-bit kernel.

JFS2 is an enhanced and updated version of the Journaled File System (JFS) from AIX Version 4.3 and previous releases. JFS2 allows for features such as file sizes of 1 terrabyte (TB) and architectural maximum file system sizes of 4 petabytes (PB) in size. JFS2 also allows you to create Enhanced Journaled File Systems on the system.

If you are using the New and Complete Overwrite installation, the installation will create JFS2 file systems in the rootvg. If your system is not 64-bit enabled, this option will not be displayed. If your system is 64-bit enabled and you do a migration installation, this option will be enabled, but it will not convert the existing file systems to JFS2.

Once you have installed the BOS, configured the Advanced Options, and the system has booted from the hard disk, the system will take you to the Configuration Assistant menu.

4.3 Configuration Assistant

After the installation is completed and the system reboots, the Configuration Assistant program, `/usr/sbin/install_assist`, is automatically started. In previous versions of AIX, the Configuration Assistant was known as the Installation Assistant or the Configuration Assistant Taskguide.

The Configuration Assistant allows you to set up basic system configurations, as shown in Figure 4-5 on page 82.

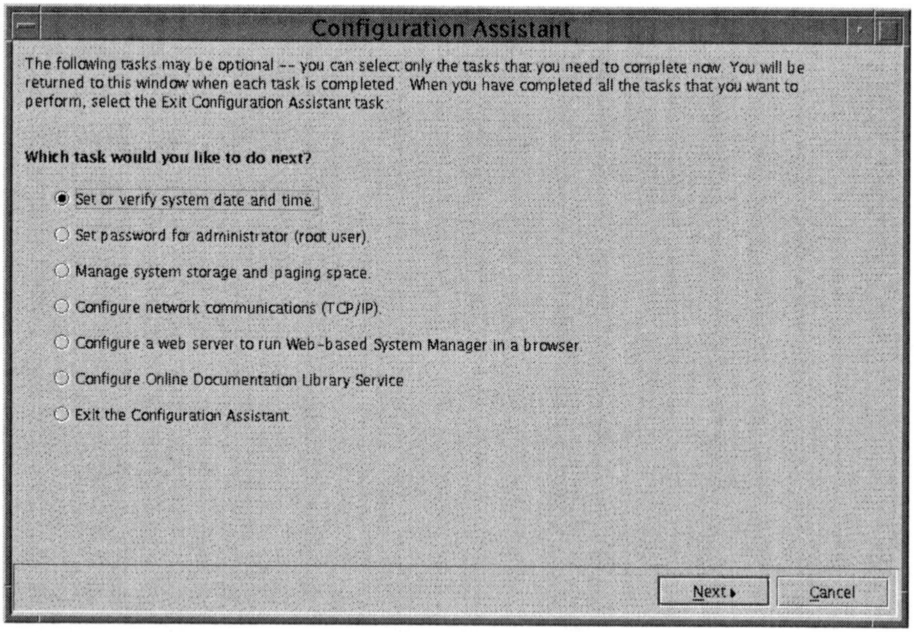

Figure 4-5 Configuration Assistant menu

On a system installed from an ASCII terminal, a similar list will appear in character format.

After completing these tasks using the Configuration Assistant, you should disable the automatic restart of the Configuration Assistant upon reboot. Otherwise, it will appear on the console every time the system is rebooted. To disable the automatic restart, do the following steps:

► Select Exit the Configuraton Assistant.

► Click Next.

► Select Finish now, and do not start Configuration Assistant when restarting the operating system.

If you need to call the Configuration Assistant again, run /usr/sbin/install_assist, or use the SMIT fast path smitty assist.

4.4 Understanding maintenance levels

Once you have installed the base operating system, you can determine the maintenance level with the oslevel command.

The general syntax of the **oslevel** command is as follows:

```
oslevel [ -l Level | -g | -q ]
```

A brief description of the **oslevel** command flags is given in Table 4-1.

Table 4-1   Command flags for oslevel

Flag	Description
-l *Level*	Lists filesets at levels earlier than the maintenance levels specified by the Level parameter.
-g	Lists filesets at levels later than the current maintenance level.
-q	Lists names of known maintenance levels that can be specified using the -l flag.

To see the current maintenance level of your system, use the **oslevel** command as follows:

```
# oslevel
4.3.2.0
```

The product name and level number identify a software product. The level of a software product in AIX Version 3.2 and later is defined as vv.rr.mmmm.ffff, where:

vv   Is a numeric field of one to two digits that identifies the version number.

rr   Is a numeric field of one to two digits that identifies the release number.

mmmm Is a numeric field of one to four digits that identifies the modification level.

ffff   Is a numeric field of one to four digits that identifies the fix level.

For example, bos.net.tcp.client 4.3.2.0 is a fileset, and bos.net.tcp.client 4.3.2.1 is an update to that fileset. If there is another fileset update, bos.net.tcp.client 4.3.2.2 is generated. This update will contain all the fixes that were in the bos.net.tcp.client 4.3.2.1. If a cumulative AIX update is generated, the modification level of the fileset will increment resulting in bos.net.tcp.client 4.3.3.0, which would contain all previous fixes.

After an update, if your system is not showing the new maintenance level, use the -l flag with the **oslevel** command to determine what filesets have not been upgraded to match the new BOS level. In Figure 4-6 on page 84, the system is at 4.3.0.0, but there are some filesets that are not at the current maintenance level.

```
# oslevel
4.3.0.0
# oslevel -q
Known Maintenance Levels
------------------------
4.3.0.0
# oslevel -g
# oslevel -l 4.3.0.0
Fileset                              Actual Level        Maintenance Level
-------------------------------------------------------------------------------
X11.msg.en_US.Dt.helpmin             4.2.0.0             4.3.0.0
X11.msg.en_US.Dt.rte                 4.2.0.0             4.3.0.0
X11.msg.en_US.apps.aixterm           4.2.0.0             4.3.0.0
X11.msg.en_US.apps.clients           4.2.0.0             4.3.0.0
X11.msg.en_US.apps.custom            4.2.0.0             4.3.0.0
X11.msg.en_US.apps.pm                4.2.0.0             4.3.0.0
X11.msg.en_US.apps.rte               4.2.0.0             4.3.0.0
X11.msg.en_US.base.common            4.2.0.0             4.3.0.0
X11.msg.en_US.base.rte               4.2.0.0             4.3.0.0
X11.msg.en_US.motif.lib              4.2.0.0             4.3.0.0
X11.msg.en_US.motif.mwm              4.2.0.0             4.3.0.0
X11.msg.en_US.vsm.rte                4.2.0.0             4.3.0.0
printers.msg.en_US.rte               4.2.0.0             4.3.0.0
#
```

Figure 4-6   Sample oslevel -l output

The **oslevel** command can also be used to verify that a system has been successfully migrated from a lower version of AIX to a higher version. For example, on a system that has just been migrated to AIX 5L Version 5.1 from AIX Version 4.3.3, the **oslevel** command would show the following:

```
# oslevel
5.1.0.0
# oslevel -l 5.1.0.0
#
```

4.5 Software packaging

Software products include those shipped with AIX and those purchased separately. Each software product can contain separately installable parts. The following explains how software products are organized.

4.5.1 Filesets

A fileset is the smallest installable base unit for the AIX operating system. A fileset includes all files that constitute a complete product, such as bos.net.uucp, or a separately installable part of a product, such as bos.net.nfs.client.

4.5.2 Packages

A package is a group of separately installable filesets that provide a set of related functions. For example, bos.net is a package.

4.5.3 Licensed Program Products

A Licensed Program Product (LPP) is a complete software product including all packages associated with that licensed program. For example, the BOS is a licensed program.

4.5.4 Bundles

A bundle is a list of software that can contain filesets, packages, and LPPs that are suited for a particular use, such as providing personal productivity software or software for a client machine in a network environment. Bundles that are used by default for the system are stored in /usr/sys/inst.data/sys_bundles. Bundles that are user-created are stored in /usr/sys/inst.data/user_bundles. The system defined bundles in AIX 5L Version 5.1 are:

► App-Dev

► CDE

► GNOME

► KDE

► Media-Defined

► Netscape

► devices

► wsm_remote

4.5.5 PTFs and APARs

PTF is an acronym for Program Temporary Fix. A PTF is an updated fileset or a fileset that fixes a previous system problem. PTFs are installed in the same way as regular filesets by the use of the **installp** command, described in Section 4.6.1, "The installp command" on page 86.

APAR is an acronym for Authorized Program Analysis Report. An APAR is an emergency fix, or e-fix, to a unique problem on the system. APARs will eventually become PTFs after testing and verification. APARs are applied to the system through the use of the **instfix** command, described in Section 4.7.3, "Displaying and updating installed software to the latest level" on page 100.

4.6 Installing optional software and service updates

Once you have installed the base operating system, only a limited number of filesets are installed on your system. For a complete listing of the software that is installed during the BOS installation, consult your AIX installation guides.

To install additional software, you can use SMIT or the command line. If you decide to use the command line to install your software, you should be familiar with the `installp` command.

4.6.1 The installp command

The `installp` command is used to install and update software. The `installp` command has a large number of flags. In the following sections, only the most important flags are shown with each command. The `installp` command is also used by all the SMIT scripts to install software.

The flags commonly used with the `installp` command are listed in Table 4-2:

Table 4-2 Command flags for installp

Flag	Description
-a	Applies one or more software products or updates. This is the default action. This flag can be used with the -c flag to apply and commit a software product update during installation.
-B	Indicates that the requested action should be limited to software updates.
-C	Cleans up after an interrupted installation and attempts to remove all incomplete pieces of the previous installation.
-c	Commits applied updates to the system.
-d *Device*	Specifies on what device the installation media can be found.
-F	Forces the installation of a software product even if there exists a previously installed version of the software product that is the same version as or newer than the one being installed.
-f *ListFile*	Reads the names of the software products from *ListFile*. If *ListFile* is a - (dash), it reads the list of names from the standard input. Output from the `installp -l` command is suitable for input to this flag.
-g	When used to install or commit, this flag automatically installs or commits, respectively, any software products or updates that are requisites of the specified software product. When used to remove or reject software, this flag automatically removes or rejects dependents of the specified software.

Flag	Description
-L	Displays the contents of the media by looking at the table of contents (.toc) and displaying the information in colon-separated output. This flag is used by SMIT to list the content of the media.
-l (lowercase L)	Lists all the software products and their separately installable options contained on the installation media to the standard output. No installation occurs.
-N	Overrides saving of existing files that are replaced when installing or updating. This flag is valid only with the -ac flags.
-p	Performs a preview of an action by running all preinstallation checks for the specified action. This flag is only valid with apply, commit, reject, and remove (-a, -c, -r, and -u) flags.
-r	Rejects all software updates that are currently applied but not committed.
-u	Removes the specified software product and any of its installed updates from the system. Removal of any bos.rte fileset is never permitted.
-V Number	Specifies the verbose option that can provide up to four levels of detail for preinstallation output, including SUCCESSES, WARNINGS, and FAILURES.
-v	Verifies that all installed files in the fileset have the correct checksum value after installation. Can be used with the -a and -ac flags to confirm a successful installation. If any errors are reported by this flag, it may be necessary to reinstall the software.
-X	Attempts to expand any file systems where there is insufficient space to do the installation.

Installing software

Software can be installed in one of two states: applied or committed. The applied state places software on the system and retains the previous version of the software. When an update is in the applied state, the previous version is stored in the /usr/lpp/*PackageName* directory. This is useful for deploying or testing new software, where it may be necessary to go back to the previous version of the software in case of errors.

The committed state places software on the system and removes all previous levels of the software from the /usr/lpp/*PackageName* directory. If committed software needs to be removed, you cannot go back to the previous version without a complete reinstall of the previous version software. We recommend you install new software in the applied state, rather than the committed state, until the new software has been thoroughly tested.

To install software in an applied state, the command syntax for the **installp** command is:

```
installp -a [ -eLogFile ] [ -V Number ] [ -dDevice ] [ -b ] [ -S ] [ -B ]
[ -D ] [ -I ] [ -p ] [ -Q ] [ -q ] [ -v ] [ -X ] [ -F | -g ] [ -O { [ r ] [ s ]
[ u ] } ] [ -tSaveDirectory ] [ -w ] [ -zBlockSize ] { FilesetName [ Level ]...
| -f ListFile | all }
```

To install software in a committed state, the command syntax is:

```
installp -ac [ -N ] [ -eLogFile ] [ -V Number ] [ -dDevice ] [ -b ] [ -S ]
[ -B ] [ -D ] [ -I ] [ -p ] [ -Q ] [ -q ] [ -v ] [ -X ] [ -F | -g ]
[ -O { [ r ] [ s ] [ u ] } ] [ -tSaveDirectory ] [ -w ]
[ -zBlockSize ] { FilesetName [ Level ]... | -f ListFile | all }
```

For example, to install all filesets within the bos.net software package in /usr/sys/inst.images directory in the applied state, with a checksum check, enter:

```
installp -avX -d/usr/sys/inst.images bos.net
```

To preview an install of all filesets within the bos.net software package in /usr/sys/inst.images directory in the committed state and to check for disk space requirements, enter:

```
installp -acpX -d/usr/sys/inst.images bos.net
```

Under the RESOURCES section in the output, you will see something similar to:

```
RESOURCES
---------
    Estimated system resource requirements for filesets being installed:
               (All sizes are in 512-byte blocks)
         Filesystem                 Needed Space          Free Space
         /                              1150                17624
         /usr                          54183                48016
         /var                              8                22424
         /tmp                            300                63280
         -----                      --------              ------
         TOTAL:                        55641               151344

NOTE:  "Needed Space" values are calculated from data available prior
to installation.  These are the estimated resources required for the
entire operation.  Further resource checks will be made during
installation to verify that these initial estimates are sufficient.
```

As shown, the /usr file system does not have enough free space for the installation, and the installation would fail.

Note: If you try to run two **installp** commands at a time from the same installation medium, it will fail with an error similar to:

```
0503-430 installp: Either there is an installp process currently running
or there is a previously failed installation. Wait for the process to
complete or run installp -C to cleanup a failed installation.
```

A record of the **installp** output can be found in /var/adm/sw/installp.summary. The following is a sample of the file:

```
# cat /var/adm/sw/installp.summary
0:bos.net.ppp:5:U:5.1.0.0:
0:bos.net.ipsec.rte:5:U:5.1.0.0:
0:bos.net.ppp:5:R:5.1.0.0:
0:bos.net.ipsec.rte:5:R:5.1.0.0:
```

Committing applied updates

The command syntax for the **installp** command to commit applied updates is:

```
installp -c [ -eLogFile ] [ -VNumber ] [ -b ] [ -g ] [ -p ] [ -v ] [ -X ]
[ -O { [ r ] [ s ] [ u ] } ] [ -w ] { FilesetName [ Level ]... | -f ListFile |
all }
```

For example, to commit all updates, enter:

```
# installp -cgX all
```

Running this command will commit all the updates and will remove the filesets for the previous version.

Rejecting applied updates

The command syntax for the **installp** command to reject the updates that are in the applied state is:

```
installp -r [ -eLogFile ] [ -VNumber ] [ -b ] [ -g ] [ -p ] [ -v ] [ -X ]
[ -O { [ r ] [ s ] [ u ] } ] [ -w ] { FilesetName [ Level ]... | -f ListFile }
```

For example, to reject all applied updates listed in the file ./reject.list, enter:

```
# installp -rBfX ./reject.list
```

Running this command will remove all the uncommitted updates listed in ./reject.list and bring the system back to the previous maintenance level.

Removing Installed software

If you want to remove an installed product, that is, remove all files that belong to that software from the system, use the **installp** command; the command syntax is:

```
installp -u [ -eLogFile ] [ -VNumber ] [ -b ] [ -g ] [ -p ] [ -v ] [ -X ]
[ -O { [ r ] [ s ] [ u ] } ] [ -w ] { FilesetName [ Level ]... | -f ListFile }
```

For example, to preview a remove of bos.net.ipsec.rte and its dependents, with a verbose display of all successes, warnings, and failures, enter:

```
# installp -ugp -V2 bos.net.ipsec.rte
```

Running this command will give you a list of files that will be removed, but will not actually remove them.

Cleaning up after failed installations

If an installation fails, **installp** will not be able to install the same software until you have removed those files that succeeded in installing prior to the failure. You can use the **installp** command as follows:

```
installp -C [ -b ] [ -eLogFile ]
```

For example, if all the prerequisites in an installation are not met, the **installp** command might fail. You will not be able to reinstall the product until you have done a cleanup. to do this, enter:

```
# installp -C
```

This will remove all the files installed in the failed installation.

Listing all installable software on media

To see what software is available on a particular media, the command syntax for the **installp** command is:

```
installp { -l | -L } [ -eLogFile ] [ -d Device ] [ -B ] [ -I ] [ -q ]
[ -zBlockSize ] [ -O { [ s ] [ u ] } ]
```

For example, to list the software that is on your CD-ROM, enter:

```
# installp -L -d /dev/cd0
```

4.6.2 Using SMIT for software maintenance

Software installation, uninstallation, and maintenance tasks can also be performed through the SMIT menus. SMIT uses the **installp** command to perform these tasks.

> **Note:** SMIT stores a record of software installation, removal, and maintenance tasks in /var/adm/sw/installp.log like the **installp** command, but SMIT also stores a more detailed record in $HOME/smit.log.

Software installation

To install software products:

1. Use the SMIT fast path **smitty install_latest**

   A screen similar to Figure 4-7 is shown.

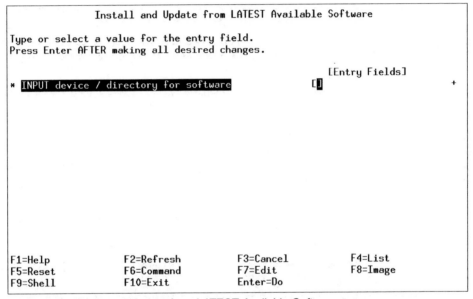

```
               Install and Update from LATEST Available Software

Type or select a value for the entry field.
Press Enter AFTER making all desired changes.

                                                        [Entry Fields]
* INPUT device / directory for software          []                        +











F1=Help            F2=Refresh        F3=Cancel         F4=List
F5=Reset           F6=Command        F7=Edit           F8=Image
F9=Shell           F10=Exit          Enter=Do
```

Figure 4-7   Install and Update from LATEST Available Software menu

2. Enter the device name for installation in the INPUT device/directory for software field. A screen similar to Figure 4-8 on page 92 is shown.

```
                Install and Update from LATEST Available Software

Type or select values in entry fields.
Press Enter AFTER making all desired changes.

                                                          [Entry Fields]
* INPUT device / directory for software                   /dev/cd0
* SOFTWARE to install                                     [_all_latest]        +
  PREVIEW only? (install operation will NOT occur)        no                   +
  COMMIT software updates?                                yes                  +
  SAVE replaced files?                                    no                   +
  AUTOMATICALLY install requisite software?               yes                  +
  EXTEND file systems if space needed?                    yes                  +
  OVERWRITE same or newer versions?                       no                   +
  VERIFY install and check file sizes?                    no                   +
  Include corresponding LANGUAGE filesets?                yes                  +
  DETAILED output?                                        no                   +
  Process multiple volumes?                               yes                  +



F1=Help              F2=Refresh          F3=Cancel          F4=List
F5=Reset             F6=Command          F7=Edit            F8=Image
F9=Shell             F10=Exit            Enter=Do
```

Figure 4-8   Install and Update from LATEST Available Software menu - more

3. In the SOFTWARE to install field, either enter the name, if you know what you
   have to install, or press F4 to get a list of all the available software. Press
   Enter once you have selected the products you want to install.

4. It is recommended that you first verify that the software you are trying to install
   meets all the prerequisite and co-requisite requirements. It is a good practice
   to set the PREVIEW only? (install operation will NOT occur) field to YES. This
   will give you a detailed listing of whether your installation will be successful or
   not.

5. It is recommended that you accept the default values for the
   AUTOMATICALLY install requisite software (default YES) and EXTEND file
   systems (default YES) fields if space is needed. Your installation might fail if
   you tell **installp** not to extend the file system. If it runs out of space, an error
   similar to the one shown below can be encountered:

   ```
   0503-008 installp: There is not enough free disk space in file system
   /usr (506935 more 512-byte blocks are required). An attempt to extend
   this file system was unsuccessful. Make more space available, then retry
   this operation.
   ```

6. Press Enter.

7. Look at the error messages, if any, at the end of the command execution
   when the command status changes to failed. It is recommended that you look
   at your smit.log even if the command status reports OK, since there may be
   filesets that you wanted to install that the system did not attempt to install.

Committing applied updates

To commit an applied software update:

1. Use the SMIT fast path`smitty install_commit`

   A screen similar to Figure 4-9 is shown.

```
                   Commit Applied Software Updates (Remove Saved Files)

Type or select values in entry fields.
Press Enter AFTER making all desired changes.

                                                            [Entry Fields]
* SOFTWARE name                                           [all]                   +
  PREVIEW only? (commit operation will NOT occur)          no                     +
  COMMIT requisites?                                       yes                    +
  EXTEND file systems if space needed?                     yes                    +
  DETAILED output?                                         no                     +




F1=Help              F2=Refresh           F3=Cancel            F4=List
F5=Reset             F6=Command           F7=Edit              F8=Image
F9=Shell             F10=Exit             Enter=Do
```

Figure 4-9   Commit Applied Software Updates (Remove Saved Files) menu

2. In the SOFTWARE to install field, either enter the name, if you know what you want to commit, or press F4 to get a list of all the available software. Press Enter once you have selected the products you want to commit. Leaving the SOFTWARE name field to all will commit all applied filesets installed on the system.

3. Press Enter. The system reports that the software is about to be committed, commits the software, and then removes the copies from the /usr/lpp/*PackageName* directory.

Rejecting applied updates

In order to reject a service update that you have installed:

1. Use the SMIT fast path `smitty install_reject`

   A screen similar to Figure 4-10 on page 94 is shown.

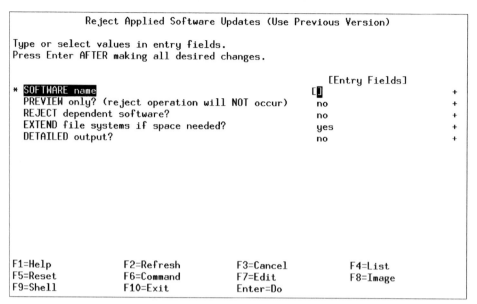

```
             Reject Applied Software Updates (Use Previous Version)

Type or select values in entry fields.
Press Enter AFTER making all desired changes.

                                                          [Entry Fields]
* SOFTWARE name                                          []                    +
  PREVIEW only? (reject operation will NOT occur)        no                    +
  REJECT dependent software?                             no                    +
  EXTEND file systems if space needed?                   yes                   +
  DETAILED output?                                       no                    +




F1=Help              F2=Refresh         F3=Cancel          F4=List
F5=Reset             F6=Command         F7=Edit            F8=Image
F9=Shell             F10=Exit           Enter=Do
```

Figure 4-10   Reject Applied Software Updates (Use Previous Version) menu

2. Press F4 on the SOFTWARE name field to select the software update you
   want to reject. All the software updates that are in the applied state will be
   listed. Select the update that you want to reject, and press Enter.

Removing installed software

You can remove installed and committed software by using the SMIT fast path:

1. `smitty install_remove`

   A screen similar to Figure 4-11 on page 95 is shown.

```
                      Remove Installed Software

Type or select values in entry fields.
Press Enter AFTER making all desired changes.

                                                  [Entry Fields]
* SOFTWARE name                                   [ ]                +
  PREVIEW only? (remove operation will NOT occur)  yes               +
  REMOVE dependent software?                       no                +
  EXTEND file systems if space needed?             no                +
  DETAILED output?                                 no                +




F1=Help          F2=Refresh        F3=Cancel         F4=List
F5=Reset         F6=Command        F7=Edit           F8=Image
F9=Shell         F10=Exit          Enter=Do
```

Figure 4-11   Remove Installed Software menu

2. Press F4 in the SOFTWARE name field to get a list of all the software that is installed on your system. Select the software you want to remove by pressing F7, followed by Enter, once you are done.

3. The PREVIEW only? (remove operation will NOT occur) field is yes by default. This allows you to preview any remove operations and confirm your choices before you actually do the remove action.

4. Once you are sure that you want to remove this software, change PREVIEW only? (remove operation will NOT occur) field to no, and press Enter. This will remove all the software that you have selected to be removed.

4.7 Maintaining optional software (applying updates)

Software that is distributed to fix a problem in a product is called an update. All software products have a version number and a release number that identify the release level of the product. In addition to this, product updates are assigned a modification level number and a fix level number to identify the level of the update. See Section 4.4, "Understanding maintenance levels" on page 82 for information on maintenance levels.

Suppose that you have your system currently running 4.3.2.0, and all the filesets are at 4.3.2.0 maintenance level. IBM has just released a latest maintenance level for systems on 4.3.2.0. You have to upgrade your system to bring it to the latest maintenance level.

Bringing a system to the latest maintenance level involves a number of steps that are listed below:

▶ Listing the maintenance level of the software

▶ Downloading fixes

▶ Displaying and updating installed software to the latest level

4.7.1 Listing the maintenance level of software

The **lslpp** command displays information about installed filesets or fileset updates. The most common flags used with the **lslpp** command are listed in Table 4-3:

Table 4-3   Command flags for lslpp

Flag	Description
-l	Displays the name, most recent level, state, and description of the specified fileset.
-f	Displays the names of the files added to the system during installation of the specified fileset.
-h	Displays the installation and update history information for the specified fileset.
-a	Displays all information about filesets specified when combined with other flags. Cannot be used with the -f flag.

In order to see what maintenance level your filesets are currently on, use the command:

```
lslpp -l
```

This will list all the software that is installed on your system showing the current maintenance level. The output will look similar to the following:

```
Fileset                     Level  State     Description
-------------------------------------------------------------------------------
Path: /usr/lib/objrepos
  IMNSearch.bld.DBCS        2.3.1.0  COMMITTED  NetQuestion DBCS Buildtime
                                                Modules
  IMNSearch.bld.SBCS        2.3.1.0  COMMITTED  NetQuestion SBCS Buildtime
                                                Modules

  IMNSearch.msg.en_US.rte.com
```

```
                               2.3.1.0  COMMITTED  Text Search Messages - U.S.
                                                   English
IMNSearch.rte.DBCS             2.3.1.0  COMMITTED  NetQuestion DBCS Search Engine
IMNSearch.rte.SBCS             2.3.1.0  COMMITTED  NetQuestion SBCS Search Engine
IMNSearch.rte.client           2.3.1.0  COMMITTED  Text Search Client
IMNSearch.rte.com              2.3.1.0  COMMITTED  Text Search Client/Server
                                                   Shared Files
IMNSearch.rte.httpdlite        2.0.0.2  COMMITTED  Lite NetQuestion Local Web
                                                   Server
IMNSearch.rte.server           2.3.1.0  COMMITTED  Text Search Server
Java130.rte.bin                1.3.0.5  COMMITTED  Java Runtime Environment
                                                   Executables
Java130.rte.lib                1.3.0.5  COMMITTED  Java Runtime Environment
                                                   Libraries
```

To list the individual files that are installed with a particular fileset, use the command:

```
lslpp -f
```

For example, if you wanted to display all files installed with the bos.64bit fileset, you would enter:

```
# lslpp -f bos.64bit
  Fileset                      File
  -------------------------------------------------------------------------
Path: /usr/lib/objrepos
  bos.64bit 5.1.0.0           /usr/lib/methods/cfg64
                              /usr/ccs/bin/shlap
                              /usr/ccs/bin/usla64
                              /usr/lib/drivers/syscalls64.ext
                              /usr/ccs/bin/usla
                              /usr/ccs/bin/shlap64

Path: /etc/objrepos
  bos.64bit 5.1.0.0           NONE
```

To list the installation and update history of filesets, use the command:

```
lslpp -h
```

For example, if you wanted to see when the bos.sysmgt.trace fileset was last updated, you would enter:

```
# lslpp -h bos.sysmgt.trace
  Fileset          Level    Action      Status       Date        Time
  --------------------------------------------------------------------------
Path: /usr/lib/objrepos
  bos.sysmgt.trace
                   4.3.3.0   COMMIT      COMPLETE     08/04/01  11:00:28
                   4.3.3.11  COMMIT      COMPLETE     08/04/01  17:00:13
```

```
Path: /etc/objrepos
  bos.sysmgt.trace
                  4.3.3.0   COMMIT      COMPLETE    06/15/00    09:57:33
                  4.3.3.11  COMMIT      COMPLETE    06/16/00    11:19:14
```

4.7.2 Downloading fixes

IBM provides a site on the Internet where you may freely download AIX-related fixes. The current anonymous FTP server is service.software.ibm.com. This site has a variety of mirrors that are listed when you FTP to the site.

To help customers browse and download fixes stored at the fix sites, IBM has released a freely available service tool called FixDist. FixDist is a tool designed to enable customers to select and download a fix and any necessary requisite fixes.

AIX 5L users should check the Web for special tools used for this Version.

FixDist and the user guide are available using an anonymous FTP from the server listed above or its mirrors. This site is also accessible through the URL http://service.software.ibm.com.

Once you have installed and set up the FixDist tool on your AIX system, the next step is to download the updates you want. On the command line, enter:

1. **fixdist**

   A screen similar to Figure 4-12 is shown.

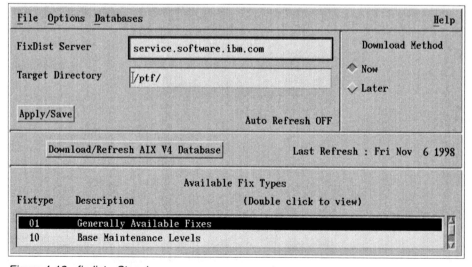

Figure 4-12 fixdist - Step 1

In this case, you have chosen to download all the PTFs to the /ptf file system. It is possible that you might be running a number of different releases of AIX in your environment. In this case, it is recommended that you keep your update downloads in different directories naming them according to the release level. In this example, set the target directory field to the /ptf directory.

2. Select Generally Available Fixes to list what updates are available from IBM. A screen similar to Figure 4-13 is shown.

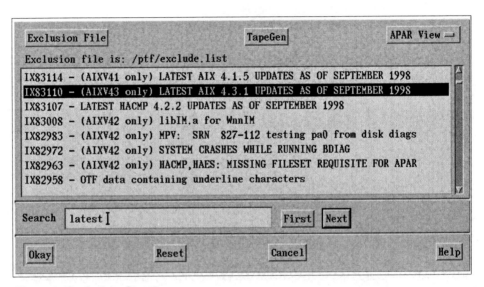

Figure 4-13   fixdist - Step 2

3. Select the updates you want to apply to your system by clicking on the name of the update/fix. In this case, since you are applying the latest updates for AIX Version 4.3.1.0, select the latest fixes for 4.3.1.0.

4. After you have selected the updates you want, you have the option to preview what will be downloaded, the estimated size of the images that will be downloaded, and other features. It is a good practice to download all your fixes into one file system.

FixDist will download all the fixes in the directory given at the start of the FixDist process as shown in Figure 4-12. All the files are downloaded in the BFF format. BFF stands for *Backup File Format*, which means that the file was created using the AIX **backup** command and can be read using the AIX **restore** command. In addition to the .bff files, .info files are also downloaded that give a brief summary of what the fileset is for and what has been fixed by this fileset.

If you apply updates frequently and keep all the updates in the same directory, then the .toc file might be outdated. The command `installp` uses the .toc file to carry out installations. To have the correct and latest software installed when you actually do the installation, it is recommended that you rebuild the .toc file. This can be done by using the `inutoc` command. The general syntax of the `inutoc` command is:

```
inutoc [Directory name]
```

The `inutoc` command creates a .toc file for directories that have backup format file install images. This command is used automatically by the `installp` command or the install script if no .toc file is present.

4.7.3 Displaying and updating installed software to the latest level

Once you have downloaded all the fixes into the /ptf directory, the next step is to install them and bring your system to the latest maintenance level. In this section, the following procedures are discussed:

► Displaying an individual fix (`instfix command`)

► Installing an individual fix by APAR

► Updating all filesets to the latest level

Displaying an individual fix (instfix command)

You can download an individual fix using FixDist following the same procedure given in Section 4.7.2, "Downloading fixes" on page 98.

In order to determine if a fix is installed on your system or to install a fix, use the `instfix` command. The general syntax of the `instfix` command is as follows:

```
instfix [ -T ] [ -s String ] [ -S ] [ -k Keyword | -f File ] [ -p ]
[ -d Device ] [ -i [ -c ] [ -q ] [ -t Type ] [ -v ] [ -F ] ] [ -a ]
```

The general flags used with `instfix` command are given in Table 4-4.

Table 4-4   Command flags for instfix

Flag	Description
-a	Displays the symptom text associated with a fix. Can be used with the -f, -i, and -k flags.
-d Device	Specifies the input device. Required for all flags except -i and -a.
-f FileName	Specifies the input file FileName containing keywords or fixes. The -T flag produces a suitable input file format for the -f flag.
-i	Displays whether fixes or keywords are installed.

Flag	Description
-k *Keyword*	Specifies an APAR number or keyword to be installed. Multiple keywords can be entered. A list of keywords entered with the -k flag must be contained in quotation marks and separated with spaces.
-s *String*	Searches for and displays fixes on the media containing a specified string.
-T	Displays the list of fixes on the media.
-v	Used with the -i flag to specify verbose mode. Displays information about each fileset associated with a fix or keyword.

The **instfix** command allows you to install a fix or set of fixes without knowing any information other than the Authorized Program Analysis Report (APAR) number or other unique keywords that identify the fix.

A fix can have a single fileset or multiple filesets. Fix information is organized in the Table of Contents (TOC) on the installation media. After a fix is installed, fix information is kept on the system in a fix database.

To list fixes that are on a CD-ROM in /dev/cd0, enter the command:

```
# instfix -T -d /dev/cd0
IX75893
```

To determine if APAR IX75893 is installed on the system, enter the command:

```
# instfix -ik IX75893
Not all filesets for IX75893 were found.
```

To examine information about APAR IX75893 and what it does, enter the command:

```
# instfix -aik IX75893
IX75893 Abstract: Process memory is made read-only unnecessarily

IX75893 Symptom Text:
 Resource handler routines not being able to store to process
  memory when a process is dumping core.


----------------------------
Not all filesets for IX75893 were found.
```

To list what maintenance levels have been installed on your system with the **instfix** command, enter the command:

```
# instfix -i | grep ML
All filesets for AIX43ML were found.
```

```
All filesets for 4.3.0.0_AIX_ML were found.
Not all filesets for 4.3.1.0_AIX_ML were found.
```

To install APAR IX75893 from /dev/cd0, enter the command:

```
# instfix -k IX75893 -d /dev/cd0
```

Note: By default, when instfix is run from the command line, the command uses stdout and stderr for reporting. If you want to generate an installation report, you will need to redirect the output. For example:

```
# instfix -aik IX75893 >/tmp/instfix.out 2>/tmp/instfix.err
```

You can also use SMIT to determine what fixes are installed on your system. Use the SMIT fast path:

1. `smitty show_apar_stat`

   A screen similar to Figure 4-14 is shown.

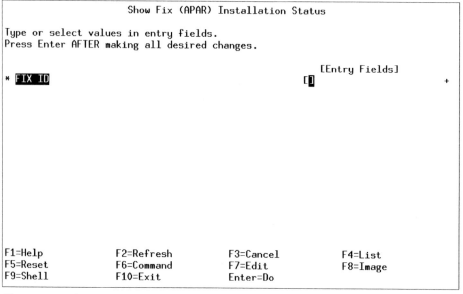

```
                      Show Fix (APAR) Installation Status

Type or select values in entry fields.
Press Enter AFTER making all desired changes.

                                                          [Entry Fields]
* FIX ID                                               []                    +




















 F1=Help            F2=Refresh        F3=Cancel         F4=List
 F5=Reset           F6=Command        F7=Edit           F8=Image
 F9=Shell           F10=Exit          Enter=Do
```

Figure 4-14   Show Fix (APAR) Installation Status menu

2. Press F4 in the FIX ID field to get a list of all the fixes that are installed on the system. The output from this command is similar to the **instfix -iv** command.

Installing an individual fix by APAR

To install the fixes using SMIT, use the SMIT fast path:

1. `smitty instfix` or `smitty update_by_fix`

2. In the INPUT device/directory for the software field, enter the name of the device (or directory if you downloaded the fixes to your system) from which to install the fixes, and press Enter. A screen similar to Figure 4-15 is shown.

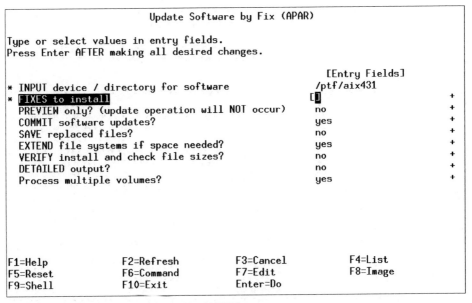

Figure 4-15   Update Software by Fix (APAR) menu

3. In the FIXES to Install field, press F4 to get a list of fixes that are available on the media and select the fixes you want to install.

4. Press Enter.

The system will update the maintenance level of the fileset you selected and upon completion you will have successfully updated the maintenance level of your software.

Updating all filesets to the latest level

To install all new fixes that are available through IBM, use the fast path:

1. `smitty update_all`

A screen similar to Figure 4-16 is shown.

```
            Update Installed Software to Latest Level (Update All)

Type or select a value for the entry field.
Press Enter AFTER making all desired changes.

                                                        [Entry Fields]
* INPUT device / directory for software           []                    +












F1=Help         F2=Refresh        F3=Cancel         F4=List
F5=Reset        F6=Command        F7=Edit           F8=Image
F9=Shell        F10=Exit          Enter=Do
```

Figure 4-16   Update Installed Software to Latest Level (Update All) menu

2. In the INPUT device/directory for software field, enter the name of the device
   (or directory if you have fixes on your hard disk) from which installation will be
   carried out.

3. Press Enter.

A screen similar to Figure 4-17 is shown.

```
              Update Installed Software to Latest Level (Update All)

Type or select values in entry fields.
Press Enter AFTER making all desired changes.

                                                      [Entry Fields]
* INPUT device / directory for software               /ptf/aix431
* SOFTWARE to update                                  _update_all
  PREVIEW only? (update operation will NOT occur)     no                    +
  COMMIT software updates?                            yes                   +
  SAVE replaced files?                                no                    +
  AUTOMATICALLY install requisite software?           yes                   +
  EXTEND file systems if space needed?                yes                   +
  VERIFY install and check file sizes?                no                    +
  DETAILED output?                                    no                    +
  Process multiple volumes?                           yes                   +




F1=Help           F2=Refresh        F3=Cancel          F4=List
F5=Reset          F6=Command        F7=Edit            F8=Image
F9=Shell          F10=Exit          Enter=Do
```

Figure 4-17   Update Installed Software to Latest Level (Update All) menu - more

4. It is best to set the PREVIEW only? (update operation will NOT occur) field to YES by pressing the Tab key. The Preview option makes a dry run of the task you are trying to perform and reports any failures that might be encountered when you do the actual installation. This will ensure that your installation does not fail.

Once you are sure that there are no prerequisites that you are missing, you can do the actual installation. This procedure will update your software to the latest maintenance level.

To view the new maintenance level of your software, enter on the command line:

```
# lslpp -l
```

This will show you the latest maintenance level of the filesets including those you just updated.

4.8 Creating installation images on a hard disk

Installable image files (or installation packages) can be copied to a hard disk for use in future installations. These image files will be copied from your installation media (tape or diskette) to a directory on the disk, so that they may be installed later using the disk directory as the input device. These files will be copied to the directory named /usr/sys/inst.images.

To create installation images on your hard disk, use the SMIT fast path:

1. `smitty bffcreate`

   A screen similar to Figure 4-18 is shown.

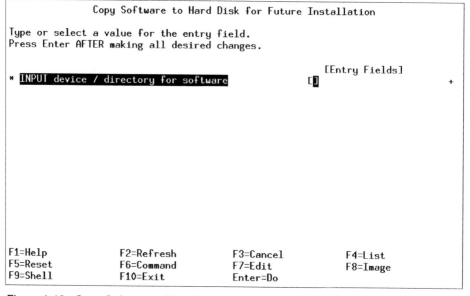

Figure 4-18   Copy Software to Hard Disk for Future Installation menu

2. In the INPUT device/directory for software field, enter the name of your source that will be used to copy the images and press Enter.

3. On the next screen, press F4 on the Software package to copy field to get a list of the software available on the media. Select the installation images you want to copy to your hard disk and press Enter.

4. All the images will be copied to your hard disk in the /usr/sys/inst.images directory, and the /usr/sys/inst.images/.toc file is updated.

For future installations, enter the /usr/sys/inst.images directory in the INPUT device / directory for software field. If for some reason your .toc file becomes corrupted, you will receive an error either in SMIT or the command line, depending on what are you using, similar to:

0503-005 The format of .toc file is invalid

In this case, simply use the `inutoc /usr/sys/inst.images/.toc` command to recreate your .toc file.

This method of creating installation images is helpful in situations where the software you are trying to install has co-requisites that are on different media and your installation process does not let you change the media it is currently processing. In such situations, your installation will fail; therefore, it is recommended to have all the prerequisites and co-requisites reside in one directory and then do the installation.

To get co-requisites that are on different media, use the `smitty bffcreate` fast path to copy required filesets from the first CD-ROM to the hard disk in /usr/sys/inst.images. Then, use the `smitty bffcreate` fast path to copy the required filesets from the additional CD-ROMs to the hard disk in /usr/sys/inst.images. After all the required filesets have been copied to the hard disk, use the `installp` command or the `smitty install_latest` fast path to install the software. Since the system reads the /usr/sys/inst.images/.toc file for installation, and all the filesets are local to the hard disk, it will not prompt you for a CD-ROM or fail the installation.

4.9 Alternate disk installation

Alternate disk installation, available in AIX Version 4.3 and later versions, allows for system installation on a system while it is still up and running, which produces install or upgrade downtime to be decreased considerably. It also allows large facilities to manage an upgrade, because systems can be installed over a longer period of time, while the systems are still running at the existing version. The switch over to the new version can then happen with a simple reboot.

4.9.1 Filesets required

Alternate disk installation requires some filesets to be installed before you are able to use the alternate disk installation functions. The bos.alt_disk_install.boot_images filesets must be installed for alternate disk `mksysb` installation, if Network Install Management (NIM) is not being used. The bos.alt_disk_install.rte fileset must be installed to clone rootvg.

Once you have installed these filesets, the alternate disk installation functions are available to you in the Software Installation and Maintenance menu. Use the SMIT fast path:

```
smitty alt_install
```

A screen similar to Figure 4-19 is shown.

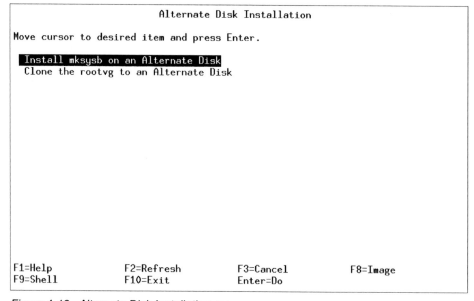

```
                        Alternate Disk Installation

Move cursor to desired item and press Enter.

    Install mksysb on an Alternate Disk
    Clone the rootvg to an Alternate Disk












F1=Help            F2=Refresh         F3=Cancel          F8=Image
F9=Shell           F10=Exit           Enter=Do
```

Figure 4-19   Alternate Disk Installation menu

Alternate disk installation can be used in one of two ways:

▶ Cloning the current running rootvg to an alternate disk.

▶ Installing a mksysb image on another disk.

4.9.2 Alternate disk rootvg cloning

Cloning the rootvg to an alternate disk can have many advantages.

▶ Having an online backup available in case of disaster. Keeping an on-line backup requires that an extra disk or disks to be available on the system.

▶ Applying new maintenance levels or updates. A copy of the rootvg is made to an alternate disk, then updates are applied to that copy. Finally, the boot list is updated to boot from the new device. The system runs uninterrupted during this time. When it is rebooted, the system will boot from the newly updated rootvg for testing. If updates cause problems, the old rootvg can be retrieved by resetting the bootlist and rebooting.

To clone your rootvg to a new disk, do the following procedure:

1. Use the SMIT fast path **smitty alt_clone**

   A screen similar to Figure 4-20 is shown.

```
                    Clone the rootvg to an Alternate Disk

Type or select values in entry fields.
Press Enter AFTER making all desired changes.

[TOP]                                           [Entry Fields]
* Target Disk(s) to install                    [ ]                      +
  Phase to execute                              all                     +
  image.data file                              [ ]                      /
  Exclude list                                 [ ]                      /

  Bundle to install                            [ ]                      +
   -OR-
  Fileset(s) to install                        [ ]

  Fix bundle to install                        [ ]
   -OR-
  Fixes to install                             [ ]

[MORE...17]

F1=Help              F2=Refresh          F3=Cancel           F4=List
F5=Reset             F6=Command          F7=Edit             F8=Image
F9=Shell             F10=Exit            Enter=Do
```

Figure 4-20   Clone the rootvg to an Alternate Disk menu

2. In the Target Disk(s) to install field, enter the name of the disk you want to use for making the clone. The target disk should be a stand-alone disk not belonging to a volume group. In addition to this, SSA disks cannot be used as your target disks.

3. The Phases to execute field defaults to all. Accept the default, for now.

4. In the Exclude list field, you can create a file that will contain the names of all the files and directories that you do not want to be copied to your cloned system.

5. Specify the name of any additional bundles or filesets and fixes that you want to install in the Bundle to install and Fix to Install fields. The use of these fields allows service to be installed as part of the clone process.

6. Specify the name of the input device in case you have selected to install any additional software in the Directory or Device with images field.

7. If you want your system to start from your alternate rootvg on the next system start-up, set the Set the bootlist to boot from this disk on next boot to YES.

8. Press Enter.

The following sequence of output is shown in SMIT while the system is cloning to the new disk:

```
Calling mkszfile to create new /image.data file.
Checking disk sizes
Creating cloned rootvg volume group and associated logical volumes
Creating Logical volume alt_hd5
Creating Logical volume alt_hd6
Creating Logical volume alt_hd8
Creating Logical volume alt_hd4
Creating Logical volume alt_hd2
Creating Logical volume alt_hd9var
Creating Logical volume alt_hd3
Creating Logical volume alt_hd1
Creating /alt_inst / file system
Creating /alt_inst/usr file system
Creating /alt_inst/var file system
Creating /alt_inst/tmp file system
Creating /alt_inst/home file system
Generating a list of files
for backup and restore into the alternate file system ...
Backing up the rootvg files and restoring them to the
alternate File Systems
Modifying ODM on cloned disk
Building boot image on cloned disk
Forced umount of /alt_inst/home
Forced umount of /alt_inst/tmp
Forced umount of /alt_inst/var
Forced umount of /alt_inst/usr
Forced umount of /alt_inst/
Changing logical volume names in Volume Group Descriptor Area
Fixing Logical Volume control blocks
Fixing File system super blocks
Bootlist is set to the bootdisk:hdisk1
```

By default, the bootlist will be set to the new cloned rootvg for the next reboot. This completes the cloning of the rootvg using the **alt_disk_install** command.

4.9.3 Alternate mksysb install

An alternate mksysb install involves installing a mksysb image that has already been created from another system onto an alternate disk of the target system. The mksysb image (AIX Version 4.3 or later) would be created on a system that was either the same hardware configuration as the target system or would have all the device and kernel support installed for a different machine type or platform or different devices.

To create the alternate mksysb system, use the SMIT fast path:

1. `smitty alt_mksysb`

   A screen similar to Figure 4-21 is shown.

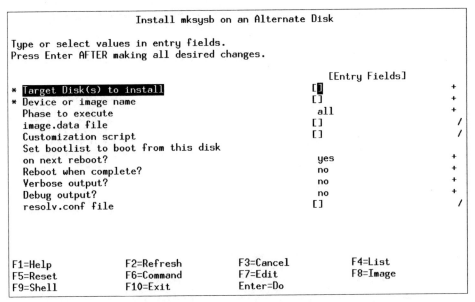

```
                    Install mksysb on an Alternate Disk

Type or select values in entry fields.
Press Enter AFTER making all desired changes.

                                                  [Entry Fields]
* Target Disk(s) to install                     []                      +
* Device or image name                          []                      +
  Phase to execute                              all                     +
  image.data file                               []                      /
  Customization script                          []                      /
  Set bootlist to boot from this disk
  on next reboot?                               yes                     +
  Reboot when complete?                         no                      +
  Verbose output?                               no                      +
  Debug output?                                 no                      +
  resolv.conf file                              []                      /




F1=Help              F2=Refresh        F3=Cancel          F4=List
F5=Reset             F6=Command        F7=Edit            F8=Image
F9=Shell             F10=Exit          Enter=Do
```

Figure 4-21   Install mksysb on an Alternate Disk menu

2. Enter the name of the disk on which you want to install the mksysb in the Target Disk(s) to install field.

3. Enter the name of the device or the image name from which you will be restoring the mksysb in the Device or image name field.

4. Press Enter.

Once the mksysb image is restored to the new disk, the system reboots from the new alternate rootvg. This completes your alternate mksysb installation.

4.10 Quiz

The following certification assessment questions help verify your understanding of the topics discussed in this chapter.

1. An AIX installation has just completed. Maintenance Level 6 has been applied to the BOS. Which command will show all installed maintenance levels concurrently?

   A. `oslevel -a`

   B. `lslpp -l | grep AIX`

   C. `smitty show_apar_stat`

   D. `instfix -ik | grep AIX`

2. How would an administrator verify that the system has all required prerequisite fixes prior to installing a software fix?

   A. Use the `lsprereq` command.

   B. Use `installp` with the preview option.

   C. View the .toc file in the root directory.

   D. Use the `inutoc` command to update the .toc file.

3. It has been determined that fix IX39714 needs to be applied to a server as soon as possible. How can this fix be obtained if the system has Internet connectivity?

   A. Use the `fixdist` utility to download the fix.

   B. FTP the fix from fixes.pseries.ibm.com.

   C. Send an E-mail to fixes.pseries.ibm.com with IX39714 in the subject line.

   D. Use the Web-Based System Manager to download the fix.

The following are additional questions created by the authors to further test your understanding of the topics.

1. During the first reboot after the AIX 5L Version 5.1 operating system installation process has completed, what is the first screen the administrator will see?

   A. Login prompt

   B. Root shell prompt

   C. Installation Assistant

   D. Configuration Assistant

2. Which of the following commands lists the current fix level of the bos.net.nfs.client fileset?

   A. `lsfs bos.net.nfs.client`

   B. `lslpp -l bos.net.nfs.client`

   C. `lppchk -l bos.net.nfs.client`

   D. `installp -ver bos.net.nfs.client`

3. Which of the following commands can be used to verify the success of an operating system upgrade?

   A. `oslevel`

   B. `lslpp -h bos.obj`

   C. `what_fileset -v`

   D. `lsattr -Vl bos.rte`

4. If bos.up displays on your machine as being at 4.3.1.7, what is the modification level?

   A. 1

   B. 3

   C. 4

   D. 7

4.10.1 Answers

The following answers are for the assessment quiz questions.

1. D

2. B

3. A

The following answers are for the additional quiz questions.

1. D

2. B

3. A

4. A

4.11 Exercises

The following exercises provide sample topics for self study. They will help ensure comprehension of this chapter.

1. Try to the run **installp** command twice at the same time on one system and see what happens.

2. You have just installed a new release of the operating system, determine the operating system level of your system.

3. What is a fileset, package, bundle? Explain.

4. Your root file system is behaving strangely; therefore, you decide to do a preserve install. However, you do not want to overwrite your /var file system. What can be done to prevent this? Perform the preserve install and save your /var file system as is.

5. Your installation is failing repeatedly because of missing prerequisites. How will you use preview option to obtain all the prerequisite information in SMIT?

6. What are the methods available to you to upgrade your system to the latest release/maintenance level yet minimize the downtime?

7. If prerequisites from two install medias point to each other, what is the best method that you can use to complete the installation without errors?

8. What are the different methods of installation available to you for installing a base operating system?

9. Use the installation assistant to set the time and paging size on your system.

10. Update your system to bring all the filesets to the latest fix level.

11. IBM has just announced a new fix pack. Obtain the fixpack from the IBM FTP site and apply the fixes to upgrade your system to the latest fix level.

12. Determine the latest fix level on your system.

13. Find out the latest fix level of a licensed program, filesets, and so on.

14. How do you use the **installp** command, and what are the different options that are available to you?

15. You have just downloaded the latest fix from IBM, but before you go into production, you want to test-run the system with the latest fix pack installed. Use the alternate disk install to make a replica of your system and test out the changes with the fix pack installed.

16. Find out what are the different filesets you have and their state using the **installp** command. Next, commit any applied software and remove any fileset that you think is not required. Also, apply a fix pack and then reject the changes made by this fixpack.

17. Download an individual fix and use SMIT to install the fix.

18. Download any package from your installation media to your disk, create a new table of contents for the /usr/sys/inst.images directory, and install the package using SMIT.

Object Data Manager

The ODM has many purposes. Its primary functions are to maintain the RISC System/6000 configuration, associated devices, and the vital product database. In addition, it provides a more robust, secure, and sharable resource than the ASCII files previously used in AIX.

System data managed by the ODM includes:

- ► Device configuration information
- ► Display information for SMIT (menus, selectors, and dialogs)
- ► Vital product data for installation and update procedures
- ► Communications configuration information
- ► System resource information

Most system object classes and objects are stored in the /usr/lib/objrepos directory; however, ODM information is stored in three directories as follows:

- ► /usr/lib/objrepos
- ► /usr/share/lib/objrepos
- ► /etc/objrepos

The basic components of the ODM are object classes and objects. To manage object classes and objects, you use the ODM commands and subroutines. Specifically, you use the create and add features of these interfaces to build object classes and objects for storage and management of your own data.

A summary of the ODM concepts is provided in Table 5-1.

Table 5-1 ODM Concepts

Item	Definition	Similar to	Similar to
ODM Object	A member of a defined ODM object class. An entity that requires management and storage of data.	An element of an array structure.	One of the fixed format records.
Object Class	A stored collection of objects with the same definition.	An array of C-Language structures.	A file with fixed format records.
ODM Database	A stored collection of ODM object classes.	A collection of structure arrays.	A directory of files.

An object class comprises one or more descriptors. Values are associated with the descriptors of an object when the object is added to an object class. The descriptors of an object and their associated values can be located and changed with the ODM facilities.

In the area of device configuration, the ODM contains information about all configured physical volumes, volume groups, and logical volumes. This information mirrors the information found in the VGDA. The process of importing a VGDA, for example, involves copying the VGDA data for the imported volume group into the ODM. When a volume group is exported, the data held in the ODM about that volume group is removed from the ODM database.

5.1 ODM commands

You can create, add, change, retrieve, display, and delete objects and object classes with ODM. ODM commands are entered on the command line.

> **Note:** ODM commands should be used only when traditional methods of system maintenance, such as SMIT, are ineffective. For a beginning system administrator, it is recommended that you perform additional reading and exercises before using these commands. Incorrect use of these commands may result in a disabled system. The ODM commands are described here for introductory purposes.

These commands are:

odmadd Adds objects to an object class. The **odmadd** command takes an ASCII stanza file as input and populates object classes with objects found in the stanza file.

odmchange Changes specific objects in a specified object class.

odmcreate Creates empty object classes. The **odmcreate** command takes an ASCII file describing object classes as input and produces C language .h and .c files to be used by the application accessing objects in those object classes.

odmdelete Removes objects from an object class.

odmdrop Removes an entire object class.

odmget Retrieves objects from object classes and puts the object information into **odmadd** command format.

odmshow Displays the description of an object class. The **odmshow** command takes an object class name as input and puts the object class information into **odmcreate** command format.

5.2 Example of an object class for an ODM database

The following is an example of the object class definition for the Customized Device Database (CuDv):

```
# odmshow CuDv
class CuDv {
        char name[16];                              /* offset: 0xc ( 12) */
        short status;                               /* offset: 0x1c ( 28) */
        short chgstatus;                            /* offset: 0x1e ( 30) */
        char ddins[16];                             /* offset: 0x20 ( 32) */
        char location[16];                          /* offset: 0x30 ( 48) */
        char parent[16];                            /* offset: 0x40 ( 64) */
        char connwhere[16];                         /* offset: 0x50 ( 80) */
        link PdDv PdDv uniquetype PdDvLn[48];       /* offset: 0x60 ( 96) */
        };
/*
```

```
descriptors:    8
structure size:    0x98 (152) bytes
data offset:    0x20001cd8
population:    50 objects (50 active, 0 deleted)
*/
```

5.3 Quiz

The following are questions created by the authors to further test your understanding of the topics.

1. A system administrator wishes to determine if a newly configured tape drive is correctly added to the ODM database. Which command would the administrator use?

   A. **odmshow**

   B. **odmadd**

   C. **odmget**

   D. **odmcreate**

2. The ODM is located in:

   A. /etc/objrepos

   B. /usr/lib/objrepos

   C. /usr/share/lib/objrepos

   D. All of the above

5.3.1 Answers

The following answers are for the quiz questions.

1. C

2. D

5.4 Exercises

The following exercises provide sample topics for self study. They will help ensure comprehension of this chapter.

1. List the uses of the ODM.

2. Using the correct ODM facility, determine the format of the Predefined Device Database (PdDv).

Storage management, LVM, and file systems

In this chapter, storage management, Logical Volume Management (LVM), and file system support issues are covered. The basic tasks that require understanding are broken down into separate sections.

6.1 Logical volume storage concepts

The five basic logical storage concepts are: Physical volumes, volume groups, physical partitions, logical volumes, and logical partitions. The relationships among these concepts are provided in Figure 6-1.

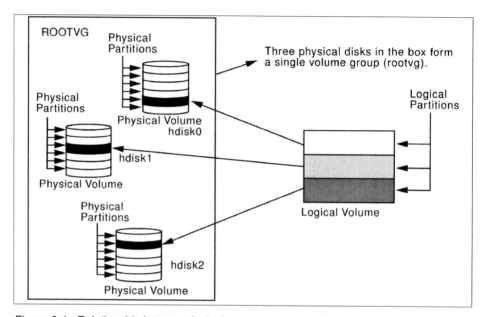

Figure 6-1   Relationship between logical storage components

The following can be said regarding Figure 6-1:

► Each individual fixed-disk drive is called a physical volume (PV) and has a name (for example: hdisk0, hdisk1, or hdisk2).

► All physical volumes belong to one volume group (VG) named rootvg.

► All of the physical volumes in a volume group are divided into physical partitions (PPs) of the same size.

► Within each volume group, one or more logical volumes (LVs) are defined. Logical volumes are groups of information located on physical volumes. Data on logical volumes appear as contiguous to the user but can be discontiguous on the physical volume.

► Each logical volume consists of one or more logical partitions (LPs). Each logical partition corresponds to at least one physical partition. If mirroring is specified for the logical volume, additional physical partitions are allocated to store the additional copies of each logical partition.

- Logical volumes can serve a number of system purposes (paging, for example), but each logical volume that holds ordinary systems, user data, or programs, contains a single journaled file system (JFS). Each JFS consists of a pool of page-size (4 KB) blocks. In AIX Version 4.1 and later, a given file system can be defined as having a fragment size of less than 4 KB (512 bytes, 1 KB, 2 KB).

After installation, the system has one volume group (the rootvg volume group), consisting of a base set of logical volumes required to start the system, and any other volume groups you specify to the installation script.

6.2 Logical Volume Manager

The set of operating system commands, library subroutines, and other tools that allow you to establish and control logical volume storage is called the Logical Volume Manager (LVM). The LVM controls disk resources by mapping data between a more simple and flexible logical view of storage space and the actual physical disks.

6.2.1 LVM configuration data

The data that describes the components of the LVM is not kept in one place. It is important to understand that this descriptive data about volume groups, logical volumes, and physical volumes is kept in several places.

Object Data Manager (ODM) database

The ODM database is the place where most of the AIX system configuration data is kept. The ODM database contains information about all configured physical volumes, volume groups, and logical volumes. This information mirrors the information found in the VGDA. For example, the process of importing a VGDA involves automatically copying the VGDA data for the imported volume group into the ODM. When a volume group is exported, the data held in the ODM about that volume group is removed from the ODM database.

The ODM data also mirrors the information held in the Logical Volume Control Block.

Volume Group Descriptor Area (VGDA)

The VGDA, located at the beginning of each physical volume, contains information that describes all the logical volumes and all the physical volumes that belong to the volume group of which that physical volume is a member. The VGDA is updated by almost all the LVM commands. The VGDA makes each volume group self-describing. An AIX system can read the VGDA on a disk, and, from that, can determine what physical volumes and logical volumes are part of this volume group.

Each disk contains at least one VGDA. This is important at vary on time. The time stamps in the VGDAs are used to determine which VGDAs correctly reflect the state of the volume group. VGDAs can get out of sync when, for example, a volume group of four disks has one disk failure. The VGDA on that disk cannot be updated while it is not operational. Therefore, you need a way to update this VGDA when the disk comes online, and this is what the vary on process will do.

The VGDA is allocated when the disk is assigned as a physical volume (with the command `mkdev`). This just reserves a space for the VGDA at the start of the disk. The actual volume group information is placed in the VGDA when the physical volume is assigned to a volume group (using the `mkvg` or `extendvg` commands). When a physical volume is removed from the volume group (using the `reducevg` command), the volume group information is removed from the VGDA.

Volume Group Status Area (VGSA)

The VGSA contains state information about physical partitions and physical volumes. For example, the VGSA knows if one physical volume in a volume group is unavailable.

Both the Volume Group Descriptor Area and the Volume Group Status Area have beginning and ending time stamps that are very important. These time stamps enable the LVM to identify the most recent copy of the VGDA and the VGSA at vary on time.

The LVM requires that the time stamps for the chosen VGDA be the same as those for the chosen VGSA.

Logical Volume Control Block (LVCB)

The LVCB is located at the start of every logical volume. It contains information about the logical volume and uses a few hundred bytes.

The following example shows the use of the **getlvcb** command to display the information held in the LVCB of logical volume hd2:

```
# getlvcb -TA hd2
AIX LVCB
intrapolicy = c
copies = 1
interpolicy = m
lvid = 00011187ca9acd3a.7
lvname = hd2
label = /usr
machine id = 111873000
number lps = 72
relocatable = y
strict = y
type = jfs
upperbound = 32
fs = log=/dev/hd8:mount=automatic:type=bootfs:vol=/usr:free=false
time created   = Tue Jul 27 13:38:45 1993
time modified = Tue Jul 27 10:58:14 1993
```

6.2.2 Disk quorum

Each physical disk in a volume group has at least one VGDA/VGSA. The number of VGDAs contained on a single disk varies according to the number of disks in the volume group as shown in Table 6-1.

Table 6-1   VGDA allocation

Condition	VGDA allocation
Single PV in a volume group	Two VGDAs on one disk.
Two PVs in a volume group	Two VGDAs on the first disk, one VGDA on the second disk.
Three or more PVs in a volume group	One VGDA on each disk

A quorum is a state in which 51 percent or more of the physical volumes in a volume group are accessible. A quorum is a vote of the number of Volume Group Descriptor Areas and Volume Group Status Areas (VGDA/VGSA) that are active. A quorum ensures data integrity in the event of a disk failure.

When a volume group is created onto a single disk, it initially has two VGDA/VGSA areas residing on the disk. If a volume group consists of two disks, one disk still has two VGDA/VGSA areas, but the other disk has one VGDA/VGSA. When the volume group is made up of three or more disks, then each disk is allocated just one VGDA/VGSA.

Figure 6-2 shows that the quorum is lost when enough disks and their VGDA/VGSA areas are unreachable so that a 51% majority of VGDA/VGSA areas no longer exists.

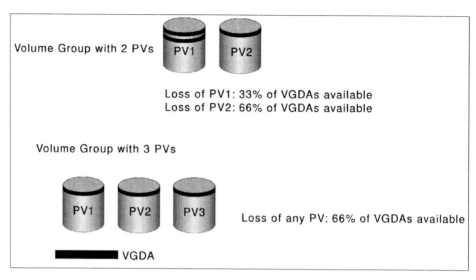

Figure 6-2 Disk quorum

When a quorum is lost, the volume group varies itself off so that the disks are no longer accessible by the Logical Volume Manager (LVM). This prevents further disk I/O to that volume group so that data is not lost or assumed to be written when physical problems occur. Additionally, as a result of the vary off, the user is notified in the error log that a hardware error has occurred and service must be performed.

This has implications when you want to use disk mirroring to ensure high availability. In a two disk mirrored system, if the first disk fails, then you have lost 66 percent of your VGDAs, and the entire volume group becomes unavailable. This defeats the purpose of mirroring. For this reason, three or more (and generally an odd number) disk units provide a higher degree of availability and are highly recommended where mirroring is desired.

> **Note:** There is the ability to turn off disk quorum protection on any volume group. Turning off quorum protection allows a volume group to remain online even when a quorum or majority of its VGDAs are not online. This would allow the volume group to remain online in the situation described previously. This capability provides for a less expensive mirroring solution but does carry the risk of data loss as, after a disk failure, data is accessible but no longer mirrored.

6.2.3 Disk mirroring

Disk mirroring is the association of two or three physical partitions with each logical partition in a logical volume. When the data is written onto the logical volume, it is also written to all the physical partitions that are associated with the logical partition. Therefore, mirroring of data increases the availability of data.

AIX and the logical volume manager provide a disk mirroring facility at a logical volume level. If mirroring is established, this can be done when a logical volume is created.

The **mklv** command allows you to select one or two additional copies for each logical volume. Mirroring can also be added to an existing logical volume using the **mklvcopy** command.

The following mirroring factors can further improve the data availability:

▶ The number of copies of data: Three copies of the data are more reliable than keeping only two copies.

▶ Location of the copies: Allocating the copies of a logical partition on different physical volumes is more reliable than allocating the copies on the same physical volume. This is because one of the most common error modes for disk subsystems is the loss of an individual physical disk. Copies can also be located across different disk adapters to further enhance isolation from failures.

The mirrorvg command

The **mirrorvg** command mirrors all the logical volumes on a given volume group. This same function may also be accomplished manually if you run the **mklvcopy** command for each individual logical volume in a volume group. As with **mklvcopy**, the target physical drives to be mirrored with data must already be members of the volume group. This command only applies to AIX Version 4.2.1 or later.

The following is the syntax for the **mirrorvg** command:

```
mirrorvg [ -S | -s ] [ -Q ] [ -c Copies] [ -m ] VolumeGroup
[ PhysicalVolume .. ]
```

By default, **mirrorvg** attempts to mirror the logical volumes onto any of the disks in a volume group. The **mirrorvg** command mirrors the logical volumes using the default settings of the logical volume being mirrored. If you wish to violate mirror strictness or affect the policy by which the mirror is created, you must execute the mirroring of all logical volumes manually with the **mklvcopy** command.

> **Note:** The `mirrorvg` command may take a significant amount of time before completing because of complex error checking, the number of logical volumes to mirror in a volume group, and the time to synchronize the new mirrored logical volumes.

Alternatively, you can also use the SMIT fast path command, `smitty mirrorvg`, to do the mirroring of volume groups.

The following examples show the use of the `mirrorvg` command:

► To triply mirror a volume group, run the following command:

```
mirrorvg -c 3 workvg
```

The logical partitions in the logical volumes held on workvg now have three copies.

► To get default mirroring of rootvg, run the following command.

```
mirrorvg rootvg
```

The rootvg volume group now has two copies of data.

> **Note:** Problems may occur when you attempt to place a disk back into the original system if the disk is removed from a volume group, updated, and then returned. There is no way to control which copy of the data will be used to resynchronize the other copy.
>
> If any LVM information is changed while the disk is in your backup system, those changes will not be known to your primary system even if the backup is used to resync the primary disk. LVM changes include: Creating, removing, or expanding any file system, paging spaces, and other logical volume.

► To replace a failed disk drive in a mirrored volume group, run the following commands:

```
unmirrorvg workvg hdisk7
reducevg workvg hdisk7
rmdev -l hdisk7 -d
```

Replace the failed disk drive with a new one, and name it hdisk7 by executing the following commands:

```
extendvg workvg hdisk7
mirrorvg workvg
```

> **Note:** By default in this example, mirrorvg will try to create two copies for the logical volumes in workvg. It will try to create the new mirrors onto the replaced disk drive. However, if the original system had been triply mirrored, there may be no new mirrors created onto hdisk7, as other copies may already exist for the logical volumes.

► The following command will synchronize the newly created mirrors:

```
mirrorvg -S -c 3 workvg
```

The -c flag specifies the minimum number of copies that each logical volume must have after the **mirrorvg** command finishes executing. The -S flag returns the **mirrorvg** command immediately and performs a background **syncvg** of the volume group. It will not be apparent when the mirrors are synchronized, but they will be immediately used by the system when ready.

► To create an exact mapped volume group, run the following command:

```
mirrorvg -m datavg hdisk2 hdisk3
```

The -m flag allows mirroring of logical volumes in the exact physical partition order that the original copy is ordered.

Rootvg mirroring

When the rootvg mirroring has completed, the following three tasks must be performed:

1. Run the **bosboot** command.

   The **bosboot** command creates a boot file (boot image) from a RAM (Random Access Memory) disk file system and a kernel. The **bosboot** command is required to customize the bootrec of the newly mirrored drive.

2. Run the **bootlist** command.

   The **bosboot** command always saves device configuration data for disk. It does not update the list of boot devices in the NVRAM (nonvolatile random access memory). The NVRAM list can be modified by using the **bootlist** command.

3. Reboot the system.

   Finally, the default of the **mirrorvg** command is for the quorum to be turned off. To turn quorum off on a rootvg volume group, the system must be rebooted.

> **Note:** Do not reboot the machine if the **bosboot** command has unsuccessfully created a boot disk. The problem should be resolved and the **bosboot** command run to successful completion. The **bosboot** command requires some space in the /tmp file system and the file system where the target image is to reside, if there is such an image.

Non-rootvg mirroring

When a non-rootvg volume group is mirrored, the quorum state is deactivated. For the deactivation of the quorum to take effect, all open logical volumes must be closed. Then vary off and vary on the volume group for the changes to take effect.

If the vary on of the volume group is not performed, although the mirroring will work correctly, no quorum changes will have taken effect.

Rootvg and non-rootvg mirroring

The system dump devices (primary /dev/hd6 and secondary /dev/sysdumpnull) should not be mirrored. On some systems, the paging device and the dump device are the same device. However, most users want the paging device mirrored. When mirrorvg detects that a dump device and the paging device are the same, the logical volume will be mirrored automatically.

If mirrorvg detects that the dump and paging devices are different logical volumes, the paging device is automatically mirrored, but the dump logical volume is not. The dump device can be queried and modified with the **sysdumpdev** command.

6.3 Managing physical volumes

The following sections discuss adding a new disk drive, changing physical volume characteristics, and monitoring the physical volumes.

6.3.1 Configuration of a physical volume

The following three methods can be used to configure a new disk drive. If the LVM will use this disk, it must also be made a physical volume.

Method 1

This method is used when it is possible to shut down and power off the system prior to attaching the disk.

When the system is booted after adding a disk drive, the `cfgmgr` command is run by the system during booting, which will automatically configure the disk. After boot-up is complete, log in as root, run **lspv**, and look for a new disk entry in the output as shown in the following example.

```
hdisk1   none                     none
```

   or

```
hdisk1   00005264d21adb2e         none
```

The 16-digit number in the second column of the preceding example is the physical volume identifier (PVID).

If the output shows the new disk with a PVID, it can be used by the LVM for configuration. If the new disk does not have a PVID, then use the procedure described in Section 6.3.2, "Making an available disk a physical volume" on page 132 to allow the disk to be used by the LVM.

Method 2

This method may be used when it is not possible to shut down or power off the system prior to attaching the disk. Perform the following tasks:

1. Run **lspv** to list the physical disks already configured on the system, as shown in the following example:

```
# lspv
hdisk0       000005265ac63976    rootvg
```

2. To configure all newly detected devices on the system (including the new disk), use the following command:

   cfgmgr

3. Run **lspv** again and look for a new disk entry in the output as shown in the following example:

```
hdisk1   none                     none
```

   or

```
hdisk1   00005264d21adb2e    none
```

Once you have determined the name of the newly configured disk, use the procedure described in Section 6.3.2, "Making an available disk a physical volume" on page 132 to allow the disk to be utilized by the LVM.

Method 3

This method may be used when it is not possible to shut down or power off the system prior to attaching the disk. This method requires the following information about the new disk:

- ► How the disk is attached (subclass).
- ► The type of the disk (type).
- ► Which system attachment the disk is connected to (parent name).
- ► The logical address of the disk (where connected).

Use the following command to configure the disk and ensure that it is available as a physical volume by using the pv=yes attribute.

mkdev -c disk -s *subclass* **-t** *type* **-p** *parentname* **-w** *whereconnected* **-a pv=yes**

The pv=yes attribute makes the disk a physical volume and writes a boot record with a unique physical volume identifier onto the disk (if it does not already have one).

6.3.2 Making an available disk a physical volume

A new disk drive is usable only when assigned to a volume group. To be used by the LVM, a disk must be configured as a physical volume. The following command will change an available disk (hdisk1) to a physical volume by assigning a physical volume identifier (PVID), if it does not already have one.

chdev -l hdisk1 -a pv=yes

This command has no effect if the disk is already a physical volume.

6.3.3 Modifying physical volume characteristics

This section discusses the two characteristics that can be changed for a physical volume using the **chpv** command.

Setting allocation permission for a physical volume

The allocation permission for a physical volume determines if physical partitions contained on this disk, which are not allocated to a logical volume yet, can be allocated for use by logical volumes. Setting the allocation permission defines whether or not the allocation of new physical partitions is permitted for the specified physical volume.

The following command is used to turn off the allocation permission for the physical volume hdisk1:

```
chpv -a n hdisk1
```

To turn the allocation permission back on, use the following command:

```
chpv -a y hdisk1
```

Setting the availability of a physical volume

The availability of a physical volume defines whether any logical input/output operations can be performed to the specified physical volume. Physical volumes should be made unavailable when they are to be removed from the system or are lost due to failure.

The following command is used to set the state of a physical volume to unavailable:

```
chpv -v r pvname
```

This will quiesce all VGDA and VGSA copies on the physical volume, and the physical volume will not take part in future vary on quorum checking. Also, information about the specified volume will be removed from the VGDAs of the other physical volumes in that volume group.

The following command will make a physical volume available to the system.

```
chpv -v a pvname
```

> **Note:** The **chpv** command uses space in the /tmp directory to store information while it is executing. If it fails, it could be due to lack of space in the /tmp directory. Create more space in that directory and try again.

6.3.4 Removing physical volumes

A physical volume must be unconfigured before it can be removed from the system. The following example shows how to unconfigure a physical volume (hdisk1) and change its state from available to defined using the **rmdev** command:

```
rmdev -l hdisk1
```

The definition of this physical volume will remain in the ODM. The -d flag removes the definition from the ODM.

6.3.5 Listing information about physical volumes

A physical volume correctly installed on the system can be assigned to a volume group and can subsequently be used to hold file systems and logical volumes.

The information about free physical partitions and their availability within different sectors on the disk can be very useful. The following section will discuss using the **lspv** command to obtain such information as is pertinent to physical volumes.

Listing physical volumes on the system

The **lspv** command, run without any flags, will produce output that will identify the physical volumes by name that are known to the system, as shown in the following example:

```
# lspv
hdisk0          00615147ce54a7ee     rootvg
hdisk1          00615147a877976a     rootvg
#
```

The **lsdev** command with the -C option and -c class will also list the physical volumes on the system along with the status of each physical volume, as shown in the following example:

```
# lsdev -C -c disk
hdisk0 Available 40-58-00-0,0 16 Bit SCSI Disk Drive
hdisk1 Available 40-58-00-1,0 16 Bit SCSI Disk Drive
hdisk2 Available 20-68-L     SSA Logical Disk Drive
hdisk3 Available 20-68-L     SSA Logical Disk Drive
hdisk4 Available 20-68-L     SSA Logical Disk Drive
hdisk5 Available 20-68-L     SSA Logical Disk Drive
hdisk6 Available 20-68-L     SSA Logical Disk Drive
```

Listing physical volume characteristics

The following example shows the use of the **lspv** command to retrieve more detailed information about a physical volume:

```
# lspv hdisk1
PHYSICAL VOLUME:    hdisk1                  VOLUME GROUP:    rootvg
PV IDENTIFIER:      00615147a877976a        VG IDENTIFIER    00615147b27f2b40
PV STATE:           active
STALE PARTITIONS:   0                       ALLOCATABLE:     yes
PP SIZE:            4 megabyte(s)           LOGICAL VOLUMES: 13
TOTAL PPs:          238 (952 megabytes)     VG DESCRIPTORS:  1
FREE PPs:           71 (284 megabytes)
USED PPs:           167 (668 megabytes)
FREE DISTRIBUTION:  48..02..00..00..21
USED DISTRIBUTION:  00..46..47..47..27
#
```

The left hand pair of columns holds information about the physical volume itself. The right hand pair displays information concerning the volume group of which the physical volume is a member.

The following are the meanings of various fields in the preceding example.

PHYSICAL VOLUME   The name of the specified physical volume.

PV IDENTIFIER   The physical volume identifier (unique to the system).

PV STATE   The state of the physical volume. This defines whether or not the physical volume is available for logical input/output operations. It can be changed using the **chpv** command.

STALE PARTITIONS   The number of stale partitions.

PP SIZE   The size of a physical partition. This is a characteristic of the volume group and is set only at the creation of the volume group as an argument to the **mkvg** command. The default size is 4 MB.

TOTAL PPs   The total number of physical partitions including both free and used partitions available on the physical volume.

FREE PPs   The number of free partitions available on the physical volume.

USED PPs   The number of used partitions on the physical volume.

FREE DISTRIBUTION   This field summarizes the distribution, of free physical partitions across the physical volume according to the sections of the physical volume on which they reside.

USED DISTRIBUTION   Same as free distribution except that it displays the allocation of used physical partitions.

VOLUME GROUP   The name of the volume group to which the physical volume is allocated.

VG IDENTIFIER	The numerical identifier of the volume group to which the physical volume is allocated.
VG STATE	State of the volume group. If the volume group is activated with the **varyonvg** command, the state is either active/complete (indicating all physical volumes are active) or active/partial (indicating some physical volumes are not active). If the volume group is not activated with the **varyonvg** command, the state is inactive.
ALLOCATABLE	Whether the system is permitted to allocate new physical partitions on this physical volume.
LOGICAL VOLUMES	The number of the logical volumes in the volume group.
VG DESCRIPTORS	The number of VGDAs for this volume group that resides on this particular physical volume.

Listing logical volume allocation within a PV

The following example shows the **lspv** command with the -l option to list the physical volume hdisk1. The output shows the names of all the logical volumes on the physical volume, the number of physical and logical partitions allocated, the distribution across the physical volume, and the mount point, if one exists:

```
# lspv -l hdisk1
hdisk1:
LV NAME           LPs   PPs   DISTRIBUTION          MOUNT POINT
rawlv             1     1     01..00..00..00..00    N/A
hd4               2     2     02..00..00..00..00    /
hd9var            1     1     01..00..00..00..00    /var
hd3               8     8     01..00..07..00..00    /tmp
lv06              5     5     00..05..00..00..00    /home2
lv07              13    13    00..13..00..00..00    /backfs
rawlv1            2     2     00..02..00..00..00    N/A
copied            2     2     00..02..00..00..00    N/A
newlv             1     1     00..01..00..00..00    N/A
fslv00            1     1     00..01..00..00..00    N/A
hd6               1     1     00..01..00..00..00    N/A
mytest            1     1     00..01..00..00..00    N/A
#
```

Listing physical partition allocation by PV region

The example provided in Figure 6-3 shows how to retrieve more detailed information about the range of physical partitions allocated to a logical volume and the region of disk used for those partitions.

```
# lspv -p hdisk1
hdisk1:
PP RANGE  STATE  REGION         LV NAME    TYPE      MOUNT POINT
   1-2    used   outer edge     hd5        boot      N/A
   3-19   free   outer edge
  20-30   used   outer edge     hd2        jfs       /usr
  31-31   used   outer edge     hd4        jfs       /
  32-103  used   outer edge     hd2        jfs       /usr
 104-143  used   outer middle   paging01   paging    N/A
 144-170  used   outer middle   hd2        jfs       /usr
 171-173  free   outer middle
 174-174  used   outer middle   hd6        paging    N/A
 175-179  free   outer middle
 180-184  used   outer middle   paging02   paging    N/A
 185-192  used   outer middle   hd1        jfs       /home
 193-195  used   outer middle   lv01       jfs       /var/dce
 196-205  used   outer middle   lv02       jfs       /var/dce/adm/dfs/
cache
 206-206  used   outer middle   hd2        jfs       /usr
 207-207  used   center         hd8        jfslog    N/A
 208-208  used   center         hd4        jfs       /
 209-217  used   center         hd2        jfs       /usr
 218-218  used   center         hd9var     jfs       /var
 219-221  used   center         hd3        jfs       /tmp
 222-222  used   center         hd1        jfs       /home
 223-285  used   center         hd2        jfs       /usr
 286-286  used   center         hd3        jfs       /tmp
 287-309  used   center         hd2        jfs       /usr
 310-412  used   inner middle   hd2        jfs       /usr
 413-447  used   inner edge     hd6        paging    N/A
 448-515  free   inner edge
# 
```

Figure 6-3   Status and characteristics of hdisk1 by physical partitions

The following is the description of the fields shown in Figure 6-3.

PP RANGE   The range of physical partitions for which the current row of data applies.

STATE   Whether or not the partitions have been allocated. Value can be either used or free.

REGION   Region of the disk within which the partitions are located.

LV NAME   Name of the logical volume to which the partitions in question have been allocated.

TYPE   Type of file system residing on the logical volume.

MOUNT POINT   Mount point of the file system if applicable.

Listing physical partition allocation table

To determine the degree of contiguity of data on the system to improve the I/O performance of a logical volume, you can use the **lspv** command with the -M option as shown in Figure 6-4. You may decide to reorganize the system after analyzing the output.

```
# lspv -M hdisk0
hdisk0:1-17
hdisk0:18          lv03:1
hdisk0:19          lv03:2
hdisk0:20          lv03:3
hdisk0:21          lv03:4
hdisk0:22-33
hdisk0:34          paging00:1
hdisk0:35          paging00:2
hdisk0:36          paging00:3
hdisk0:37          paging00:4
hdisk0:38          paging00:5
hdisk0:39          paging00:6
hdisk0:40          paging00:7
hdisk0:41          paging00:8
hdisk0:42          paging00:9
hdisk0:43          paging00:10
hdisk0:44          paging00:11
hdisk0:45          paging00:12
hdisk0:46          paging00:13
hdisk0:47          paging00:14
hdisk0:48          paging00:15
hdisk0:49          paging00:16
hdisk0:50          paging00:17
hdisk0:51          paging00:18
hdisk0:52          paging00:19
hdisk0:53          paging00:20
hdisk0:54          paging00:21
hdisk0:55          paging00:22
hdisk0:56          paging00:23
hdisk0:57          paging00:24
hdisk0:58-81
#
```

Figure 6-4   Physical partition allocation by disk region

The first column indicates the physical partition (if a group of contiguous partitions are free, it will indicate a range of partitions) for a particular hard disk. The second column indicates which logical partition of which logical volume is associated with that physical partition.

Migrating the contents of a physical volume

The physical partitions belonging to one or more specified logical volumes can be moved from one physical volume to one or more other physical volumes within a volume group using the **migratepv** command.

> **Note:** The `migratepv` command cannot move data between different volume groups, as shown in Figure 6-5. See Section 6.5.5, "Copying a logical volume" on page 161 for examples on how to move data between volume groups.

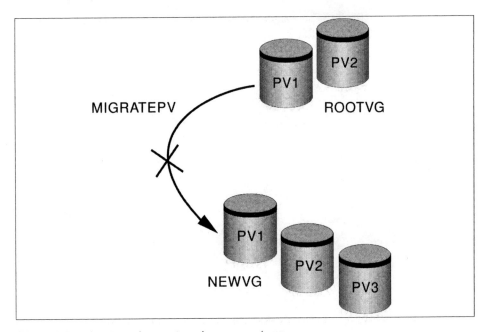

Figure 6-5   migratepv does not work across volume groups

The following procedure describes how to move the data from a failing disk before it is removed for repair or replacement:

1. Determine which disks are in the volume group. Make sure that the source and destination physical volumes are in the same volume group. If the source and destination physical volumes are in the same volume group, proceed to step 3.

```
# lsvg -p rootvg
rootvg:
    PV_NAME    PV STATE    TOTAL PPs    FREE PPs    FREE DISTRIBUTION
    hdisk0     active      159          0           00..00..00..00..00
```

2. If you are planning to migrate to a new disk, such as when you have a failing disk, perform the following steps:

   a. Make sure the disk is available by entering the following:

   ```
   # lsdev -Cc disk
   hdisk0  Available  00-08-00-30  670 MB  SCSI  Disk Drive
   hdisk1  Available  00-08-00-20  857 MB  SCSI  Disk Drive
   ```

   b. If the disk is listed and in the available state, make sure it does not belong to another volume group using the following command. In the following example, hdisk1 can be used as a destination disk:

   ```
   # lspv
   hdisk0    0000078752249812    rootvg
   hdisk1    000000234ac56e9e    none
   ```

   c. If the disk is not listed or is not available, you need to check or install the disk.

   d. Add the new disk to the volume group using the command:

   ```
   extendvg VGName hdiskNumber
   ```

3. Make sure that you have enough room on the target disk for the source that you want to move.

   a. Determine the number of physical partitions on the source disk by using the following command. SourceDiskNumber will be of the form hdiskNumber:

   ```
   lspv SourceDiskNumber | grep "USED PPs"
   ```

   The output will look similar to the following:

   ```
   USED PPs:      159 (636 megabytes)
   ```

   In this example, you would need 159 free PPs on the destination disk to successfully complete the migration.

   b. Determine the number of free physical partitions on the destination disk or disks using the following command for each destination disk (DestinationDiskNumber will be of the form hdiskNumber).

   ```
   lspv DestinationDiskNumber | grep "FREE PPs"
   ```

   Add the free PPs from all of the destination disks. If the sum is larger than the number of USED PPs from step 3a, you will have enough space for the migration.

4. Follow this step only if you are migrating data from a disk in the rootvg volume group. If you are migrating data from a disk in a user-defined volume group, proceed to step 5.

   Check to see if the boot logical volume (hd5) is on the source disk:

   ```
   lspv -l SourceDiskNumber | grep hd5
   ```

If you get no output, the boot logical volume is not located on the source disk. Continue to step 5.

If you get output similar to the following:

```
hd5          2    2    02..00..00..00..00    /blv
```

then run the following command:

```
migratepv -l hd5 SourceDiskNumber DestinationDiskNumber
```

> **Note:**
>
> ► The **migratepv** command is not allowed if the volume group is varied on in a concurrent mode.
>
> ► The **migratepv** command cannot migrate striped logical volumes. If this is the case, to move data from one physical volume to another, use the **cplv** command to copy the data, and then use the **rmlv** command to remove the old copy.
>
> ► You must either have root user authority or be a member of the system group to run the **migratepv** command.

Next, you will get a message warning you to perform the **bosboot** command on the destination disk.

> **Note:** When the boot logical volume is migrated from a physical volume, the boot record on the source should be cleared. Failure to clear this record may result in a system hang. When you run the **bosboot** command, you must also run: **mkboot -c**

Run the **mkboot -c** command to clear the boot record on the source. Do the following on pre-AIX Version 4.2 systems:

```
bosboot -a -d /dev/DestinationDiskNumber
```

then:

```
bootlist -m normal DestinationDiskNumber
```

then:

```
mkboot -c -d /dev/SourceDiskNumber
```

5. Executing the SMIT fast path command **smitty migratepv** to migrate the data will show a screen similar to Figure 6-6 on page 142.

```
                    Move Contents of a Physical Volume
Type or select values in entry fields.
Press Enter AFTER making all desired changes.

                                                      [Entry Fields]
* SOURCE physical volume name                         hdisk1
* DESTINATION physical volumes                        [hdisk4]              +
  Move only data belonging to this                    []                    +
     LOGICAL VOLUME?




F1=Help              F2=Refresh          F3=Cancel          F4=List
F5=Reset             F6=Command          F7=Edit            F8=Image
F9=Shell             F10=Exit            Enter=Do
```

Figure 6-6   smitty migratepv command

6. List the physical volumes by pressing F4, and select the source physical volume you examined previously.

7. Go to the DESTINATION physical volume field. If you accept the default, all the physical volumes in the volume group are available for the transfer. Otherwise, select one or more disks with adequate space for the partitions you will be moving (from step 4).

8. If you wish, go to the Move only data belonging to this LOGICAL VOLUME field and list and select a logical volume. You will move only the physical partitions allocated to the logical volume specified that are located on the physical volume selected as the source physical volume.

9. Press Enter to move the physical partitions.

10. To remove the source disk from the volume group, such as when it is failing, enter the following command:

   reducevg VGNname SourceDiskNumber

11. Before physically removing the source disk from the system, such as when it is failing, enter the following command:

   rmdev -l SourceDiskNumber -d

The following are additional examples of using the **migratepv** command:

▶ Use the following command to move physical partitions from hdisk1 to hdisk6 and hdisk7 (all physical volumes are in one volume group):

```
migratepv hdisk1 hdisk6 hdisk7
```

▶ Use the following command to move physical partitions in logical volume lv02 from hdisk1 to hdisk6:

```
migratepv -l lv02 hdisk1 hdisk6
```

6.4 Managing volume groups

This section discusses the functions that can be performed on volume groups. As with physical volumes, volume groups can be created and removed, and their characteristics can be modified. Additional functions, such as activating and deactivating volume groups, can also be performed.

6.4.1 Adding a volume group

Before a new volume group can be added to the system, one or more physical volumes not used in other volume groups, and in an available state, must exist on the system.

It is important to decide upon certain information, such as the volume group name and the physical volumes to use, prior to adding a volume group.

New volume groups can be added to the system by using the **mkvg** command or by using SMIT. Of all the characteristics set at creation time of the volume group, the following are the most important:

▶ The volume group names must be unique on the system.

▶ The names of all physical volumes to be used in the new volume group.

▶ The maximum number of physical volumes that can exist in the volume group.

▶ The physical partition size for the volume group.

▶ The flag to activate the volume group automatically at each system restart.

The following example shows the use of the **mkvg** command to create a volume group, myvg, using the physical volumes hdisk1 and hdisk5, with a physical partition size of 4 KB. The volume group is limited to a maximum of 10 physical volumes.

```
mkvg -y myvg -d 10 -s 8 hdisk1 hdisk5
```

Alternatively, you can use the SMIT fast path command `smitty mkvg` to obtain the screen shown in Figure 6-7 and enter the characteristics of the volume group to be created in the fields.

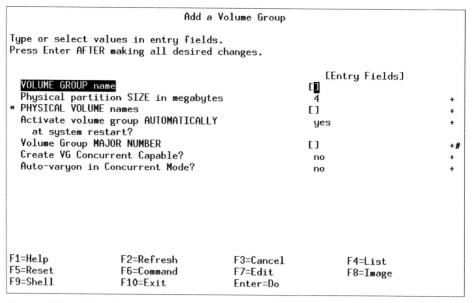

```
                          Add a Volume Group

Type or select values in entry fields.
Press Enter AFTER making all desired changes.

                                                     [Entry Fields]
  VOLUME GROUP name                                 []
  Physical partition SIZE in megabytes              4                +
* PHYSICAL VOLUME names                             []               +
  Activate volume group AUTOMATICALLY               yes              +
    at system restart?
  Volume Group MAJOR NUMBER                          []              +#
  Create VG Concurrent Capable?                     no               +
  Auto-varyon in Concurrent Mode?                   no               +




F1=Help           F2=Refresh          F3=Cancel          F4=List
F5=Reset          F6=Command          F7=Edit            F8=Image
F9=Shell          F10=Exit            Enter=Do
```

Figure 6-7   smitty mkvg command

The `smitty mkvg` command will automatically activate the volume group by calling the `varyonvg` command. Moreover, the SMIT command limits the following functions, as compared to executing from the command line:

- `smitty mkvg` does not provide the -d flag to set the maximum number of physical volumes. It uses a default value of 32.

- `smitty mkvg` does not provide the -m flag to set the maximum size of the physical volume. This flag will determine how many physical partitions are used. It uses a set value of 1016 partitions.

- `smitty mkvg` always uses the -f flag to force the creation of the volume group.

Note: For a new volume group to be successfully added to the system using the `mkvg` command, the root file system should have about 2 MB of free space. Check this using the `df` command. This free space is required because a file is written in the directory /etc/vg each time a new volume group is added.

6.4.2 Modifying volume group characteristics

The following sections discuss the tasks required to modify a volume group's characteristics.

Modifying volume group activation characteristics

The following command allows the volume group, newvg, to be varied on automatically each time a system is restarted:

```
chvg -ay newvg
```

The following command will turn off the automatic varying on of the volume group, newvg, at the system restart:

```
chvg -an newvg
```

Unlocking a volume group

A volume group can become locked when an LVM command terminates abnormally, due to a system crash while an LVM operation was being performed on the system.

In AIX Version 4 and later, it is also possible to unlock a volume group. The following example shows the command to unlock the newvg volume group.

```
chvg -u newvg
```

Adding a physical volume

It may be necessary to increase the free space available in a volume group, so that existing file systems and logical volumes within the volume group can be extended, or new ones can be added. This requires additional physical volumes be made available within the volume group.

It is possible to add physical volumes to a volume group up to the maximum specified at creation time. A physical volume can be added using the **extendvg** command. The following example shows the command to add the physical volume hdisk3 to volume group newvg.

```
extendvg newvg hdisk3
```

> **Note:** The **extendvg** command will fail if the physical volume being added already belongs to a varied on volume group on the current system. Also, if the physical volume being added belongs to a volume group that is currently not varied on, the user will be asked to confirm whether or not to continue.

Alternatively, you can use the SMIT fast path command smitty vgsc and select Add a Physical Volume to a Volume Group.

Removing a physical volume

The volume group must be varied on before it can be reduced. The following example shows how to remove the physical volume, hdisk3, from the volume group, myvg.

```
reducevg myvg hdisk3
```

Alternatively, you can use the SMIT fast path command **smitty reducevg** to remove a physical volume from a volume group.

> **Note:** The **reducevg** command provides the -d and -f flags.
>
> ► The -d flag can be dangerous because it automatically deletes all logical volume data on the physical volume before removing the physical volume from the volume group. If a logical volume spans multiple physical volumes, the removal of any of those physical volumes may jeopardize the integrity of the entire logical volume.
>
> ► The -f flag makes the -d flag even more dangerous by suppressing interaction with a user requesting confirmation that the logical volume should be deleted.

If the logical volumes on the physical volume specified to be removed also span other physical volumes in the volume group, the removal operation may destroy the integrity of those logical volumes regardless of the physical volume on which they reside.

When you remove all physical volumes in a volume group, the volume group itself is also removed.

Removing a physical volume reference

Sometimes a disk is removed from the system without first running **reducevg VolumeGroup PhysicalVolume**. The VGDA still has the removed disk's reference, but the physical volume name no longer exists or has been reassigned. To remove references to the disk that has been removed, you can still use the **reducevg** command using the PVID of the physical volume removed. The following command will remove the reference of a physical volume (with PVID of 000005265ac63976) from the volume group newvg.

```
reducevg VolumeGroup 000005265ac63976
```

6.4.3 Importing and exporting a volume group

There may be times when a volume group needs to be moved from one RS/6000 or @server pSeries system to another, so that logical volume and file system data in the volume group can be accessed directly on the target system.

To remove the system definition of a volume group from the ODM database, the volume group needs to be exported using the **exportvg** command. This command will not remove any user data in the volume group, but will only remove its definition from the ODM database.

Similarly, when a volume group is moved, the target system needs to add the definition of the new volume group. This can be achieved by importing the volume group by using the **importvg** command, which will add an entry to the ODM database.

The following example shows the export of the volume group myvg.

```
exportvg myvg
```

And, the following example shows the import of the volume group myvg.

```
importvg -y myvg hdisk12
```

You can also use the SMIT fast path commands, **smitty exportvg** or **smitty importvg**, to export or import a volume group.

If the specified volume group name is already in use, the **importvg** command will fail with an appropriate error message since duplicate volume group names are not allowed. In this instance, the command can be rerun with a unique volume group name specified. The command can also be rerun without the -y flag or the volume group name, which gives the imported volume group a unique system default name.

It is also possible that some logical volume names may also conflict with those already on the system. The **importvg** command will automatically reassign these with system default names. The important thing to remember when moving volume groups from system to system is that the **exportvg** command is always run on the source system prior to importing the volume group to the target system.

Consider that a volume group is imported on system Y without actually performing an **exportvg** on system X. If system Y makes a change to the volume group, such as removing a physical volume from the volume group, and the volume group is imported back onto system X, the ODM database on system X will not be consistent with the changed information for this volume group.

However, it is worth noting that a volume group can be moved to another system without first being exported on the source system.

You can also use **exportvg** and **importvg** to change the name of a user-defined volume group, as shown in the following example:

```
# lspv
hdisk0          006151409772fa27    rootvg
hdisk1          00382642e0e14dbd    vg00
# varyoffvg vg00
# exportvg vg00
# importvg -y cadsvg hdisk1
cadsvg
# lspv
hdisk0          006151409772fa27    rootvg
hdisk1          00382642e0e14dbd    cadsvg
```

> **Note:**
>
> ▶ The **importvg** command changes the name of an imported logical volume if there currently is a logical volume with the same name already on the system. An error message is printed to standard error if an imported logical volume is renamed. The **importvg** command also creates file mount points and entries in /etc/filesystems, if possible (if there are no conflicts).
>
> ▶ A volume group that has a paging space volume on it cannot be exported while the paging space is active. Before exporting a volume group with an active paging space, ensure that the paging space is not activated automatically at system initialization by running the following command:
>
> chps -a n *paging_space_name*
>
> Then, reboot the system so that the paging space is inactive. AIX 5L Version 5.1 enhances paging space deactivation. See "Deactivating paging spaces" on page 202 for more information.
>
> ▶ If you do not activate the volume group through **smitty importvg**, you must run the **varyonvg** command to enable access to the file systems and logical volumes.
>
> ▶ If you imported a volume group that contains file systems, or if you activated the volume group through **smitty importvg**, it is highly recommended that you run the **fsck** command before you mount the file systems. If you are moving the volume group to another system, be sure to unconfigure the disks before moving them.
>
> ▶ The **smitty exportvg** command deletes references to file systems in /etc/filesystems, but it leaves the mount points on the system.

6.4.4 Varying on and varying off a volume group

Once a volume group exists, it can be made available for use for system administrative activities using the **varyonvg** command. This process involves the following steps:

1. Each VGDA on each physical volume in a volume group is read.

2. The header and trailer time stamps within each VGDA are read. These time stamps must match for a VGDA to be valid.

3. If a majority of VGDAs (called the quorum) are valid, then the vary on process proceeds. If they are not, then the vary on fails.

4. The system will take the most recent VGDA (the one with the latest time stamp) and write it over all other VGDAs so they all match.

5. The **syncvg** command is run to resynchronize any stale partition present (in the case where mirroring is in use).

The **varyonvg** command has the following options that can be used to overcome damage to the volume group structure or give status information:

▶ The -f flag can be used to force a volume group to be varied on even when inconsistencies are detected. These inconsistencies are generally differences between the configuration data for each volume group held in the ODM database and VGDA.

▶ The -n flag will suppress the invocation of the **syncvg** command at vary on time. When a volume group is varied on, and stale partitions are detected, the vary on process will invoke the **syncvg** command to synchronize the stale partitions. This option is of value when you wish to carefully recover a volume group and you want to ensure that you do not accidentally write bad mirrored copies of data over good copies.

▶ The -s flag allows a volume group to be varied on in the maintenance or system management modes. Logical volume commands can operate on the volume group, but no logical volume can be opened for input or output.

The following example shows the command to activate the volume group newvg.

```
varyonvg newvg
```

You can also use the SMIT fast path command, **smitty varyonvg**, to obtain output similar to what is presented in Figure 6-8 on page 150. Enter the name of the volume group to be varied on, along with all the options.

```
                    Activate a Volume Group
Type or select values in entry fields.
Press Enter AFTER making all desired changes.

                                                  [Entry Fields]
* VOLUME GROUP name                            []                         +
  RESYNCHRONIZE stale physical partitions?     yes                        +
  Activate volume group in SYSTEM              no                         +
    MANAGEMENT mode?
  FORCE activation of the volume group?        no                         +
   Warning--this may cause loss of data
   integrity.
  Varyon VG in Concurrent Mode?                no                         +




F1=Help            F2=Refresh          F3=Cancel          F4=List
F5=Reset           F6=Command          F7=Edit            F8=Image
F9=Shell           F10=Exit            Enter=Do
```

Figure 6-8   smitty varyonvg command

The **varyoffvg** command will deactivate a volume group and its associated
logical volumes. This requires that the logical volumes be closed, which requires
that file systems associated with logical volumes be unmounted. The **varyoffvg**
command also allows the use of the -s flag to change the volume group from
being active to being in the maintenance or systems management mode.

> **Note:** In AIX Version 4 and later, when a volume group is imported, it is
> automatically varied on; while in AIX Version 3, the volume group has to be
> varied on separately.

The following example shows the command to deactivate the volume group
myvg.

```
varyoffvg myvg
```

You can also use the SMIT fast path command, **smitty varyoffvg,** which will
show a screen is similar to that shown in Figure 6-9 on page 151. You can enter
the name of the volume group to be varied off, and you can also put the volume
group into system management mode.

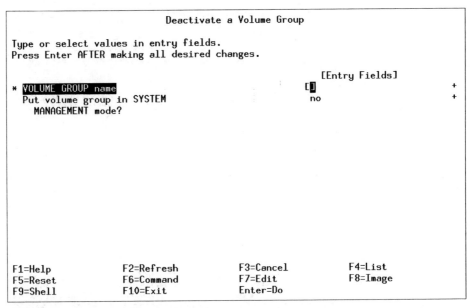

```
                        Deactivate a Volume Group

Type or select values in entry fields.
Press Enter AFTER making all desired changes.

                                                        [Entry Fields]
* VOLUME GROUP name                              [ ]                    +
    Put volume group in SYSTEM                    no                    +
        MANAGEMENT mode?




F1=Help          F2=Refresh          F3=Cancel          F4=List
F5=Reset         F6=Command          F7=Edit            F8=Image
F9=Shell         F10=Exit            Enter=Do
```

Figure 6-9   smitty varyoffvg command

6.4.5 Monitoring volume groups

The **lsvg** command interrogates the ODM database for all volume groups
currently known to the system. The following are a few examples showing the
use of the **lsvg** command to monitor volume groups.

Listing the volume groups

The following example shows the use of the **lsvg** command without any flag to
list all the volume groups known to the system:

```
# lsvg
rootvg
altinst_rootvg
datavg
testvg
#
```

The following example shows how to list the volume groups that are currently
active (varied on):

```
# lsvg -o
testvg
datavg
rootvg
```

Listing the characteristics of a volume group

The example in Figure 6-10 shows the command used to list detailed information and status about the volume group's characteristics.

```
# lsvg rootvg
VOLUME GROUP:    rootvg           VG IDENTIFIER:    00615151e5394126
VG STATE:        active           PP SIZE:          4 megabyte(s)
VG PERMISSION:   read/write       TOTAL PPs:        596 (2384 megabytes)
MAX LVs:         256              FREE PPs:         146 (584 megabytes)
LVs:             14               USED PPs:         450 (1800 megabytes)
OPEN LVs:        13               QUORUM:           2
TOTAL PVs:       2                VG DESCRIPTORS:   3
STALE PVs:       0                STALE PPs:        0
ACTIVE PVs:      2                AUTO ON:          yes
MAX PPs per PV: 1016              MAX PVs:          32
# ▮
```

Figure 6-10   lsvg rootvg command

Listing the logical volumes in a volume group

The example in Figure 6-11 shows the command used to display the names, characteristics, and status of all the logical volumes in the volume group rootvg.

```
# lsvg -l rootvg
rootvg:
LV NAME       TYPE     LPs   PPs   PVs  LV STATE      MOUNT POINT
hd5           boot     2     2     1    closed/syncd  N/A
hd6           paging   36    36    1    open/syncd    N/A
hd8           jfslog   1     1     1    open/syncd    N/A
hd4           jfs      2     2     1    open/syncd    /
hd2           jfs      309   309   1    open/syncd    /usr
hd9var        jfs      1     1     1    open/syncd    /var
hd3           jfs      4     4     1    open/syncd    /tmp
hd1           jfs      9     9     1    open/syncd    /home
paging00      paging   24    24    1    open/syncd    N/A
paging01      paging   40    40    1    open/syncd    N/A
lv01          jfs      3     3     1    open/syncd    /var/dce
lv02          jfs      10    10    1    open/syncd    /var/dce/adm/dfs/c
lv03          jfs      4     4     1    open/syncd    /usr/vice/cache
paging02      paging   5     5     1    open/syncd    N/A
# ▮
```

Figure 6-11   lsvg -l rootvg command

List the physical volume status within a volume group

The example shown in Figure 6-12 shows the use of the **lsvg** command with the -p flag to display a list of physical volumes contained in a volume group, as well as some status information including physical partition allocation. This form of the **lsvg** command is useful for summarizing the concentrations of free space on the system.

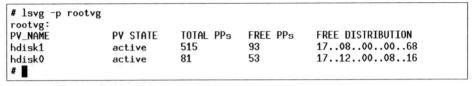

```
# lsvg -p rootvg
rootvg:
PV_NAME         PV STATE    TOTAL PPs   FREE PPs    FREE DISTRIBUTION
hdisk1          active      515         93          17..08..00..00..68
hdisk0          active      81          53          17..12..00..08..16
#
```

Figure 6-12   lsvg -p vgname command

The following is the description of the various fields shown in Figure 6-12.

PV_NAME   The name of the physical volume.

PV STATE   Whether or not this physical volume is active.

TOTAL PPs   The total number of physical partitions on this physical volume.

FREE PPs   The total number of unused physical partitions on this physical volume.

FREE DISTRIBUTION   The location of the free physical partitions on the physical volumes. There are five columns, one for each disk region, in the following order: Outside edge, Outside middle, Center, Inside middle, Inside edge.

6.4.6 Reorganizing a volume group

The **reorgvg** command is used to reorganize the physical partition allocation for a volume group according to the allocation characteristics of each logical volume.

The following is the syntax of the **reorgvg** command:

reorgvg [-i] *VolumeGroup* [*LogicalVolume* ...]

The volume group must be varied on and must have free partitions before you can use the **reorgvg** command. The relocatable flag of each logical volume must be set to y using the **chlv -r** command for the reorganization to take effect; otherwise, the logical volume is ignored.

Note:

1. The **reorgvg** command does not reorganize the placement of allocated physical partitions for striped logical volumes.

2. At least one free physical partition must exist on the specified volume group for the **reorgvg** command to run successfully.

3. In AIX Version 4.2, or later, if you enter the **reorgvg** command with the volume group name and no other arguments, it will only reorganize the first logical volume in the volume group. The first logical volume is the one listed by the `lsvg -l VolumeName` command.

You can also use the SMIT fast path command, `smitty reorgvg`, to do the same task.

See Table 6-2 for details on a flag for the **reorgvg** command.

Table 6-2   reorgvg command flags

Flag	Description
-i	Specifies physical volume names read from standard input. Only the partitions on these physical volumes are organized.

Examples of reorganizing volume groups are as follows:

► The following command reorganizes the logical volumes lv03, lv04, and lv07 on volume group vg02:

```
reorgvg vg02 lv03 lv04 lv07
```

Only the listed logical volumes are reorganized on vg02.

► The following example shows how to reorganize the partitions located on physical volumes hdisk04 and hdisk06 that belong to the logical volumes lv203 and lv205:

```
echo "hdisk04 hdisk06" | reorgvg -i vg02 lv203 lv205
```

Only the partitions located on physical volumes hdisk04 and hdisk06 of volume group vg02, which belong to the logical volumes lv203 and lv205, are reorganized.

6.4.7 Synchronizing a volume group

The **syncvg** command is used to synchronize logical volume copies that are not current (stale).

The following is the syntax of **syncvg** command:

```
syncvg [ -f ] [ -i ] [ -H ] [ -P NumParallelLps ] { -l | -p | -v }
Name ...
```

The **syncvg** command synchronizes the physical partitions, which are copies of the original physical partition that are not current. The **syncvg** command can be used with logical volumes, physical volumes, or volume groups, with the Name parameter representing the logical volume name, physical volume name, or volume group name. The synchronization process can be time consuming depending on the hardware characteristics and the amount of data.

When the -f flag is used, an uncorrupted physical copy is chosen and propagated to all other copies of the logical partition whether or not they are stale.

Unless disabled, the copies within a volume group are synchronized automatically when the volume group is activated by the **varyonvg** command. The commonly used flags with the **syncvg** command are shown in Table 6-3.

Table 6-3   Key flags for the syncvg command

Flag	Description
-p	Specifies that the Name parameter represents a physical volume device name.
-v	Specifies that the Name parameter represents a volume group device name.

The following examples show the use of the **syncvg** command:

► To synchronize the copies on physical volumes hdisk04 and hdisk05, run the following command:

```
syncvg -p hdisk04 hdisk05
```

► To synchronize the copies on volume groups vg04 and vg05, run the following command:

```
syncvg -v vg04 vg05
```

6.5 Managing logical volumes

Physical volumes and volume groups are normally not addressed directly by users and applications to access data, and they cannot be manipulated to provide disk space for use by users and applications. However, logical volumes provide the mechanism to make disk space available for use, giving users and applications the ability to access data stored on them.

When you create a logical volume, you specify the number of logical partitions for the logical volume. A logical partition maps to one, two, or three physical partitions, depending on the number of copies of your data you want to maintain. For example, you can specify a logical volume to be mirrored and have more than one copy as shown in Figure 6-13. One copy of the logical volume (the default) indicates that there is a direct mapping of one logical partition to one physical partition.

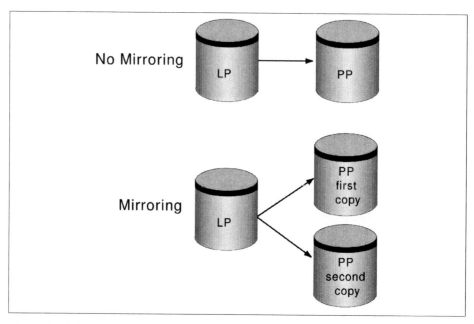

Figure 6-13   Mapping of LP to PP for mirrored and non-mirrored data

The management of logical volumes is, therefore, the management of disk space that is available for use. This section will review the functions that can be performed by users on logical volumes.

6.5.1 Adding a logical volume

You can create additional logical volumes with the `mklv` command. This command allows you to specify the name of the logical volume and define its characteristics including the number of the logical partitions to allocate for it. The default maximum size for a logical volume at creation is 128 logical partitions.

Creating a logical volume using the command line

The `mklv` command is used to create a new logical volume. The following is the syntax of the `mklv` command, and the most commonly used flags are shown in Table 6-4.

```
mklv [ -a Position ] [ -b BadBlocks ] [ -c Copies ] [ -d Schedule ]
[ -e Range ] [ -i ] [ -L Label ] [ -m MapFile ] [ -r Relocate ] [ -s Strict ]
[ -t Type ] [ -u UpperBound ] [ -v Verify ] [ -w MirrorWriteConsistency ]
[ -x Maximum ] [ -y NewLogicalVolume | -Y Prefix ] [ -S StripeSize ]
[ -U Userid ] [ -G Groupid ] [-P Modes ] VolumeGroup Number
[ PhysicalVolume ... ]
```

Table 6-4   mklv command flags

Flag	Description
-c *copies*	Sets the number of physical partitions allocated for each logical partition. The copies variable can be set to a value from 1 to 3; the default is 1.
-i	Reads the PhysicalVolume parameter from standard input. Use the -i flag only when PhysicalVolume is entered through standard input.
-L	Sets the logical volume label. The default label is None. The maximum size of the label file is 127 characters. If the logical volume is going to be used as a journaled file system (JFS), then the JFS will use this field to store the mount point of the file system on that logical volume for future reference.
-P *Modes*	Specifies permissions (file modes) for the logical volume special file.
-t *Type*	Sets the logical volume type. The standard types are JFS (file systems), JFSLOG (journal file system logs), and paging (paging spaces), but a user can define other logical volume types with this flag. You cannot create a logical volume of type boot. The default is JFS. If a log is manually created for a file system, the user must run the `logform` command to clean out the new JFSLOG before the log can be used. Use the following command to format the logical volume logdev: `logform /dev/logdev` where /dev/logdev is the absolute path to the logical volume.

Flag	Description
-y *NewLV*	Specifies the logical volume name to use instead of using a system-generated name. Logical volume names must be unique names system-wide and can range from 1 to 15 characters. If the volume group is varied on in concurrent mode, the new name should be unique across all the concurrent nodes the volume group is varied on. The name cannot begin with a prefix already defined in the PdDv class in the Device Configuration Database for other devices.

The following example shows the use of **mklv** command to create a new logical volume, newlv. This will create a logical volume called newlv in the rootvg, and it will have 10 logical partitions, and each logical partition consists of two physical partitions.

```
mklv -y newlv -c 2 rootvg 10
```

Creating a logical volume using SMIT

You can use the following SMIT dialog to create a logical volume.

1. Run the command **smitty mklv**

2. Press F4 to get a list of all the volume groups that are defined in the system. A screen similar to Figure 6-14 will be shown:

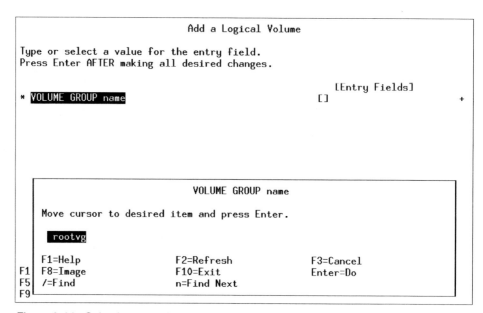

Figure 6-14   Selecting the volume group to hold the new logical volume

3. Use the arrow keys to select the volume group in which you want to create your new logical volume and press Enter. A screen similar to Figure 6-15 will be shown.

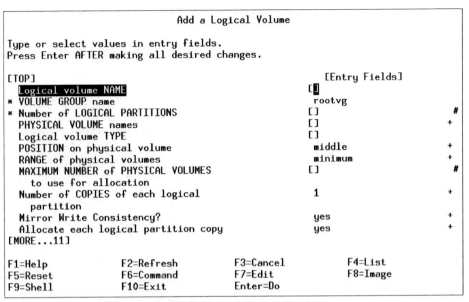

```
                        Add a Logical Volume

Type or select values in entry fields.
Press Enter AFTER making all desired changes.

[TOP]                                              [Entry Fields]
  Logical volume NAME                              []
* VOLUME GROUP name                                rootvg
* Number of LOGICAL PARTITIONS                     []                        #
  PHYSICAL VOLUME names                            []                        +
  Logical volume TYPE                              []
  POSITION on physical volume                      middle                    +
  RANGE of physical volumes                        minimum                   +
  MAXIMUM NUMBER of PHYSICAL VOLUMES               []                        #
    to use for allocation
  Number of COPIES of each logical                 1                         +
    partition
  Mirror Write Consistency?                        yes                       +
  Allocate each logical partition copy             yes                       +
[MORE...11]

F1=Help            F2=Refresh        F3=Cancel         F4=List
F5=Reset           F6=Command        F7=Edit           F8=Image
F9=Shell           F10=Exit          Enter=Do
```

Figure 6-15   Setting characteristics of the new logical volume

4. In the Logical volume NAME field, enter the name of the logical volume you are creating (newlv, in this case).

5. In the Number of LOGICAL PARTITIONS field, enter the number of logical partitions you want to assign to your new logical volume (10, in this case). Each logical partition corresponds to one or more physical partitions depending upon the number of copies of data you want to keep.

6. In the PHYSICAL VOLUME names field, enter the physical volumes that you want to use for this logical volume. If you do not specify any names, the first PV in the system will be used to place all the data on.

7. In the Number of COPIES of each logical partition field, enter the number of LP copies that you want for your data. A value of 1 to 3 is allowed.

8. Press Enter to create the logical volume.

6.5.2 Removing a logical volume

You may need to remove a logical volume if it is no longer in use for storage purposes by users and applications. The **rmlv** command can be used to remove a logical volume.

Removing a logical volume using the command line

The `rmlv` command is used to remove a logical volume. The following shows the general syntax of the command, and its commonly used flags are shown in Table 6-5.

rmlv [-f] [-p *PhysicalVolume*] *LogicalVolume* ...

Table 6-5   rmlv command flags

Flag	Description
-f	Removes the logical volumes without requesting confirmation.
-p *PhysicalVolume*	Removes only the logical partition on the PhysicalVolume. The logical volume is not removed unless there are no other physical partitions allocated.

The following shows the command to remove a logical volume, newlv:

```
# rmlv newlv
Warning, all data on logical volume newlv will be destroyed.
rmlv: Do you wish to continue? y(es) n(o) y
#
```

Entering a y as the response to this dialogue and pressing Enter will complete the process of deletion of a logical volume.

Removing a logical volume using SMIT

Alternatively, you can use the SMIT fast path command `smitty rmlv` to remove a logical volume.

6.5.3 Reducing the size of a logical volume

The following steps can be performed to reduce the size of a logical volume to free up excess logical partition allocation:

1. Back up all data in the logical volume.

2. Remove the logical volume.

3. Recreate the logical volume with the reduced logical partition allocation.

4. Restore the data.

The resulting free space could be put to better use by allocating it to other logical volumes requiring it.

6.5.4 Increasing the size of a logical volume

An existing logical volume can be increased in size by using the **extendlv** command or SMIT.

If the logical volume is used by a journaled file system, you can also use the **chfs** command or the SMIT fast path command **smitty chjfs** to increase the size of the logical volume.

Extending a logical volume using the command line

The **extendlv** command is used to increase the size of a logical volume. The following is the general syntax of the command and its commonly used flags:

```
extendlv [ -a Position ] [ -e Range ] [ -u Upperbound ] [ -s Strict ]
LogicalVolume Partitions [ PhysicalVolume ... ]
```

The following example shows the use of the **extendlv** command to add three more logical partitions to the logical volume you created:

```
extendlv newlv 3
```

Extending a Logical Volume Using SMIT

The SMIT fast path **smitty extendlv** command can be used to increase the size of a logical volume.

6.5.5 Copying a logical volume

Logical volumes may need to be copied for a number of reasons. If a disk is to be removed and replaced with a new disk, the logical volumes on that disk will need to be copied to the new disk. Logical volumes can be copied to new logical volumes or to existing logical volumes that are then overwritten.

Copying a logical volume using the command line

The following example shows the use of the **cplv** command to copy a logical volume:

```
cplv -v myvg -y newlv oldlv
```

This copies the contents of oldlv to a new logical volume, called newlv, in the volume group myvg. If the volume group is not specified, the new logical volume will be created in the same volume group as the old logical volume. This command creates a new logical volume.

The following example demonstrates how to copy a logical volume to an existing logical volume:

```
cplv -e existinglv oldlv
```

This copies the contents of oldlv to the logical volume existinglv in the same volume group. Confirmation for the copy will be requested, since all data in existinglv will be overwritten.

If existinglv is smaller than oldlv, then data will be lost probably resulting in corruption.

> **Note:** Do not copy from a larger logical volume containing data to a smaller one. Doing so results in a corrupted file system, because some data is not copied. This command will fail if the `cplv` creates a new logical volume, and the volume group is varied on in concurrent mode.

Copying a logical volume using SMIT

Alternatively, you can use the SMIT fast path command, `smitty cplv`, to obtain a screen similar to that shown in Figure 6-16.

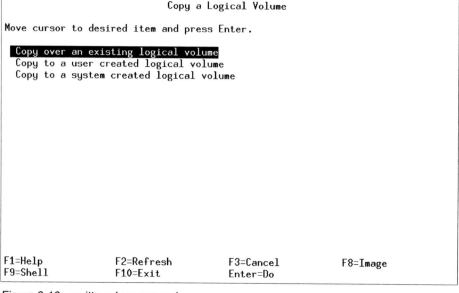

```
                         Copy a Logical Volume

Move cursor to desired item and press Enter.

  Copy over an existing logical volume
  Copy to a user created logical volume
  Copy to a system created logical volume

















F1=Help            F2=Refresh         F3=Cancel          F8=Image
F9=Shell           F10=Exit           Enter=Do
```

Figure 6-16   smitty cplv command

1. Select Copy over an existing logical volume. A screen similar to Figure 6-17 will be shown.

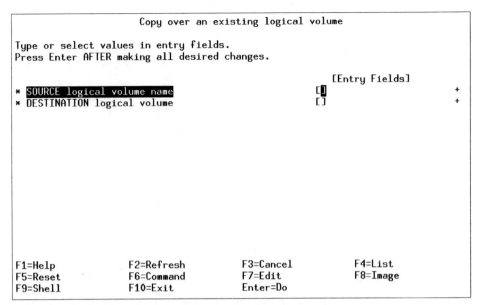

```
                      Copy over an existing logical volume

Type or select values in entry fields.
Press Enter AFTER making all desired changes.

                                                    [Entry Fields]
* SOURCE logical volume name                       []                    +
* DESTINATION logical volume                       []                    +




F1=Help            F2=Refresh        F3=Cancel        F4=List
F5=Reset           F6=Command        F7=Edit          F8=Image
F9=Shell           F10=Exit          Enter=Do
```

Figure 6-17   Selecting source and destination logical volumes

2. Enter the name of the logical volume you want to copy in the SOURCE logical volume name field.

3. Enter the name of the logical volume on which you want to copy your existing logical volume onto in the DESTINATION logical volume name field. This name can be of an existing logical volume that you have already created, or it can be a new logical volume that you want to create. Press Enter to complete this step.

> **Note:** You might encounter the following error:
>
> ```
> cplv : Destination logical volume must have type set to copy
> ```
>
> If this is the case, use the following command:
>
> ```
> chlv -t copy Destination_Logical_Volume_Name
> ```
>
> Return to your SMIT session. Now the system will allow you to copy the logical volume. This has been done to ensure extra security so that you do not overwrite your data accidently.

6.5.6 Splitting copies of a logical volume

The `splitlvcopy` command splits copies from one logical volume and creates a new and separate logical volume from them. The general syntax of the `splitlvcopy` command is as follows:

```
splitlvcopy [ -f ] [ -y NewLogicalVolumeName ] [ -Y Prefix ] LogicalVolume
Copies [ PhysicalVolume ... ]
```

> **Note:** Although the `splitlvcopy` command can split logical volumes that are open, including logical volumes containing mounted file systems, this is not recommended. You may lose consistency between LogicalVolume and NewLogicalVolume if the logical volume is accessed by multiple processes simultaneously. When splitting an open logical volume, you implicitly accept the risk of potential data loss and data corruption associated with this action. To avoid the potential corruption window, unmount file systems and close logical volumes before splitting them.

To split one copy of each logical partition belonging to the logical volume named oldlv which currently has 3 copies of each logical partition, and create the logical volume newlv, use the `splitlvcopy` command as follows:

```
splitlvcopy -y newlv oldlv 2
```

Each logical partition in the logical volume oldlv now has two physical partitions. Each logical partition in the logical volume newlv now has one physical partition.

6.5.7 Listing logical volumes

The following logical volumes are automatically created at system installation time:

hd5	This is the boot logical volume that holds the boot code. It is available only at system startup time.
hd6	This is the default paging space logical volume that is used by the system to perform paging.
hd8	This logical volume is used as the default logging space for the journaled file systems.
hd4	This logical volume in used by the /, root file system.
hd2	This logical volume is used by the /usr file system.
hd9var	This logical volume is used by the /var file system.
hd3	This logical volume used by the /tmp file system.
hd1	This logical volume is used by the /home file system.

The following command will list all the logical volumes defined on the system, as shown in Figure 6-18:

```
lsvg | lsvg -il
```

```
rootvg:
LV NAME            TYPE     LPs   PPs   PVs  LV STATE      MOUNT POINT
hd5                boot     2     2     1    closed/syncd  N/A
hd6                paging   32    32    1    open/syncd    N/A
hd8                jfslog   1     1     1    open/syncd    N/A
hd4                jfs      4     4     1    open/syncd    /
hd2                jfs      123   123   1    open/syncd    /usr
hd9var             jfs      1     1     1    open/syncd    /var
hd3                jfs      4     4     1    open/syncd    /tmp
hd1                jfs      1     1     1    open/syncd    /home
lv00               jfs      4     4     1    closed/syncd  /usr/vice/cache
lv01               jfs      3     3     1    open/syncd    /var/dce
lv02               jfs      10    10    1    closed/syncd  /var/dce/adm/dfs/c
ache
lvtest             ???      3     6     1    open/syncd    /test
lvbkup             ???      3     3     1    closed/syncd  N/A
lv03               jfs      108   108   1    closed/syncd  /export/lpp_source
_1
lv04               jfs      53    53    1    closed/syncd  /export/spot_1
lv05               jfs      158   158   1    closed/syncd  /work
lv06               jfs      5     5     1    closed/syncd  /home2
lv07               jfs      1     1     1    open/syncd    /auto1
lv08               jfs      1     1     1    closed/syncd  /auto2
Standard input
```

Figure 6-18   Logical volume listing

The **lslv** command can be used to view all the attributes related to a logical volume (newlv) as shown in Figure 6-19 on page 166.,

```
# lslv newlv
LOGICAL VOLUME:        newlv                    VOLUME GROUP:     rootvg
LV IDENTIFIER:         00615147b27f2b40.26      PERMISSION:       read/write
VG STATE:              active/complete          LV STATE:         closed/syncd
TYPE:                  jfs                      WRITE VERIFY:     off
MAX LPs:               512                      PP SIZE:          4 megabyte(s)
COPIES:                1                        SCHED POLICY:     parallel
LPs:                   1                        PPs:              1
STALE PPs:             0                        BB POLICY:        relocatable
INTER-POLICY:          minimum                  RELOCATABLE:      yes
INTRA-POLICY:          middle                   UPPER BOUND:      32
MOUNT POINT:           N/A                      LABEL:            None
MIRROR WRITE CONSISTENCY: on
EACH LP COPY ON A SEPARATE PV ?: yes
#
```

Figure 6-19   Logical volume attributes

6.5.8 Logical volume size

The size of a logical volume is the space that is allocated to the logical volume and is a factor of the number of logical partitions that are allocated to the logical volume and the number of copies that you have told the system to maintain. Therefore, the total space taken up by the logical volume is determined by the following formula:

Total LV size=PP size * LPs assigned to LV * Number of copies of the LV

The following example shows how to calculate the logical volume size.

If PP size is 4 MB, LPs assigned to the logical volume are 10, and the number of copies of the logical volume are 2, then the total space that will be allocated to this logical volume will be 80 MB (4*10*2).

6.6 Managing journaled file systems

A file system is a set of files, directories, and other structures. File systems maintain information and identify the location of a file or directory's data. In addition to files and directories, file systems may contain a boot block, a superblock, bitmaps, and one or more allocation groups. An allocation group contains disk i-nodes and fragments.

The following three types of file systems are supported on an AIX system:

Journaled File System   This native file system type is called the journaled file system (JFS). Each journaled file system resides on a separate logical volume. The operating system mounts some journaled file systems during initialization (those that are required to boot and run the system) and mounts others at that time only if directed to do so in /etc/filesystems.

Network File System   The network file system (NFS) is a distributed file system that allows users to access files and directories located on remote computers and use those files and directories as though they are local.

CD-ROM File System   The CD-ROM file system (CDRFS) is a file system type that allows you to access the contents of a CD-ROM through the normal file system interfaces.

The Journaled File System (JFS) divides the logical volume into a number of fixed size units called logical blocks. The logical blocks in the file system are organized as follows:

Logical Block 0   The first logical block in the file system is reserved and available for a bootstrap program or any other required information; this block is unused by the file system.

Superblock   The first and thirty-first logical blocks are reserved for the superblock (logical block 31 being a backup copy). The super block contains information, such as the overall size of the file system in 512 byte blocks, the file system name, file system log device address (logs will be covered later in this section), version number, and the file system state.

Allocation Groups   The rest of the logical blocks in the file system are divided into a number of allocation groups. An allocation group consists of data blocks and i-nodes to reference those data blocks when they are allocated to directories or files. These groups can be used to tailor the physical placement of data on a disk.

6.6.1 Characteristics of the journaled file system

The size for a Journaled File System (JFS) is defined when the file system is created considering the following parameters:

- ► Number of i-nodes
- ► Allocation group size
- ► File system fragment addressability
- ► Journaled File System log size
- ► Maximum Journaled File System size

Number of i-nodes

The total number of i-nodes in a file system limits the total number of files and the total size of the file system. The JFS provides the nbpi (number of bytes per i-node) parameter that affects the number of i-nodes in a file system. JFS supports nbpi values of 512, 1024, 2048, 4096, 8192, 16384, 32768, 65536, and 131072. The values 32768, 65536, and 131072 only apply to AIX Version 4.2 or later.

For example, to create an 8 MB file system with an nbpi value of 4096, an i-node will be generated for each 4096 bytes of data. This would result in a maximum of 2048 i-nodes for an 8 MB file system, which means that if every file in the file system is ideally 4 KB in length, a maximum of 2048 files can be created in the file system.

The JFS restricts all file systems to 16 MB (2^{24}) i-nodes.

Allocation group size

AIX Version 4.2 and later supports various allocation group sizes. The JFS segregates file system space into groupings of i-nodes and disk blocks for user data. These groupings are called allocation groups. The allocation group size can be specified when the file system is created. The allocation group sizes are 8 MB, 16 MB, 32 MB, and 64 MB. Each allocation group size has an associated nbpi range. The ranges are defined in Table 6-6.

Table 6-6   Allowable nbpi values

Allocation Group size in MB	Maximum number of i-nodes
8	512, 1024, 2048, 4096, 8192, and 16384
16	1024, 2048, 4096, 8192, 16384, and 32768
32	2048, 4096, 8192, 16384, 32768, and 65536
64	4096, 8192, 16384, 32768, 65536, and 131072

File system fragment addressability

The JFS supports four fragment sizes: 512, 1024, 2048, and 4096 byte units of contiguous disk space. The JFS maintains fragment addresses in i-nodes and indirect blocks as 28-bit numbers. Each fragment must be addressable by a number from 0 to 2^{28}. If a file system predominately has 400-byte files, a fragment size of 512 would be the most efficient, since 4096-byte fragments would be wasted space. The fragment is the smallest addressable unit of storage.

The Journaled File System log

Multiple Journaled File Systems use a common log, called a JFS log, configured to be 4 MB in size. For example, after initial installation, all file systems within the root volume group use the logical volume hd8 as a common JFS log. The default logical volume partition size is 4 MB, and the default log size is one partition; therefore, the root volume group normally contains a 4 MB JFS log. When file systems exceed 2 GB, or when the total amount of file system space using a single log exceeds 2 GB, the default log size needs to be increased. The JFS log is limited to a maximum size of 256 MB.

Maximum Journaled File System size

The maximum JFS size is defined when the file system is created. For example, selecting a fragment size of 512 will limit the file system to a size of 8 GB (512 * 2^{24} = 8 GB). When creating a JFS file system, the factors listed (nbpi, fragment size, and allocation group size) need to be weighed carefully. The file system size limitation is the minimum of NPBI * 2^{24} or Fragment Size * 2^{28}.

6.6.2 Creating a file system

Every file system in AIX corresponds to a logical volume. To create a Journaled File System, use the following SMIT hierarchy:

1. Executing the SMIT fast path command `smitty crjfs` will show a screen similar to Figure 6-20 on page 170.

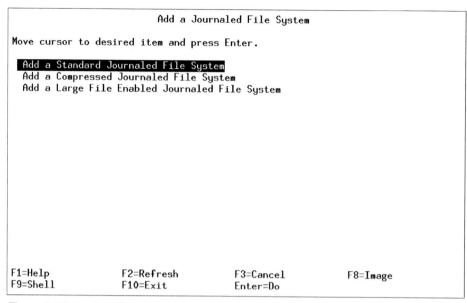

Figure 6-20   smitty crjfs command

2. Select Add a Standard Journaled File System to add a new Journaled File System. A screen similar to Figure 6-21 is displayed.

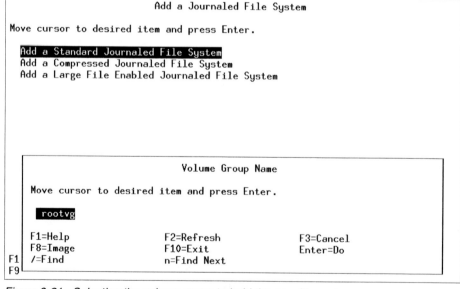

Figure 6-21   Selecting the volume group to hold the new file system

3. Select the volume group you want to add the new file system to by using the arrow keys. In this case, since there is only one volume group (rootvg), only rootvg is displayed. Select rootvg as your target volume group by pressing the Enter key.

4. Once you select the target volume group, a screen similar to Figure 6-22 is displayed.

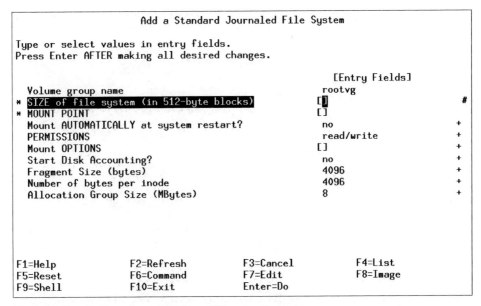

Figure 6-22   Setting characteristics of the new file system

5. In the Size of file system (in 512 byte blocks) field, enter the size of the file system you want to create. For example, if you want to create a file system of 4 MB in size, you can simply multiply the number of megabytes (four, in this case) with 2048 to get the number of 512-byte blocks you will need to specify to create a file system this large (8192, in this case).

Note: In AIX, all of the I/O is in 4 KB blocks; however, space is allocated in multiples of 512 byte blocks. This is done just to remain consistent with other UNIX systems. The smallest file system that you can create is equal to one PP; therefore, even if you specify that the number of blocks to be less than one PP, the system will still create a file system equal to one PP. The following example shows how to calculate the number of blocks for a given amount of space in MB:

Since,	512 bytes = 1 block
Therefore,	1024 bytes = 2 blocks
and	1 MB = 2*1024 blocks
Therefore,	x MB = x * 2048 blocks **(Answer)**

This indicates that the equivalent number of blocks for a file system of 2 MB are 4096 (enter this number in the Size of File System field).

6. Next, in the MOUNT POINT field, enter the full path where you want your file system to attach itself to the file system hierarchy. A mount point is a directory or file at which the new file system, directory, or file is made accessible.

7. Press Enter to create the Journaled File System. The screen shown in Figure 6-23 indicates the successful completion of the process.

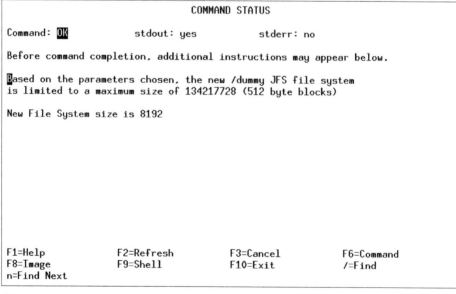

Figure 6-23   smitty crjfs results

Alternatively, you can perform the same task on the command line using the following command:

```
crfs -v jfs -g rootvg -a size=8192 -m /dummy
```

This will create a journaled file system of 4 MB with /dummy as the mount point in the rootvg volume group.

6.6.3 Mounting a file system

Mounting is a concept that makes file systems, files, directories, devices, and special files available for use at a particular location. It is the only way a file system is made accessible. Once you have created the file system, the next task is to make it available to your users. To do that, you must know how AIX manages the patching of the newly created file systems into its file tree using the mount points.

Figure 6-24 shows a file system mount point (/u/kenzie) before a file system is mounted over it.

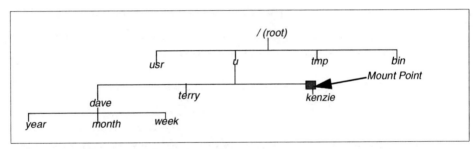

Figure 6-24   File tree view before mounting

Figure 6-25 shows a mounted file system /u/kenzie over the /u/kenzie mount point.

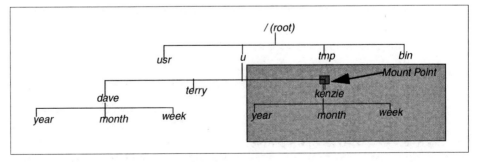

Figure 6-25   File tree view after mounting

> **Note:**
>
> ► When a file system is mounted over a directory, the permissions of the root directory of the mounted file system takes precedence over the permissions of the mount point.
>
> ► A common problem is failure of the **pwd** command. Without search permission in the mounted-over directory, the **pwd** command returns the following message:
>
> ```
> pwd: Permission denied
> ```
>
> This problem can be avoided by always setting the permissions of the mounted-over directory to at least 111.

Mounting a file system using the command line

The following command shows how to mount a file system (/FileSystemX).

```
mount /FileSystemX
```

Alternatively, if you know the name of the device associated with your file system, you can use the device name to mount your newly created file system.

If you want to mount all the file systems, you can use the following command to mount all the file systems at one time.

```
mount {-a|all}
```

Mounting a file system using SMIT

A file system can be also be mounted using the following SMIT fast path hierarchy.

1. Executing **smitty mount** will display the screen shown in Figure 6-26 on page 175.

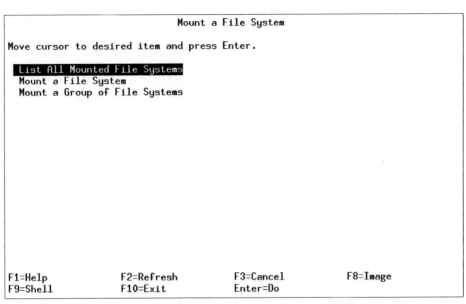

```
                        Mount a File System

Move cursor to desired item and press Enter.

   List All Mounted File Systems
   Mount a File System
   Mount a Group of File Systems

F1=Help              F2=Refresh          F3=Cancel           F8=Image
F9=Shell             F10=Exit            Enter=Do
```

Figure 6-26   smitty mount command

2. Use the arrow keys to move the cursor down and select Mount a File System by pressing the Enter key. A screen similar to Figure 6-27 is shown:

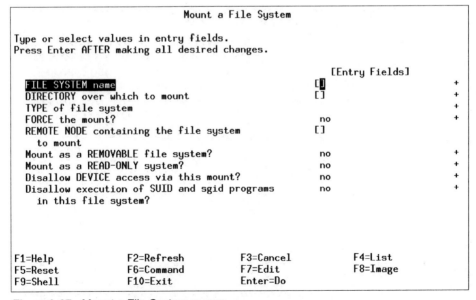

```
                        Mount a File System

Type or select values in entry fields.
Press Enter AFTER making all desired changes.

                                                     [Entry Fields]
   FILE SYSTEM name                                  []                  +
   DIRECTORY over which to mount                     []                  +
   TYPE of file system                                                   +
   FORCE the mount?                                  no                  +
   REMOTE NODE containing the file system            []
      to mount
   Mount as a REMOVABLE file system?                 no                  +
   Mount as a READ-ONLY system?                      no                  +
   Disallow DEVICE access via this mount?            no                  +
   Disallow execution of SUID and sgid programs      no                  +
      in this file system?

F1=Help              F2=Refresh          F3=Cancel           F4=List
F5=Reset             F6=Command          F7=Edit             F8=Image
F9=Shell             F10=Exit            Enter=Do
```

Figure 6-27   Mount a File System screen

3. Use the arrow keys to move down to DIRECTORY over which to mount.

4. Press F4 to get a list of the mount points that you have defined for your file system (refer to Section 6.6.2, "Creating a file system" on page 169, to see how you created a file system, and notice that you created a mount point for your file system. You will use the same mount point to make your file system available to the users). Pressing F4 shows a screen similar to Figure 6-28.

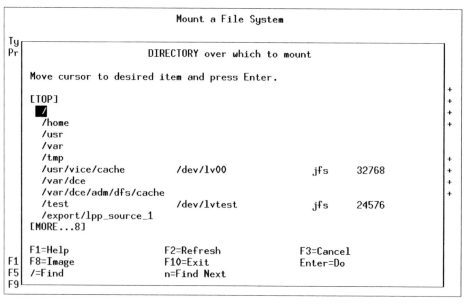

```
                          Mount a File System

 Ty┌─────────────────────────────────────────────────────────────────────┐
 Pr│                   DIRECTORY over which to mount                      │
   │                                                                     │
   │ Move cursor to desired item and press Enter.                        │
   │                                                                   + │
   │ [TOP]                                                             + │
   │ ▮  /                                                              + │
   │   /home                                                           + │
   │   /usr                                                              │
   │   /var                                                              │
   │   /tmp                                                            + │
   │   /usr/vice/cache          /dev/lv00              jfs     32768   + │
   │   /var/dce                                                        + │
   │   /var/dce/adm/dfs/cache                                          + │
   │   /test                    /dev/lvtest            jfs     24576     │
   │   /export/lpp_source_1                                              │
   │ [MORE...8]                                                          │
   │                                                                     │
   │ F1=Help              F2=Refresh             F3=Cancel               │
 F1│ F8=Image             F10=Exit               Enter=Do                │
 F5│ /=Find               n=Find Next                                    │
 F9└─────────────────────────────────────────────────────────────────────┘
```

Figure 6-28   Selecting the mount point

5. Use the arrow keys to select the file system you want to mount. Press Enter to make the selection. This will display the mount point you just selected in the DIRECTORY over which to mount field.

6. Press Enter again and wait for the SMIT OK prompt, which indicates the successful completion of the process.

Automatic mounting

Mounts can be set to occur automatically during system initialization. There are two types of automatic mounts:

► Those mounts that are required to boot and run the system. These file systems are explicitly mounted by the boot process. The stanzas of such file systems in the /etc/filesystems file have mount=automatic. When the multi-user initialization starts, the /etc/rc script does not try to mount these file systems again when it runs the **mount all** command. Similarly, when the **umount all** command is run, these file systems are not unmounted.

- The second type of automatic mount is user-controlled. These file systems are mounted during initialization by the /etc/rc script when it issues the **mount all** command. The stanzas of user-controlled automatic mounts contain mount=true in /etc/filesystems.

You can specify that a file system is to be mounted automatically by either the **mount all** command or by the /etc/rc script at the initialization time. You do this by setting the Mount AUTOMATICALLY at system restart field to TRUE when you are creating a file system (see Figure 6-22 on page 171), or by using the **chfs -A yes** *file_system* command. The following stanza from /etc/filesystems shows a file system, which is mounted automatically:

```
/opt:
        dev             = /dev/hd10opt
        vfs             = jfs
        log             = /dev/hd8
        mount           = true
        check           = true
```

Displaying mounted file systems

The following example shows the use of the **mount** command without a flag to display information about all the currently mounted file systems.

```
# mount
node        mounted          mounted over    vfs       date        options
--------  ---------------  ---------------   ------    ------------ ---------------
            /dev/hd4         /               jfs       Oct 25 18:20 rw,log=/dev/hd8
            /dev/hd2         /usr            jfs       Oct 25 18:20 rw,log=/dev/hd8
            /dev/hd9var      /var            jfs       Oct 25 18:20 rw,log=/dev/hd8
            /dev/hd3         /tmp            jfs       Oct 25 18:20 rw,log=/dev/hd8
            /dev/lv01        /var/dce        jfs       Oct 25 18:21 rw,log=/dev/hd8
            /dev/hd1         /home           jfs       Oct 27 15:14 rw,log=/dev/hd8
            /dev/lvtest      /test           jfs       Oct 27 15:17 rw,log=/dev/hd8
            /dev/lv07        /auto1          jfs       Oct 27 15:34 rw,log=/dev/hd8
```

6.6.4 Removing a file system

The following example shows the steps involved to remove a file system:

1. Using the **mount** command to check the file systems that are currently mounted will display the following screen:

```
# mount
node        mounted          mounted over    vfs       date        options
--------  ---------------  ---------------   ------    ------------ ---------------
            /dev/hd4         /               jfs       Oct 25 18:20 rw,log=/dev/hd8
            /dev/hd2         /usr            jfs       Oct 25 18:20 rw,log=/dev/hd8
            /dev/hd9var      /var            jfs       Oct 25 18:20 rw,log=/dev/hd8
            /dev/hd3         /tmp            jfs       Oct 25 18:20 rw,log=/dev/hd8
```

```
/dev/lv01        /var/dce       jfs    Oct 25 18:21 rw,log=/dev/hd8
/dev/hd1         /home          jfs    Oct 27 15:14 rw,log=/dev/hd8
/dev/lvtest      /test          jfs    Oct 27 15:17 rw,log=/dev/hd8
/dev/lv07        /auto1         jfs    Oct 27 15:34 rw,log=/dev/hd8
```

2. Identify if the file system you want to remove is shown in the list.

    Yes   Continue with Step 3.

    No   Go to Step 5.

3. Unmount the file system by using the **umount** command.
   ```
   # umount filesystem_name
   ```

4. Repeat Step 1 to check whether the file system has successfully been unmounted.

5. Using the SMIT fast path command `smitty rmjfs` to remove a Journaled File System will display a screen similar to the one shown in Figure 6-29.

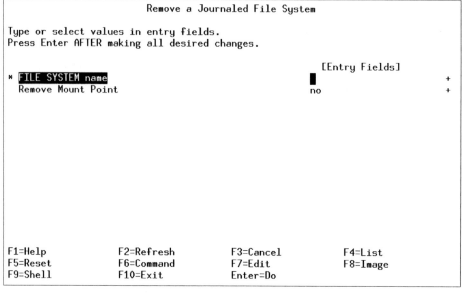

Figure 6-29   smitty rmjfs command

6. Press F4 to get a list of all the file systems that are defined on the system. You will obtain a screen similar to Figure 6-30 on page 179.

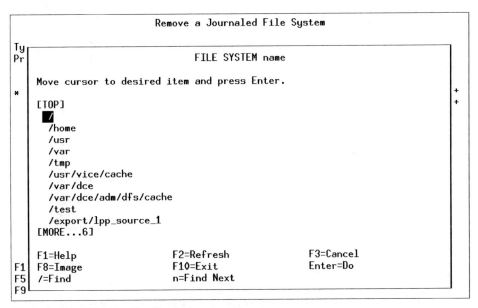

```
                    Remove a Journaled File System
Ty
Pr ┌──────────────────────────────────────────────────────────────┐
   │                        FILE SYSTEM name                        │
   │                                                                │
   │  Move cursor to desired item and press Enter.                  │
 * │                                                              + │
   │  [TOP]                                                       + │
   │     ▓                                                          │
   │     /home                                                      │
   │     /usr                                                       │
   │     /var                                                       │
   │     /tmp                                                       │
   │     /usr/vice/cache                                            │
   │     /var/dce                                                   │
   │     /var/dce/adm/dfs/cache                                     │
   │     /test                                                      │
   │     /export/lpp_source_1                                       │
   │  [MORE...6]                                                    │
   │                                                                │
   │  F1=Help              F2=Refresh            F3=Cancel          │
F1 │  F8=Image             F10=Exit              Enter=Do           │
F5 │  /=Find               n=Find Next                             │
F9 └──────────────────────────────────────────────────────────────┘
```

Figure 6-30   Selecting the file system to remove

7. Select the file system to be removed using the arrow keys and press Enter.

8. The name of the file system you just selected will be shown in the FILE SYSTEM name field.

9. If you want to keep the directory name that was used to mount this file system, press Enter to complete the command, otherwise, change the Remove Mount Point field to YES and press Enter to complete the process.

Alternatively, you could replace steps 5 through 9 with the **rmfs** command.

   #rmfs *filesystem_name*

To remove the mount point when the file system is removed, add the -r flag.

6.6.5 Increasing the size of a file system

AIX provides you with the ability to increase the size of a file system dynamically provided you have enough free space available on your disk. File systems that are low on space might create unanticipated problems.

> **Note:** Whenever a file system is full, the system cannot write to it, and returns the following error:
>
> There is not enough room in the file system

Increasing file system size using the command line

A file system can be increased by using the **chfs** command, as shown in the following steps:

1. Use the **df** command to find out the current size of the file system.

2. Calculate the number of blocks you need to add.

3. On the command line, enter the following command:

```
chfs -a size=new_size_in_512-byte_blocks file_system_name
Filesystem size changed to new_size_in_512-byte_blocks
```

Increasing file system size using SMIT

To increase the file system size using SMIT, perform the following steps:

1. Run the **smitty chjfs** command to display a screen similar to Figure 6-31.

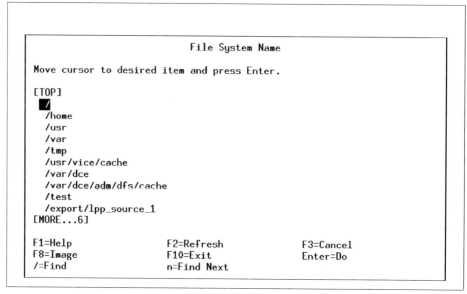

Figure 6-31   smitty chjfs command

2. Use the arrow keys to select the file system you want to change and press the Enter key. A screen similar to Figure 6-32 on page 181 will be shown, which will report the current file system attributes.

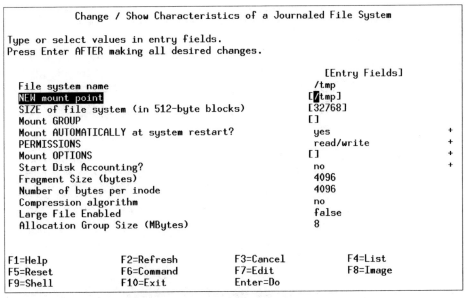

```
                Change / Show Characteristics of a Journaled File System

Type or select values in entry fields.
Press Enter AFTER making all desired changes.

                                                            [Entry Fields]
     File system name                                        /tmp
     NEW mount point                                         [/tmp]
     SIZE of file system (in 512-byte blocks)                [32768]
     Mount GROUP                                             []
     Mount AUTOMATICALLY at system restart?                  yes              +
     PERMISSIONS                                             read/write       +
     Mount OPTIONS                                           []               +
     Start Disk Accounting?                                  no               +
     Fragment Size (bytes)                                   4096
     Number of bytes per inode                               4096
     Compression algorithm                                   no
     Large File Enabled                                      false
     Allocation Group Size (MBytes)                          8


F1=Help            F2=Refresh         F3=Cancel          F4=List
F5=Reset           F6=Command         F7=Edit            F8=Image
F9=Shell           F10=Exit           Enter=Do
```

Figure 6-32   Setting new characteristics of a file system

3. Enter the new file system size that you calculated in the SIZE of file system (in 512 byte block) field.

4. Press Enter. The SMIT OK prompt will indicate the successful completion of the process.

6.6.6 Reducing the size of a file system

You might increase the size of a file system for a variety of reasons. For example, you may increase the size of your /myfs file system to install a new product. If you later de-install this product, the free space in the /myfs file system will increase. Since this space has been allocated to the /myfs file system, it cannot be used by any other file system.

The following example shows how to reduce the size of the /myfs file system.:

1. Make a backup of the /usr file system using any one of the following commands:

   - **cpio**

   - **backup**

   - **tar** - See Section 8.2.2, "How to backup the current directory" on page 225. This section also covers the **backup** and **cpio** commands.

- **savevg** - See Section 8.2.1, "Backing up a single volume group" on page 224.

2. Remove the file system (/myfs) using the procedure discussed in Section 6.6.4, "Removing a file system" on page 177.

3. Create a new file system using the same name and reduced size. You can refer to Section 6.6.2, "Creating a file system" on page 169.

> **Note:** If you enter a value that is less than the minimum size required to contain the current data (indicated in the LV_MIN_LPs entry), the reinstallation process will fail. Use the **df -k** command to see the current blocks used in the file systems, then divide this number by 1024 to get the total MB of the file system.

4. Restore the backup of the file system into this reduced file system by using the procedure discussed in Section 8.3.3, "How to restore a directory" on page 231.

Using a mksysb to reduce a file system

During the process of restoring the rootvg volume group from a mksysb, one of the options is to *shrink* file systems on the disks where you install them. When you choose this option, the logical volumes and file systems within the volume group are recreated to the minimum size required to contain the data. User-defined volume groups can also be restored in this manner by using the -s flag of the **restvg** command.

6.6.7 Checking file system consistency

The **fsck** command checks file system consistency and interactively repairs the file system. The general syntax of the **fsck** command is as follows:

```
fsck [ -n ] [ -p ] [ -y ] [ -dBlockNumber ] [ -f ] [ -ii-NodeNumber ]
[ -o Options ] [ -tFile ] [ -V VfsName ] [ FileSystem1 - FileSystem2 ... ]
```

The flags commonly used with the **fsck** command and their meanings are shown in Table 6-7.

Table 6-7   fsck command flags

Flag	Description
-f	Performs a fast check. Under normal circumstances, the only file systems likely to be affected by halting the system without shutting down properly are those that are mounted when the system stops. The -f flag prompts the **fsck** command not to check file systems that were unmounted successfully. The **fsck** command determines this by inspecting the s_fmod flag in the file system superblock. This flag is set whenever a file system is mounted and cleared when it is unmounted successfully. If a file system is unmounted successfully, it is unlikely to have any problems. Because most file systems are unmounted successfully, not checking those file systems can reduce the checking time.
-p	Does not display messages about minor problems but fixes them automatically. This flag does not grant the wholesale license that the -y flag does and is useful for performing automatic checks when the system is started normally. You should use this flag as part of the system startup procedures, whenever the system is being run automatically. This flag also allows parallel checks by group. If the primary superblock is corrupt, the secondary superblock is verified and copied to the primary superblock.
-t*File*	Specifies a file parameter as a scratch file on a file system other than the one being checked if the **fsck** command cannot obtain enough memory to keep its tables. If you do not specify the -t flag, and the **fsck** command needs a scratch file, it prompts you for the name of the scratch file. However, if you have specified the -p flag, the **fsck** command will be unsuccessful. If the scratch file is not a special file, it is removed when the **fsck** command ends.
-y	Assumes a yes response to all questions asked by the **fsck** command. This flag lets the **fsck** command take any action it considers necessary. Use this flag only on severely damaged file systems.

The **fsck** command checks and interactively repairs inconsistent file systems. You should run this command before mounting any file system. You must be able to read the device file on which the file system resides (for example, the /dev/hd0 device).

Normally, the file system is consistent, and the `fsck` command merely reports on the number of files, used blocks, and free blocks in the file system. If the file system is inconsistent, the `fsck` command displays information about the inconsistencies found and prompts you for permission to repair them. If the file system cannot be repaired, restore it from backup.

Mounting an inconsistent file system may result in a system crash. If you do not specify a file system with the *FileSystem* parameter, the `fsck` command will check all the file systems with attribute check=TRUE in /etc/filesystems.

> **Note:** By default, the /, /usr, /var, and /tmp file systems have the check attribute set to False (check=false) in their /etc/filesystem stanzas. The attribute is set to False for the following reasons:
>
> 1. The boot process explicitly runs the `fsck` command on the /, /usr, /var, and /tmp file systems.
>
> 2. The /, /usr, /var, and /tmp file systems are mounted when the /etc/rc file is run. The `fsck` command will not modify a mounted file system, and `fsck` results on mounted file systems are unpredictable.

6.6.8 Initializing the JFS log device

The `logform` command initializes a logical volume for use as a JFS log device, which stores transactional information about file system metadata changes and can be used to roll back incomplete operations if the machine crashes. The following is the general syntax of the `logform` command:

```
logform LogName
```

> **Note:**
>
> ▶ The `logform` command is destructive; it wipes out all data in the logical volume.
>
> ▶ Accidentally running this on a file system completely destroys the file system's data. If a log device is open due to its use by a mounted file system, the file system should be unmounted prior to running `logform` against the log device. The `logform` command destroys all log records on existing log devices, which may result in file system data loss. You can check to ensure that the log device is closed by running the following:
>
> ```
> lsvg -l VGname
> ```

6.6.9 Placement of the JFS log device

The JFS log logical volume should be placed on a different physical volume from the most active file system, preferably on the disk with the lowest I/O utilization, to increase parallel resource usage. Using a separate JFS log for each file system is also supported. Special consideration, however, should be taken with the placement of multiple JSF logs on the same physical disk, and avoided if possible.

6.6.10 Large file enabled file systems

AIX Version 4.3 and later provides support for file sizes in excess of 2 GB. 64-bit processes can open files without specifically indicating that they understand large files.

With the large file support in AIX Version 4.2, there was no underlying support for a file size in excess of 2 GB.

In file systems enabled for large files, file data stored before the 4 MB file offset is allocated in 4096 byte blocks and the file data stored beyond the 4 MB file offset is allocated with large disk blocks of 128 KB in size. The large disk blocks are actually 32 contiguous 4096 byte blocks.

For example, a 132 MB file in a file system enabled for large files has 1024 4 KB disk blocks and 1024 128 KB disk blocks. In a regular file system, the 132 MB file would require 33 single indirect blocks (each filled with 1024 number of 4 KB disk addresses). However, the large file geometry requires only two single indirect blocks for the 132 MB file.

Determining large file enabled file systems

You can determine large file enabled file systems using the lsfs -q *file_system* command as shown in Figure 6-33.

```
# lsfs -q /tmp/evar
Name            Nodename   Mount Pt             VFS   Size    Options     Auto Accounting
/dev/lv14        --        /tmp/evar            jfs   8192    rw          yes  no
  (lv size: 8192, fs size: 8192, frag size: 4096, nbpi: 4096, compress: no, bf: true, ag: 4)
#
```

Figure 6-33   lsfs -q command output

The bf: output field in Figure 6-33 indicates a big file. This field specifies the file system is a large file enabled, if it has a value of true.

6.7 Troubleshooting file system problems

This section will discuss some of the problems encountered while managing LVM and how to resolve them.

6.7.1 Recovering from super block errors

If you receive one of the following errors from the **fsck** or **mount** commands, the problem may be a corrupted (or *dirty*) superblock.

```
fsck: Not an AIX3 file system
fsck: Not an AIXV3 file system
fsck: Not an AIX4 file system
fsck: Not an AIXV4 file system
fsck: Not a recognized file system type
mount: invalid argument
```

The problem can be resolved by restoring the backup of the superblock over the primary superblock using one of the following commands:

```
dd count=1 bs=4k skip=31 seek=1 if=/dev/lv00 of=/dev/lv00
```

The following command works only for AIX Version 4:

```
fsck -p /dev/lv00
```

Once the restoration process is completed, check the integrity of the file system by issuing the **fsck** command.

```
fsck /dev/lv00
```

In many cases, restoration of the backup of the superblock to the primary superblock will recover the file system. If this does not resolve the problem, recreate the file system and restore the data from a backup.

6.7.2 Cannot unmount file systems

A file system cannot be unmounted if any reference is still active within that file system. The following error message will be displayed:

```
Device busy
```

or

```
A device is already mounted or cannot be unmounted
```

The following situations can leave an open references to a mounted file system:

► Files are open within a file system. Close these files before the file system can be unmounted. The **fuser** command is often the best way to determine what is still active in the file system. The **fuser** command will return the process IDs for all processes that have open references within a specified file system as shown in the following example:

```
# fuser -xc /tmp
/tmp: 2910 3466 11654 26400
```

The process having an open reference can be killed by using the **kill** command, and the unmount can be accomplished.

► If the file system is still busy and still cannot be unmounted, this could be due to a kernel extension that is loaded but exists within the source file system. The **fuser** command will not show these kinds of references since a user process is not involved. However, the **genkex** command will report on all loaded kernel extensions.

► File systems are still mounted within the file system. Unmount these file systems before the file system can be unmounted. If any file system is mounted within a file system, this leaves open references in the source file system at the mount point of the other file system. Use the **mount** command to get a list of mounted file systems. Unmount all the file systems that are mounted within the file system to be unmounted.

► A process is using a directory within the file system as its current working directory. The **fuser** command appends a c to the process IDs of all processes that are using a directory as their current working directory, and the -u flag identifies the owner of the process. It can be used with the **find** command as shown in the following example:

```
# find /home -type d -exec fuser -u {} \;
/home:
/home/lost+found:
/home/guest:
/home/kenzie:    3548c(kenzie)
```

For an interactive process, have the identified user change their current working directory to a directory outside the file system, otherwise kill the process, and the **umount** can be accomplished.

6.8 Summary of LVM commands

This section summarizes the key commands that have been used in different sections of this chapter.

6.8.1 PV commands

The following commands are most commonly used with physical volume related tasks.

`lsdev`	Lists devices in the ODM.
`chdev`	Changes the characteristics of a device.
`mkdev`	Adds a device to the system.
`chpv`	Changes the state of the physical volume.
`lspv`	Displays information about a physical volume within a volume group.
`migratepv`	Moves allocated physical partitions from one physical volume to one or more other physical volumes.

6.8.2 VG commands

The following commands are most commonly used with volume group related tasks:

`mkvg`	Creates a new volume group.
`extendvg`	Adds a physical volume to a volume group.
`reducevg`	Removes a physical volume from a volume group.
`chvg`	Changes a volume group.
`lsvg`	Displays information about a volume group.
`importvg`	Installs a volume group.
`exportvg`	Removes a volume group.
`reorgvg`	Reorganizes a volume group.
`syncvg`	Synchronizes a volume group.
`varyonvg`	Makes a volume group available for use.
`varyoffvg`	Makes a volume group unavailable for use.

6.8.3 LV commands

The following are some of the most commonly used logical volume commands:

`mklv`	Creates a logical volume.
`lslv`	Lists the characteristics of a logical volume.
`rmlv`	Removes a logical volume.
`extendlv`	Increases the size of a logical volume.

`chlv`	Changes the characteristic of a logical volume.
`mklvcopy`	Adds copies to a logical volume.
`rmlvcopy`	Removes copies from a logical volume.

6.8.4 File system commands

The following is the list of file systems commands that have been discussed in this chapter:

`chfs`	Changes the characteristics of a file system.
`crfs`	Adds a file system.
`lsfs`	Displays the characteristics of a file system.
`rmfs`	Removes a file system.
`mount`	Makes a file system available for use.
`fsck`	Checks file system consistency and interactively repairs the file system.
`umount`	Unmounts a previously mounted file system, directory, or file.
`df`	Reports information about space on file systems.

6.9 Quiz

The following certification assessment questions help verify your understanding of the topics discussed in this chapter.

1. While using the SMIT install menus to install an LPP, the response *yes* has been selected for the option: EXTEND file systems if space needed. After successfully installing the LPP, the /usr file system appears to be unnecessarily large. Which of the following actions can be performed to reduce the size of the /usr file system?

    A. Backup, unmount, remove, recreate and restore the file system.

    B. Unmount, run **defragfs** /usr and the **reducefs -size XXX /usr commands**.

    C. Boot from **mksysb** tape and follow the procedure to reduce the file system.

    D. Update /etc/filesystems with the desired size for /usr and reboot the system.

2. A system administrator's daily monitoring has revealed a failing disk drive. While examining the system, the administrator identified an unallocated drive. Which of the following actions should be performed first to migrate the data from the failing drive to the unallocated drive?

   A. Migrate logical volumes to the new drive.

   B. Add the unallocated drive to the volume group.

   C. Create a copy of the file systems to the new drive.

   D. Create a mirror of the logical volumes to the new drive.

3. Due to high I/O volume to several file systems, the system administrator has decided to create a second JFS log volume to balance the I/O requests. After creating the logical volume to serve as the JFS log, what must be done to make the jfslog available for use?

   A. Use the **chvg** command to enable the JFS log volume.

   B. Use the **chjfs** command to enable the JFS log volume.

   C. Use the **logform** command to format the logical volume.

   D. Edit /etc/filesystems and add the logical volume name.

4. A system has been recovered from a hard disk failure and the failed disk has been replaced with a new unformatted one. When the system administrator varies on the volume group, an error message about a missing or unavailable disk matches the one the system administrator replaced. Which of the following commands will eliminate this error message?

   A. **cfgmgr**

   B. **export** *VGName*

   C. **mkdev -1 hdisk3**

   D. **reducevg -df** *VGName* **PVID**

The following are additional questions created by the authors to further test your understanding of the topics.

1. The system administrator has created 20 file systems that are set to mount each time the system boots. Which of the following is the *quickest* method to mount these file systems?

   A. **mount -a**

   B. Reboot the system.

   C. /usr/lib/methods/cfgfs

   D. Mount each individual file system.

2. To increase the size of a file system, the system administrator must:

   A. Unmount the file system.

   B. Boot the system into single user mode.

   C. Have enough free physical partitions within the volume group.

   D. Back up the file system, change the size, and restore the file system.

3. To decrease the size of the /home file system, the system administrator must:

   A. Use the `chfs` command.

   B. Use the `reducefs` command.

   C. Run the `defragfs` command and then use the `reducefs` command.

   D. Back up, delete, redefine, and restore the file system.

4. What is the correct sequence of steps to mirror a volume group?

   1. extendvg

   2. mirroring

   3. `syncvg`

   4. set quorum

   5. `mkfscopy`

   6. `reorgvg`

   A. 1, 2, 3, 4

   B. 1, 5, 3, 4

   C. 1, 2, 4, 6

   D. 6, 5, 4, 3

5. Several error log entries indicate that hdisk5 is going bad. Before it completely fails, the system administrator decides to copy the information from that disk to the other five hard disks in that volume group. Which of the following commands should be used?

   A. `copyfs`

   B. `movelv`

   C. `populatefs`

   D. `migratepv`

6. A system has one internal disk drive (hdisk0) and one external disk drive (hdisk1).

   - hdisk0 is a 2.2 GB SCSI/2 Fastwide disk drive and contains a volume group called rootvg.
   - hdisk1 is a 4.5 GB SSA drive and contains a volume group called appsvg.
   - The external SSA drive has over 3.0 GB of free space.

   The system administrator would like to make a mirrored copy of a 500 MB logical volume that currently is on hdisk0. What would prohibit the system administrator from establishing a mirrored copy between the internal and external disk drives?

   A. The disks are not the same physical size.

   B. The disks are not within the same volume group.

   C. AIX does not support mirroring logical volume mirroring.

   D. The disks are not the same drive type (for example, SSA verses SCSI/2).

7. Which of the following commands displays the status of a physical volume (hdisk1) before adding it to a volume group called cdvg?

   A. `lsvg cdvg`

   B. `chvg cdvg`

   C. `lspv hdisk1`

   D. `chpv hdisk1`

8. What step must be taken prior to removing a file system?

   A. Unmount the file system.

   B. Remove the logical volume.

   C. Delete the data from the file system.

   D. Remove the NFS export for the file system.

6.9.1 Answers

The following answers are for the assessment quiz questions.

1. C
2. B
3. C
4. C

The following answers are for the additional quiz questions.

1. A
2. C
3. D
4. A
5. D
6. B
7. C
8. A

6.10 Exercises

The following exercises provide sample topics for self study. They will help ensure comprehension of this chapter.

1. List all the physical volumes, volume groups, logical volumes, physical partitions, and file systems on your system.
2. Determine which disks the rootvg volume group resides on.
3. Add a new physical volume to your system and check to make sure the drive is available.
4. Create a volume group named datavg on this new physical volume.
5. Create a file system named datafiles.
6. Unmount the datafiles file system.
7. Create a mirror of datavg.
8. Determine whether you have a disk quorum.
9. Determine how many VGDA and VGSA are there for your system.
10. Increase the size of the file system, datafiles.

11. Reduce the file system, datafiles.

12. List the disks that a file system, datafiles, and a volume group, datavg, reside on.

13. Remove the mirror of datavg and check to make sure the logical volume isn't mirrored.

14. Remove the datavg volume group.

15. Migrate data from any volume group other than rootvg to an unallocated drive.

System paging space

To accommodate a large virtual memory space with a limited real memory space, the system uses real memory as a work space and keeps inactive data and programs on a disk. The area of the disk that contains this data is called the system paging space. This chapter discusses the management of system paging space related functions.

7.1 Paging space overview

A page is a unit of virtual memory that holds 4 KB of data and can be transferred between real and auxiliary storage.

A paging space, also called a swap space, is a logical volume with the attribute type equal to paging. This type of logical volume is referred to as a paging space logical volume or simply paging space. When the amount of free real memory in the system is low, programs or data that have not been used recently are moved from real memory to paging space to release real memory for other activities.

The installation creates a default paging logical volume (hd6) on drive hdisk0, also referred as primary paging space.

The default paging space size is determined during the system customizing phase of AIX installation according to the following standards:

- Paging space can use no less than 16 MB, except for hd6. In AIX Version 4.2.1, hd6 can use no less than 32 MB, and in AIX Version 4.3 and later, no less than 64 MB.

- Paging space can use no more than 20 percent of the total disk space.

- If real memory is less than 256 MB, paging space is two times real memory.

- If real memory is greater than or equal to 256 MB, paging space is 512 MB.

7.1.1 Paging space considerations

The amount of paging space required by an application depends on the type of activities performed on the system. If paging space runs low, processes may be lost. If paging space runs out, the system may panic. When a paging space low condition is detected, additional paging space should be defined. The system monitors the number of free paging space blocks and detects when a paging space shortage exists. The **vmstat** and **topas** commands obtain statistics related to this condition. When the number of free paging space blocks falls below a threshold known as the paging space warning level, the system informs all processes (except the kernel process) of the low paging space condition.

Placement of paging spaces

The I/O from and to the paging spaces is random and is mostly one page at a time. The reports from the **vmstat** and **topas** commands indicate the amount of paging space I/O that is taking place. A sample output of the **vmstat** command is shown in Figure 7-1 on page 197.

```
# vmstat 5
kthr      memory              page                faults          cpu
----- ----------- ------------------------ ------------ -----------
 r  b   avm   fre  re  pi  po  fr   sr  cy   in   sy  cs us sy id wa
 0  0 16690  422   0   0   0   0    0   0  127  369  27  0  1 99  1
 0  0 16690  422   0   0   0   0    0   0  118   18  24  0  0 99  0
 0  0 16692  418   0   0   0   0    0   0  124   83  35  0  1 98  0
 0  0 16692  418   0   0   0   0    0   0  120   35  25  0  1 99  0
 0  0 16692  493   0   0   3  16   45   0  145 1812  61 15 13 64  8
 0  0 16692  493   0   0   0   0    0   0  142   13  24  0  1 99  0
 0  0 16692  493   0   0   0   0    0   0  213   24  27  0  0 99  0
█
```

Figure 7-1   vmstat command output

The **topas** command was introduced in AIX Version 4.3.3. A sample output of the **topas** command is shown in Figure 7-2.

```
Topas Monitor for host:      server1            EVENTS/QUEUES      FILE/TTY
Fri Aug 31 11:52:48 2001    Interval:  2        Cswitch        35  Readch        78
                                                Syscall        76  Writech     3252
Kernel    0.1  |                             |  Reads           1  Rawin          0
User      0.0  |                             |  Writes          3  Ttyout         0
Wait      0.0  |                             |  Forks           0  Igets          0
Idle     99.8  |############################|  Execs           0  Namei          0
                                                Runqueue      0.0  Dirblk         0
Network   KBPS   I-Pack  O-Pack   KB-In  KB-Out Waitqueue     0.0
tr0        3.5      3.0     3.0     0.2     3.3
lo0        0.0      0.0     0.0     0.0     0.0  PAGING             MEMORY
                                                Faults          0  Real,MB      511
Disk      Busy%    KBPS      TPS KB-Read KB-Writ Steals         0  % Comp      24.5
hdisk0     0.0      0.0      0.0     0.0     0.0  PgspIn          0  % Noncomp   19.8
hdisk1     0.0      0.0      0.0     0.0     0.0  PgspOut         0  % Client     0.5
                                                PageIn          0
Name       PID  CPU% PgSp  Owner                 PageOut         0  PAGING SPACE
topas    13284   0.1  0.8  root                  Sios            0  Size,MB      512
xterm    15076   0.0  0.9  root                                     % Used       1.2
dtexec   22776   0.0  0.7  root                  NFS (calls/sec)    % Free      98.7
dtscreen 21362   0.0  0.6  root                  ServerV2        0
syncd     5956   0.0  0.3  root                  ClientV2        0  Press:
X         5454   0.0  3.1  root                  ServerV3        0  "h" for help
dtsession 5198   0.0  2.7  root                  ClientV3        0  "q" to quit
```

Figure 7-2   topas command output

To improve paging performance, you should use multiple paging spaces and locate them on separate physical volumes whenever possible. More than one paging space can be located on the same physical volume, however, we do not recommend it.

Sizes of paging spaces

The general recommendation is that the sum of the sizes of the paging spaces should be equal to at least twice the size of the real memory of the machine, up to a memory size of 256 MB (512 MB of paging space). For memories larger than 256 MB, the following rule is recommended:

Total paging space = 512 MB + (memory size - 256 MB) * 1.25

Ideally, there should be several paging spaces of roughly equal size each on a different physical disk drive. If you decide to create additional paging spaces, create them on physical volumes that are more lightly loaded than the physical volume in rootvg.

While the system is booting, only the primary paging space (hd6) is active. Consequently, all paging-space blocks allocated during boot are on the primary paging space. This means that the primary paging space should be somewhat larger than the secondary paging spaces. The secondary paging spaces should all be of the same size to ensure that the round-robin algorithm can work effectively.

The `lsps -a` command provides a snapshot of the current utilization of each of the paging spaces on a system, while the `lsps -s` command provides a summary of the total active paging space and its current utilization.

Limitations of volume groups having paging space

Avoid adding paging space to the volume groups on portable disks in systems prior to AIX 5L Version 5.1. Removing a disk that is online with an active paging space will require a reboot to deactivate the paging space and, therefore, cause user disruption.

> **Note:** In versions prior to AIX 5L Version 5.1, a volume group that has a paging space volume on it cannot be varied off or exported while the paging space is active. Before deactivating a volume group having an active paging space volume, ensure that the paging space is not activated automatically at system initialization and then reboot the system.

7.2 Managing paging spaces

The following commands are used to manage paging space:

chps	Changes the attributes of a paging space.
lsps	Displays the characteristics of a paging space.
mkps	Creates an additional paging space.
rmps	Removes an inactive paging space.
swapon	Activates a paging space.
swapoff	Deactivates one or more paging spaces.

The **swapon** command is used during early system initialization (/sbin/rc.boot) to activate the initial paging-space device. During a later phase of initialization, when other devices become available, the **swapon** command is used to activate additional paging spaces so that paging activity occurs across several devices.

Active paging spaces cannot be removed. To remove an active paging space, it must first be made inactive. To accomplish this in AIX versions up to AIX Version 4.3, use the **chps** command so the paging space is not used on the next system restart. Then, after restarting the system, the paging space is inactive and can be removed using the **rmps** command. In AIX 5L Version 5.1, use the **swapoff** command to dynamically deactivate the paging space, then proceed with the **rmps** command.

> **Note:** In AIX versions up to AIX Version 4.3, paging space cannot be deactivated dynamically. It requires a system reboot. So, any maintenance task that requires removal of paging space will have to be scheduled at an appropriate time to minimize user disruption.

The paging-space devices that are activated by the **swapon -a** command are listed in the /etc/swapspaces file as shown in the following example. A paging space is added to this file when it is created by the **mkps -a** command, removed from the file when it is deleted by the **rmps** command, and added or removed by the **chps -a** command.

```
# pg /etc/swapspaces
* /etc/swapspaces
*
* This file lists all the paging spaces that are automatically put into
* service on each system restart (the 'swapon -a' command executed from
* /etc/rc swaps on every device listed here).
*
* WARNING: Only paging space devices should be listed here.
*
```

```
* This file is modified by the chps, mkps and rmps commands and referenced
* by the lsps and swapon commands.

hd6:
        dev = /dev/hd6

paging00:
        dev = /dev/paging00
```

7.2.1 Displaying paging space characteristics

The **lsps** command displays the characteristics of paging spaces, such as the paging space name, physical volume name, volume group name, size, percentage of the paging space used, whether the space is active or inactive, and whether the paging space is set to automatic. The paging space parameter specifies the paging space whose characteristics are to be shown.

The following examples show the use of the **lsps** command with various flags to obtain the paging space information. The -c flag will display the information in colon format and paging space size in physical partitions.

```
# lsps -a -c
#Psname:Pvname:Vgname:Size:Used:Active:Auto:Type
paging00:hdisk1:rootvg:20:1:y:y:lv
hd6:hdisk1:rootvg:64:1:y:y:lv
# lsps -a
Page Space  Physical Volume  Volume Group   Size   %Used  Active  Auto  Type
paging00    hdisk1           rootvg         80MB     1     yes     yes   lv
hd6         hdisk1           rootvg         256MB    1     yes     yes   lv
# lsps -s
Total Paging Space    Percent Used
        336MB              1%
```

7.2.2 Adding and activating a paging space

To make a paging space available to the operating system, you must add the paging space, and then activate it. The total space available to the system for paging is the sum of the sizes of all active paging-space logical volumes.

> **Note:** You should not add paging space to volume groups on portable disks because removing a disk with an active paging space will cause the system to crash.

The following example shows the steps to create a new 20 MB paging space logical volume:

1. Run the SMIT fast path **smitty mkps** to obtain a screen, as shown in Figure 7-3.

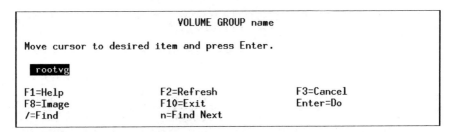

```
                              VOLUME GROUP name

Move cursor to desired item and press Enter.

   rootvg

F1=Help             F2=Refresh              F3=Cancel
F8=Image            F10=Exit                Enter=Do
/=Find              n=Find Next
```

Figure 7-3   smitty mkps command

2. Use the Arrow keys to highlight the rootvg volume group name, and then press the Enter key to obtain a screen, as shown in Figure 7-4.

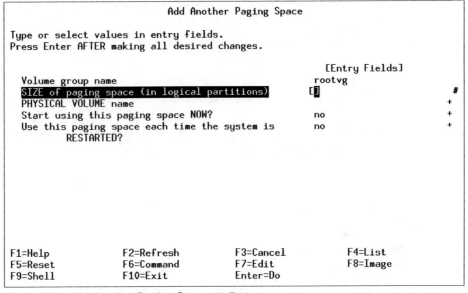

```
                          Add Another Paging Space

Type or select values in entry fields.
Press Enter AFTER making all desired changes.

                                                    [Entry Fields]
   Volume group name                               rootvg
   SIZE of paging space (in logical partitions)    []                #
   PHYSICAL VOLUME name                                              +
   Start using this paging space NOW?              no               +
   Use this paging space each time the system is   no               +
           RESTARTED?




F1=Help             F2=Refresh          F3=Cancel          F4=List
F5=Reset            F6=Command          F7=Edit            F8=Image
F9=Shell            F10=Exit            Enter=Do
```

Figure 7-4   Add Another Paging Space attributes

3. Type 5 for the field SIZE of paging space (in logical partitions), 5 times 4 MB results in a 20 MB paging logical volume.

4. Use the Tab key to toggle the field Start using this paging space NOW? from no to yes, or use the F4 key to select it.

5. Use the Tab key to toggle the field Use this paging space each time the system is RESTARTED? from no to yes.

6. Press the Enter key to create the paging logical volume.

7. SMIT returns the new device name, paging01, with an OK prompt. Press the F10 key to return to the command line.

8. You can now use the command **lsps -a** to check that the new device (paging01) is added and active.

```
# lsps -a
Page Space  Physical Volume  Volume Group   Size  %Used  Active  Auto  Type
paging01    hdisk1           rootvg         20MB    1      yes     yes   lv
paging00    hdisk1           rootvg         80MB    1      yes     yes   lv
hd6         hdisk1           rootvg        256MB    1      yes     yes   lv
```

7.2.3 Changing attributes of a paging space

You can change only the following two attributes for a paging space logical volume.

▶ Deactivate or activate a paging space for the next reboot.

▶ Increase the size of an already existing paging space.

AIX 5L Version 5.1 adds the abilities to deactivate a paging space and to decrease the size of a paging space without having to reboot.

Deactivating paging spaces

The following example shows how to deactivate a paging logical volume, paging03:

1. Run the SMIT fast path command, **smitty chps**, to get to a PAGING SPACE name prompt screen as shown in Figure 7-5.

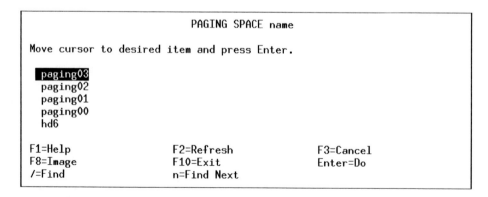

Figure 7-5   smitty chps command

2. Use the Arrow keys to highlight the paging03 paging space name and then press the Enter key.

3. Use the Tab key to toggle the field Use this paging space each time the system is RESTARTED? from yes to no, as shown in Figure 7-6.

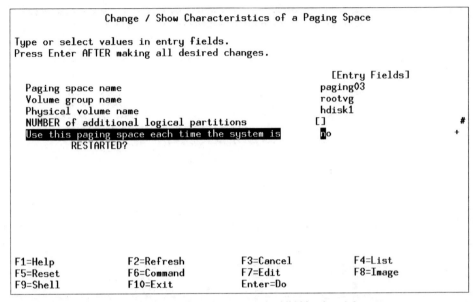

```
                 Change / Show Characteristics of a Paging Space

Type or select values in entry fields.
Press Enter AFTER making all desired changes.

                                                          [Entry Fields]
    Paging space name                                     paging03
    Volume group name                                     rootvg
    Physical volume name                                  hdisk1
    NUMBER of additional logical partitions               []                      #
    Use this paging space each time the system is         no                      +
                RESTARTED?




F1=Help            F2=Refresh          F3=Cancel          F4=List
F5=Reset           F6=Command          F7=Edit            F8=Image
F9=Shell           F10=Exit            Enter=Do
```

Figure 7-6   Changing attributes of paging space in AIX Version 4.3

4. Press Enter to change the paging03 paging logical volume.

5. When SMIT returns an OK prompt, you can press the F10 key to return to the command line.

6. Reboot the system and run the **lsps -a** command to confirm that status of paging03 has changed to inactive.

Dynamically deactivating a paging space in AIX 5L Version 5.1

The **swapoff** command deactivates paging spaces without requiring a reboot.

The **swapoff** command syntax is as follows:

```
# swapoff DeviceName { DeviceName ... }
```

Use the command **swapoff /dev/paging03** to deactivate paging space paging03, or use the SMIT fast path **smitty swapoff** as shown in Figure 7-7 on page 204.

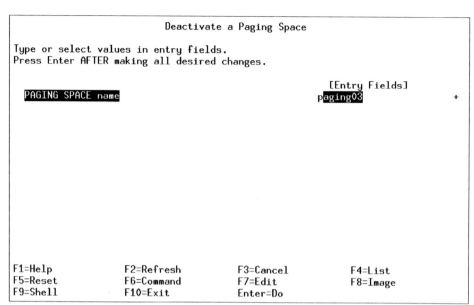

```
                        Deactivate a Paging Space

Type or select values in entry fields.
Press Enter AFTER making all desired changes.

                                                    [Entry Fields]
PAGING SPACE name                                   paging03                +




F1=Help          F2=Refresh        F3=Cancel         F4=List
F5=Reset         F6=Command        F7=Edit           F8=Image
F9=Shell         F10=Exit          Enter=Do
```

Figure 7-7   smitty swapoff command

Note: It is necessary to move all pages in use on the paging space being deactivated to other paging spaces, therefore there must be enough space available in the other active paging spaces.

Increasing the size of a paging space

The following example shows how to increase the size of an already existing paging space, paging03, by 20 MB.

1. Run the SMIT fast path command `smitty chps` to get to a PAGING SPACE name prompt screen, as shown in Figure 7-5 on page 202.

2. Use the Arrow keys to highlight the paging03 paging space name, and then press the Enter key.

3. Type 5 for the field NUMBER of additional logical partitions, as 5 times 4 MB will result in a 20 MB increase in paging space.

4. Press the Enter key to change the paging03 paging logical volume.

5. When SMIT returns an OK prompt, you can press the F10 key to return to the command line.

6. Run the `lsps -a` command to confirm that the size of paging03 has increased.

Decreasing the size of a paging space

AIX 5L Version 5.1 introduces the **chps -d** command. This allows the size of a paging space to be decreased without having to deactivate it, then reboot, then remove the paging space, then recreate it with a smaller size, and then reactivate it.

Use the **chps -d** command to decrease the size of paging03 by 2 logical partitions as shown in the following example:

```
# chps -d 2 paging03
shrinkps: Temporary paging space paging04 created.
shrinkps: Paging space paging03 removed.
shrinkps: Paging space paging03 recreated with new size.
```

7.2.4 Removing a paging space (except hd6)

The following example shows the steps involved in removing an existing paging space, paging00, in AIX versions up to AIX Version 4.3.

> **Note:** Removing default paging spaces incorrectly can prevent the system from restarting. This procedure should only be attempted by experienced system administrators. You must deactivate the paging space before you can remove it, which requires a reboot.
>
> Check the primary dump device you are using by executing the command **sysdumpdev -l**. You cannot remove the default dump device. You must change the default dump device to another paging space or logical volume before removing the paging space. To change the default dump device, use the following command:
>
> sysdumpdev -P -p */dev/new_dump_device*

1. Refer to Section 7.2.3, "Changing attributes of a paging space" on page 202 to change the attributes of paging space, paging00, so that it will not be active after a reboot.

2. Reboot the system by executing the **shutdown -Fr** command.

3. When the system is up, login in as root and run the fast path **smitty rmps** to get to the menu with the title Remove a Paging Space. Alternatively, you can use SMIT by executing the following commands:

   a. Run **smitty**.

   b. Select System Storage Management (Physical & Logical Storage).

   c. Select Logical Volume Manager.

   d. Select Paging Space.

e. Select Remove a Paging Space to get to the same menu.

4. Press the F4 key to generate a list of paging logical volumes.

5. Use the Arrow keys to highlight the paging00 logical volume name, and then press the Enter key three times (once to enter the name in the field, once to get the warning, and the third time to run the command).

6. When SMIT returns an OK prompt with the following message, you can press the F10 key to return to the command line.

```
rmlv:Logical volume paging00 is removed
```

The following example shows the error message you get when you try to remove an active paging space, paging01.

```
# lsps -a
Page Space   Physical Volume   Volume Group   Size    %Used   Active   Auto   Type
paging03     hdisk1            rootvg          4MB       0       no      no     lv
paging01     hdisk1            rootvg         20MB       1      yes     yes     lv
paging00     hdisk1            rootvg         80MB       1      yes     yes     lv
hd6          hdisk1            rootvg        256MB       1      yes     yes     lv
# rmps paging01
0517-062 rmps: Paging space paging01 is active.
0517-061 rmps: Cannot remove paging space paging01.
```

The following example shows how you would remove paging space paging00 in AIX 5L Version 5.1:

```
# swapoff /dev/paging00
# rmps paging00
rmlv: Logical volume paging00 is removed.
```

7.2.5 Managing default paging space (hd6)

The default installation creates a paging logical volume (hd6) on drive hdisk0, which contains part or all of the busy / (root) and /usr file systems. System administrators may want to reduce the default paging space or move it to a less busy hard disk to:

▶ Enhance storage system performance by forcing paging and swapping to other disks in the systems that are less busy.

▶ Conserve disk space on hdisk0.

A special procedure is required to remove the default paging space (hd6). This paging space is activated during boot time by shell scripts that configure the system. To remove one of the default paging spaces, these scripts must be altered, and a new boot image must be created.

The following example shows the command to check your logical volume and file system distribution across a physical volume, hdisk1:

```
# lspv -l hdisk1
hdisk1:
LV NAME          LPs  PPs  DISTRIBUTION           MOUNT POINT
hd5              2    2    02..00..00..00..00     N/A
hd6              64   64   00..64..00..00..00     N/A
paging01         5    5    00..05..00..00..00     N/A
hd8              1    1    00..00..01..00..00     N/A
hd4              1    1    00..00..01..00..00     /
hd2              73   73   00..00..73..00..00     /usr
hd9var           1    1    00..00..01..00..00     /var
hd3              4    4    00..00..04..00..00     /tmp
hd1              1    1    00..00..01..00..00     /home
paging00         20   20   00..00..20..00..00     N/A
paging03         1    1    00..00..01..00..00     N/A
```

Reducing the size of hd6 paging space

The following example shows the steps involved in reducing the size of paging space hd6 from 160 MB to 120 MB. The steps in the following procedures are all necessary - even those not directly related to hd6. The additional steps are needed because a paging space cannot be deactivated while the system is running.

> **Note:**
>
> ► AIX Version 4.2.1 and later does not support reducing the size of hd6 below 32 MB. If this is done, the system will not boot.
>
> ► If you decide to reduce hd6, you must leave enough space for the software in rootvg. A rule of thumb for reducing hd6 paging space is to leave enough space to match physical memory. To find out the amount of physical memory, use the following command:
>
> ```
> lsattr -E -l sys0 -a realmem
> ```

1. Create a temporary paging space on rootvg by executing the following command:

   ```
   mkps -a -n -s 30 rootvg hdisk0
   ```

   This command outputs the name of the paging space (paging00 if no others exist).

2. Use the following command to deactivate the hd6 paging spaces in preparation for the reboot later in the procedure.

   ```
   chps -a n hd6
   ```

3. Change the paging space entry in the /sbin/rc.boot file from:

```
swapon /dev/hd6
```

to

```
swapon /dev/paging00.
```

4. Run the following command to check the primary dump device designation.

```
# sysdumpdev -l
primary            /dev/hd6
secondary          /dev/sysdumpnull
copy directory     /var/adm/ras
forced copy flag   TRUE
always allow dump  FALSE
```

5. If the primary dump device is hd6, change it to some other paging space. The following command shows how to change the primary dump device to paging00:

```
# sysdumpdev -P -p /dev/paging00
primary            /dev/paging00
secondary          /dev/sysdumpnull
copy directory     /var/adm/ras
forced copy flag   TRUE
always allow dump  FALSE
```

6. Create a bootable image with the **bosboot** command for a hard disk image. This step is required to update the system image used during initialization to reflect the changes made to rc.boot.

```
bosboot -d /dev/hdisk0 -a
```

7. Put the system key (if present) in the normal position and use the following command, which will both shutdown the operating system and reboot it.

```
shutdown -r
```

8. After the system reboots, remove the hd6 paging space.

```
rmps hd6
```

9. Create a new paging space logical volume of the size 120 MB for the hd6 paging space.

```
mklv -t paging -y hd6 rootvg 30
```

10. Use the **lsps -a** command to verify the reduced size of the default paging space hd6.

11. Change the primary dump device designation back to be the paging space hd6.

```
sysdumpdev -P -p /dev/hd6
```

12. Change the paging space entry in the /sbin/rc.boot file from:

```
swapon /dev/paging00
```

to

```
swapon /dev/hd6.
```

13. Create a bootable image with the **bosboot** command for a hard disk image.

```
bosboot -d /dev/hdisk0 -a
```

14. Run the following command to make the new hd6 paging space automatically activate when the system reboots.

```
chps -a y hd6
```

15. Run the following command to change the attribute of temporary paging space, paging00, so that it does not automatically activate after the next reboot.

```
chps -a n paging00
```

16. Put the system key (if present) in the normal position and use the following command to shutdown and reboot the system:

```
shutdown -r
```

17. After the system reboots, remove the temporary paging space.

```
rmps paging00
```

Reducing hd6 in AIX 5L Version 5.1

You can use the **chps -d** command to dynamically reduce the size of the primary paging space hd6. This command will prevent you from decreasing the size of hd6 below 32 MB or actually deleting it. If you decrease the primary paging space, a temporary boot image and a temporary /sbin/rc.boot pointing to this temporary primary paging space will be created to make sure the system is always in a state where it can be safely rebooted.

Moving the hd6 paging space to another volume group

Moving a paging space with the name hd6 from rootvg to another volume group is not recommended because the name is hard-coded in several places.

Only the paging spaces in rootvg will be active during the second phase of the boot process, and having no paging space in rootvg could severely affect system boot performance. If you want the majority of paging space on other volume groups, it is better to make hd6 as small as possible (the same size as physical memory) and then create larger paging spaces on other volume groups.

Moving the hd6 paging space within the same VG

Moving the default paging space from hdisk0 to a different disk within the same volume group does not require a system reboot.

The following example shows the command to move the default (hd6) paging space from hdisk0 to hdisk1.

```
migratepv -l hd6 hdisk0 hdisk1
```

This may take a few minutes depending upon the size of the paging space.

7.3 Quiz

The following are questions created by the authors to further test your understanding of the topics.

1. The system administrator realizes that paging space, paging12, must first be removed from hdisk12. Which of the following is the correct sequence of events?

   A. `chps -an paging12`, reboot, `rmps paging12`

   B. `swapoff paging12`, `rmps paging12`

   C. `swapoff paging12`, reboot, `rmps paging12`

   D. `chps -an paging12`, `swapoff paging12`, `rmps paging12`

2. A customer would like to remove an unneeded, but active, paging space called paging00. What is proper sequence of steps to accomplish this?

   A. Remove the paging space by using the **rmps** command and reboot the system.

   B. Disable the paging space by using the **chps** command, reboot the system, and remove the paging00 logical volume by using the **rmps** command.

   C. Disable the paging space by using the **chps** command, remove the paging00 logical volume by using the **rmps** command, and reboot the system.

   D. Disable the paging space by using the **chps** command, reboot the system, and remove the paging00 logical volume by using the **rmlv** command.

3. A system administrator would like to list all of the paging spaces residing on the server. What is the correct syntax of the command to accomplish this?

   A. `lsps -a`

   B. `lsps -s`

   C. `lsps -l`

   D. `lsps -all`

7.3.1 Answers

The following answers are for the quiz questions.

1. A

2. B

3. A

7.4 Exercises

The following exercises provide sample topics for self study. They will help ensure comprehension of this chapter.

1. Determine the paging spaces on a system by using the `lsps` command.

2. Add a new paging space logical volume of size of 5 MB to the system.

3. Discuss all the steps involved in decreasing the size of the default paging space.

4. Discuss the precautions you would take before removing a paging space.

5. How can you change the primary dump device?

6. How can you move the hd6 paging space from one hdisk to another within the same volume group?

7. Which command will display the paging activity status on the system?

8. Increase the paging space logical volume size by 10 MB.

9. Discuss how the process of decreasing the hd6 paging space is different from decreasing any other paging space on the system.

System backup, restores, and availability

There are various commands you can use to make backups of systems. The following is a list of the most common commands for backups. A short description of each is given here with a list of their respective flags in Table 8-1 on page 214.

tar The **tar** command manipulates archives by writing files to, or retrieving files from, an archive storage medium. The files used by the **tar** command are represented by the File parameter. If the File parameter refers to a directory, then that directory and, recursively, all files and directories within it are referenced as well.

cpio The **cpio** command copies files into and out of archive storage and directories.

dd The **dd** command reads the *InFile* parameter or standard input, does the specified conversions, then copies the converted data to the *OutFile* parameter or standard output. The input and output block size can be specified to take advantage of raw physical I/O.

pax The **pax** command should be the archive of choice for system dumps and images greater than 2 GB in size.

mksysb The **mksysb** command creates an installable image of the root volume group either in a file or onto a bootable tape.

savevg The savevg command saves non-root volume groups.

backup   The **backup** command creates copies of your files on a backup medium, such as a magnetic tape or diskette. The copies are in one of the two backup formats: Either specific files backed up (using the -i flag), or the entire file system backed up by i-node.

restore   The **restore** command reads archives created by the backup command and extracts the files stored on them. These archives can be in either file-name or file-system format.

restvg   Use the **restvg** command to restore a volume group.

tctl   Use the **tctl** command to control a tape device.

Table 8-1   List of backup commands and flags

Command	Flags	Description
tar	-x	Extracts the files from the archive.
	-c	Creates a new archive and writes the files specified.
	-t	Lists the files in the order in which they appear in the archive.
	-f *Archive*	Uses the Archive variable as the archive to be read or written. For example, /dev/fd0.
	-p	Says to restore fields to their original modes ignoring the current umask.
	-v	Lists the name of each file as it is processed.
cpio	-i	Reads from standard input an archive file created by the **cpio -o** command and copies from it the files with names that match the Pattern parameter.
	-o	Reads file path names from standard input and copies these files to standard output.
	-c	Reads and writes header information in ASCII character form. If a **cpio** archive was created using the -c flag, it must be extracted with a -c flag.
	-v	Lists file names.
	-d	Creates directories as needed.
	-u	Copies unconditionally. An older file now replaces a newer file with the same name.
	-m	Retains previous file modification time. This flag does not work when copying directories.

Command	Flags	Description
	-B	Performs block input and output using 512 bytes to a record.
dd	if=*InFile*	Specifies the input file name; standard input is the default.
	of=*OutFile*	Specifies the output file name; standard output is the default.
	skip=*SkipInput Blocks*	Skips the specified SkipInputBlocks value of input blocks before starting to copy.
pax	-a	Appends files to the end of an archive.
	-f *Archive*	Specifies the path of an archive file to be used instead of standard input (when the -w flag is not specified) or standard output (when the -w flag is specified but the -r flag is not).
	-r	Reads an archive file from the standard input.
	-v	Writes information about the process. If neither the -r or -w flags are specified, the -v flag produces a verbose table of contents; otherwise, archive member path names are written to standard error.
	-w	Writes files to the standard output in the specified archive format.
	-x *Format*	Specifies the output archive format. If no format is provided, pax uses the pax format by default.
mksysb	-e	Excludes files listed in the /etc/exclude.rootvg file from being backed up.
	-i	Calls the mkszfile command, which generates the /image.data file automatically during a backup.
	-m	Calls the mkszfile command to generate map files.
	-X	Automatically expands /tmp as necessary.
savevg	-i	Creates the data file by calling the mkvgdata command.
	-f *Device*	Specifies the device or file name on which the image is to be stored. The default is the /dev/rmt0 device.
	-e	Excludes files specified in the /etc/exclude.*vgname* file from being backed up by this command.

Command	Flags	Description
backup	-i	Specifies that files be read from standard input and archived by file name.
	-p	Specifies that the files be packed, or compressed, before they are archived. Only files of less than 2 GB are packed. This option should only be used when backing up files from an inactive file system. Modifying a file when a backup is in progress may result in corruption of the backup and an inability to recover the data. When backing up to a tape device that performs compression, this option can be omitted.
	-q	Indicates that the removable medium is ready to use. When you specify the -q flag, the backup command proceeds without prompting you to prepare the backup medium. Press the Enter key to continue.
	-u	Updates /etc/dumpdates with time, date, and level of the last incremental backup.
	-v	Causes the backup command to display additional information about the backup.
restore	-d	Indicates that, if the File parameter is a directory, all files in that directory should be restored. This flag can only be used when the archive is in filename format.
	-f *Device*	Specifies the input device. To receive input from a named device, specify the *Device* variable as a path name (such as /dev/rmt0). To receive input from the standard output device, specify a - (minus sign).
	-q	Specifies that the first volume is ready to use and that the restore command should not prompt you to mount the volume and press Enter.
	-r	Restores all files in a file system archive.
	-s *SeekBackup*	Specifies the backup to seek and restore on a multiple-backup tape archive. The -s flag is only applicable when the archive is written to a tape device. To use the -s flag properly, a no-rewind-on-close and no-retension-on-open tape device, such as /dev/rmt0.1 or /dev/rmt0.5, must be specified.

Command	Flags	Description
	-t	Displays information about the backup archive. If the archive is in file-system format, a list of files found on the archive is written to standard output.
	-T	Displays information about the backup archive. If the archive is in file-name format, the information contained in the volume header and a list of files found on the archive are written to standard output.
	-v	Displays additional information when restoring.
	-x	Restores individually named files specified by the File parameter.
restvg	-f Device	Specifies the device name of the backup media. The default is /dev/rmt0.
	-p PPsize	Specifies the number of megabytes in each physical partition. If not specified, restvg uses the best value for the PPsize, dependent upon the largest disk being restored to.
	-s	Specifies that the logical volumes be created at the minimum size possible to accommodate the file systems.
tctl	-b	Specifies, in bytes, the block size used to read and write to the tape device.
	-f	Specifies the tape device to use.

8.1 The mksysb command

The mksysb command creates a bootable image of all mounted file systems on the rootvg volume group. You can use this backup command to reinstall a system to its original state.

The tape format includes a BOS boot image, a BOS install image, and a dummy table of contents (TOC) followed by the system backup (root volume group) image. The root volume group image is in backup-file format starting with the data files and then any optional map files.

User-defined paging spaces and raw devices are not backed up.

8.1.1 The data layout of a mksysb tape

The layout of a mksysb tape is shown in Figure 8-1.

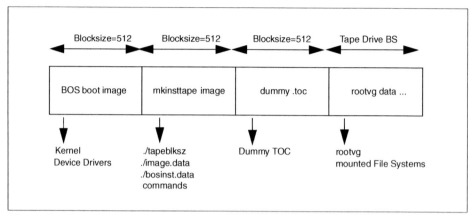

Figure 8-1   Layout of a mksysb tape

The BOS boot image contains a copy of the system's kernel and device drivers needed to boot from the mksysb tape. It is created by the **bosboot** command.

There are three important files in the mkinsttape image (the second image of the **mksysb** tape): ./tapeblksz, ./bosinst.data and ./image.data. The ./tapeblksz file contains the block size the tape drive was set to when the **mksysb** command was run.

The ./bosinst.data file allows you to specify the requirements at the target system and how the user interacts with the target system. This file contains the customized BOS install procedures and dictates how the BOS install program will behave. You can customize this file before issuing the **mksysb** command or use a procedure to customize this file after the image backup is done.

The ./image.data file contains information describing the image installed during the BOS installation process. This information includes the sizes, names, maps, and mount points of logical volumes and file systems in the rootvg. You can customize this file before using the **mksysb** command, or run **mksysb -i** to generate a new ./image.data file on the tape during a backup. The **mkszfile** command generates the ./image.data file. The ./image.data file is arranged in stanza format. Each stanza contains one or more fields. The most important fields are:

SHRINK   When set to YES, causes the system to create the smallest file systems required to contain all the data in the file system.

BOSINST_FILE   Provides the full path name of a file or command to execute
                after the BOS install completes.

EXACT_FIT   When set to YES, causes the system to place logical volumes
                on the disk according to the physical partition maps that were
                generated with -m flag of the mksysb command.

The dummy table of contents (TOC) is used so that the mksysb tape contain the
same number of images as a BOS install tape.

The rootvg data area contains all data in the rootvg volume group backed up by
the mksysb command. The mksysb command uses the **backup** command to save
the contents of mounted JFS data in rootvg, excluding raw data.

8.1.2 Excluding file systems from a backup

When you need to make a mksysb backup of a system, and you want to exclude
some data file systems from the system, you need to edit the /etc/exclude.rootvg
file. If, for example, you want to exclude the file systems /usr and /tmp from your
mksysb backup, add the following:

```
/usr/
/tmp/
```

Make sure there are no empty lines in this file. You can list the contents of the file
as follows:

```
# cat /etc/exclude.rootvg
/usr/
/tmp/
```

Then run the mksysb command using the -e flag to exclude the contents of the
exclude.rootvg file as follows:

```
mksysb -e /dev/rmt0
```

8.1.3 How to create a bootable system backup

The mksysb command creates a bootable image of the rootvg file system either
in a file system directory onto a bootable tape, and is used to restore a system
after a system failure or for system cloning.

To use smitty to create a bootable system backup, follow the steps below:

1. Run the smitty Command. Select the System Storage Management
   (Physical & Logical Storage) field as shown in Figure 8-2 on page 220.

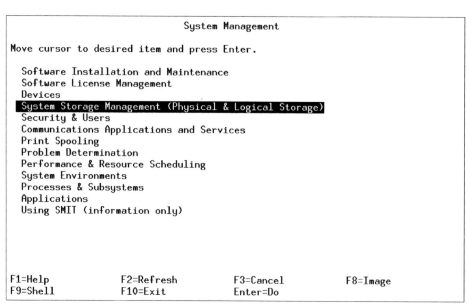

Figure 8-2   *System Management menu*

2. Once in the System Storage Management menu, select the System Backup Manager field as shown in Figure 8-3.

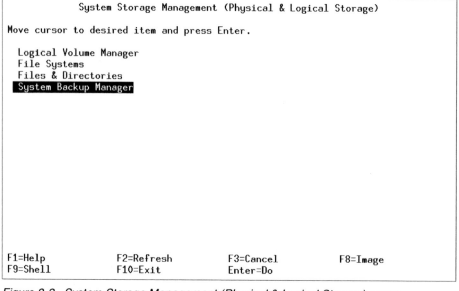

Figure 8-3   *System Storage Management (Physical & Logical Storage) menu*

3. In the System Backup Manager window, select the Back Up the System field as shown in Figure 8-4.

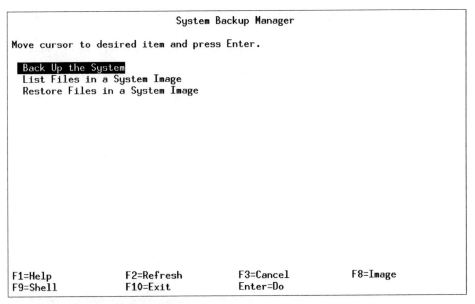

```
                        System Backup Manager

Move cursor to desired item and press Enter.

   Back Up the System
   List Files in a System Image
   Restore Files in a System Image












F1=Help            F2=Refresh         F3=Cancel          F8=Image
F9=Shell           F10=Exit           Enter=Do
```

Figure 8-4   System Backup Manager menu

4. In the Back Up the System menu, select Backup DEVICE or FILE field. This is where you would select your backup device. If you press F4, it will give you a list of backup devices. Choose the device you want, and then press Enter as shown in Figure 8-5 on page 222.

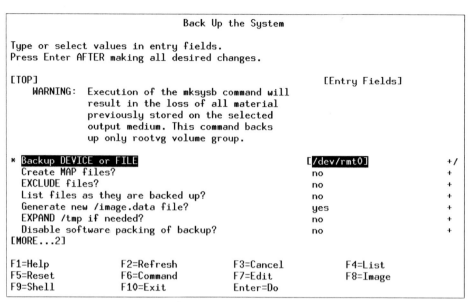

```
                              Back Up the System
   Type or select values in entry fields.
   Press Enter AFTER making all desired changes.

   [TOP]                                                    [Entry Fields]
        WARNING:   Execution of the mksysb command will
                   result in the loss of all material
                   previously stored on the selected
                   output medium. This command backs
                   up only rootvg volume group.

   * Backup DEVICE or FILE                                 [/dev/rmt0]            +/
     Create MAP files?                                      no                    +
     EXCLUDE files?                                         no                    +
     List files as they are backed up?                      no                    +
     Generate new /image.data file?                         yes                   +
     EXPAND /tmp if needed?                                 no                    +
     Disable software packing of backup?                    no                    +
   [MORE...2]

   F1=Help            F2=Refresh           F3=Cancel              F4=List
   F5=Reset           F6=Command           F7=Edit                F8=Image
   F9=Shell           F10=Exit             Enter=Do
```

Figure 8-5   Back Up the System menu

5. The COMMAND STATUS screen is now displayed. Figure 8-6 on page 223 is a screen of what information is being displayed during the backup process. In Figure 8-7 on page 223 is the display for the successful completion of the backup process.

6. The system has now created a bootable system backup.

```
                              COMMAND STATUS

Command: running        stdout: yes           stderr: no

Before command completion, additional instructions may appear below.


Creating information file (/image.data) for rootvg.......

Creating tape boot image....................█
```

Figure 8-6   COMMAND STATUS screen during operation

```
                              COMMAND STATUS

Command: OK             stdout: yes           stderr: no

Before command completion, additional instructions may appear below.

[TOP]
█
Creating information file (/image.data) for rootvg.......

Creating tape boot image....................

Creating list of files to back up...............................................
.....
Backing up 37601 files...............................
28 of 37601 files (0%)..............................
97 of 37601 files (0%)..............................
6267 of 37601 files (16%)..............................
15247 of 37601 files (40%)..........................
[MORE...6]

F1=Help              F2=Refresh          F3=Cancel          F6=Command
F8=Image             F9=Shell            F10=Exit           /=Find
n=Find Next
```

Figure 8-7   COMMAND STATUS screen after operation

8.1.4 Using mksysb to back up a user volume group

You can run **mksysb** on rootvg; You cannot run **mksysb** against a user volume group. If you want to back up a user volume group, you must use **savevg**, **tar**, **cpio**, or **backup**.

8.2 Backing up user information

To backup user information, you can use one of the following commands:

savevg   Finds and backs up all files belonging to a specified volume group.

tar   Manipulates archives by writing files to, or retrieving files from, an archive storage medium.

cpio   Copies files into and out of archive storage and directories.

backup   Creates copies of your files on a backup medium.

8.2.1 Backing up a single volume group

The **savevg** command finds and backs up all files belonging to a specified volume group. A volume group must be varied on, and the file systems must be mounted. The **savevg** command uses the data file created by the **mkvgdata** command.

To back up the uservg volume group and create a new uservg.data file, do the following:

1. Check which volume group you want to back up.

   ```
   # lsvg
   rootvg
   uservg
   ```

2. If you are satisfied that the volume group that must be backed up is uservg, proceed with the backup as follows:

   ```
   # savevg -if /dev/rmt0 uservg
   Creating list of files to back up....
   Backing up 9077 files.................................
   4904 of 9077 files (54%)...................................
   8798 of 9077 files (96%)...................................
   8846 of 9077 files (97%)...................................
   9029 of 9077 files (99%)...................................
   0512-038 savevg: Backup Completed Successfully.
   ```

8.2.2 How to backup the current directory

To back up your current directory to the tape device /dev/rmt0, use the following example. First, check that you are in the correct directory and then list the contents of the directory:

```
# cd /userdirectory
# pwd
/userdirectory
# ls -l
total 1808
-rw-r--r--    1 root      system         0 Oct 22 18:20 DKLoadLog
-rw-r--r--    1 root      system         0 Oct 22 18:20 adnan.gif
-rw-r--r--    1 root      system         0 Oct 22 18:20 aixhelp
-rw-r--r--    1 root      system     51200 Oct 22 18:20 backup1
-rw-r--r--    1 root      system         0 Oct 22 18:20 cde-help
-rw-r--r--    1 root      system         0 Oct 22 18:20 cde-main
-rw-r-----    1 root      system        25 Oct 22 18:20 cfgvg.out
-rw-r--r--    1 root      system         0 Oct 22 18:20 dtappint.log
-rw-r--r--    1 root      system         0 Oct 22 18:20 filelist
-rw-r--r--    1 root      system         0 Oct 22 18:20 httpd-pid
-rw-r--r--    1 root      system         0 Oct 22 18:20 mk_netboot
-rw-r--r--    1 root      system         0 Oct 22 18:20 nim1.gif
-rw-r--r--    1 root      system         0 Oct 22 18:20 nimM.gif
drwxr-xr-t    2 root      system      1024 Oct 22 18:20 tmp
-rw-r--r--    1 root      system         0 Oct 22 18:20 xlogfile
-rwxr-x--x    1 root      system    864256 Oct 22 18:20 xv
```

Now that you know what is in the directory, you can now back it up using the following command:

```
# tar -cvf /dev/fd0 *
a DKLoadLog 0 blocks.
a adnan.gif 0 blocks.
a aixhelp 0 blocks.
a backup1 100 blocks.
a cde-help 0 blocks.
a cde-main 0 blocks.
a cfgvg.out 1 blocks.
a dtappint.log 0 blocks.
a filelist 0 blocks.
a httpd-pid 0 blocks.
a mk_netboot 0 blocks.
a nim1.gif 0 blocks.
a nimM.gif 0 blocks.
a tmp
a tmp/.strload.mutex 0 blocks.
a tmp/.oslevel.mlinfo.cache 53 blocks.
a xlogfile 0 blocks.
a xv 1688 blocks.
```

The flags used are -c to create the archive, -v to list the archive contents, and -f to select the device. A more comprehensive list of flags can be found in Table 8-1 on page 214.

> **Note:** The `tar` command is one of very few commands that does not require a - (minus) sign before a flag.

There are two other commands that you can use to create backups. Using the scenario of backing up /userdirectory, you can either use `backup` or `cpio`.

► Using the `backup` command:

```
# cd /userdirectory
# find . -depth | backup -i -f /dev/rmt0
```

This will do a backup using relative path names, which means that when you restore the information using the `restore` command, you need to be in the /userdirectory directory, or else it will restore the information into your current directory.

> **Note:** The -print flag for the `find` command can be interchanged with the -depth flag equally for backup commands.

► Using the `cpio` command:

```
# cd /
# find /userdirectory -print | cpio -o -c -v -B > /dev/rmt0
```

This will back up the information using absolute path names. This information is restored using the `cpio` command with the -i flag. You can restore this from anywhere, and it will restore to the directory /userdirectory.

Relative or absolute path names can be used by either the `backup` command or the `cpio` command.

8.2.3 Incremental backups

The `backup` command can allow an administrator to make sets of incremental backups over periods of time. This is useful for storing data that changes often on the system. The syntax for the command is shown in the following example:

```
# backup -0 -uf /dev/rmt0 /home
```

When the -u flag is used with the **backup** command, the system will do an incremental backup of user data according to the *-level* number specified. A level 0 backup will back up all system data in the specified file systems. Each subsequent level will back up only the data that has changed since the previous level backup. For example, a level 5 backup will only back up the data that has changed after the level 4 backup was made. Levels can range from 0 to 9. By default, the **backup** command without any parameters will run a level 9 backup.

If you want to design a weekly backup schedule to back up data that has changed in the /data file system nightly, with a full backup done every Sunday, the **backup** command can easily do this task.

On Sunday, the system would run:

```
# backup -0 -uf /dev/rmt0 /data
```

On Monday, the system would run:

```
# backup -1 -uf /dev/rmt0 /data
```

On Saturday, the system would run:

```
# backup -6 -uf /dev/rmt0 /data
```

Information regarding the date, time, and level of each incremental backup is written to the /etc/dumpdates file. Data is stored in the following format:

```
/dev/lv01 0 Mon Jun 04 14:00:00 2001
/dev/lv01 1 Wed Dec 05 14:00:00 2001
```

8.3 Restoring information from backup media

When you restore information, you are taking information that you backed up in the previous section and using one of the restore methods discussed in the following sections.

8.3.1 The tctl command

The **tctl** command sends subcommands to a streaming tape device, like /dev/rmt0. This command can manipulate tapes easily for data restoration. The general syntax of the **tctl** command is as follows:

```
tctl [ -f Device ] [ eof | weof | fsf | bsf | fsr | bsr | rewind | offline |
rewoffl | erase | retension | reset | status ] [ Count ]
```

If you do not specify the *Device* variable with the -f flag, the TAPE environment variable is used. The most common subcommands are shown in Table 8-2 on page 228.

Table 8-2 Common tctl subcommands

Subcommand	Description
rewind	Rewinds the tape.
rewoffl or offline	Rewinds the tape and takes the tape drive offline. This will unload or eject the tape when appropriate. The tape must be reinserted, or another tape must be loaded before the device can be used again.
status	Displays status information about the specified tape device.
reset	Sends a bus device reset (BDR) to the tape device. The BDR will only be sent if the device cannot be opened and is not busy. Once complete, the system will return the cursor to a prompt without any notification.
fsf *Count*	Moves the tape forward by the number of file marks specified by the *Count* parameter, and positions it on the end-of-tape (EOT) side of the file mark.
bsf *Count*	Moves the tape backward by the number of file marks specified by the *Count* parameter, and positions it on the beginning-of-tape (BOT) side of the file mark. If the bsf subcommand attempts to move the tape past the beginning, the tape will rewind and the tctl command returns EIO.

8.3.2 How to restore a file

For this example, you will restore the file /etc/hosts from a tape device /dev/rmt0.

You can use one of the following commands, depending on what command was used to do the backup:

▶ `mksysb`

There are three images (the BOS boot image, mkinsttape image, and dummy TOC) that precede the **backup** files in a `mksysb`. You can move past them using **mt** or **tctl** and the no-rewind option on the tape, or you can use the -s4 flag in the restore command.

Rewind the tape to the beginning by using the following:

```
tctl -f /dev/rmt0 rewind
```

List the information on the backup media by using the following:

```
# restore -T -d -v -q -s4 -f /dev/rmt0.1
New volume on /dev/rmt0.1:
Cluster size is 51200 bytes (100 blocks).
The volume number is 1.
The backup date is: Tue Oct 27 10:15:25 CST 1998
Files are backed up by name.
The user is root.
.......... (Lines Removed)
       528 ./tmp/vgdata/rootvg/hd1.map
       972 ./tmp/vgdata/rootvg/hd2.map
        48 ./tmp/vgdata/rootvg/hd3.map
        36 ./tmp/vgdata/rootvg/hd4.map
   588 ./tmp/vgdata/rootvg/hd9var.map
   0 ./etc
   901 ./etc/hosts
   0 ./home
         0 ./home/lost+found
         0 ./home/guest
         0 ./home/ftp
       254 ./home/ftp/.profile
         0 ./home/ftp/bin
     18774 ./home/ftp/bin/ls
         0 ./home/ftp/etc
         0 ./home/ftp/pub
    150841 ./home/ftp/pub/aix-1-let.ps
.......... (Lines Removed)
The total size is 509575953 bytes.
The number of archived files is 37773.
```

This screen scrolls down showing you all the files on the backup medium. If you want to show only the header information, you can leave out the -T and -v flags.

Change to the /etc/ directory and list all files with the word hosts in them. Notice that the hosts file is missing.

```
# cd /etc
# ls -l hosts*
-rw-r--r--   1 root      system       2060 Aug 25 09:41 hosts.equiv
-rw-rw-r--   1 root      system       1906 Aug 25 09:41 hosts.lpd
```

Change to the root directory and check your current directory as in the following:

```
# cd /
# pwd
/
```

Rewind the tape device using the following command:

```
tctl -f /dev/rmt0 rewind
```

Restore the file that you want. Notice the . (point) before /etc/hosts; this needs to be part of the **restore** command.

```
# restore -x -d -v -q -s4 -f /dev/rmt0.1 ./etc/hosts
New volume on /dev/rmt0.1:
Cluster size is 51200 bytes (100 blocks).
The volume number is 1.
The backup date is: Tue Oct 27 10:15:25 CST 1998
Files are backed up by name.
The user is root.
x          1848 ./etc/hosts
The total size is 1848 bytes.
The number of restored files is 1.
```

The information from the tape device during the restore operation is displayed.

Change your directory to /etc and list the files beginning with hosts.

```
# cd /etc
# ls -l hosts*
-rw-rw-r--  1 root     system    1848 Sep 10 13:44 hosts
-rw-r--r--  1 root     system    2060 Aug 25 09:41 hosts.equiv
-rw-rw-r--  1 root     system    1906 Aug 25 09:41 hosts.lpd
```

Check if the file has been restored.

► **tar**

The following example shows the command syntax you would use to restore the file /etc/hosts using the **tar** command.

```
tar -x -v -f /dev/rmt0 /etc/hosts
```

► **cpio**

The following shows the command syntax you would use to restore the file /etc/hosts using the **cpio** command. Notice that " (quotes) are used in your file selection.

```
cpio -i -c -v -d -u -m -B < /dev/rmt0 "/etc/hosts"
```

► **restore**

The next two examples show the command syntax you would use to restore the file /etc/hosts using the **restore** command.

The following shows how to restore the file /etc/hosts from a backup that was made using the -i flag option during a backup by file name. Notice the -d flag is used to restore the file:

```
restore -x -d -v -q -f /dev/rmt0 /etc/hosts
```

The following shows how to restore the file /etc/hosts when a file system backup was used to make the backup:

```
restore -x -v -q -f /dev/rmt0 /etc/hosts
```

8.3.3 How to restore a directory

For this example, you will restore the directory /var and its contents from a tape device /dev/rmt0.

You can use one of the following commands, depending on what command was used to do the backup.

▶ **mksysb**

There are three images (the BOS boot image, mkinsttape image, and dummy TOC) that precede the **backup** files in a **mksysb**. Move past them using either the **mt** or **tctl** commands with the norewind option on the tape or use the -s4 flag in the **restore** command.

Rewind the tape to the beginning by using the **tctl** command:

```
tctl -f /dev/rmt0 rewind
```

List the files on the backup media by using the **restore** command:

```
# restore -T -d -v -q -s4 -f /dev/rmt0.1
New volume on /dev/rmt0.1:
Cluster size is 51200 bytes (100 blocks).
The volume number is 1.
The backup date is: Tue Oct 27 10:15:25 CST 1998
Files are backed up by name.
The user is root.
.......... (Lines Removed)
       528 ./tmp/vgdata/rootvg/hd1.map
       972 ./tmp/vgdata/rootvg/hd2.map
        48 ./tmp/vgdata/rootvg/hd3.map
        36 ./tmp/vgdata/rootvg/hd4.map
        24 ./tmp/vgdata/rootvg/hd5.map
       768 ./tmp/vgdata/rootvg/hd6.map
        12 ./tmp/vgdata/rootvg/hd8.map
       588 ./tmp/vgdata/rootvg/hd9var.map
         0 ./home
         0 ./home/lost+found
         0 ./home/guest
         0 ./home/ftp
       254 ./home/ftp/.profile
         0 ./home/ftp/bin
     18774 ./home/ftp/bin/ls
         0 ./home/ftp/etc
         0 ./home/ftp/pub
```

```
 150841 ./home/ftp/pub/aix-1-let.ps
3404039 ./home/ftp/pub/aix-2-let.ps
9210123 ./home/ftp/pub/aix-3-let.ps
4690937 ./home/ftp/pub/aix-6-let.ps
6512370 ./home/ftp/pub/aix-7-let.ps
......... (Lines Removed)
The total size is 509575953 bytes.
The number of archived files is 37773.
```

This scrolls down the screen showing all of the files on the backup medium. If you want to show only the header information you can leave out the -T and -v flags.

Change to the /var directory and check the present working directory as in the following:

```
# cd /var
# pwd
/var
```

List the contents of the current directory using the following command:

```
# ls -l
total 13
drwxrwxr-x   8 root    adm        512 Oct 22 09:14 adm
drwxr-xr-x   2 bin     bin        512 Aug 25 16:47 cifs
dr-xr-xr-x   3 bin     bin       1024 Aug 26 13:37 ifor
drwxrwxrwx   2 root    system     512 Oct 22 09:15 locks
drwx------   2 root    system     512 Aug 25 09:21 lost+found
drwxrwxrwx   2 bin     bin        512 Aug 25 09:23 msgs
drwxrwxrwx   2 bin     bin        512 Aug 25 09:23 news
drwxrwxrwx   2 bin     bin        512 Sep 21 16:40 preserve
dr-xr-x---   2 root    system     512 Aug 25 09:39 security
drwxrwxr-x  12 bin     bin        512 Sep 23 09:09 spool
drwxrwxrwt   2 bin     bin        512 Oct 27 14:28 tmp
```

Change directory to the root directory and check the present working directory:

```
# cd /
# pwd
/
```

Rewind the tape and start the restore of directory /var/dt. Notice the . (point) before the directory name; this is always needed when restoring from a **mksysb** backup:

```
# tctl -f /dev/rmt0 rewind
# restore -x -d -v -s4 -f/dev/rmt0.1 ./var/dt
New volume on /dev/rmt0.1:
Cluster size is 51200 bytes (100 blocks).
The volume number is 1.
The backup date is: Tue Oct 27 10:15:25 CST 1998
```

```
Files are backed up by name.
The user is root.
.......... (Lines Removed)
x          117 ./var/dt/Xerrors
x            5 ./var/dt/Xpid
x           44 ./var/dt/A:0-oActaa
x           44 ./var/dt/A:0-IdcsMa
x           44 ./var/dt/A:0-WqcsMa
x           44 ./var/dt/A:0-UzcsUa
x           44 ./var/dt/A:0-V7csUa
x           44 ./var/dt/A:0-kAcsUa
x           44 ./var/dt/A:0-YYcsUa
x           44 ./var/dt/A:0-Xoctia
.......... (Lines Removed)
The total size is 1065 bytes.
The number of restored files is 32.
```

The preceding is the information from the tape device during the restore operation listing all the files restored.

Change your directory to /var and list the contents of the /var directory.

```
# cd /var
# ls -l
total 14
drwxrwxr-x   8 root    adm       512 Oct 22 09:14 adm
drwxr-xr-x   2 bin     bin       512 Aug 25 16:47 cifs
drwxr-xr-x   4 bin     bin       512 Oct 29 10:26 dt
dr-xr-xr-x   3 bin     bin      1024 Aug 26 13:37 ifor
drwxrwxrwx   2 root    system    512 Oct 22 09:15 locks
drwx------   2 root    system    512 Aug 25 09:21 lost+found
drwxrwxrwx   2 bin     bin       512 Aug 25 09:23 msgs
drwxrwxrwx   2 bin     bin       512 Aug 25 09:23 news
drwxrwxrwx   2 bin     bin       512 Sep 21 16:40 preserve
dr-xr-x---   2 root    system    512 Aug 25 09:39 security
drwxrwxr-x  12 bin     bin       512 Sep 23 09:09 spool
drwxrwxrwt   2 bin     bin       512 Oct 27 14:28 tmp
```

Verify that the directory /var/dt has been restored.

► **tar**

The following command restores the directory and the directory contents using the **tar** command:

```
tar -x -v -f /dev/rmt0 /var/dt
```

► **cpio**

The following command restores the directory and the directory contents using the **cpio** command:

```
cpio -i -c -v -d -u -m -B < /dev/rmt0 "/var/dt/*"
```

▶ **restore**

The next two commands show additional ways to restore a directory and its contents using the **restore** command.

The following shows how to restore the directory from a filename backup:

```
restore -x -d -v -q -f /dev/rmt0 /var/dt
```

The following shows how to restore the directory where a file system backup was done:

```
restore -x -v -q -f /dev/rmt0 /var/dt
```

8.3.4 Errors on restore, incorrect block size

A typical problem with moving tapes between systems is an incorrect block size. Incorrect block sizes can cause the tape to be temporarily unreadable. For example, a tar backup is placed on a tape with a 512 byte block size. When the tape is placed into a system with a 2048 byte block size, and a restore is attempted, the system displays:

```
# tar -tvf /dev/rmt0
tar: 0511-193 An error occurred while reading from the media.
There is an input or output error.
```

There are two methods to determine tape block size:

▶ Method 1

Use the **tcopy** command as follows:

```
# tcopy /dev/rmt0
tcopy : Tape File: 1; Records: 1 to 7179 ; size:512
tcopy : Tape File: 1; End of file after :7179 records; 3675648 bytes
tcopy : Tape File: 2; Records: 1 to 2900 ; size:512
tcopy : Tape File: 2; End of file after 2900 records, 76890 bytes
...
```

This will give you a list of all the files found on the media with their byte count and the block size (shown in bold) used.

▶ Method 2

Use the **dd** command to read a single block from the device and find out what block size is used for the archive:

```
dd if=/dev/rmt0 bs=128k count=1 | wc -c
```

This will return the size in bytes of the block being read.

To change the block size, use the **chdev** command, as follows:

```
# chdev -l rmt0 -a block_size=512
rmt0 changed
```

```
# tar tvf /dev/rmt0
-rw-rw-r--   0 0     1817 Jun 09 16:24:17 2000 /etc/hosts
```

8.3.5 Using the rmfs command

The rmfs command removes a file system. Though it is not a normal command to be included in a backup chapter, you can use this command once you have restored a backup to clean up file systems that are no longer required, or unintentionally mounted during backup time. To run the command, enter:

```
rmfs userfs
```

8.4 Cloning your system

A mksysb image enables you to clone one system image onto multiple target systems. The target systems might not contain the same hardware devices or adapters, require the same kernel (uniprocessor or microprocessor), or be the same hardware platform (rs6k, rspc, or chrp) as the source system.

Use this procedure to install a mksysb backup on a target system it was not created on. Be sure to boot from the product media appropriate for your system and at the same maintenance level of BOS as the installed source system that the mksysb backup was made on. For example, you can use BOS Version 4.2.1 product media with a mksysb backup from a BOS Version 4.2.1 system. This procedure is to be used when installing a backup tape to a different system.

After booting from product media, complete the following steps when the Welcome to the Base Operating System Installation and Maintenance screen is displayed.

1. Select the Start Maintenance Mode for System Recovery option.

2. Select the Install from a System Backup option.

3. Select the drive containing the backup tape and insert the media for that device. The system reads the media and begins the installation.

4. You will be prompted again for the BOS install language, and the Welcome screen is displayed. Continue with the Prompted Installation process, as cloning is not supported for Nonprompted Installations.

Note:

► Booting from tape product media is not supported on some rspc platform systems. When a backup tape is created on one of these systems, the **mksysb** command will display a message indicating that the system does not support tape boot. To determine what your platform system is, enter the following command:

```
bootinfo -p
```

or

```
lscfg -vp | grep Arch
```

► If you are cloning from the product tape to restore a backup tape, create a diskette that contains a ./bosinst.data file with SWITCH_TO_PRODUCT_TAPE=yes in the control_flow stanza if this was not set prior to making the mksysb.

► If SWITCH_TO_PRODUCT_TAPE is set to yes, the system will prompt you to remove the **mksysb** media and insert the product media after the **mksysb** backup has been restored.

After the **mksysb** backup installation completes, the installation program automatically installs additional devices and the kernel (uniprocessor or microprocessor) on your system using the original product media you booted from. Information is saved in BOS installation log files. To view BOS installation log files, enter **cd /var/adm/ras** and view the devinst.log file in this directory.

If the source system does not have the correct passwords and network information, you may make modifications on the target system now. Also, some products ship device-specific files such as graPHIGS. If your graphics adapter is different on the target system, verify that the device-specific filesets for graphics-related LPPs are installed.

If the system you have cloned is using OpenGL or graPHIGS, there may be some device filesets from these LPPs that must be installed after a clone.

8.5 Creating a duplicate copy of a diskette

The **dd** command reads the *InFile* parameter or standard input, performs any specified conversions, then copies the converted data to the *OutFile* parameter or standard output.

To make a duplicate copy of a diskette, you first use the **dd** command to copy the contents of the diskette into a temporary file. Once the temporary file has been created, use the **dd** command to copy the temporary file onto the /dev/fd0 device, thus, creating a duplicate of your diskette. The following commands demonstrate this:

```
# dd if=/dev/fd0 of=/tmp/ddcopy
2880+0 records in.
2880+0 records out.
# dd if=/tmp/ddcopy of=/dev/fd0
2880+0 records in.
2880+0 records out.
```

8.6 Duplicating a magnetic tape

The **tcopy** command also copies magnetic tapes. Source and target file names are specified by the Source and Destination parameters. The **tcopy** command assumes that there are two tape marks at the end of the tape, and it ends when it finds the double file marks.

To copy from one tape device to another, enter:

```
# tcopy /dev/rmt0 /dev/rmt1
tcopy: Tape File: 1; Records: 1 to 74; Size: 2097152.
tcopy: Tape File: 1; Record: 75; Size 1574912.
tcopy: File: 1; End of File after: 75 Records, 156764160 Bytes.
tcopy: The end of the tape is reached.
tcopy: The total tape length is 156764160 bytes.
```

The duplication of the tape cartridge is now complete.

8.7 Special file notes for rmt

The purpose of the device rmt is to provide access to the sequential-access bulk storage medium device driver.

Magnetic tapes are used primarily for backup, file archives, and other off-line storage. Tapes are accessed through the /dev/rmt0, ..., /dev/rmt255 special files. The r in the special file name indicates raw access through the character special file interface. A tape device does not lend itself well to the category of a block device. Only character interface special files are therefore provided.

Table 8-3 is a list of the tape device special file characteristics; /dev/rmt* can be from /dev/rmt0 to /dev/rmt255.

Table 8-3   Tape device special file characteristics

Special file name	Rewind-on-close	Retension-on-open	Bytes per inch
/dev/rmt*	Yes	No	Density setting #1
/dev/rmt*.1	No	No	Density setting #1
/dev/rmt*.2	Yes	Yes	Density setting #1
/dev/rmt*.3	No	Yes	Density setting #1
/dev/rmt*.4	Yes	No	Density setting #2
/dev/rmt*.5	No	No	Density setting #2
/dev/rmt*.6	Yes	Yes	Density setting #2
/dev/rmt*.7	No	Yes	Density setting #2

The following can be said about the characteristics shown:

► The values of density setting #1 and density setting #2 come from tape drive attributes that can be set using SMIT. Typically, density setting #1 is set to the highest possible density for the tape drive, while density setting #2 is set to a lower density. However, density settings are not required to follow this pattern.

► The density value (bytes per inch) is ignored when using a magnetic tape device that does not support multiple densities. For tape drives that do support multiple densities, the density value only applies when writing to the tape. When reading, the drive defaults to the density at which the tape is written.

► Older tape drives use a 512-byte block size. The 8 mm tape drive uses a minimum block size of 1024 bytes. Using SMIT to lower the block size may waste space.

8.8 High Availability Cluster Multi-Processing (HACMP)

HACMP for AIX is an application solution that can link up to eight RS/6000 servers or SP nodes into highly available clusters. With the enhanced scalability feature, up to 16 SP nodes can be linked. Clustering servers or nodes enables parallel access to their data, which can help provide the redundancy and fault resilience required for business critical applications. HACMP includes graphical user interface-based tools to help install, configure, and manage your clusters in a highly productive manner.

HACMP is flexible in configuration and use. Uniprocessors, symmetric multiprocessors (SMPs) and SP nodes can all participate in highly available clusters. Micro Channel and PCI-based systems are supported under AIX. You can mix and match system sizes and performance levels as well as network adapters and disk subsystems to satisfy your application, network, and disk performance needs.

HACMP clusters can be configured in several modes for different types of processing requirements. Concurrent access mode suits environments where all of the processors must work on the same workload and share the same data at the same time. In a mutual takeover mode, the processors share the workload and back each other up. Idle standby allows one node to back up any of the other nodes in the cluster.

Whichever mode you choose, HACMP provides data access and backup plans to help optimize application execution and scalability while helping to guard against costly unplanned outages and down time. HACMP also enables server clusters to be configured for application recovery/restart to provide a measure of fault resilience for your business critical applications through redundancy.

Understanding HACMP is a lesson in fault tolerant systems. If you do not want to commit all the resources required for an HACMP installation, you can still eliminate many of the potential exposures for system downtime by adding redundancy to disk drives, adapter cards, network connections, and by implementing software RAS features, such as disk mirroring and system monitoring as described in an HACMP installation.

8.9 Quiz

The following certification assessment questions help verify your understanding of the topics discussed in this chapter.

1. What is the purpose of the -i flag with the `mksysb` command?

   A. It creates/updates the /.fsdata.

   B. It reports the size of a file in bytes.

   C. It creates a bootable system backup.

   D. It creates or updates the /image.data file.

2. The administrator of the Widget company has decided that doing full backups of the /apps directory each night is taking much more time than originally assumed and that incrementals should be done during the week with one Full backup each Saturday night. Which file *if present* can be used to manage this during the week?

   A. /last_full_backup

   B. /etc/last_full_backup

   C. /etc/incremental_dump_dates

   D. /etc/incremental_file_backup

The following are additional questions created by the authors to further test your understanding of the topics.

1. What is the purpose of the `mkszfile` command?

   A. It creates or updates the /image.data file.

   B. It reports the size of a file in bytes.

   C. It creates a bootable system backup.

   D. It creates/updates the /.fsdata.

2. After creating a `tar` archive on a tape and verifying that the backup was successful, a system administrator then inserts the tape into another machine to access the data and receives the following error:

   `"Media Read Error - I/O Error"`

   Which of the following is the most likely cause of the error?

   A. The blocksize or density setting is incorrect.

   B. There is a lack of disk space in the root file system.

   C. The tape is not read/writable.

   D. There is a bad cable on the tape drive.

3. A system administrator would like to restore the third image from a `mksysb` tape. To position the tape to the correct image, which of the following commands should be run?

   A. `lsattr`

   B. `tctl`

   C. `ffwd`

   D. `chdev`

4. The finance group at the Widget Company has just approved a new financial package that runs on an RS/6000. They will be converting their old data to the new system. Currently, they have 10 GB of data but will be growing to 18 GB with the new system because they want to maintain one year of history online. The new system they have ordered is an F50 with 128 MB of RAM, an SSA card, two 9.1 GB SSA drives, and a single FDDI card.

   What would be the best addition to this system for redundancy?

   1. One SSA card

   2. Two 9.1 GB SSA disks

   3. Error correcting RAM

   4. Two additional processors

   A. 3 and 1

   B. 4 and 1

   C. 4 and 2

   D. 1 and 2

8.9.1 Answers

The following answers are for the assessment quiz questions.

1. D

2. B

The following answers are for the additional quiz questions.

1. A

2. A

3. B

4. D

8.10 Exercises

The following exercises provide sample topics for self study. They will help ensure comprehension of this chapter.

1. Use **mksysb** to back up the volume group uservg.

2. Exclude file systems from a **mksysb** backup.

3. Design a sound backup schedule and strategy for your system.

4. Create a bootable system backup.

5. Retrieve a file from a **mksysb**, a **tar** backup, and a **cpio** backup.

6. Retrieve a directory from a **mksysb**, a **tar** backup, and a **cpio** backup.

7. Back up a current directory using **tar**.

8. What makes the **mkszfile** command so important?

9. Back up a single volume group.

10. Clone a system. Why use the **rmfs** command?

11. Make a copy of a diskette and then make a copy of a tape.

12. Position a **mksysb** backup at a the end of the third image.

System Resource Controller administration

The System Resource Controller (SRC) provides a set of commands and subroutines to make it easier for the system manager and programmer to create and control subsystems. A subsystem is any program or process or set of programs or processes that is capable of operating independently or with a controlling system. A subsystem is designed as a unit to provide a designated function. A subserver is a program or process that belongs to a subsystem.

The SRC is designed to minimize the need for operator intervention. It provides a mechanism to control subsystem processes using a common command line and the C interface. This mechanism includes the following:

▶ Consistent user interface for start, stop, and status inquiries.

▶ Logging of the abnormal termination of subsystems.

▶ A notification program called at the abnormal system termination of related processes.

▶ Tracing of a subsystem, a group of subsystems, or a subserver.

▶ Support for control of operations on a remote system.

▶ Refreshing of a subsystem (such as after a configuration data change).

The SRC is useful if you want a common way to start, stop, and collect status information on processes.

9.1 Starting the SRC

The System Resource Controller (SRC) is started during system initialization with a record for the /usr/sbin/srcmstr daemon in the /etc/inittab file. The default /etc/inittab file already contains such a record, so starting the SRC may be unnecessary. You can, if needed, start the SRC from the command line, a profile, or a shell script, but there are several reasons for starting it during initialization:

▶ Starting the SRC from the /etc/inittab file allows the **init** command to restart the SRC should it stop for any reason.

▶ The SRC is designed to simplify and reduce the amount of operator intervention required to control subsystems. Starting the SRC from any source other than the /etc/inittab file would be counter-productive to that goal.

▶ The default /etc/inittab file contains a record for starting the print scheduling subsystem (qdaemon) with the **startsrc** command. Typical installations have other subsystems started with **startsrc** commands in the /etc/inittab file as well. Since the **startsrc** command requires the SRC to be running, removing the srcmstr daemon from the /etc/inittab file would cause these **startsrc** commands to fail.

Refer to the manual page using the command **man srcmstr** for the configuration requirements to support remote SRC requests.

If the /etc/inittab file does not already contain a record for the srcmstr daemon, you can add one using the following procedure:

1. Make a record for the srcmstr daemon in the /etc/inittab file using the **mkitab** command. For example, to make a record identical to the one that appears in the default /etc/inittab file, enter:

```
mkitab -i fbcheck srcmstr:2:respawn:/usr/sbin/srcmstr
```

The -i fbcheck flag ensures that the record is inserted before all subsystems records.

2. Tell the **init** command to reprocess the /etc/inittab file by entering:

```
telinit q
```

When **init** revisits the /etc/inittab file, it processes the newly entered record for the srcmstr daemon and starts the SRC.

9.1.1 The telinit command

The `telinit` command directs the actions of the init process (process ID 1) by taking a one-character argument and signaling the init process to perform the appropriate action. In general, the `telinit` command sets the system at a specific run level. A run level is a software configuration that allows only a selected group of processes to exist. The following arguments serve as directives that the `telinit` command passes to the init process:

0-9   Tells the init process to put the system in one of the run levels 0-9.

S,s,M,m   Tells the init process to enter the maintenance mode.

a,b,c   Tells the init process to examine only those records in the /etc/inittab file with a, b, or c in the run level field.

Q,q   Tells the init process to re-examine the entire /etc/inittab file.

N   Sends a signal that stops processes from being respawned.

9.2 Restarting the SRC

Normally, you do not need to restart srcmstr. The default record in /etc/inittab for AIX 5L Version 5.1 is shown in Table 9-1.

Table 9-1   Default srcmstr record in the /etc/inittab file

Field	Value
Identifier	srcmstr
RunLevel	23456789
Action	respawn
Command	/usr/sbin/srcmstr

In previous versions of AIX, srcmstr had a RunLevel value of 2.

If the srcmstr daemon terminates abnormally, the respawn action specified in the /etc/inittab restarts the srcmstr daemon. The srcmstr daemon then determines which SRC subsystems were active during the previous invocation. The daemon reestablishes communication with these subsystems (if it existed previously) and initializes a private kernel extension and the srcd daemon to monitor the subsystem processes. Note that the process ID is changed after srcmstr is terminated and restarted automatically as shown in Figure 9-1 on page 246.

```
# ps -ef |grep srcmstr
    root   2650     1    0 09:59:48      -   0:00 /usr/sbin/srcmstr
    root 13922 11870    2 10:33:04   pts/2  0:00 grep srcmstr
# kill -9 2650
# ps -ef |grep srcmstr
    root   6246     1    0 10:33:09      -   0:00 /usr/sbin/srcmstr
    root 13700 11870    0 10:33:13   pts/2  0:00 grep srcmstr
# ▮
```

Figure 9-1   Restart of the srcmstr daemon

However, if you have edited the /etc/inittab file adding the -r or -B flag to
/usr/sbin/srcmstr, you must use the command `init -q` to reexamine /etc/inittab
or reboot to make the new flags effective. The -r flag prevents srcmstr from
responding to remote requests, and -B runs srcmstr in a pre-AIX Version 4.3.1
mode.

9.3 The startsrc command

The `startsrc` command sends the System Resource Controller (SRC) a request
to start a subsystem or a group of subsystems or to pass on a packet to the
subsystem that starts a subserver.

If a start subserver request is passed to the SRC, and the subsystem to which
the subserver belongs is not currently active, the SRC starts the subsystem and
transmits the start subserver request to the subsystem.

The flags for the `startsrc` command are shown in Table 9-2.

Table 9-2   Flags for the startsrc command

Flag	Description	Example
To start a subsystem		
-a *argument*	Specifies an argument string that is passed to the subsystem when the subsystem is executed.	`startsrc -s srctest -a "-D DEBUG"` This starts the srctest subsystem with "-D DEBUG" as two arguments to the subsystem.

Flag	Description	Example

-e *Environment*	Specifies an environment string that is placed in the subsystem environment when the subsystem is executed.	`startsrc -s srctest -e`
		`"TERM=dumb HOME=/tmp"`
		This starts the srctest subsystem with "TERM=dumb", "HOME=/tmp" in its environment to the subsystem.

-g *Group*	Specifies a group of subsystems to be started.	`startsrc -g nfs` This starts all the subsystems in the subsystem nfs group
-s *Subsystem*	Specifies a subsystem to be started.	`startsrc -s srctest`
To start either a subsystem or a subserver		
-h *Host*	Specifies the foreign host on which this start action is requested. The local user must be running as root. The remote system must be configured to accept remote System Resource Controller requests.	`startsrc -g nfs -h itsosmp` This starts all the subsystems in the nfs group on the itsosmp machine.
To start a subserver		
-t *Type*	Specifies that a subserver is to be started.	`startsrc -t tester` This sends a start subserver request to the subsystem that owns the tester subsystem.
-o *Object*	Specifies that a subserver object is to be passed to the subsystem as a character string. It is the subsystem's responsibility to determine the validity of the Object string.	`startsrc -o tester -p 1234` The subserver tester is passed as a character string to the subsystem with a PID of 1234.
-p *SubsystemPID*	Specifies a particular instance of the subsystem to which the start subserver request is to be passed.	`startsrc -t tester -p 1234` This starts the tester subserver that belongs to the srctest subsystem with a subsystem PID of 1234.

9.4 The syslogd daemon

The syslog function on AIX is provided by the syslogd daemon. The syslogd daemon reads a datagram socket and sends each message line to a destination described by the /etc/syslog.conf configuration file. The syslogd daemon reads the configuration file when it is activated or when it receives a hangup signal.

9.4.1 Starting the syslogd daemon

The syslogd daemon is started during system IPL by srcmstr. The stanza in ODM is shown in Figure 9-2.

```
#odmget -q subsysname=syslogd SRCsubsys

SRCsubsys:
        subsysname = "syslogd"
        synonym = ""
        cmdargs = ""
        path = "/usr/sbin/syslogd"
        uid = 0
        auditid = 0
        standin = "/dev/console"
        standout = "/dev/console"
        standerr = "/dev/console"
        action = 2
        multi = 0
        contact = 3
        svrkey = 0
        svrmtype = 0
        priority = 20
        signorm = 0
        sigforce = 0
        display = 1
        waittime = 20
        grpname = "ras"
#
```

Figure 9-2   Syslogd stanza in ODM

9.4.2 syslog configuration file

The configuration file informs the syslogd daemon where to send a system message depending on the message's priority level and the facility that generated it.

If you do not use the -f flag to specify an alternate configuration file, the default configuration file /etc/syslog.conf file is used.

The syslogd daemon ignores blank lines and lines beginning with a # (pound sign).

Lines in the configuration file for the syslogd daemon contain a selector field and an action field separated by one or more tabs.

The selector field names a facility and a priority level. Separate facility names with a , (comma). Separate the facility and priority-level portions of the selector field with a . (period). Separate multiple entries in the same selector field with a ; (semicolon). To select all facilities, use an * (asterisk).

The action field identifies a destination (file, host, or user) to receive the messages. If routed to a remote host, the remote system will handle the message as indicated in its own configuration file. To display messages on a user's terminal, the destination field must contain the name of a valid, logged-in system user.

The last part of the default /etc/syslog.conf is shown in Figure 9-3.

```
# /etc/syslog.conf - control output of syslogd
#
#
# Each line must consist of two parts:-
#
# 1) A selector to determine the message priorities to which the
#    line applies
# 2) An action.
#
# The two fields must be separated by one or more tabs or spaces.
#
# format:
#
# <msg_src_list>                  <destination>
#
# where <msg_src_list> is a semicolon separated list of <facility>.<priority>
# where:
#
# <facility> is:
#        * - all (except mark)
#        mark - time marks
#        kern,user,mail,daemon, auth,... (see syslogd(AIX Commands Reference))
#
# <priority> is one of (from high to low):
#        emerg/panic,alert,crit,err(or),warn(ing),notice,info,debug
#        (meaning all messages of this priority or higher)
#
# <destination> is:
#        /filename - log to this file
#        username[,username2...] - write to user(s)
#        @hostname - send to syslogd on this machine
#        * - send to all logged in users
#
# example:
# "mail messages, at debug or higher, go to Log file. File must exist."
# "all facilities, at debug and higher, go to console"
# "all facilities, at crit or higher, go to all users"
#    mail.debug            /usr/spool/mqueue/syslog
#    *.debug               /dev/console
#    *.crit                        *
#
```

Figure 9-3 Sample syslog configuration file

If you decide to capture the warning messages from all users in the /var/spool/syslog file, you should do the following:

1. Add the following line to the /etc/syslog.conf file as the last line of the file.

   ```
   *.warning                /var/spool/syslog
   ```

2. Create the /var/spool/syslog file.

   ```
   touch /var/spool/syslog
   ```

3. Change the permission bits of /var/spool/syslog so that all users are allowed to write warning messages to this file.

   ```
   chmod 666 /var/spool/syslog
   ```

4. Refresh the syslogd daemon to make the update to the syslog configuration file effective.

   ```
   refresh -s syslogd
   ```

9.4.3 Recycling and refreshing the syslogd daemon

The syslogd daemon reads the configuration file when it is activated or when it receives a hangup signal. A refresh keeps the current process ID and is a less intrusive method of reading the configuration file. A recycle is useful when you feel there is a problem with the service and a complete restart is required. You can recycle the syslogd daemon by stopping and then starting it.

```
# stopsrc -s syslogd
# startsrc -s syslogd
```

Alternatively, you can refresh the syslogd daemon by sending a HUP signal.

```
ps -ef |grep syslogd
```

Note the PID of the syslogd process, in this example is 5682.

```
kill -1 5682
```

9.4.4 Collecting syslog data from multiple systems

The syslogd daemon logs messages received from remote hosts unless you use the -r flag to suppress it.

In the /etc/syslog.conf of the remote hosts, instead of specifying the full path name of a file in the destination part, put in @Host where Host is the host name of the remote system.

9.5 Refreshing a daemon

Use the **refresh** command to tell a System Resource Controller (SRC) resource, such as a subsystem or a group of subsystems, to refresh itself.

The prerequisites for using the **refresh** command are:

- ► The SRC must be running.
- ► The resource you want to refresh must not use the signals communications method.
- ► The resource you want to refresh must be programmed to respond to the refresh request.

The **refresh** command sends the System Resource Controller a subsystem refresh request that is forwarded to the subsystem. The refresh action is subsystem-dependent.

To start the Lotus Domino Go Webserver, use the following command:

```
startsrc -s httpd
```

To allow users to open a homepage, index.html, in a new directory, /newdir, you have added a directory mapping in the /etc/httpd.conf file:

```
pass          /*          /newdir/*
```

To refresh the Web server, enter:

```
refresh -s httpd
```

After this, the users will be able to access the new homepage by entering the following URL in their Web browser:

```
http://server_name[:port_number]/newdir/index.html
```

9.6 The cron daemon

The cron daemon runs shell commands at specified dates and times. The following event types are scheduled by the cron daemon:

- ► **crontab** command events
- ► **at** command events
- ► **batch** command events
- ► sync subroutine events
- ► **ksh** command events

► **csh** command events

The way these events are handled is specified in the /var/adm/cron/queuedefs file.

Regularly scheduled commands can be specified according to the instructions contained in the crontab files. You can submit your crontab file with the `crontab` command. Use the `at` command to submit commands that are to be run only once. Because the cron daemon never exits, it should be run only once.

The cron daemon examines crontab files and `at` command files only when the cron daemon is initialized. When you make changes to the crontab files using the `crontab` command, a message indicating the change is sent to the cron daemon. This eliminates the overhead of checking for new or changed files at regularly scheduled intervals.

When the TZ environment variable is changed, either with the `chtz` command, a Web-based System Management application, or through SMIT, the cron daemon must be restarted. This enables the cron daemon to use the correct timezone and summer time change information for the new TZ environment variable.

The cron daemon creates a log of its activities in the /var/adm/cron/log file.

9.6.1 Crontab file record format

A crontab file contains entries for each cron job. Entries are separated by newline characters. Each crontab file entry contains six fields separated by spaces or tabs in the following form:

```
minute  hour  day_of_month  month  weekday  command
```

These fields accept the following values:

minute	0 through 59
hour	0 through 23
day_of_month	1 through 31
month	1 through 12
weekday	0 through 6 for Sunday through Saturday
command	a shell command

You must specify a value for each field. Except for the command field, these fields can contain the following:

► A number in the specified range. To run a command in May, specify 5 in the month field.

- Two numbers separated by a dash to indicate an inclusive range. To run a cron job on Tuesday through Friday, place 2-5 in the weekday field.

- A list of numbers separated by commas. To run a command on the first and last day of a month, you would specify 1,31 in the day_of_month field.

- An * (asterisk), meaning all allowed values. To run a job every hour, specify an asterisk in the hour field.

Blank lines and lines whose first non-blank character is # (number sign) are ignored.

> **Note:** Any character preceded by a backslash (including the %) causes that character to be treated literally.

For example, if you have written a script fullbackup stored in the /root directory, and you want to schedule it to run at 1 am on the 15th of every month, use the **crontab -e** command to add an entry as follows:

```
0 1 15 * * /fullbackup
```

> **Note:** The execute permission bit of the /fullbackup file must be on.

9.6.2 Allowing access to the crontab command

The /var/adm/cron/cron.allow and /var/adm/cron/cron.deny files control which users can use the **crontab** command. A root user can create, edit, or delete these files. Entries in these files are user login names with one name to a line.

If the cron.allow file exists, only users whose login names appear in it can use the **crontab** command.

> **Note:** The root user name must appear in the cron.allow file if the file exists.

You can explicitly stop a user from using the **crontab** command by listing the user's login name in the cron.deny file. If only the cron.deny file exists, any user whose name does not appear in the file can use the **crontab** command.

A user cannot use the **crontab** command if one of the following is true:

- The cron.allow file and the cron.deny file do not exist (allows root user only).

- The cron.allow file exists but the user's login name is not listed in it.

- The cron.deny file exists and the user's login name is listed in it.

If neither the cron.allow nor the cron.deny file exists, only the root user can submit a job with the **crontab** command.

9.6.3 Housekeeping

When you have logged in as root, or used the **su** command to become root, the **crontab -l** command shows that there are three commented entries in the crontab file. They are:

▶ #0 3 * * * /usr/sbin/skulker

▶ #45 2 * * 0 /usr/lib/spell/compress

▶ #45 23 * * * ulimit 5000; /usr/lib/smdemon.cleanu > /dev/null

These are housekeeping jobs that you can enable to clean up your system. Use the **crontab -e** command to remove the # mark in column 1 to enable the jobs. Also, you may change the time when you want the job to run. A sample crontab file is shown in Figure 9-4.

```
# crontab -l
# @(#)08        1.15.1.3   src/bos/usr/sbin/cron/root, cmdcntl, bos430, 9737A_430
2/11/94 17:19:47
# IBM_PROLOG_BEGIN_TAG
# This is an automatically generated prolog.
#
# bos430 src/bos/usr/sbin/cron/root 1.15.1.3
#
# Licensed Materials - Property of IBM
#
# (C) COPYRIGHT International Business Machines Corp. 1989,1994
# All Rights Reserved
#
# US Government Users Restricted Rights - Use, duplication or
# disclosure restricted by GSA ADP Schedule Contract with IBM Corp.
#
# IBM_PROLOG_END_TAG
#
# COMPONENT_NAME: (CMDCNTL) commands needed for basic system needs
#
# FUNCTIONS:
#
# ORIGINS: 27
#
# (C) COPYRIGHT International Business Machines Corp. 1989,1994
# All Rights Reserved
# Licensed Materials - Property of IBM
#
# US Government Users Restricted Rights - Use, duplication or
# disclosure restricted by GSA ADP Schedule Contract with IBM Corp.
#
#0 3 * * * /usr/sbin/skulker
#45 2 * * 0 /usr/lib/spell/compress
#45 23 * * * ulimit 5000; /usr/lib/smdemon.cleanu > /dev/null
0 11 * * * /usr/bin/errclear -d S,O 30
0 12 * * * /usr/bin/errclear -d H 90
0 4 * * * /usr/bin/rmxcred -d 4 1>/dev/null 2>/dev/null
# █
```

Figure 9-4   Sample crontab file

The skulker command

The `skulker` command is a command file for periodically purging obsolete or unneeded files from file systems. Candidate files include files in the /tmp directory, files older than a specified age, a.out files, core files, or ed.hup files.

The `skulker` command is normally invoked daily, often as part of an accounting procedure run by the `cron` command during off-peak periods. Modify the `skulker` command to suit local needs following the patterns shown in the distributed version. System users should be made aware of the criteria for automatic file removal.

The `find` command and the `xargs` command form a powerful combination for use in the `skulker` command. Most file selection criteria can be expressed conveniently with find expressions. The resulting file list can be segmented and inserted into `rm` commands using the `xargs` command to reduce the overhead that would result if each file were deleted with a separate command.

> **Note:** Because the `skulker` command is run by a root user and its whole purpose is to remove files, it has the potential for unexpected results. Before installing a new `skulker` command, test any additions to its file removal criteria by running the additions manually using the `xargs -p` command. After you have verified that the new `skulker` command removes only the files you want removed, you can install it.

To enable the `skulker` command, you should use the `crontab -e` command to remove the comment statement by deleting the # (pound sign) character from the beginning of the /usr/sbin/skulker line in the /var/spool/cron/crontabs/root file.

The /usr/lib/spell/compress command

This is *not* the AIX `compress` command. The `/usr/lib/spell/compress` command is a shell script to compress the spell program log.

To enable the `/usr/lib/spell/compress` command, you should use the `crontab -e` command to remove the comment statement by deleting the # (pound sign) character from the beginning of the `/usr/lib/spell/compress` line in the /var/spool/cron/crontabs/root file.

The script is shown in Figure 9-5 on page 256.

```
# cat /usr/lib/spell/compress
#!/bin/bsh
# @(#)60        1.5  src/cmdtext/usr/bin/spell/compress.sh, cmdtext, cmdtext430,
 9737A_430 5/17/91 10:04:52
#
# COMPONENT_NAME: (CMDTEXT) Text Formatting Services
#
# FUNCTIONS:
#
# ORIGINS: 3
#
#        compress - compress the spell program log

trap 'rm -f /usr/tmp/spellhist;exit' 1 2 3 15
echo "COMPRESSED `date`" > /usr/tmp/spellhist
grep -v ' ' /usr/lib/spell/spellhist | sort -fud >> /usr/tmp/spellhist
cp /usr/tmp/spellhist /usr/lib/spell
rm -f /usr/tmp/spellhist
#
```

Figure 9-5   /usr/lib/spell/compress script

This script removes all duplicated words in the /usr/lib/spell/spellhist file. This file is updated when the users invoke the **spell** command.

The /usr/lib/smdemon.cleanu command

The **smdemon.cleanu** command is a shell procedure that cleans up the **sendmail** command queue and maintains the /var/spool/mqueue/log file.

To enable the **smdemon.cleanu** command, you must remove the comment statement by deleting the # (pound sign) character from the beginning of the smdemon.cleanu line in the /var/spool/cron/crontabs/root file. If the /var/spool/mqueue directory does not exist, do not change the /var/spool/cron/crontabs/root file.

Be careful that the average size of a log file for each smdemon.cleanu session multiplied by the number of log files does not use more space than you need. You can arrange the number of log files to suit your needs.

> **Note:** The **smdemon.cleanu** command is not usually entered on the command line. The command is executed by the cron daemon.

9.7 Quiz

The following certification assessment question helps verify your understanding of the topics discussed in this chapter.

1. The system administrator would like to log messages related to user login failures to a file. How could this be accomplished?

    A. Issue the command: `alog -f /etc/security/failedlogin -q`

    B. Modify the /etc/security/login to add an auth_method for logging.

    C. Add a line to the /etc/syslog.conf file to capture this information.

    D. Set log=true in the default stanza in the /etc/security/user file.

The following are additional questions created by the authors to further test your understanding of the topics.

1. A system administrator would like to collect a log file of **su** activity on all hosts across a network. The central logfile will reside on host mars. The syslog daemon is already operational on host mars. Which of the following is the first step in accomplishing this task?

    A. Edit the /var/adm/sulog file on all hosts except mars adding the line:

       `remote:mars`

    B. Edit the /etc/syslog.conf file on all hosts except mars adding the line:

       `auth.debug @mars`

    C. Edit the /var/adm/syslog file on all hosts except mars adding the line:

       `sulog = mars`

    D. Edit the /etc/security/user file on all hosts except mars adding the following line to the default stanza:

       `sulog = mars`

2. An overwrite installation has just been completed to bring the machine up to the latest AIX version. Which of the following is the next step to take in order to enable operation of skulker?

    A. Run the command: `startsrc -s skulker`

    B. Run the command: `chitab "skulker:2:wait:/etc/rc.skulker"`

    C. Remove the comment from the skulker entry of the root crontab

    D. Remove the comment from the skulker entry in the inetd.conf and refresh inetd.

9.7.1 Answers

The following answer is for the assessment quiz questions.

1. C

The following answers are for the additional quiz questions.

1. B
2. C

9.8 Exercises

The following exercises provide sample topics for self study. They will help ensure comprehension of this chapter.

1. What is needed to restart the SRC in AIX Version 4.3.2 or AIX Version 4.2.1? Is a reboot needed? Can it be done by refresh or other commands?

2. What is the **startsrc** command and what are the use of its major flags?

3. Start the syslog and examine the results.

4. What is the syslog configuration file? What should be done to refresh the daemon?

5. Collect syslog data from many systems.

6. Refresh the syslogd daemon to pick up modifications.

7. Refresh a daemon.

8. Explain the configuration file for cron jobs.

9. Enable the skulker, or other commented daemons.

## 10

Network administration

A network is the combination of two or more computers and the connecting links between them. A physical network is the hardware (equipment, such as adapter cards, cables, and concentrators) that makes up the network. The software and the conceptual model make up the logical network.

You will find important aspects of administrating TCP/IP on the system in this section, including IP addressing, network daemons, and basic network security. Note that this does not present the full scope of network administration.

10.1 Network startup at boot time

At IPL time, the /init process will run /etc/rc.tcpip after starting the SRC. The /etc/rc.tcpip file is a shell script that, when executed, uses SRC commands to initialize selected daemons. It can also be executed at any time from the command line.

Most of the daemons that can be initialized by the rc.tcpip file are specific to TCP/IP. These daemons are:

- inetd (started by default)
- gated
- routed
- named
- timed
- rwhod

> **Note:** Running the gated and routed daemons at the same time on a host may cause unpredictable results.

There are also daemons specific to the base operating system or to other applications that can be started through the rc.tcpip file. These daemons are:

- lpd
- portmap
- sendmail
- syslogd (started by default)

10.2 Stopping and restarting TCP/IP daemons

The subsystems started from rc.tcpip can be stopped using the `stopsrc` command and restarted using the `startsrc` command.

10.2.1 Stopping TCP/IP daemons using the /etc/tcp.clean command

The script `/etc/tcp.clean` can be used to stop TCP/IP daemons. It will stop the following daemons and remove the /etc/locks/lpd TCP/IP lock files:

- ndpd-host
- lpd

- routed
- gated
- sendmail
- inetd
- named
- timed
- rwhod
- iptrace
- snmpd
- rshd
- rlogind
- telnetd
- syslogd

Note that the script /etc/tcp.clean does not stop the portmap and nfsd daemons. If you want to stop the portmap and the nfsd daemons, use the **stopsrc -s portmap** and the **stopsrc -s nfsd** commands. The execution bit of this /etc/tcp.clean file is not on by default. You will have to invoke it by issuing:

```
sh /etc/tcp.clean
```

10.2.2 Restarting TCP/IP daemons

The /etc/rc.tcpip script can be used to restart TCP/IP daemons. Alternatively, you can use the **startsrc -s** command to start individual TCP/IP daemons.

> **Note:** Do *not* restart TCP/IP daemons using the command:
>
> ```
> startsrc -g tcpip
> ```
>
> It will start all subsystems defined in the ODM for the tcpip group, which includes both routed and gated.

10.3 System boot without starting rc.tcpip

TCP/IP is a peer-to-peer, connection-oriented protocol. There are no master/slave relations. The applications, however, use a client/server model for communications.

Removing the rc.tcpip entry in /etc/inittab means that you are not starting any server applications during IPL.

> **Note:** If you have a graphic console, make sure you also remove the rc.dt and rc.tcpip entries in the /etc/inittab file. Otherwise, your console will hang when you login. Unless you have an ASCII terminal connected to the serial port, there is no way you can recover since you will not be able to communicate with the machine through the **telnet** or **rlogin** commands with no TCP/IP server application started.

Without the server applications started, you will not be able to **telnet** or **ftp** to this machine from another host.

However, as long as you have not brought down the network interface, you can still utilize the client network services. You can still **ping** other hosts, you can still **telnet** to other hosts, and you can still **ftp** to other hosts.

The **ping** command sends an Internet Control Message Protocol (ICMP) ECHO_REQUEST to obtain an ICMP ECHO_RESPONSE from a host and does not need a server application. Therefore, even without starting any server application, the machine will still respond to a **ping** request from other hosts.

10.4 The inetd daemon

The /usr/sbin/inetd daemon provides Internet service management for a network. This daemon reduces system load by invoking other daemons only when they are needed and by providing several simple Internet services internally without invoking other daemons.

10.4.1 Starting and refreshing inetd

When the daemon starts, it reads its configuration information from the file specified in the Configuration File parameter. If the parameter is not specified, the inetd daemon reads its configuration information from the /etc/inetd.conf file. Once started, the inetd daemon listens for connections on certain Internet sockets in the /etc/inetd.conf and either handles the service request itself or invokes the appropriate server once a request on one of these sockets is received.

The /etc/inetd.conf file can be updated by using the System Management Interface Tool (SMIT), the System Resource Controller (SRC), or by editing the /etc/inetd.conf.

If you change the /etc/inetd.conf using SMIT, then the inetd daemon will be refreshed automatically and will read the new /etc/inetd.conf file. If you change the file using an editor, run the `refresh -s inetd` or `kill -1 InetdPID` commands to inform the inetd daemon of the changes to its configuration file. You will not receive a message if you use the `kill -1` command as shown in Figure 10-1.

```
# refresh -s inetd
0513-095 The request for subsystem refresh was completed successfully.
# ps -ef |grep inetd
    root 17840  2900   0 09:17:31     -   0:00 /usr/sbin/inetd
    root 20606 20016   1 09:19:14  pts/2 0:00 grep inetd
# kill -1 17840
# ps -ef |grep inetd
    root 17482 20016   2 09:19:37  pts/2 0:00 grep inetd
    root 17840  2900   0 09:17:31     -   0:00 /usr/sbin/inetd
# █
```

Figure 10-1   Refreshing the inetd daemon using refresh or kill

10.4.2 Subservers controlled by inetd

The inetd daemon is a subsystem that controls the following daemons (subservers):

► comsat daemon

► ftpd daemon

► fingerd daemon

► rlogind daemon

► rexecd daemon

► rshd daemon

► talkd daemon

► telnetd daemon

► tftpd daemon

► uucpd daemon

The ftpd, rlogind, rexecd, rshd, talkd, telnetd, and uucpd daemons are started by default. The tftpd, fingerd, and comsat daemons are not started by default.

To start any one of them, remove the pound (#) sign in column one of the respective entry in the /etc/inetd.conf file. You can check the details of subservers started in inetd by using the `lssrc -ls` command, as shown in Figure 10-2 on page 264.

```
# lssrc -ls inetd
Subsystem          Group              PID     Status
 inetd             tcpip              17840   active

Debug              Not active

Signal             Purpose
 SIGALRM           Establishes socket connections for failed services.
 SIGHUP            Rereads the configuration database and reconfigures services.

 SIGCHLD           Restarts the service in case the service ends abnormally.

Service            Command                     Description            Status
 xmquery           /usr/bin/xmservd            xmservd -p3            active
 ttdbserver        /usr/dt/bin/rpc.ttdbserver  rpc.ttdbserver 100083 1  active
 cmsd              /usr/dt/bin/rpc.cmsd        cmsd 100068 2-5        active
 dtspc             /usr/dt/bin/dtspcd          /usr/dt/bin/dtspcd     active
 time              internal                                           active
 daytime           internal                                           active
 discard           internal                                           active
 echo              internal                                           active
 time              internal                                           active
 daytime           internal                                           active
 chargen           internal                                           active
 discard           internal                                           active
 pcnfsd            /usr/sbin/rpc.pcnfsd        pcnfsd 150001 1-2      active
 sprayd            /usr/lib/netsvc/spray/rpc.sprayd sprayd 100012 1               active
 rwalld            /usr/lib/netsvc/rwall/rpc.rwalld rwalld 100008 1               active
 rusersd           /usr/lib/netsvc/rusers/rpc.rusersd rusersd 100002 1-2             active
 rstatd            /usr/sbin/rpc.rstatd        rstatd 100001 1-3      active
 ntalk             /usr/sbin/talkd             talkd                 active
 klogin            /usr/sbin/krlogind          krlogind              active
 login             /usr/sbin/rlogind           rlogind               active
 kshell            /usr/sbin/krshd             krshd                 active
 shell             /usr/sbin/rshd              rshd                  active
 telnet            /usr/sbin/telnetd           telnetd               active
 ftp               /usr/sbin/ftpd              ftpd                  active
#
```

Figure 10-2   Subservers started in inetd

10.4.3 The /etc/services file

The /etc/services file contains information about the known services used in the DARPA Internet network by inetd. Each service listed in /etc/services runs on a specific port number for communications, in a specific format, such as TCP or UDP.

Each service is listed on a single line corresponding to the form:

```
ServiceName PortNumber/ProtocolName Aliases
```

A sample section from /etc/services may look like the following:

```
echo        7/tcp
echo        7/udp
discard     9/tcp        sink null
```

```
discard       9/udp     sink null
daytime      13/tcp
daytime      13/udp
chargen      19/tcp     ttytst source
chargen      19/udp     ttytst source
ftp          21/tcp
time         37/tcp     timeserver
time         37/udp     timeserver
```

If you edit the /etc/services file, run the **refresh -s inetd** command, in order for your changes to be used.

10.4.4 Stopping inetd

Use the command **stopsrc -s inetd** to stop the inetd daemon as shown in Figure 10-3.

```
# stopsrc -s inetd
0513-044 The stop of the /usr/sbin/inetd Subsystem was completed successfully.
#
```

Figure 10-3 Stopping inetd

When the inetd daemon is stopped, the previously started subserver processes are not affected. However, new service requests for the subservers can no longer be satisfied. If you try to **telnet** or **ftp** to the server with inetd down, you will see messages as shown in Figure 10-4.

```
$ telnet sv1166f
Trying...
telnet: connect: A remote host refused an attempted connect operation.
$ ftp sv1166f
ftp: connect: A remote host refused an attempted connect operation.
ftp> bye
$
```

Figure 10-4 Telnet and FTP when inetd on sv1166f is down

In other words, existing sessions are not affected when the inetd daemon is stopped, but no new **telnet** and **ftp** sessions can be established without first restarting the inetd daemon.

10.5 The portmap daemon

The portmap daemon converts remote procedure call (RPC) program numbers into Internet port numbers.

When an RPC server starts up, it registers with the portmap daemon. The server tells the daemon which port number it is listening to and which RPC program numbers it serves. Thus, the portmap daemon knows the location of every registered port on the host and which programs are available on each of these ports.

A client consults the portmap daemon only once for each program the client tries to call. The portmap daemon tells the client which port to send the call to. The client stores this information for future reference.

Since standard RPC servers are normally started by the inetd daemon, the portmap daemon must be started before the inetd daemon is invoked.

Note: If the portmap daemon is stopped or comes to an abnormal end, all RPC servers on the host must be restarted.

The nfsd is a common RPC server.

10.6 Internet addressing

If you want your machines to communicate with each other across the TCP/IP network, you must give them unique IP addresses. Each host is assigned a unique 32-bit logical address (in the case of IPv4) that is divided into two main parts: the network number and the host number. The network number identifies a logical network to which the host belongs and must be the same across the subnet. The host number identifies a host on the specific logical network.

10.6.1 IP address format

The IP address is the 32-bit address, grouped eight bits at a time, separated by dots and represented in decimal format called dotted decimal notation. Each bit in the octet has a binary weight (128, 64, 32,16, 8, 4, 2, 1). The minimum value for an octet is 0, and the maximum value for an octet is 255. Figure 10-5 on page 267 illustrates the basic format of an IP address.

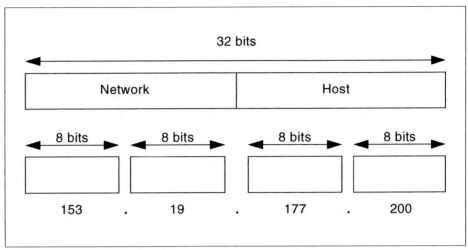

Figure 10-5   IP address format

10.6.2 Binary to decimal conversion

The decimal value of the bits ranges from high to low with the left-most bit in every byte having the highest value of 128. To convert from binary value to decimal value, add decimal values on the position where the bits have value of 1. An example is shown in Figure 10-6.

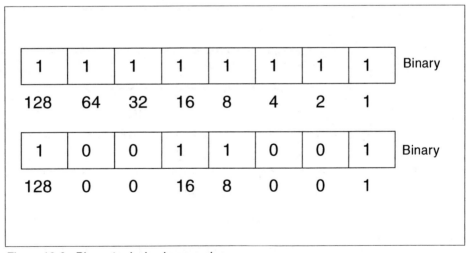

Figure 10-6   Binary to decimal conversion

To convert numbers to and from binary format, you can use the **bc** command. To make the conversion of value 195 to binary format, enter:

```
# bc
obase=2
195
11000011
```

To convert the binary number 11001100 to a decimal format, enter:

```
# bc
ibase=2
11001100
204
```

10.6.3 Internet address classes

IP addressing supports five different address classes: A, B, C, D, and E. Classes A, B, and C are available for commercial use. You can determine the network class of an IP address by checking the bits in the first octet of a network address.

By converting all of the bits of an IP address to binary format and calculating the number of hosts and networks available, you will receive data similar to that shown in Figure 10-7.

		7 bits	24 bits
CLASS A	O	Network address	Host address

		14 bits	16 bits
CLASS B	1O	Network address	Host address

		21 bits	8 bits
CLASS C	11O	Network address	Host address

		28 bits	
CLASS D	111O	Multicast address	

Figure 10-7   IP address classes

To determine the class of an IP address, refer to Table 10-1 on page 269.

Table 10-1   IP address classes

IP address class	Format	First octet	Address range	Number bits network/ host	Number of hosts
A	N.H.H.H	0	1.0.0.0 127.0.0.0	7 / 24	2^{24} - 2
B	N.N.H.H	10	128.1.0.0 191.254.0.0	14 / 16	2^{16} - 2
C	N.N.N.H	110	192.0.1.0 223.255.254.0	22 / 8	2^{8} - 2
D	-	1110	224.0.0.0 239.255.255.255	-	-
N - Network number H - Host number					

For example, in the IP address 195.116.119.2, the first octet is 195. Because 195 falls between 192 and 223, 195.116.119.2 is a class C address.

Class A, B, and C addresses also provide address ranges that are useful to define a private network without INTERNIC authorization. A private network can have the following address ranges:

Class A   10.0.0.0 to 10.255.255.255

Class B   172.16.0.0 to 172.31.255.255

Class C   192.168.0.0 to 192.168.255.255

10.6.4 Special Internet addresses

There are a few IP addresses that cannot be used as host addresses. Those addresses are used for special occasions.

The loopback interface allows a client and server on the same host to communicate with each other using TCP/IP. The network class A with network address 127 is reserved for the loopback interface lo0. AIX assigns the IP address 127.0.0.1 to this interface and assigns it the name localhost. To check attributes of any interface use the **ifconfig** or **lsattr** commands as follows:

```
# ifconfig lo0
lo0:
flags=e08084b<UP,BROADCAST,LOOPBACK,RUNNING,SIMPLEX,MULTICAST,GROUPRT,64BIT>
```

```
            inet 127.0.0.1 netmask 0xff000000 broadcast 127.255.255.255
            inet6 ::1/0
# lsattr -El lo0
netaddr    127.0.0.1 Internet Address                        True
state      up        Current Interface Status                True
netmask              Subnet Mask                             True
mtu        16896     Maximum IP Packet Size for This Device  True
netaddr6   ::1       N/A                                     True
prefixlen            Subnet Mask                             True
```

The network address is an IP address with all host address bits set to 0. If you have the IP address 195.116.119.2, the network address for this will be 195.116.119.0. This type of address is used in the routing table as the network destination address. An example routing table is shown in the following (0 is omitted in the routing tables).

```
# netstat -nr
Routing tables
Destination       Gateway         Flags  Refs     Use  If   PMTU  Exp  Groups

Route Tree for Protocol Family 2 (Internet):
default           9.3.240.1       UGc       0       0  tr0    -    -
9.3.240/24        9.3.240.58      U        30  130787  tr0    -    -
127/8             127.0.0.1       U        54    1300  lo0    -    -
195.116.119/24    195.116.119.2   U         0       2  en0    -    -
```

The limited broadcast address is 255.255.255.255 (an address with all host address and network address bits set to 1). This can be used as the destination address for all hosts regardless of their network number. Routers never forward a limited broadcast; it only appears on the local cable.

The directed broadcast address is an IP address, with all the host address bits set to 1. It is used to simultaneously address all hosts within the same network. For example, consider an IP address 195.116.119.2; because it is class C address, the network address for this address is 195.116.119. Therefore, the directed broadcast for this network will be 195.116.119.255. To check the broadcast setting for interface en0, enter:

```
# ifconfig en0
en0:
flags=e080863<UP,BROADCAST,NOTRAILERS,RUNNING,SIMPLEX,MULTICAST,GROUPRT,64BIT>
inet 195.116.119.2 netmask 0xffffff00 broadcast 195.116.119.255
```

The last column of Table 10-1 on page 269 shows the number of hosts in the appropriate network class. Notice that the two hosts were subtracted. This was done so that one address is reserved for the broadcast address, and one address is reserved for the network address.

10.6.5 Subnetting

Subnet addressing allows an autonomous network made up of multiple systems to share the same Internet address class. The subnetwork capability of TCP/IP also makes it possible to divide a single network into multiple logical networks (subnets). This makes sense for class A and class B addresses, since attaching thousands of hosts to a single network is impossible.

A standard IP address has two fields (see "IP address format" on page 266): a network address and a host address. A subnet address is created by borrowing bits from the host field and designating them as the subnet field. The number of borrowed subnet bits varies and it depends of the chosen subnet mask. Figure 10-8 shows how bits are borrowed from the host address field to create the subnet address field and how the subnet mask works.

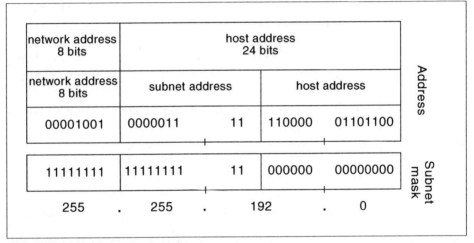

Figure 10-8   Subnetting example

When deciding how to partition the host address into the subnet address and host address, you should consider the number of subnets and the number of hosts on those subnets.

You have great flexibility when assigning subnet addresses and host addresses. The bits of the host address can be divided according to the needs and potential growth of the organization and its network structure. The only restrictions are:

▶ The network address is constant for all its subnets.

▶ The subnet address is constant throughout the physical network.

▶ The host address is a field that is normally at least 2-bits wide.

If the width of the subnet address field is 0, the network is not organized into subnets, and addressing to the network is performed using the Internet network address as mentioned in Section 10.6.1, "IP address format" on page 266.

> **Note:** It is generally desirable for the subnet bits to be contiguous and located as the most significant bits of the host address.

10.6.6 Subnet masks

The subnet mask tells the system what the subnet partitioning scheme is. This bit mask consists of the network address portion and subnet address portion of the IP address.

When a host sends a message to a destination, the system must determine whether the destination is on the same network as the source or if the destination must be reached through a gateway. The system compares the destination address to the host address using the subnet mask. If the destination is not on the local network, the system sends the packet to a gateway. The gateway performs the same comparison to see if the destination address is on a network it can reach locally.

Table 10-2 shows how to calculate the subnet mask from binary format to the dotted decimal notation.

Table 10-2 Subnet mask calculation

Bits of octet								Mask
128	64	32	16	8	4	2	1	
1	0	0	0	0	0	0	0	128
1	1	0	0	0	0	0	0	192
1	1	1	0	0	0	0	0	224
1	1	1	1	0	0	0	0	240
1	1	1	1	1	0	0	0	248
1	1	1	1	1	1	0	0	252
1	1	1	1	1	1	1	0	254
1	1	1	1	1	1	1	1	255

A subnet mask is 32 bits long. A bit set to 1 in the subnet mask indicates that bit position is part of the network address portion of the IP address. A bit set to 0 in the subnet mask indicates that bit position is part of the host address portion of the IP address.

There are default subnet mask sets (Figure 10-9) for each network class address. Using an address with a default subnet mask for an address class indicates that subnets are not set up for the network.

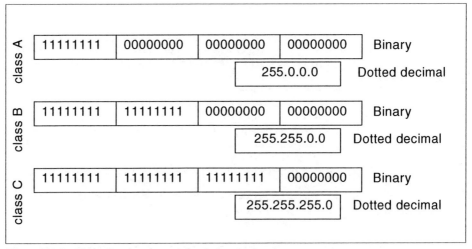

Figure 10-9   Default subnet mask for network classes

The class B address subnetting example

The default subnet mask for a class B address that has no subnetting is 255.255.0.0, while the subnet mask for a class B address 172.16.0.0 that specifies 3 bits of subnetting is 255.255.224.0. The reason for this is that 3 bits of subnetting give $2^3 - 2 = 6$ (1 for the network address and 1 for the broadcast address) subnets possible. You have 5 bits from the 3rd octet and 8 bits from the last octet forming a total of 13 bits for the hosts address. This gives you $2^{13} - 2 = 8190$ hosts per subnet. Figure 10-10 on page 274 shows a subnetting scenario for this address.

255	255	224	0	
11111111	11111111	**111**00000	00000000	Subnet mask 255.255.224.0

172	16	32	0	
10101100	00010000	**00**100000	00000000	1st subnet

172	16	32	1	
10101100	00010000	**00**100000	00000001	1st host in this subnet

172	16	63	255	
11111111	00010000	**00**111111	**11111111**	Subnet broadcast

172	16	64	0	
10101100	00010000	**01**000000	00000000	2nd subnet

172	16	64	1	
10101100	00010000	**01**000000	00000001	1st host in this subnet

172	16	95	255	
10101100	00010000	**01**011111	**11111111**	Subnet broadcast

Figure 10-10   Subnetting scenario

Table 10-3 shows the subnet mask, the number of subnets and the number of hosts based on the number of bits for the subnet for network class B.

Table 10-3   Class B subnetting reference chart

Numbers of bits for subnet	Subnet mask	Number of subnets	Number of hosts
2	255.255.192.0	2	16382
3	255.255.224.0	6	8190
4	255.255.240.0	14	4094
5	255.255.248.0	30	2046
6	255.255.252.0	62	1022
7	255.255.254.0	126	510
8	255.255.255.0	254	254

Numbers of bits for subnet	Subnet mask	Number of subnets	Number of hosts
9	255.255.255.128	510	126
10	255.255.255.192	1022	62
11	255.255.255.224	2046	30
12	255.255.255.240	4096	14
13	255.255.255.248	8190	6
14	255.255.255.252	16382	2

The class C address subnetting example

The subnet mask for a class C address 192.168.2.0 that specifies 5 bits of subnetting is 255.255.255.248. With 5 bits available for subnetting, $2^5 - 2 = 30$ subnets possible. Now you have 3 bits left for the hosts part and it gives $2^3 - 2 = 6$ hosts per subnet. Table 10-4 shows the number of hosts, number of subnets, and subnet mask based on the numbers of bits for subnet.

Table 10-4   Class C subnetting reference chart

Number of bits for subnet	Subnet mask	Number of subnets	Number of hosts
2	255.255.255.192	2	62
3	255.255.255.224	6	30
4	255.255.255.240	14	14
5	255.255.255.248	30	6
6	255.255.255.252	62	2

10.7 Host name resolution

TCP/IP provides a naming system that supports both flat and hierarchical network organizations so that users can use meaningful, easily remembered names instead of Internet addresses.

In flat TCP/IP networks, each machine on the network has a file (/etc/hosts) containing the name-to-Internet-address mapping information for every host on the network.

When TCP/IP networks become very large, as on the Internet, naming is divided hierarchically. Typically, the divisions follow the network's organization. In TCP/IP, hierarchical naming is known as the domain name system (DNS) and uses the DOMAIN protocol. The DOMAIN protocol is implemented by the named daemon in TCP/IP.

The default order in resolving host names is:

1. BIND/DNS (named)

2. Network Information Service (NIS)

3. Local /etc/hosts file

The default order can be overwritten by creating the configuration file, /etc/netsvc.conf and specifying the desired order. Both the default and /etc/netsvc.conf can be overwritten with the environment variable NSORDER.

You can override the default order by creating the /etc/netsvc.conf file with an entry. If /etc/netsvc.conf does not exist, the default will be as though you made the following entry:

```
hosts = bind,nis,local
```

You can override the default or the configuration file order by changing the NSORDER environment variable. If it is not set, the default will be as though you issued the command:

```
export NSORDER=bind,nis,local
```

10.7.1 The /etc/resolv.conf file

The /etc/resolv.conf file defines Domain Name Protocol (DOMAIN) name-server information for local resolver routines. If the /etc/resolv.conf file does not exist, then BIND/DNS is considered to be not set up or running and, therefore, not available. The system will attempt name resolution using the default paths, the /etc/netsvc.conf file, or the NSORDER environment variable.

A sample /etc/resolv.conf file is shown in Figure 10-11.

```
# cat /etc/resolv.conf
nameserver      9.3.1.74
domain  itsc.austin.ibm.com
search  itsc.austin.ibm.com austin.ibm.com
#
```

Figure 10-11   Sample /etc/resolv.conf file

In this case, there is only one name server defined, with an address of 9.3.1.74. The system will query this domain name server for name resolution. The default domain name to append to names that do not end with a . (period) is itsc.austin.ibm.com. The search entry defines the list of domains to search when resolving a name; in the above example, they are itsc.austin.ibm.com and austin.ibm.com.

10.7.2 Related problems with /etc/resolv.conf

When you have problems resolving a host name, and you are using a name server, you should:

1. Verify that you have a /etc/resolv.conf file specifying the correct domain name and Internet address of a name server. If you try to access a host by name with an incorrect entry in /etc/resolv.conf, and if the host is also not defined in /etc/hosts, you will get an error message, as shown in the following example:

```
# ping olympus
0821-062 ping: host name olympus NOT FOUND
```

2. If /etc/resolv.conf contains the correct data, verify that the host acting as the local name server is up by issuing the **ping** command with the IP address of the name server found in the /etc/resolv.conf file.

3. If the local name server is up, verify that the named daemon on that local system is active by issuing the **lssrc -s named** command on that host.

4. If you are running the syslogd daemon, there could be error messages logged. The output for these messages is defined in the /etc/syslog.conf file.

10.7.3 The nslookup command

The **nslookup** command queries domain name servers for information about various hosts and domains. The **nslookup** command is useful for determining host names of servers of systems on the Internet by IP address, host name, or domain. The **nslookup** command can be run as follows:

```
# nslookup [IPAddress | HostName]
```

For example, to determine the host name of the system with the IP address of 207.25.253.26, you would enter:

```
# nslookup 207.25.253.26
Server:  dhcp001.itsc.austin.ibm.com
Address: 9.3.240.2

Name:    service.boulder.ibm.com
Address: 207.25.253.26
```

In this example, the host name of the system with the IP address of 207.25.253.26 is service.boulder.ibm.com.

The nslookup command can also determine IP addresses of systems by host name. For example, to display the IP address of service.software.ibm.com, you would enter:

```
# nslookup service.software.ibm.com
Server:  dhcp001.itsc.austin.ibm.com
Address:  9.3.240.2

Non-authoritative answer:
Name:    service.boulder.ibm.com
Address:  207.25.253.26
Aliases:  service.software.ibm.com
```

In this example, the IP address of service.software.ibm.com is 207.25.253.26. The **nslookup** output also shows that service.software.ibm.com is an alias for service.boulder.ibm.com.

10.8 New adapter considerations

Changing network adapters in a machine may require additional configuration steps after the basic hardware installation. Consider the following tasks as the additional steps required to configure a new adapter.

1. If you missed the informational messages from the **cfgmgr** command invoked during system boot, you should invoke the command again to check if the required device-dependent software is missing.

2. Install the required device software, if needed using the **smitty devices** command.

3. Invoke the **diag -a** command to confirm that the new adapter resource is added in the hardware configuration.

4. Rerun **cfgmgr**.

5. Ensure that the adapter is available on the system by invoking the **lsdev -Cl** command on the adapter. For example:

   ```
   # lsdev -Cl ent0
   ```

6. Obtain the IP address and netmask from your network architect.

7. Configure the network interface using the SMIT fast path **smit inet**. Do not use **smit mktcpip**. It is only used for configuring TCP/IP for the first time.

8. Enable IP forwarding if the machine is connected to two networks.

9. Add a route to those systems that need access from any private networks.

10.8.1 Configuring a network adapter using SMIT

To change advanced features of network adapters, including ring speed, duplex settings, and queue sizes for transmitting and receiving information, use the SMIT fast path **smit chgenet** for Ethernet adapters, and **smit chgtok** for token ring adapters. A sample screen of **smit chgenet** is shown in Figure 10-12.

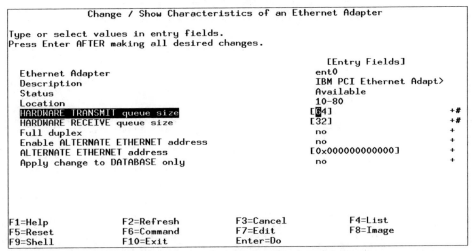

```
                  Change / Show Characteristics of an Ethernet Adapter

Type or select values in entry fields.
Press Enter AFTER making all desired changes.
                                                             [Entry Fields]
                                                           ent0
    Ethernet Adapter
    Description                                            IBM PCI Ethernet Adapt>
    Status                                                 Available
    Location                                               10-80
    HARDWARE TRANSMIT queue size                           [64]                   +#
    HARDWARE RECEIVE queue size                            [32]                   +#
    Full duplex                                            no                     +
    Enable ALTERNATE ETHERNET address                      no                     +
    ALTERNATE ETHERNET address                             [0x000000000000]       +
    Apply change to DATABASE only                          no                     +




F1=Help              F2=Refresh           F3=Cancel            F4=List
F5=Reset             F6=Command           F7=Edit              F8=Image
F9=Shell             F10=Exit             Enter=Do
```

Figure 10-12   Change/Show Characteristics of an Ethernet Adapter menu

10.8.2 Configuring a network interface using SMIT

The SMIT fast path command used to configure TCP/IP is **smit tcpip**. You can configure a network interface using the fast path **smit inet**. For these examples, we will be using an Ethernet interface, en0.

1. Check whether the en0 interface exists by selecting List All Network Interfaces. If en0 does not exist, select Add a Network Interface, and then select Add a Standard Ethernet Network Interface. You should see a panel similar to in Figure 10-13 on page 280.

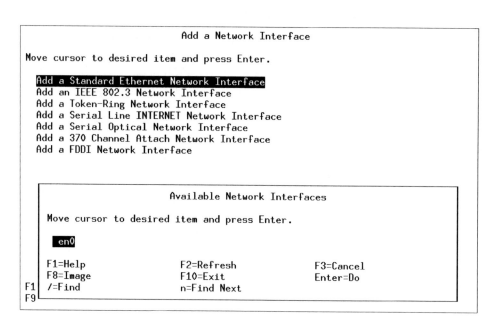

```
                       Add a Network Interface

  Move cursor to desired item and press Enter.

     Add a Standard Ethernet Network Interface
     Add an IEEE 802.3 Network Interface
     Add a Token-Ring Network Interface
     Add a Serial Line INTERNET Network Interface
     Add a Serial Optical Network Interface
     Add a 370 Channel Attach Network Interface
     Add a FDDI Network Interface


    ┌─────────────────────────────────────────────────────────────┐
    │                 Available Network Interfaces                  │
    │                                                               │
    │  Move cursor to desired item and press Enter.                 │
    │                                                               │
    │    en0                                                        │
    │                                                               │
    │  F1=Help              F2=Refresh            F3=Cancel         │
    │  F8=Image             F10=Exit              Enter=Do          │
  F1│  /=Find               n=Find Next                             │
  F9└─────────────────────────────────────────────────────────────┘
```

Figure 10-13   Available Network Interfaces submenu

2. Press Enter to select en0 and fill in the following dialog screen.

   Choose the interface that you need to configure and fill in the necessary information. A sample screen is shown in Figure 10-14 on page 281.

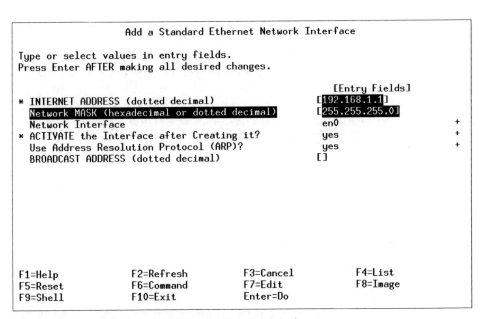

```
                  Add a Standard Ethernet Network Interface

Type or select values in entry fields.
Press Enter AFTER making all desired changes.

                                                         [Entry Fields]
* INTERNET ADDRESS (dotted decimal)                      [192.168.1.1]
  Network MASK (hexadecimal or dotted decimal)           [255.255.255.0]
  Network Interface                                       en0                 +
* ACTIVATE the Interface after Creating it?               yes                 +
  Use Address Resolution Protocol (ARP)?                  yes                 +
  BROADCAST ADDRESS (dotted decimal)                      []




F1=Help            F2=Refresh         F3=Cancel          F4=List
F5=Reset           F6=Command         F7=Edit            F8=Image
F9=Shell           F10=Exit           Enter=Do
```

Figure 10-14   Add a Standard Ethernet Network Interface menu

3. On completion of adding the standard Ethernet network interface, you should
   see the message en0 Available.

4. If en0 already exists, select Change/Show Characteristics of a Network
   Interface. The SMIT fast path is **smit chinet**. A sample screen is shown in
   Figure 10-15 on page 282.

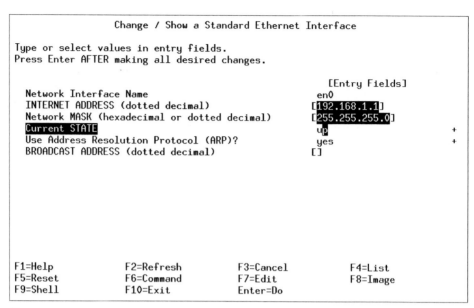

```
                    Change / Show a Standard Ethernet Interface

Type or select values in entry fields.
Press Enter AFTER making all desired changes.

                                                    [Entry Fields]
    Network Interface Name                          en0
    INTERNET ADDRESS (dotted decimal)               [192.168.1.1]
    Network MASK (hexadecimal or dotted decimal)    [255.255.255.0]
    Current STATE                                   up                  +
    Use Address Resolution Protocol (ARP)?          yes                 +
    BROADCAST ADDRESS (dotted decimal)              []




    F1=Help             F2=Refresh          F3=Cancel          F4=List
    F5=Reset            F6=Command          F7=Edit            F8=Image
    F9=Shell            F10=Exit            Enter=Do
```

Figure 10-15   Change/Show a Standard Ethernet Interface menu

5. On completion of changing the standard Ethernet interface, you should see a
   message that the en0 interface has been changed.

10.9 Enabling IP forwarding

To allow other systems to access a different network through a machine
containing two network adapters, you must enable IP forwarding on that
machine. The system will now act as a gateway between network A and network
B.

IP forwarding is a runtime attribute. The default value of 0 (zero) prevents
forwarding of IP packets when they are not for the local system. A value of 1
(one) enables forwarding. Enable IP forwarding using the command:

```
no -o ipforwarding=1
```

This setting will be lost following a system reboot.

10.10 Adding network routes

For those systems that need to access a private network, use the SMIT fast path `smit route` or `smit mkroute` to add a route to the private network through the gateway between two networks. A sample of `smit mkroute` is shown in Figure 10-16.

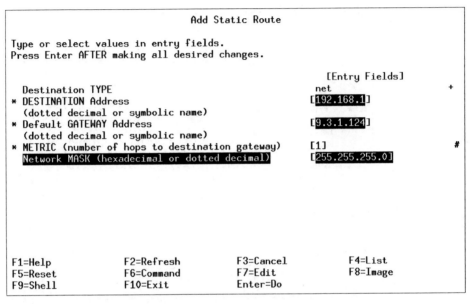

```
                          Add Static Route

Type or select values in entry fields.
Press Enter AFTER making all desired changes.

                                                    [Entry Fields]
  Destination TYPE                                  net                      +
* DESTINATION Address                               [192.168.1]
  (dotted decimal or symbolic name)
* Default GATEWAY Address                           [9.3.1.124]
  (dotted decimal or symbolic name)
* METRIC (number of hops to destination gateway)    [1]                      #
  Network MASK (hexadecimal or dotted decimal)      [255.255.255.0]




F1=Help          F2=Refresh        F3=Cancel        F4=List
F5=Reset         F6=Command        F7=Edit          F8=Image
F9=Shell         F10=Exit          Enter=Do
```

Figure 10-16   Adding a Static Route menu

Instead of using SMIT, you can also use the command:

`route add -net 192.168.1 -netmask 255.255.255.0 9.3.1.124`

The procedure, shown in Figure 10-17 on page 284, illustrates:

▶ A host cannot access the IP addresses 192.168.1.1 and 192.168.1.2.

▶ A route is added using the **route add** command specifying that 9.3.1.124 should be used as the gateway to the network 192.168.1.

▶ The **traceroute** command shows the route taken to reach both 192.168.1.1 and 192.168.1.2.

```
# ping 192.168.1.1
PING 192.168.1.1: (192.168.1.1): 56 data bytes
^C
----192.168.1.1 PING Statistics----
2 packets transmitted, 0 packets received, 100% packet loss
# ping 192.168.1.2
PING 192.168.1.2: (192.168.1.2): 56 data bytes
^C
----192.168.1.2 PING Statistics----
2 packets transmitted, 0 packets received, 100% packet loss
# ping 9.3.1.124
PING 9.3.1.124: (9.3.1.124): 56 data bytes
64 bytes from 9.3.1.124: icmp_seq=0 ttl=255 time=1 ms
64 bytes from 9.3.1.124: icmp_seq=1 ttl=255 time=1 ms
^C
----9.3.1.124 PING Statistics----
2 packets transmitted, 2 packets received, 0% packet loss
round-trip min/avg/max = 1/1/1 ms
# route add -net 192.168.1 -netmask 255.255.255.0 9.3.1.124
9.3.1.124 net 192.168.1: gateway 9.3.1.124
# traceroute 192.168.1.2
trying to get source for 192.168.1.2
source should be 9.3.1.33
traceroute to 192.168.1.2 (192.168.1.2) from 9.3.1.33 (9.3.1.33), 30 hops max
outgoing MTU = 1492
 1  192.168.1.2 (192.168.1.2)  13 ms  2 ms  2 ms
# traceroute 192.168.1.1
trying to get source for 192.168.1.1
source should be 9.3.1.33
traceroute to 192.168.1.1 (192.168.1.1) from 9.3.1.33 (9.3.1.33), 30 hops max
outgoing MTU = 1492
 1  sv1166f.itsc.austin.ibm.com (9.3.1.124)  13 ms  2 ms  2 ms
 2  192.168.1.1 (192.168.1.1)  5 ms  4 ms  3 ms
# █
```

Figure 10-17   Adding a route using the route add command

10.11 Changing IP addresses using SMIT

If you are moving your machine from one network segment to another, and need
to change IP addresses, use `smit mktcpip` the same way as the first time you
configured TCP/IP. You may need to change the host name, IP address, and the
default gateway address. A sample screen is shown in Figure 10-18 on
page 285.

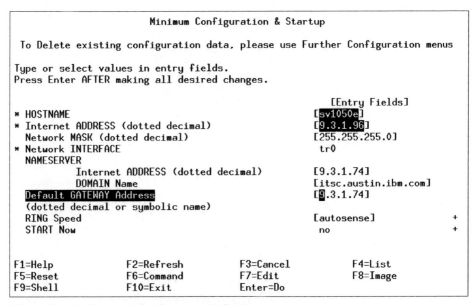

```
                    Minimum Configuration & Startup

   To Delete existing configuration data, please use Further Configuration menus

   Type or select values in entry fields.
   Press Enter AFTER making all desired changes.

                                                    [Entry Fields]
   * HOSTNAME                                       [sv1050e]
   * Internet ADDRESS (dotted decimal)             [9.3.1.96]
     Network MASK (dotted decimal)                 [255.255.255.0]
   * Network INTERFACE                              tr0
     NAMESERVER
             Internet ADDRESS (dotted decimal)     [9.3.1.74]
             DOMAIN Name                           [itsc.austin.ibm.com]
     Default GATEWAY Address                       [9.3.1.74]
     (dotted decimal or symbolic name)
     RING Speed                                    [autosense]          +
     START Now                                      no                  +


   F1=Help          F2=Refresh        F3=Cancel         F4=List
   F5=Reset         F6=Command        F7=Edit           F8=Image
   F9=Shell         F10=Exit          Enter=Do
```

Figure 10-18   Minimum Configuration & Startup menu

Note: Do not perform this task in a Telnet session, as you will lose your connection when the change is made.

If you are not moving across network segments, and simply want to change the IP address, you can change the field START Now shown in Figure 10-18 to yes. This will start the TCP/IP daemons automatically or refresh them if they are already started.

10.12 The ifconfig command

The **ifconfig** command can allow you to configure and modify properties of network interfaces directly, without the use of SMIT. Often, administrators find this easier than using the SMIT panels for network administration.

The syntax of the **ifconfig** command for configuring and modifying network interfaces is as follows:

ifconfig *Interface* [*AddressFamily* [*Address* [*DestinationAddress*]]] [*Parameters...*]]

There are three address families that can be used with the **ifconfig** command:

inet The default dotted decimal notation for a system that is part of the DARPA-Internet. This is the address family that **ifconfig** uses by default.

inet6 The default dotted decimal notation for a system that is part of the DARPA-Internet running IPv6.

ns The default dotted hexadecimal notation for a system that is part of a Xerox Network Systems family.

Table 10-5 is a list of common command parameters and their functions for the **ifconfig** command.

Table 10-5   Common parameters for ifconfig

Parameter	Description
alias	Establishes an additional network address for the interface.
delete	Removes the specified network address from the interface.
detach	Removes an interface from the network interface list.
down	Marks an interface as inactive (down), which keeps the system from trying to transmit messages through that interface.
mtu *Value*	Sets the maximum IP packet size to *Value* bytes, (maximum transmission unit), ranging from 60 to 65535.
netmask *Mask*	Specifies how much of the address to reserve for subdividing networks into subnetworks.
up	Marks an interface as active (up).

10.12.1 Identifying network interfaces

Before you use the **ifconfig** command to perform administration on network interfaces, it is helpful to identify all interfaces on your server. There are two ways to identify network interfaces on your server. The first command that you can run is:

```
# lsdev -Cc if
```

This will produce a simple list of all interfaces on the system, whether they are being actively used by the system or not. For example:

```
# lsdev -Cc if
en0 Defined    10-80 Standard Ethernet Network Interface
en1 Defined    20-60 Standard Ethernet Network Interface
et0 Defined    10-80 IEEE 802.3 Ethernet Network Interface
et1 Defined    20-60 IEEE 802.3 Ethernet Network Interface
lo0 Available        Loopback Network Interface
```

```
tr0 Available 10-68 Token Ring Network Interface
```

The second command that you can run is:

```
# ifconfig -a
```

This will produce a list of all network interfaces on the system that have IP addresses assigned and are actively being used by the system. For example:

```
# ifconfig -a
tr0: flags=e0a0043<UP,BROADCAST,RUNNING,ALLCAST,MULTICAST,GROUPRT,64BIT>
        inet 10.1.2.2 netmask 0xffffff00 broadcast 10.1.2.255
lo0:
flags=e08084b<UP,BROADCAST,LOOPBACK,RUNNING,SIMPLEX,MULTICAST,GROUPRT,64BIT
>
        inet 127.0.0.1 netmask 0xff000000 broadcast 127.255.255.255
        inet6 ::1/0
```

To get information about one specific network interface, including state, IP address, and netmask, run the command:

```
# ifconfig Interface
```

To get information about tr0, for example, run the command:

```
# ifconfig tr0
tr0: flags=e0a0043<UP,BROADCAST,RUNNING,ALLCAST,MULTICAST,GROUPRT,64BIT>
        inet 10.1.2.2 netmask 0xffffff00 broadcast 10.1.2.255
```

10.12.2 Activating a network interface

Before messages can be transmitted through a network interface, the interface must be placed in the up or active state. To activate an interface using **ifconfig**, run the command:

```
# ifconfig Interface [Address] [netmask Netmask] up
```

To activate a network interface using **ifconfig**, such as tr0, run the command:

```
# ifconfig tr0 up
```

To activate a network interface, such as the loopback interface (lo0) and assign it an IP address, run the command:

```
# ifconfig lo0 127.0.0.1 up
```

To activate a network interface, such as a token ring interface (tr0), and assign it an IP address and netmask, run the command:

```
# ifconfig tr0 10.1.2.3 netmask 255.255.255.0 up
```

10.12.3 Deactivating a network interface

To stop messages from being transmitted through an interface, the interface must be placed in the down or inactive state. To deactivate an interface using **ifconfig**, run the command:

```
# ifconfig Interface down
```

For example, to deactivate the network interface tr0, run the command:

```
# ifconfig tr0 down
```

Note: This command does not remove any IP addresses assigned to the interface from the system, nor does it remove the interface from the network interface list.

10.12.4 Deleting an address from a network interface

To remove a network address from an interface, the address must be deleted from the interface definition. To delete a network address from an interface using **ifconfig**, run the command:

```
# ifconfig Interface [Address] [netmask Netmask] delete
```

For example, to delete the network address from tr0, run the command:

```
# ifconfig tr0 delete
```

Note: This command does not place the interface in the down state, nor does it remove the interface from the network interface list.

10.12.5 Detaching a network interface

To remove an interface from the network interface list, the interface must be detached from the system. This command can be used when a network interface card has physically been removed from a system or when an interface no longer needs to be defined within the system. To detach a network interface from the system using **ifconfig,** run the command:

```
# ifconfig Interface detach
```

For example, to remove the interface tr0 from the network interface list, run the command:

```
# ifconfig tr0 detach
```

Note: This command removes all network addresses assigned to the interface and removes the interface from the output of the `ifconfig -a` command. To add an interface back to the system, or to add a new interface to the network interface list, run the command:

```
# ifconfig Interface
```

where *Interface* is the network interface you want to add.

10.12.6 Creating an IP alias for a network interface

Through the `ifconfig` command, you can bind multiple network addresses to a single network interface by defining an alias. This is a useful tool for such activities as providing two different initial home pages through a Web server application. To bind an alias to a network interface, run the command:

```
# ifconfig Interface Address [netmask Netmask] alias
```

For example, to bind the IP address of 10.1.2.3 to tr0 with a netmask of 255.255.255.0, run the command:

```
# ifconfig tr0 10.1.2.3 netmask 255.255.255.0 alias
```

Note: There will be no ODM record created of the alias by this command. You will need to invoke the same command every time you reboot your system to preserve the alias. If your system configuration has a local startup script defined in the /etc/inittab file, this command should be included in that local startup script.

When this alias is no longer required, you can remove it using the command:

```
ifconfig tr0 10.1.2.3 netmask 255.255.255.0 delete
```

Note: If you do not specify which alias is to be removed from a network interface, the system will default and remove the primary network address from the interface. After this occurs, the first alias in the list of network addresses for the interface will become the primary network address for the interface. To remove all aliases from an interface, you must delete each alias individually.

10.12.7 Changing the MTU size of a network interface

When messages are transmitted through a network interface, they travel in bundles of information called packets. These packets can vary in length from 60 bytes to 65535 bytes per packet. By default, a 16 Mb token-ring interface will transmit packets that are 1492 bytes long, and Ethernet interfaces will transmit packets that are 1500 bytes long. For AIX systems, these packets are governed by the maximum transmission unit (MTU) size variable.

Note: The minimum and maximum MTU sizes for specific interfaces may vary. See "Automatic Configuration of Network Interfaces" in the *AIX 5L Version 5.1 System Management Guide: Communications and Networks* as part of the AIX product documentation for more information.

The MTU size is critical for proper network communications. Packets that are too small in length may be lost during transmission. Packets that are too long in length may collide with other packets that are being transmitted. These factors can lead to slower transmission rates and other network problems as packets must then be retransmitted.

To determine the MTU size for a network interface, run the command:

```
# lsattr -El Interface
```

The output will look similar to the following:

```
# lsattr -El tr1
mtu          1492       Maximum IP Packet Size for This Device        True
mtu_4        1492       Maximum IP Packet Size for 4 Mbit ring speed   True
mtu_16       1492       Maximum IP Packet Size for 16 Mbit ring speed  True
mtu_100      1492       Maximum IP Packet Size for 100 Mbit ring speed True
...
```

The **ifconfig** command can adjust the MTU size for a network interface. To change the MTU size, run the command:

```
# ifconfig Interface mtu Value
```

For example, to change the MTU size of tr1 to 12000 bytes in length, run the command:

```
# ifconfig tr1 mtu 12000
```

Note: The MTU size cannot be changed while the interface is in use. All systems that are on the same local area network (LAN) must have the same MTU size, so all systems must change MTU size simultaneously to prevent problems.

10.13 Network security

Network security is a prevalent issue for system administrators. There is a great need for secure connections, trusted networks, and other ways of communications that do not allow for unauthorized system access. This section briefly describes some of the more common ways you can prevent unauthorized access to your systems over your networks.

10.13.1 Trusted and non-trusted processes

A trusted program, or trusted process, is a shell script, a daemon, or a program that meets a particular standard of security. These security standards are set and maintained by the U.S. Department of Defense, which also certifies some trusted programs.

TCP/IP contains several trusted daemons and many non-trusted daemons. The trusted daemons have been tested to ensure that they operate within particular security standards, such as granting users a particular level of access and only permitting users to perform certain tasks.

Examples of trusted daemons are:

► ftpd

► rexecd

► telnetd

The trusted types of daemons require verification and authentication of the user wishing to communicate with the server. Typically, this is done through the use of a login and password.

Examples of non-trusted daemons are:

► rshd

► rlogind

► tftpd

The non-trusted types of daemons do not always require verification or authentication of the user wishing to communicate with the server. A login and password is not necessarily required for the use of these types of daemons. Caution should be used in enabling these processes to run on your system.

10.13.2 The $HOME/.netrc file

The $HOME/.netrc file contains information used by the automatic login feature of the **rexec** and **ftp** commands. It is a hidden file in a user's home directory and must be owned either by the user executing the command or by the root user. If the .netrc file contains a login password, the file's permissions must be set to 600 (read and write by owner only). The login password is in plain text. Even with permissions set to 600, passwords for remote systems are vulnerable to being revealed to any user with root authority.

Entries in the $HOME/.netrc file are stored in the following format (separated by spaces, tabs, or new lines):

machine *HostName*	The *HostName* variable is the name of a remote host. This entry begins the definition of the automatic login process for the specified host. All following entries up to the next machine entry or the end of the file apply to that host.
login *UserName*	The *UserName* variable is the full domain user name for use at the remote host. If this entry is found, the automatic login process initiates a login using the specified name. If this entry is missing, the automatic login process is unsuccessful.
password *Password*	The *Password* variable is the login password to be used. The automatic login process supplies this password to the remote server. A login password must be established at the remote host, and that password must be entered in the .netrc file. Otherwise, the automatic login process is unsuccessful, and the user is prompted for the login password.
account *Password*	The *Password* variable is the account password to be used. If this entry is found, and an account password is required at the remote host, the automatic login process supplies the password to the remote server. If the remote host requires an account password, but this entry is missing, the automatic login process prompts for the account password.
macdef *MacroName*	The *MacroName* variable is the name of an FTP subcommand macro. The macro is defined to contain all of the following FTP subcommands up to the next blank line or the end of the file. If the macro is named init, the **ftp** command executes the macro upon successful completion of the automatic login process. The **rexec** command does not recognize a macdef entry.

A sample $HOME/.netrc file is shown Figure 10-19.

```
$ cat .netrc
machine service.software.ibm.com login anonymous password pw0rd@ macdef init
bin
lcd /ptf/
site exec lfixdist "devices.buc.00004001.rte.4.3.1.1:0:0:202615808:125:IBM:fixdi
stm:0:usrname@hostname"
get /aix/fixes/v4/os/bos.64bit.4.3.1.4.bff bos.64bit.4.3.1.4.bff
get /aix/fixes/v4/os/bos.64bit.4.3.1.4.info bos.64bit.4.3.1.4.info
quit

$ █
```

Figure 10-19 A sample .netrc file

Note: The maximum size of the .netrc file is 4096 bytes. If you need to use more than 4096 bytes, you have to split up your file into multiple parts and write a script to automate functions like FTP jobs.

10.13.3 The /etc/hosts.equiv and $HOME/.rhosts files

The /etc/hosts.equiv file, along with any local $HOME/.rhosts files, defines the hosts (computers on a network) and user accounts that can invoke remote commands on a local host without supplying a password. A user or host that is not required to supply a password is considered trusted, though the daemons that initiate the connections may be nontrusted in nature (for example, rlogind).

When a local host receives a remote command request, the appropriate local daemon first checks the /etc/hosts.equiv file to determine if the request originates with a trusted user or host. For example, if the local host receives a remote login request, the rlogind daemon checks for the existence of a hosts.equiv file on the local host. If the file exists, but does not define the host or user, the system checks the appropriate $HOME/.rhosts file. This file is similar to the /etc/hosts.equiv file, except that it is maintained for individual users.

Note: If a remote command request is made by the root user, the /etc/hosts.equiv file is ignored and only the /.rhosts file is read.

Both files, /etc/hosts.equiv and $HOME/.rhosts, must have permissions denying write access to group and other (600). If either group or other have write access to a file, that file will be ignored. Do not give write permission to the /etc/hosts.equiv file to group and others, as this can lead to security vulnerabilities and undesired user access to the local host.

The format of the /etc/hosts.equiv and $HOME/.rhosts files is as follows:

```
[ + | - ] HostName [ + | - ] UserName or @NetGroup
```

Note: Both /etc/hosts.equiv and $HOME/.rhosts are read top to bottom, so the order of placing entries into these files can change the desired results. The deny, or - (minus sign), statements must precede the accept, or + (plus sign), statements in the lists.

For example, to allow all the users on the hosts toaster and machine to log in to the local host, you would enter:

```
toaster
machine
```

To only allow the user bob to log in from the host machine, you would enter:

```
toaster
machine bob
```

To allow the user lester to log in from any host, you would enter:

```
toaster
machine bob
+ lester
```

To allow all users from the host tron to log in, while requesting users joel and mike for a password to log in, you would enter:

```
toaster
machine bob
+ lester
tron -joel
tron -mike
tron
```

To deny all members of the forum netgroup from logging in automatically, you would enter:

```
toaster
machine bob
+ lester
tron -joel
tron -mike
tron
- @forum
```

> **Note:** Netgroups is a feature of NIS and of AIX 5L Version 5.1 that allows an administrator to easily classify hosts and users into common groups. The use of netgroups is outside the scope of this book. More information on netgroups can be found in the *AIX 5L Version 5.1 System Management Guide: Communications and Networks* that is part of the AIX product documentation.

10.13.4 The securetcpip command

The `securetcpip` command provides enhanced security for the network on a host. It performs the following tasks:

▶ Disables the nontrusted commands and daemons: `rcp`, `rlogin`, `rlogind`, `rsh`, rshd, tftp, and tftpd. The disabled commands and daemons are not deleted; instead, they are changed to mode 0000. You can enable a particular command or daemon by re-establishing a valid mode. The /.netrc file is not used by any programs when the `securetcpip` command has been run on your system.

▶ Adds a TCP/IP security stanza to the /etc/security/config file. The stanza is in the following format:

```
tcpip:
    netrc = ftp,rexec    /* functions disabling netrc */
```

> **Note:** Before running the `securetcpip` command, quiesce the system by logging in as root and executing the `killall` command to stop all network daemons. The `killall` command kills all processes except the calling process. If users are logged in or applications are running, have them exit or finish before executing the `killall` command.

After issuing the `securetcpip` command, shut down and restart your system. All of your TCP/IP commands and network interfaces should be properly configured after the system restarts.

10.13.5 Anonymous FTP

Anonymous FTP is a feature that allows users to transfer files in some file directories on your system through **ftp** without having a unique login for each user. This is a useful tool in areas such as releasing patches for software, when large quantities of users worldwide may need access to a specific system. The user only needs to use the login name *anonymous* and password of *guest* or some other common password convention (typically the user's Internet e-mail ID)

To setup anonymous FTP on a server running AIX 5L Version 5.1, run the script:

```
# /usr/samples/tcpip/anon.ftp
```

This will create the appropriate users and directories for using anonymous FTP.

10.13.6 FTP logging

By default, FTP does not log connections or file transfers from users accessing the system. This can be a security risk when users use anonymous FTP to transfer files to or from your system. To enable FTP logging, do the following:

1. Edit the /etc/syslog.conf file and add the line:

```
daemon.info FileName
```

where *FileName* is the name of the log file that will track FTP activity, both by the anonymous and other user IDs. *FileName* must exist before you perform the next step of this process.

2. Run the command **refresh -s syslogd** to refresh the syslogd daemon.

3. Edit the /etc/inetd.conf file, and modify the line containing ftpd as follows:

```
ftp      stream tcp6   nowait  root    /usr/sbin/ftpd          ftpd -1
```

4. Run the command **refresh -s inetd** to refresh the inetd daemon.

When users use the **ftp** command to access your system, their login and file transfer activity will be logged in *FileName*. This log will look similar to the following:

```
Sep  5 13:56:47 localhost ftpd[17958]: connection from server2.example.ibm.com
at Wed Sep  5 13:56:47 2001
Sep  5 13:56:52 localhost ftpd[17958]: ANONYMOUS FTP LOGIN FROM
server2.example.ibm.com, sampleid@server1.example.ibm.com
Sep  5 13:57:17 localhost ftpd[17958]: FTPD: IMPORT file local testfile, remote
```

In this sample, a user established an anonymous FTP connection from server1.example.ibm.com. As a password, the user provided the e-mail address of sampleid@server1.example.ibm.com. The user used the FTP command **put** to upload the file *testfile* to server2.

FTP logging does not record when a user quits an FTP session. To determine if someone is still logged onto your system, run a **ps -fp** on the PID provided within the brackets ([17958]).

FTP log files will grow in proportion to how many users access your system and how many file transfers take place. We recommend that you monitor the growth of your FTP log to prevent potential system problems.

10.14 The uname command

Apart from the **hostname** command, you can also use the **uname -n** command to display the host name of your system. Without any flags, the **uname** command will display the operating system that your are using.

You can also use the **uname -x** command to display:

► The operating system that your are using

► The host name

► The machine ID number of the hardware running the system

► The release number of the operating system

► The operating system version

► The system model name

A few examples of the use of the **uname** command are shown in Figure 10-20.

```
$ uname
AIX
$ uname -n
rs1800a
$ uname -x
AIX rs1800a 1632719180 3 4 006151514C00
$ ▋
```

Figure 10-20   The uname command

10.15 Basic network problem determination

When a user informs you that a certain system cannot be accessed, check for various network problems. Typically, you will go through these TCP/IP problem determination topics using whichever is applicable to your environment:

► Communication problems

► Name resolution problems

► Routing problems

► Problems with System Resource Controller (SRC) support

► Telnet or rlogin problems

► Configuration problems

► Common problems with network interfaces

► Problems with packet delivery

► Problems with Dynamic Host Configuration Protocol (DHCP)

However, there are other considerations outside the network area that you should check also:

► The server system may be down.

This will usually reveal itself when you check for communication problems. The `ping` command will lead you to the problem system. The whole system may be down or the network interface may be down.

► The paging space may be full.

If a user has logged in, this will be fairly obvious as there is usually a system message stating not enough paging space or not enough memory. However, if a user is trying to `telnet` or `ftp` to the system, there will be time outs as the system cannot create additional processes, or the system may be busy killing processes.

► A file system may be full.

If the user can access the system, but there are problems with certain functions, you should check all areas in the system. If the user cannot start the Web Based System Manager (WSM), the /tmp filesystem may be full.

► A file system may not have been mounted.

Usually, the user will mention losing all his files.

Not all problems are caused by the network and the network function. Make sure you understand your user's problem before concluding that it is a network problem.

10.16 Quiz

The following are additional questions created by the authors to further test your understanding of the topics.

1. Which of the following actions allow a System Administrator to configure anonymous FTP?

   A. `smit ftp`

   B. `/usr/samples/tcpip/anon.ftp`

   C. `startsrc -s ftp -a anonymous`

   D. add the FTP anonymous user using smit

2. A System Administrator is given only one Ethernet network card (en0) in a system, with an IP address of 192.168.1.3. A user wants to host two different initial home pages on the Web server. The System Administrator has verified that the Web server does support multiple IP Addresses. To add another IP address to the already configured interface, which of the following choices should be selected?

    A. `smitty chgenet`

    B. `smitty add_interface`

    C. `ifconfig en0` *newipaddress* `netmask` *netmask* `alias`

    D. This task cannot be accomplished without adding a new Ethernet interface.

3. When a RPC (remote procedural call) server starts up, it registers itself with which of the following daemons?

    A. yp daemons

    B. nfs daemons

    C. inetd daemons

    D. portmap daemon

The following are additional questions created by the authors to further test your understanding of the topics.

1. Which of the following actions will allow the system administrator to stop and restart the TCP/IP daemons manually?

    A. Use the `netstat` command.

    B. Use the SRC utility to stop and restart.

    C. Use the `netconfig` utility menu.

    D. Issue the `rmdev` command on the appropriate network adapter.

2. Two Web servers need to be configured on a single machine that has only one network interface. Each Web server needs to have its own unique IP address. How should an administrator accomplish this?

    A. Use the `smitty alias` command

    B. Add it in /etc/defaults

    C. Use the `newaliases 192.127.10.10` command

    D   Use the `ifconfig en0 alias 192.127.10.10` command

10.16.1 Answers

The following answers are for the assessment quiz questions.

1. B
2. C
3. D

The following answers are for the additional quiz questions.

1. B
2. D

10.17 Exercises

The following exercises provide sample topics for self study. They will help ensure comprehension of this chapter.

1. After installing a new network adapter or after replacing a Token Ring adapter with an Ethernet adapter, what are the steps to restart TCP/IP?
2. Configure a network interface using SMIT.
3. Start and stop TCP/IP daemons using /etc/rc.tcpip and /etc/tcp.clean.
4. Name the SMIT fast paths needed for networking, such as tcpip, route, and others.
5. Change the IP address using SMIT.
6. Describe the inetd, portmap, and other TCP/IP daemons. What errors will users experience when any one of the TCP/IP daemons is not started?
7. What are the errors if the /etc/resolv file is incorrect?
8. How do you add a route?
9. Create and delete an IP alias using the `ifconfig` command.
10. Does ping work without starting TCP/IP?
11. Use the $HOME/.netrc file to eliminate the user login and password prompts for the **rexec** and **ftp** commands.

Network File System administration

The Network File System (NFS) is a distributed file system that allows users to access files and directories of remote servers as if they were local. For example, the user can use operating systems commands to create, remove, read, write, and set file attributes for remote files and directories. NFS is independent of machine types, operating systems, and network architectures through the use of remote procedure calls (RPC). This section discusses the tasks that can be performed by an administrator in an NFS environment.

11.1 NFS services

NFS provides its services through a client-server relationship. The computers that make their file systems, directories, and other resources available for remote access are called *servers*. The act of making file systems available is called exporting. The computers, or the processes they run, that use a server's resources are considered *clients*. Once a client mounts a file system that a server exports, the client can access the individual server files. Access to exported directories can be restricted to specific clients.

The following are a list of terms that are used throughout this discussion:

Server   A computer that makes its file systems, directories, and other resources available for remote access.

Clients   The computers, or their processes, that use a server's resources.

Export   The act of making file systems available to remote clients.

Mount   The act of a client accessing the file systems that a server exports.

The major services provided by NFS are:

Mount   From the /usr/sbin/rpc.mountd daemon on the server and the **/usr/sbin/mount** command on the client. The mountd daemon is a Remote Procedure Call (RPC) that answers a client request to mount a file system. The mountd daemon finds out which file systems are available by reading the /etc/xtab file. In addition, the mountd daemon provides a list of currently mounted file systems and the clients on which they are mounted.

Remote file access From the /usr/sbin/nfsd daemon on the server and the /usr/sbin/biod daemon on the client. Handles client requests for files. The biod daemon runs on all NFS client systems. When a user on a client wants to read or write to a file on a server, the biod daemon sends this request to the server.

Boot parameters Provides boot parameters to SunOS diskless clients from the /usr/sbin/rpc.bootparamd daemon on the server.

PC authentication Provides a user authentication service for PC-NFS from the /usr/sbin/rpc.pcnfsd daemon on the server.

An NFS server is *stateless*. That is, an NFS server does not have to remember any transaction information about its clients. In other words, NFS transactions are atomic: A single NFS transaction corresponds to a single, complete file operation. NFS requires the client to remember any information needed for later NFS use.

Figure 11-1 is an illustration of the NFS configuration discussed in this section.

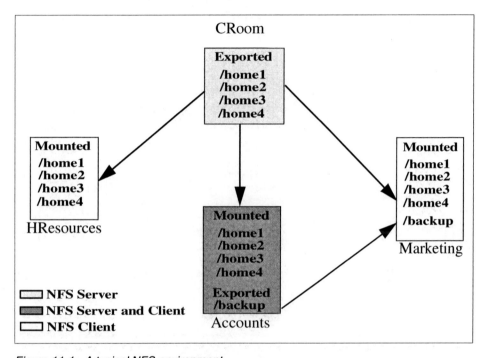

Figure 11-1   A typical NFS environment

The environment illustrated in Figure 11-1 includes two NFS servers and three clients where one system is both a server and a client. The CRoom server exports its directories allowing all other systems to have access to them. The Accounts server shares one directory that only Marketing has access to. The following section references the scenario illustrated and discusses any challenges and tasks that arise while administrating NFS in this environment.

11.2 Planning, installation, and configuration of NFS

There are no specific installation tasks needed for NFS, as the Base Operating System (BOS) Installation also includes the default installation of network services, such as TCP/IP and NFS.

Before starting the configuration of NFS on any of the systems, perform the following tasks:

1. Identify which systems in the network will be servers and which will be clients. As shown in Figure 11-1, CRoom and Accounts are servers, and HResources, Accounts, and Marketing are clients. Note that Accounts is both a client and server.

2. Start the NFS daemons for each system (whether client or server). The NFS daemons, by default, are not started on a newly installed system. When a system is first installed, all of the files are placed on the system, but the steps to activate NFS are not taken. The daemons can be started by:

   − Using the SMIT fast path `smitty mknfs`

   − Using the `mknfs` command to start the NFS daemons immediately, and this should produce the following:

```
# mknfs -N
0513-059 The portmap Subsystem has been started. Subsystem PID is 23734.
Starting NFS services:
0513-059 The biod Subsystem has been started. Subsystem PID is 27264.
0513-059 The nfsd Subsystem has been started. Subsystem PID is 30570.
0513-059 The rpc.mountd Subsystem has been started. Subsystem PID is 28350.
0513-059 The rpc.statd Subsystem has been started. Subsystem PID is 15298.
0513-059 The rpc.lockd Subsystem has been started. Subsystem PID is 30976.
#
```

Table 11-1 lists the most common flags of the `mknfs` command.

Table 11-1   Flags for the mknfs command

Flag	Description
-B	Adds an entry to the inittab file to execute the /etc/rc.nfs file on system restart. The mknfs command also executes the /etc/rc.nfs file immediately to start the NFS daemons. This flag is the default.
-I	Adds an entry to the inittab file to execute the /etc/rc.nfs file on system restart.
-N	Starts the /etc/rc.nfs file to start the NFS daemons immediately. When started this way, the daemons run until the next system restart.

The -B and -I options place an entry in the inittab file so that the /etc/rc.nfs script is run each time the system restarts. This script, in turn, starts all NFS daemons required for a particular system.

Use the following instructions to configure CRoom and Accounts as an NFS server:

1. Start the NFS daemons using SRC if not already started.

The NFS daemons can be started individually or all at once. Use the following command to start NFS daemons individually:

```
startsrc -s daemon
```

where *daemon* is any one of the SRC controlled daemons (See Section 11.4, "NFS files, commands, and daemons reference" on page 319). For example, to start the nfsd daemon:

```
startsrc -s nfsd
```

Use the following command to start all of the NFS daemons:

```
startsrc -g nfs
```

> **Note:** If the /etc/exports file does not exist, the nfsd and the rpc.mountd daemons will not be started. You can create an empty /etc/exports file by running the command **touch /etc/exports**. This will allow the nfsd and the rpc.mountd daemons to start, although no file systems will be exported.

2. Create the exports in the /etc/exports file.

11.2.1 Exporting NFS directories

This section discusses the use of the **exportfs** command.

Exporting an NFS directory using SMIT

To export file systems using SMIT, follow this procedure:

1. Verify that NFS is already running on CRoom and Accounts servers using the command **lssrc -g nfs**. As in the following example, the output should indicate that the nfsd and the rpc.mountd daemons are active. If they are not, start NFS using the instructions in Section 11.2, "Planning, installation, and configuration of NFS" on page 303.

```
# lssrc -g nfs
Subsystem        Group          PID     Status
 biod            nfs            15740   active
 nfsd            nfs            11376   active
 rpc.mountd      nfs            5614    active
 rpc.statd       nfs            16772   active
 rpc.lockd       nfs            15496   active
#
```

2. Use `smitty mknfsexp` to export the directory; the SMIT screen is as shown in Figure 11-2.

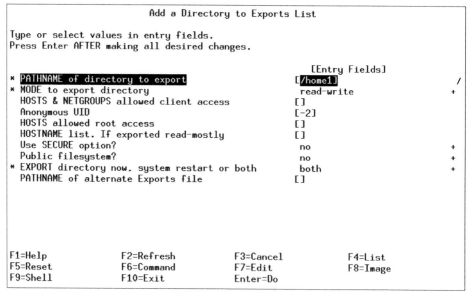

```
                        Add a Directory to Exports List

Type or select values in entry fields.
Press Enter AFTER making all desired changes.

                                                          [Entry Fields]
* PATHNAME of directory to export                      [/home1]                  /
* MODE to export directory                              read-write               +
  HOSTS & NETGROUPS allowed client access               []
  Anonymous UID                                         [-2]
  HOSTS allowed root access                             []
  HOSTNAME list. If exported read-mostly                []
  Use SECURE option?                                     no                      +
  Public filesystem?                                     no                      +
* EXPORT directory now, system restart or both          both                    +
  PATHNAME of alternate Exports file                    []




F1=Help            F2=Refresh          F3=Cancel          F4=List
F5=Reset           F6=Command          F7=Edit            F8=Image
F9=Shell           F10=Exit            Enter=Do
```

Figure 11-2   Adding a directory to the export list

3. For CRoom Server, specify /home1, and on Accounts /backup in the PATHNAME of directory to export field, set the MODE to export directory field to read-write, and set the EXPORT directory now, system restart, or both field to both.

4. Specify any other optional characteristics you want, or accept the default values by leaving the remaining fields as they are. For this illustration, for Accounts, set the Hosts and NetGroups allowed client access field to Marketing and keep the default for everything else.

5. When you have finished making your changes, SMIT updates the /etc/exports file. If the /etc/exports file does not exist, it will be created.

6. Repeat steps 3 through 5 for directories /home2, /home3, /home4 on CRoom. Accounts is only exporting /backup; there is no need to do any other exports.

7. If NFS is currently running on the servers, enter:

   `/usr/sbin/exportfs -a`

   The -a option tells the **exportfs** command to send all information in the /etc/exports file to the kernel. If NFS is not running, start NFS using the instructions in Section 11.2, "Planning, installation, and configuration of NFS" on page 303.

8. Verify that all file systems have been exported properly as follows:

For the CRoom Server:

```
# showmount -e CRoom
export list for CRoom:
/home1      (everyone)
/home2      (everyone)
/home3      (everyone)
/home4      (everyone)
#
```

For the Accounts Server:

```
# showmount -e Accounts
export list for Accounts:
/backup Marketing
#
```

Exporting an NFS directory using a text editor

To export file systems using a text editor, follow this procedure:

1. Open the /etc/exports file with your favorite text editor.

   ```
   vi /etc/exports
   ```

2. Create an entry for each directory to be exported by using the full path name of the directory as shown in Figure 11-3.

```
/home1
/home2
/home3
/home4
~
~
~
~
~
~
~
~
~
~
~
~
~
~
~
~
~
~
~
~
"/etc/exports" 4 lines, 28 characters
```

Figure 11-3   Content of /etc/exports for CRoom server

3. List each directory to be exported starting in the left margin. No directory should include any other directory that is already exported. Save and close the /etc/exports file.

4. If NFS is currently running on the servers, enter:

```
/usr/sbin/exportfs -a
```

Exporting an NFS directory temporarily

A file system can be exported when needed, and as such, does not change the /etc/exports file. This is done by entering:

```
exportfs -i /dirname
```

where /dirname is the name of the file system you want to export. The **exportfs -i** command specifies that the /etc/exports file is not to be checked for the specified directory, and all options are taken directly from the command line.

For each system that is to be a client (HResources, Accounts, and Marketing), the following steps will ensure that they have access to directories and files on the CRoom and Accounts Servers.

1. Verify that NFS is the default remote file system. If this is not done, you will need to specify the -v nfs flag when using the **mount** command. Using a text editor, open the /etc/vfs file and search for the following entries:

```
%defaultvfs jfs nfs
nfs 2 /sbin/helpers/nfsmnthelp none remote
```

If pound signs (#) appear at the beginning of the previous lines, delete the pound signs.

2. Save and close the /etc/vfs file.

3. Start NFS using the instructions in Section 11.2, "Planning, installation, and configuration of NFS" on page 303.

4. Go to Section 11.2.3, "Mounting an NFS directory" on page 309.

11.2.2 Unexporting an NFS directory

You can unexport an NFS directory by using one of the following procedures:

► To unexport an NFS directory using SMIT:

a. On the CRoom Server, enter the following command to remove /home4 export:

```
smitty rmnfsexp
```

b. Enter /home4 in the PATHNAME of exported directory to be removed field.

The directory is now removed from the /etc/exports file and is unexported.

▶ To unexport an NFS directory using a text editor:

a. Open the /etc/exports file with a text editor.

b. Find the entry for the directory you wish to unexport, that is, /home4, and then delete that line.

c. Save and close the /etc/exports file.

d. If NFS is currently running, enter:

```
exportfs -u dirname
```

where *dirname* is the full path name of the directory (/home4) you just deleted from the /etc/exports file.

11.2.3 Mounting an NFS directory

There are three types of NFS mounts: Predefined, explicit, and automatic.

Predefined mounts are specified in the /etc/filesystems file. Each stanza (or entry) in this file defines the characteristics of a mount, as shown in Figure 11-4.

```
/home1:
        dev          = "/home1"
        vfs          = nfs
        nodename     = CRoom
        mount        = true
        options      = bg,hard,intr
        account      = false
```

Figure 11-4   Example NFS stanza in the /etc/filesystems file

Data, such as the host name, remote path, local path, and any mount options, are listed in this stanza. Predefined mounts should be used when certain mounts are always required for proper operation of a client.

Explicit mounts serve the needs of the root user. Explicit mounts are usually done for short periods of time when there is a requirement for occasional unplanned mounts. Explicit mounts can also be used if a mount is required for special tasks, and that mount should not be generally available on the NFS client. These mounts are usually fully qualified on the command line by using the **mount** command with all needed information.

Explicit mounts do not require updating the /etc/filesystems file. File systems mounted explicitly remain mounted unless explicitly unmounted with the **umount** command or until the system is restarted.

Automatic mounts are controlled by the **automount** command, which causes the AutoFS kernel extension to monitor specified directories for activity. If a program or user attempts to access a directory that is not currently mounted, then AutoFS intercepts the request, arranges for the mount of the file system, and then services the request.

NFS mounting process

Clients access files on the server by first mounting a server's exported directories. When a client mounts a directory, it does not make a copy of that directory. Rather, the mounting process uses a series of remote procedure calls to enable a client to access the directories on the server transparently. The following describes the mounting process:

1. When the server starts, the /etc/rc.nfs script runs the **exportfs** command, which reads the server /etc/exports file and then tells the kernel which directories are to be exported and which access restrictions they require.

2. The rpc.mountd daemon and several nfsd daemons (eight, by default) are then started by the /etc/rc.nfs script.

3. When the client starts, the /etc/rc.nfs script starts several biod daemons (eight, by default), which forward client mount requests to the appropriate server.

4. Then the /etc/rc.nfs script executes the **mount** command, which reads the file systems listed in the /etc/filesystems file.

5. The **mount** command locates one or more servers that export the information the client wants and sets up communication between itself and that server. This process is called *binding*.

6. The **mount** command then requests that one or more servers allow the client to access the directories in the client /etc/filesystems file.

7. The server rpc.mountd daemon receives the client mount requests and either grants or denies them. If the requested directory is available to that client, the rpc.mountd daemon sends the client's kernel an identifier called a *file handle*.

8. The client kernel then ties the file handle to the mount point (a directory) by recording certain information in a mount record.

Once the file system is mounted, the client can perform file operations. When the client does a file operation the biod daemon sends the file handle to the server, where the file is read by one of the nfsd daemons to process the file request. Assuming the client has access to perform the requested file operation, the nfsd daemon returns the necessary information to the client's biod daemon.

The following procedure helps to complete the scenario shown in Figure 11-1 on page 303.

1. On HResources, establish the local mount point for /home1 on server CRoom using the **mkdir** command.

   ```
   mkdir /home1
   ```

   This directory should be empty. This mount point can be created like any other directory, and no special attributes are needed for this directory.

   > **Note:** The mount points for all NFS mounts must exist on your system before you can mount a file system with one exception. If the automount daemon is used, it may not be necessary to create mount points. See "Mounting an NFS directory automatically" on page 315.

2. On HResources, establish and mount the predefined mounts by following the instructions in "Establishing predefined NFS mounts" on page 311.

Establishing predefined NFS mounts

You can establish predefined NFS mounts using one of the following procedures.

> **Note:** Define the bg (background) and intr (interruptible) options in the /etc/filesystems file when establishing a predefined mount that is to be mounted during system startup. Mounts that are non-interruptible and running in the foreground can hang the client if the network or server is down when the client system starts up. If a client cannot access the network or server, the user must start the machine again in maintenance mode and edit the appropriate mount requests.

To establish predefined mounts through SMIT (Figure 11-5 on page 312), use the following command:

```
smitty mknfsmnt
```

```
                         Add a File System for Mounting

Type or select values in entry fields.
Press Enter AFTER making all desired changes.

[TOP]                                                     [Entry Fields]
* PATHNAME of mount point                                 [ ]                    /
* PATHNAME of remote directory                            [ ]
* HOST where remote directory resides                     [ ]
  Mount type NAME                                         [ ]
* Use SECURE mount option?                                no                     +
* MOUNT now, add entry to /etc/filesystems or both?       now                    +
* /etc/filesystems entry will mount the directory         no                     +
  on system RESTART.
* MODE for this NFS file system                           read-write             +
* ATTEMPT mount in foreground or background               background             +
  NUMBER of times to attempt mount                        [ ]                    #
  Buffer SIZE for read                                    [ ]                    #
  Buffer SIZE for writes                                  [ ]                    #
[MORE...26]


F1=Help            F2=Refresh          F3=Cancel            F4=List
F5=Reset           F6=Command          F7=Edit              F8=Image
F9=Shell           F10=Exit            Enter=Do
```

Figure 11-5   Add a File System for Mounting screen

Specify values in this screen for each mount you want predefined. You must
specify a value for each required field (those marked with an asterisk (*) in the
left margin). You may specify values for the other fields or accept their default
values. This method creates an entry in the /etc/filesystems file for the desired
mount and attempts the mount.

To establish the NFS default mounts by editing the /etc/filesystems file (only use
this method under special circumstances), perform the following:

1. Open the /etc/filesystems file on HResources with a text editor. Add entries for
   each of the remote file systems that you want mounted when the system is
   started. For example:

   /home1:
   dev = /home1
   mount = false
   vfs = nfs
   nodename = CRoom
   options = ro,soft
   type = nfs_mount

This stanza directs the system to mount the /home1 remote directory over the local mount point of the same name. The file system is mounted as read-only (ro). Because it is also mounted as soft, an error is returned in the event the server does not respond. By specifying the type parameter as nfs_mount, the system attempts to mount the /home1 file system (along with any other file systems that are specified in the type = nfs_mount group) when the **mount -t nfs_mount** command is issued.

The following example stanza directs the system to mount the /home2 file system at system startup time. If the mount fails, the bg option tells the system to continue attempting the mount in the background.

```
/home2:
dev = /home2
mount = true
vfs = nfs
nodename = CRoom
options = ro,soft,bg
type = nfs_mount
```

Note: See "Parameters" on page 316 for additional parameters.

2. Remove any directory entries that you do not want to mount automatically at system startup.

3. Save and close the file.

4. Run the **mount -a** command to mount all the directories specified in the /etc/filesystems file.

5. On Marketing, repeat mount for /backup directory from Accounts

The NFS directory is now ready to use.

Mounting an NFS directory explicitly

To mount an NFS directory explicitly, use the following procedure:

1. Verify that the NFS server has exported the directory, using:

```
showmount -e ServerName
```

For Server CRoom:

```
# showmount -e CRoom
export list for CRoom:
/home1     (everyone)
/home2     (everyone)
/home3     (everyone)
/home4     (everyone)
#
```

where *ServerName* is the name of the NFS server. This command displays the names of the directories currently exported from the NFS server. If the directory you want to mount is not listed, export the directory from the server.

2. Establish the local mount point using the `mkdir` command. For NFS to complete a mount successfully, a directory that acts as the mount point of an NFS mount must be present. This directory should be empty. This mount point can be created like any other directory, and no special attributes are needed for this directory.

3. On the HResources machine, enter the following SMIT fast path:

   `smitty mknfsmnt`

4. Make changes to the following fields that are appropriate for your network configuration. Your configuration may not require completing all of the entries on this screen.
   - PATHNAME of mount point.
   - PATHNAME of remote directory.
   - HOST where remote directory resides.
   - MOUNT now, add entry to /etc/filesystems
   - /etc/filesystems entry will mount the directory on system RESTART.
   - MODE for this NFS.

   Note: If you are using the ASCII SMIT interface, press the Tab key to change to the correct value for each field, but do not press Enter until you get to step 7.

5. Use the default values for the remaining entries or change them depending on your NFS configuration.

6. When you finish making all the changes on this screen, SMIT mounts the NFS.

7. When the Command: field shows the OK status, exit SMIT.

The NFS is now ready to use.

Mounting an NFS directory automatically

AutoFS relies on the use of the **automount** command to propagate the automatic mount configuration information to the AutoFS kernel extension and start the automountd daemon. Through this configuration propagation, the extension automatically and transparently mounts file systems whenever a file or a directory within that file system is opened. The extension informs the automountd daemon of mount and unmount requests, and the automountd daemon actually performs the requested service.

Because the name-to-location binding is dynamic within the automountd daemon, updates to a Network Information Service (NIS) map used by the automountd daemon are transparent to the user. Also, there is no need to pre-mount shared file systems for applications that have hard-coded references to files and directories, nor is there a need to maintain records of which hosts must be mounted for particular applications.

AutoFS allows file systems to be mounted as needed. With this method of mounting directories, all file systems do not need to be mounted all of the time, only those being used are mounted.

For example, to mount the /backup NFS directory automatically:

1. Verify that the NFS server has exported the directory by entering:

   ```
   # showmount -e Accounts
   export list for Accounts:
   /backup Marketing
   #
   ```

   This command displays the names of the directories currently exported from the NFS server.

2. Create an AutoFS map file. AutoFS will mount and unmount the directories specified in this map file. For example, suppose you want to use AutoFS to mount the /backup directory as needed from the Accounts server onto the remote /backup directory. In this example, the map file name is /tmp/mount.map. An example of a map file can be found in /usr/samples/nfs.

3. Ensure that the AutoFS kernel extension is loaded and the automountd daemon is running. This can be accomplished in two ways:

   a. Using SRC, enter:

      ```
      lssrc -s automountd
      ```

      If the automountd subsystem is not running, issue: **startsrc -s automountd**

b. Using the **automount** command, issue **/usr/sbin/automount -v**. Define the map file using the command line interface by entering:

```
/usr/sbin/automount -v /backup /tmp/mount.map
```

where /backup is the AutoFS mount point on the client. Now, if a user runs the **cd /backup** command, the AutoFS kernel extension will intercept access to the directory and will issue a remote procedure call to the automountd daemon, which will mount the /backup directory and then allow the **cd** command to complete.

4. To stop the automountd, issue the **stopsrc -s automountd** command.

If, for some reason, the automountd daemon was started without the use of SRC, issue:

```
kill automountd_PID
```

where automountd_PID is the process ID of the automountd daemon. (Running the **ps -e** command will display the process ID of the automountd daemon.) The **kill** command sends a SIGTERM signal to the automountd daemon.

Parameters

The parameters required for stanzas pertaining to NFS mounts are:

dev=*file_system_name*   Specifies the path name of the remote file system being mounted.

mount=[true|false]   If true, specifies that the NFS will be mounted when the system boots. If false, the NFS will not be mounted when the system boots.

nodename=*hostname*   Specifies the host machine on which the remote file system resides.

vfs=nfs   Specifies that the virtual file system being mounted is an NFS.

If you do not set the following options, the kernel automatically sets them to the following default values:

► biods=6

► fg

► retry=10000

► rsize=8192

► wsize=8192

► timeo=7

► retrans=3

- ▶ port=NFS_PORT
- ▶ hard
- ▶ secure=off
- ▶ acregmin=3
- ▶ acregmax=60
- ▶ acdirmin=30
- ▶ acdirmax=60

11.3 Administration of NFS servers and clients

In this section, we will discuss the operations performed by a system administrator working with NFS. The topics being discussed are:

- ▶ The status of the NFS daemons
- ▶ Changing exported NFSs
- ▶ Using the **unmount** command

11.3.1 Getting the Current Status of the NFS Daemons

You can get the current status of the NFS daemons individually or all at once. To get the current status of the NFS daemons individually, enter:

```
lssrc -s daemon
```

where *daemon* is any one of the SRC controlled daemons. For example, to get the current status of the rpc.lockd daemon, enter:

```
lssrc -s rpc.lockd
```

To get the current status of all NFS daemons at once, enter:

```
lssrc -g nfs
```

11.3.2 Changing an exported file system

This section explains how you can change an exported NFS.

Changing an exported NFS directory using SMIT

The following procedure will guide you through changing an exported file system using SMIT.

1. Unexport the file system on the CRoom server by entering:

   ```
   exportfs -u /dirname
   ```

   where */dirname* is the name of the file system you want to change. In this case, /home3.

2. On the CRoom server, enter:

   ```
   smitty chnfsexp
   ```

   The resulting screen is shown in Figure 11-6.

3. Enter the appropriate path name in the PATHNAME of exported directory field. In this case, /home3.

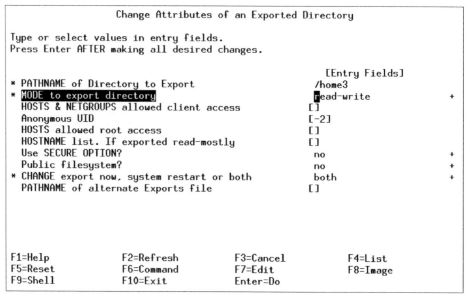

```
                   Change Attributes of an Exported Directory

Type or select values in entry fields.
Press Enter AFTER making all desired changes.

                                                       [Entry Fields]
* PATHNAME of Directory to Export                      /home3
* MODE to export directory                             read-write            +
  HOSTS & NETGROUPS allowed client access              []
  Anonymous UID                                        [-2]
  HOSTS allowed root access                            []
  HOSTNAME list. If exported read-mostly               []
  Use SECURE OPTION?                                   no                    +
  Public filesystem?                                   no                    +
* CHANGE export now, system restart or both            both                  +
  PATHNAME of alternate Exports file                   []




F1=Help            F2=Refresh         F3=Cancel          F4=List
F5=Reset           F6=Command         F7=Edit            F8=Image
F9=Shell           F10=Exit           Enter=Do
```

Figure 11-6   Change the Attributes of an Exported Directory

Make whatever changes you need then press Enter.

4. Exit SMIT.

5. Re-export the file system by entering:

```
exportfs /dirname
```

where */dirname* is the name of the file system you just changed, in this case /home3.

Changing an exported NFS directory using a text editor

The following procedure will guide you through changing an exported file system using a text editor.

1. Unexport the file system by entering:

```
exportfs -u /dirname
```

where */dirname* is the name of the file system you want to change, in this case /home3.

2. Open the /etc/exports file with your favorite text editor.

3. Make whatever changes you want.

4. Save and close the /etc/exports file.

5. Re-export the file system by entering:

```
exportfs /dirname
```

where */dirname* is the name of the file system you just changed, in this case /home3.

11.3.3 Unmounting a mounted file system

To unmount an explicitly or automatically mounted NFS directory, enter **umount** **/directory** or **unmount /directory**, for example:

```
umount /backup
```

The **rmfs** command can be used to remove any file systems you created.

11.4 NFS files, commands, and daemons reference

In this section, the key NFS files, commands, and daemons are defined.

11.4.1 List of NFS Files

The following is a list of key NFS files.

/etc/bootparams   Lists servers that diskless clients can use for booting.

/etc/exports   Lists the directories that can be exported to NFS clients.

/etc/networks	Contains information about networks on the Internet network.
/etc/pcnfsd.conf	Options for the rpc.pcnfsd daemon.
/etc/rpc	Contains database information for Remote Procedure Call (RPC) programs.
/etc/xtab	Lists directories that are currently exported.
/etc/filesystems	Lists all file systems that can potentially be mounted and their mounting configuration.

List of NFS commands

The following is a list of NFS Commands.

chnfs	Starts a specified number of biod and nfsd daemons.
mknfs	Configures the system to run NFS and starts NFS daemons.
nfso	Configures NFS network options.
automount	Mounts an NFS automatically.
chnfsexp	Changes the attributes of an NFS-exported directory.
chnfsmnt	Changes the attributes of an NFS-mounted directory.
exportfs	Exports and unexports directories to NFS clients.
lsnfsexp	Displays the characteristics of directories that are exported with NFS.
lsnfsmnt	Displays the characteristics of mounted NFS systems.
mknfsexp	Exports a directory using NFS.
mknfsmnt	Mounts a directory using NFS.
rmnfs	Changes the configuration to stop the NFS daemons.
rmnfsexp	Removes NFS-exported directories from a server's list of exports.
rmnfsmnt	Removes NFS-mounted file systems from a client's list of mounts.

List of NFS daemons

The following is a list of NFS Locking daemons.

| /usr/sbin/rpc.lockd | Processes lock requests through the RPC package. |
| /usr/sbin/rpc.statd | Provides crash-and-recovery functions for the locking services on NFS. |

The following is a list of NFS Network Service daemons and utilities.

/usr/sbin/biod Sends the client's read and write requests to the server. The biod daemon is SRC controlled.

/usr/sbin/rpc.mountd Answers requests from clients for file system mounts. The mountd daemon is SRC controlled.

/usr/sbin/nfsd Starts the daemons that handle a client's request for file system operations. nfsd is SRC controlled.

/usr/sbin/nfsstat Displays information about a machine's ability to receive calls.

/usr/sbin/portmap Maps RPC program numbers to Internet port numbers. portmap is inetd Controlled.

/usr/bin/rpcgen Generates C code to implement an RPC protocol.

/usr/bin/rpcinfo Reports the status of RPC servers.

/usr/sbin/rpc.rstatd Returns performance statistics obtained from the kernel.

/usr/bin/showmount Displays a list of all clients that have mounted remote file systems.

/usr/sbin/rpc.pcnfsd Handles service requests from PC-NFS clients.

11.5 NFS problem determination

Troubleshooting NFS problems involves a strategy for tracking NFS problems, recognizing NFS-related error messages, and selecting the appropriate solutions. When tracking down an NFS problem, isolate each of the three main points of failure to determine which is not working: The server, the client, or the network itself.

11.5.1 Identifying NFS problems checklist

If a client is having NFS trouble, perform the following tasks:

1. Verify that the network connections are functioning properly.

2. Verify that the inetd, portmap, and biod daemons are running on the client (see Section 11.3.1, "Getting the Current Status of the NFS Daemons" on page 317).

3. Verify that a valid mount point exists on the client system for the file system to be mounted. For more information, see "Establishing predefined NFS mounts" on page 311.

4. Verify that the server is up and running, by executing the following command at the shell prompt of the client machine:

```
/usr/bin/rpcinfo -p server_name
```

where *server_name* is the name of the server being verified.

If the server is up, a list of programs, versions, protocols, and port numbers is displayed similar to the following:

```
program  vers proto    port
100000    2   tcp      111   portmapper
100000    2   udp      111   portmapper
100005    1   udp     1025   mountd
100001    1   udp     1030   rstatd
100001    2   udp     1030   rstatd
100001    3   udp     1030   rstatd
100002    1   udp     1036   rusersd
100002    2   udp     1036   rusersd
100008    1   udp     1040   walld
100012    1   udp     1043   sprayd
100005    1   tcp      694   mountd
100003    2   udp     2049   nfs
100024    1   udp      713   status
100024    1   tcp      715   status
100021    1   tcp      716   nlockmgr
100021    1   udp      718   nlockmgr
100021    3   tcp      721   nlockmgr
100021    3   udp      723   nlockmgr
100020    1   udp      726   llockmgr
100020    1   tcp      728   llockmgr
100021    2   tcp      731   nlockmgr
```

If a similar response is not returned, log in to the server at the server console and check the status of the NFS daemons by following the instructions in Section 11.3.1, "Getting the Current Status of the NFS Daemons" on page 317.

5. Verify that the mountd, portmap, and nfsd daemons are running on the NFS server by entering the following commands at the client shell prompt:

- **/usr/bin/rpcinfo -u *server_name* mount.**
  As shown in the following example:

```
# /usr/bin/rpcinfo -u CRoom mount
program 100005 version 1 ready and waiting
program 100005 version 2 ready and waiting
program 100005 version 3 ready and waiting
#
```

- **/usr/bin/rpcinfo -u *server_name* portmap.**
  As shown in the following example:

```
# /usr/bin/rpcinfo -u CRoom portmap
program 100000 version 2 ready and waiting
program 100000 version 3 ready and waiting
program 100000 version 4 ready and waiting
#
```

- **/usr/bin/rpcinfo -u *server_name* nfs.**
  As shown in the following example:

```
# /usr/bin/rpcinfo -u CRoom nfs
program 100003 version 2 ready and waiting
program 100003 version 3 ready and waiting
#
```

The program numbers correspond to the commands, respectively, as shown in step 4. If a similar response is not returned, log in to the server at the server console and check the status of the daemons by following the instructions in Section 11.3.1, "Getting the Current Status of the NFS Daemons" on page 317.

6. Verify that the /etc/exports file on the server lists the name of the file system that the client wants to mount and that the file system is exported. Do this by entering the command:

```
showmount -e server_name
```

This command will list all the file systems currently exported by the server_name.

11.5.2 Checking network connections

If the biod daemons are working, check the network connections. The **nfsstat** command determines whether you are dropping packets. Use the **nfsstat -c** and **nfsstat -s** commands to determine if the client or server is retransmitting large blocks. Retransmissions are always a possibility due to lost packets or busy servers. A retransmission rate of 5 percent is considered high.

The probability of retransmissions can be reduced by changing the communication adapter transmit queue parameters (xmt_que_size), or **no** settings, to name two. SMIT or the **chdev** and **no** commands can be used to change these parameters.

11.5.3 NFS error messages

The following sections explain error codes that can be generated while using NFS.

Hard-mounted and soft-mounted file problems

When the network or server has problems, programs that access hard-mounted remote files fail differently from those that access soft-mounted remote files.

If a server fails to respond to a hard-mount request, NFS prints the message:

```
NFS server hostname not responding, still trying
```

If a server fails to respond to a soft-mount request, NFS prints the message:

```
Connection timed out
```

Bad sendreply error message

Insufficient transmit buffers on your network can cause the following error message:

```
nfs_server: bad sendreply
```

To increase transmit buffers, use the SMIT fast path **smitty commodev**. Then select your adapter type and increase the number of transmit buffers.

Server not responding

Use the procedure in Section 11.5.1, "Identifying NFS problems checklist" on page 321 to troubleshoot this error. The error usually occurs if the NFS daemons have not been started or have been stopped. If the mountd or the nfsd daemons were not started or were stopped on the server, then when a client tries to mount an exported file system, an 1831-010 error message is displayed.

For example, if the rpc.mountd daemon dies after starting, and this error is received at a client machine, then do the following:

1. **Telnet** to the server and log in as root.

2. **cd** to the /etc directory

3. Enter **stopsrc -g nfs**.

4. Enter **stopsrc -s portmap**.

5. Enter `rm -rf state sm sm.bak xtab rmtab`.

6. Enter `startsrc -s portmap`.

7. Enter `startsrc -g nfs`.

8. Enter `exportfs -a`.

9. `showmount -e` *servername*.

The `rm -rf` command clears the mountd files that may be too large for mountd to handle. If this procedure does not work, then refer to Section 11.5, "NFS problem determination" on page 321.

Remote mounting errors

The following list provides common mounting errors and their probable causes.

A remote mounting process can fail in several ways. The error messages associated with mounting failures are as follows:

1. `mount: ... already mounted`

   The file system that you are trying to mount is already mounted.

2. `mount: ... not found in /etc/filesystems`

   The specified file system or directory name cannot be matched.

   If you issue the **mount** command with either a directory or file system name but not both, the command looks in the /etc/filesystems file for an entry whose file system or directory field matches the argument. If the **mount** command finds an entry, such as the following:

   ```
   /danger.src:
   dev=/usr/src
   nodename = danger
   type = nfs
   mount = false
   ```

   then it performs the mount as though you had entered the following at the command line:

   ```
   /usr/sbin/mount -n danger -o rw,hard /usr/src /danger.src
   ```

3. If you receive the following message:

   ```
   mount... not in hosts database
   ```

   a. On a network without Network Information Service (NIS), this message indicates that the host specified to the **mount** command is not in the /etc/hosts file. On a network running NIS, the message indicates that NIS could not find the host name in the /etc/hosts database or that the NIS ypbind daemon on your machine has terminated. If the /etc/resolv.conf file exists, so that a name server is being used for host name resolution, there may be a problem in the named database.

Check the spelling and the syntax in your **mount** command. If the command is correct, and your network does not run NIS, and you only get this message for this host name, check the entry in the /etc/hosts file.

b. If your network is running NIS, make sure that the ypbind daemon is running by entering the following at the command line:

```
ps -ef | grep ypbind
```

You should see an entry for the ypbind daemon. Try using the **rlogin** command to log in remotely to another machine, or use the **rcp** command to remote-copy something to another machine. If this also fails, your ypbind daemon is probably stopped or hung.

If you only get this message for this host name, you should check the /etc/hosts entry on the NIS server.

4. `mount: ... server not responding: port mapper failure - RPC timed out`

Either the server you are trying to mount from is down, or its port mapper is stopped or hung. Try restarting the inetd, portmap, and ypbind daemons.

If you cannot log in to the server remotely with the **rlogin** command, but the server is up, you should check the network connection by trying to log in remotely to some other machine. You should also check the server's network connection.

5. `1831-019 mount: ... server not responding: program not registered`

This means that the **mount** command got through to the port mapper, but the rpc.mountd NFS mount daemon was not registered.

6. `mount: access denied...`

Your machine name is not in the export list for the file system you are trying to mount from the server.

You can get a list of the server's exported file systems by running the following command at the command line:

```
showmount -e host_name
```

If the file system you want is not in the list, or your machine name or netgroup name is not in the user list for the file system, log in to the server and check the /etc/exports file for the correct file system entry. A file system name that appears in the /etc/exports file, but not in the output from the **showmount** command, indicates a failure in the mountd daemon. Either the daemon could not parse that line in the file, it could not find the directory, or the directory name was not a locally mounted directory. If the /etc/exports file looks correct and your network runs NIS, check the server's ypbind daemon. It may be stopped or hung.

7. `mount: ...: Permission denied`

This message is a generic indication that some part of authentication failed on the server. It may be that, as in the previous example, you are not in the export list, the server could not recognize your machine's ypbind daemon, or that the server does not accept the identity you provided.

Check the server's /etc/exports file and, if applicable, the ypbind daemon. In this case, you can just change your host name with the **hostname** command and retry the **mount** command.

8. `mount: ...: Not a directory`

Either the remote path or the local path is not a directory. Check the spelling in your command, and try to run it on both the remote and local paths.

9. `mount: ...: You are not allowed`

You must have root authority or be a member of the system group to run the **mount** command on your machine, because it affects the file system for all users on that machine. NFS mounts and unmounts are only allowed for root users and members of the system group.

11.6 Quiz

The following certification assessment question helps verify your understanding of the topics discussed in this chapter.

1. An AIX system administrator decides to experiment with NFS. She exports /home and /var, two file systems from a system called *pluto*. The system administrator now is on system called *mars*, another AIX machine on the same subnet as pluto. She now wishes to mount the exported file systems from pluto onto mars. Which of the following commands will she use to view the export list of 'pluto'?

A. **exportlist pluto**

B. **rpcinfo -p pluto**

C. **showmount -e mars**

D. **showmount -e pluto**

The following are additional questions created by the authors to further test your understanding of the topics.

1. A system administrator has been working on a project for the last couple of months that requires writing different scripts on Server A. These scripts, which have been run nightly, have been collecting data within log files in a journaled file system called /project22. The system administrator would now like to access this JFS from a remote server called Server B.

   The system administrator has issued the command `lssrc -g nfs` and discovered that the daemons are inoperative on Server A. Which of the following actions should be performed to correct this situation?

   A. Run the `nfs.start` command.

   B. Run the `startsrc -g nfs` command.

   C. Run the `refresh -s nfsd` command.

   D. Log out and then log back into the system.

2. The same scenario from question one still applies.

   Which of the following actions should be performed by the system administrator to give Server B access to Server A's file system?

   A. Run the `chfs` command on Server A.

   B. Run the `chfs` command on Server B.

   C. Run the `exportfs` command on Server A.

   D. Run the `exportfs` command on Server B.

11.6.1 Answers

The following answer is for the assessment quiz questions.

1. D

The following answers are for the additional quiz questions.

1. B
2. C

11.7 Exercises

The following exercises provide sample topics for self study. They will help ensure comprehension of this chapter.

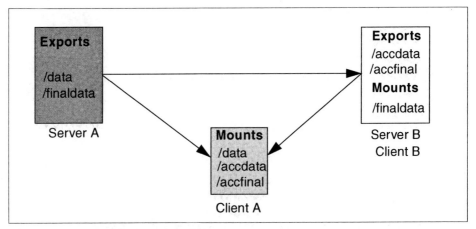

Figure 11-7   Exhibit for NFS Exercises

1. You are required to recreate the environment in Figure 11-7. Take into consideration the following:
   - Client A and Client B are allowed access to the /finaldata directory.
   - /data and /accdata are predefined mounts. Use a text editor to create the /data mount in the /etc/filesystems file.
   - /finaldata is an explicit mount.
   - /accfinal is an automatic mount.
   - On Client A /data and /accdata are mounted over mount point /user/data and /user/accdata, respectively.
2. Determine the availability of NFS on each system.
3. From Client A, look at the directories exported on Server A and B, respectively.
4. Unexport /accfinal from Server B. Refresh the NFS daemons on Server B.
5. Unmount /finaldata from Client B.
6. Disallow Client A access to /finaldata on Server A.
7. Determine all automatically mounted file systems.
8. Stop NFS daemon on Server A. From Client A, try to access /data on Server A. Make note of any messages displayed. Restart the NFS daemons on Server A. Retry accessing the /data export from Client A.

## 12

System performance

For any system, continued customer satisfaction and purchasing decisions depend strongly on performance. Part of the job of the system administrator is performance analysis: To understand the system behavior and identify the usage of resources.

This section provides information on concepts, tools, and techniques for assessing and tuning the performance of AIX on RS/6000 systems. Topics covered include assessment of CPU use, memory use, disk I/O, and communications I/O. The concepts, tools, and techniques discussed in this section are not intended to be a total list, and, as such, you are encouraged to seek additional information from the appropriate AIX product documentation.

12.1 System dynamics and workload

An accurate and complete definition of the system's workload is critical to predicting or understanding its performance. A difference in workload can cause far more variation in the measured performance of a system than differences in CPU clock speed or RAM size. The workload definition must include not only the type and rate of requests to the system but also the exact software packages and in-house application programs to be executed.

Whenever possible, normal usage of existing applications should be observed to get authentic, real-world measurements of the rates at which users interact with their workstations or terminals.

Make sure that you include the work load that your system is doing behind the scenes. For example, if your system contains file systems that are NFS-mounted and frequently accessed by other systems, handling those accesses is probably a significant fraction of the overall workload even though your system is not officially a *server*.

12.1.1 System dynamics

It is not enough to have the most efficient programs. In many cases, the actual programs being run are outside of the control of the person who is responsible for meeting the organization's performance objectives. Once the application programs have been acquired or implemented as efficiently as possible, further improvement in the overall performance of the system becomes a matter of system tuning. The main components that are subject to system-level tuning are:

Fixed disk The Logical Volume Manager (LVM) controls the placement of file systems and paging spaces on the disk, which can significantly affect the amount of seek latency the system experiences. The disk device drivers control the order in which I/O requests are acted on.

Real memory The Virtual Memory Manager (VMM) controls the pool of free real-memory frames and determines when and from whom to steal frames to replenish the pool.

Running thread The scheduler determines which dispatchable entity should receive control next. (In AIX Version 4, the dispatchable entity changes from a process to a thread.)

Communications I/O Depending on the type of workload and the type of communications link, it may be necessary to tune one or more of the communications device drivers, TCP/IP, or NFS.

12.1.2 Classes of workloads

Workloads tend to fall naturally into a small number of classes. The types that follow are sometimes used to categorize systems. However, since a single system is often called upon to process multiple classes, *workload* seems more apt in the context of performance.

Workstation   A workload that consists of a single user submitting work through the native keyboard and receiving results on the native display of the system. Typically, the highest-priority performance objective of such a workload is minimum response time to the user's requests.

Multiuser   A workload that consists of a number of users submitting work through individual terminals. Typically, the performance objectives of such a workload are either to maximize system throughput while preserving a specified worst-case response time or to obtain the best possible response time for a fairly constant workload.

Server   A workload that consists of requests from other systems. For example, a file-server workload is mostly disk read/write requests. In essence, it is the disk-I/O component of a multiuser workload (plus NFS or DFS activity); so, the same objective of maximum throughput within a given response-time limit applies. Other server workloads consist of compute-intensive programs, database transactions, print jobs, and so on.

When a single system is processing workloads of more than one type, there must be a clear understanding between the users and the performance analyst as to the relative priorities of the possibly conflicting performance objectives of the different workloads.

12.1.3 General performance and availability guidelines

There are some basic guidelines that can help with the configuration of systems, depending on their intended use. These are outlined briefly as follows:

► Multi-threaded applications benefit the most from multiple CPUs.

► I/O intensive applications benefit the most from multiple I/O adapters and many disk drives.

► Additional memory is never disadvantageous.

► Data availability can be increased by using hardware or software mirroring.

► When intending to have a backup server for use in case of a failure in the primary server, it should be as identical to the primary server as possible, preferably an exact duplicate.

12.2 Overview of system performance

The AIX Base Operating System contains a number of monitoring and tuning tools that have historically been part of UNIX systems or are required to manage the implementation-specific features of AIX. The BOS functions and commands that are most important to performance analysts are:

`iostat`	Reports CPU and I/O statistics.
`vmstat`	Reports virtual-memory activity and other system statistics.
`netstat`	Displays the contents of network-related data structures.
`ps`	Displays the status of processes.
`lsattr`	Displays the attributes of devices.
`lslv`	Displays information about a logical volume or the logical volume allocations of a physical volume.
`nfsstat`	Displays statistics about Network File System (NFS) and Remote Procedure Call (RPC) activity.
`nice`	Runs a command at higher- or lower-than-normal priority.
`no`	Displays or sets network options.
`renice`	Changes the priority of one or more processes.
`reorgvg`	Reorganizes the physical-partition allocation within a volume group.
`sar`	Collects and reports or records system-activity information.
`schedtune`	Sets parameters for CPU scheduler and Virtual Memory Manager processing.
`svmon`	Captures and analyzes a snapshot of virtual memory.
`time`	Prints the elapsed execution time and the user and system processing time attributed to a command.
`tprof`	Reports CPU usage for individual programs and the whole system.
`trace`	Records and reports selected system events.

In the following section, a subset of these functions and commands is discussed.

12.3 Base Operating System tools

The following commands are the focus throughout this section.

► `vmstat`

► `iostat`

- netstat

- sar

12.3.1 Using the vmstat command

The **vmstat** command syntax is as follows:

vmstat [-f] [-i] [-s] [*PhysicalVolume* ...] [*Interval* [*Count*]]

The **vmstat** command reports statistics about kernel threads, virtual memory, disks, traps, and CPU activity. Reports generated by the **vmstat** command can be used to balance system load activity. These system-wide statistics (among all processors) are calculated either as averages for values expressed as percentages, or as sums.

The PhysicalVolume parameter can be used to specify one to four names. Transfer statistics are given for each specified drive in the order specified. This count represents logical and physical requests to the physical device. It does not imply an amount of data that was read or written. Several logical requests can be combined into one physical request.

If the **vmstat** command is invoked without flags, the report contains a summary of the virtual memory activity since system startup. If the -f flag is specified, the **vmstat** command reports the number of forks since system startup. The PhysicalVolume parameter specifies the name of the physical volume.

The Interval parameter specifies the amount of time in seconds between each report. The first report contains statistics for the time since system startup. Subsequent reports contain statistics collected during the interval since the previous report. If the Interval parameter is not specified, the **vmstat** command generates a single report and then exits.

The Count parameter can only be specified with the Interval parameter. If the Count parameter is specified, its value determines the number of reports generated and the number of seconds apart. If the Interval parameter is specified without the Count parameter, reports are continuously generated. A Count parameter of zero (0) is not allowed.

The kernel maintains statistics for kernel threads, paging, and interrupt activity, which the **vmstat** command accesses. The disk input/output statistics are maintained by device drivers. For disks, the average transfer rate is determined by using the active time and number of transfers information. The percent active time is computed from the amount of time the drive is busy during the report.

Note: Both the -f and -s flags can be entered on the command line, but the system will only accept the first flag specified and will override the second flag.

Table 12-1 provides the key flags for the **vmstat** command:

Table 12-1   Key flags for the vmstat command

Flag	Description
-f	Reports the number of forks since system startup.
-i	Displays the number of interrupts taken by each device since system startup.
-s	Writes to standard output the contents of the sum structure, which contains an absolute count of paging events since system initialization. The -s option is exclusive of the other **vmstat** command options.

Examples

The following are some examples using the **vmstat** command.

1. To display a summary of the statistics since boot, enter **vmstat**. A sample output follows:

```
# vmstat
kthr      memory              page                  faults         cpu
----- ----------- ----------------------- ------------- -----------
 r  b   avm   fre  re  pi  po  fr    sr  cy  in   sy  cs us sy id wa
 0  0 19046  1554   0   0   0   0     0   0 117  310  30  0  1 99  1
#
```

2. To display five summaries at 2-second intervals, enter **vmstat 2 5**. A sample output follows:

```
# vmstat 2 5
kthr      memory              page                  faults         cpu
----- ----------- ----------------------- ------------- -----------
 r  b   avm   fre  re  pi  po  fr    sr  cy  in   sy  cs us sy id wa
 0  0 19097  1498   0   0   0   0     0   0 117  310  30  0  1 99  1
 0  0 19097  1498   0   0   0   0     0   0 121  168  34  0  1 99  0
 0  0 19097  1498   0   0   0   0     0   0 126  118  34  0  0 99  0
 0  0 19097  1498   0   0   0   0     0   0 121  118  38  0  0 99  0
 0  0 19097  1498   0   0   0   0     0   0 122  121  34  0  0 99  0
#
```

The first summary (line one of the report) contains statistics for the time since boot.

3. To display a summary of the statistics since boot, including statistics for logical disks hdisk0 and hdisk1, enter: **vmstat hdisk0 hdisk1**. A sample output follows:

```
# vmstat hdisk0 hdisk1
kthr      memory              page                    faults        cpu        disk xfer
----- -----------  -----------------------  ------------  -----------  ----------
 r  b   avm   fre  re pi po  fr   sr  cy  in    sy  cs us sy id wa  1  2  3  4
 0  0 18461  3284   0  0  0   0    0   0 117   310  30  0  1 99  1  0  0
#
```

4. To display fork statistics, enter: **vmstat -f**. A sample output follows:

```
# vmstat -f
      13887 forks
#
```

5. To display the count of various events, enter: **vmstat -s**. A sample output follows:

```
# vmstat -s
    2205645 total address trans. faults
      46745 page ins
     135567 page outs
       7088 paging space page ins
      16737 paging space page outs
          0 total reclaims
     950333 zero filled pages faults
      12659 executable filled pages faults
     233034 pages examined by clock
         15 revolutions of the clock hand
      48272 pages freed by the clock
      27557 backtracks
          0 lock misses
         10 free frame waits
          0 extend XPT waits
      38657 pending I/O waits
     163907 start I/Os
     163907 iodones
   12734979 cpu context switches
   49535570 device interrupts
          0 software interrupts
          0 traps
  130379165 syscalls
#
```

vmstat report output

Table 12-2 contains the column headings and their description for vmstat output.

Table 12-2   vmstat output parameters

Parameter	Description
Kthr: Kernel thread state	
r	Number of kernel threads waiting in run queue. This value is zero in an idle system and higher in a CPU bound system.
b	Number of kernel threads waiting on the wait queue (awaiting resource, awaiting input/output).
Memory: Usage of virtual and real memory	
avm	Active virtual pages, that is, the total number of pages allocated in page space. A high value is not an indicator of poor performance.
fre	Size of the free list RAM pages
Page: Page faults and paging activity	
re	Pager input/output list
pi	Pages paged in from paging space
po	Pages paged out to paging space.
fr	Pages freed (page replacement)
sr	Pages scanned by page-replacement algorithm
cy	Clock cycles used by page-replacement algorithm
Faults: Trap and interrupt rate averages per second	
in	Device interrupts
sy	System calls
cs	Kernel thread context switches
CPU: % usage of CPU time	
us	User time
sy	System time
id	CPU idle time
wa	CPU cycles to determine that the current process is wait, and there is pending disk input/output.

Parameter	Description
	Disk: Provides the number of transfers per second to the specified physical volumes that occurred in the sample interval

Note: A large portion of real memory is utilized as a cache for file system data. It is not unusual for the size of the free list to remain small.

12.3.2 Using the iostat command

The `iostat` command syntax is as follows:

```
iostat [ -d | -t ] [ PhysicalVolume ... ] [ Interval [ Count ] ]
```

The `iostat` command is used for monitoring system input/output device loading by observing the time the physical disks are active in relation to their average transfer rates. The `iostat` command generates reports that can be used to determine what changes should be made to the system configuration to better balance the input/output load between physical disks.

The first report generated by the `iostat` command provides statistics concerning the time since the system was booted.

Each subsequent report covers the time since the previous report. All statistics are reported each time the `iostat` command is run. The report consists of a TTY and CPU header row followed by a row of TTY and CPU statistics. On multiprocessor systems, CPU statistics are calculated system-wide as averages among all processors. A disks header row is displayed followed by a line of statistics for each disk that is configured. If the PhysicalVolume parameter is specified, only those names specified are displayed.

If the PhysicalVolume parameter is specified:

► One or more physical volumes can be specified.

► The TTY and CPU reports are displayed.

► The disk report contains statistics for the specified drives.

The first character in the PhysicalVolume parameter cannot be numeric.

The Interval parameter specifies the amount of time in seconds between each report. The first report contains statistics for the time since system startup (boot). Each subsequent report contains statistics collected during the interval since the previous report.

The Count parameter can be specified in conjunction with the Interval parameter. If the Count parameter is specified, the value of count determines the number of reports generated at Interval seconds apart. If the Interval parameter is specified without the Count parameter, the `iostat` command generates reports continuously.

The `iostat` command is useful in determining whether a physical volume is becoming a performance bottleneck and if there is potential to improve the situation. The % utilization field for the physical volumes indicates how evenly the file activity is spread across the drives. A high percentage utilization on a physical volume is a clear indication that there may be contention for this resource. Since the CPU utilization statistics are also available with the `iostat` report, the percentage of time the CPU is in I/O wait can be determined at the same time. Consider distributing data across drives if the I/O wait time is significant, and the disk utilization is not evenly distributed across volumes.

> **Note:** Some amount of system resources are consumed in maintaining disk I/O history for the `iostat` command. Use the sysconfig subroutine or SMIT to stop history accounting.

Table 12-3 provides a list of common `iostat` command flags.

Table 12-3 Key flags for the iostat command

Flag	Description
-d	The -d option is exclusive of the -t option and displays only the disk utilization report.
-t	The -t option is exclusive of the -d option and displays only the TTY and CPU usage reports.

Examples

The following are examples of the `iostat` command usage.

1. To display a single history since boot report for all tty, CPU, and Disks, enter:

```
#iostat
tty:       tin           tout      avg-cpu:  % user    % sys    % idle    % iowait
           0.1           32.9                5.9       17.0     32.3      44.8

Disks:     % tm_act      Kbps      tps       Kb_read   Kb_wrtn
hdisk1     3.7           34.5      1.9       4664      128
hdisk0     46.5          526.3     40.2      68116     5048
cd0        0.0           0.0       0.0       0         0
#
```

2. To display a continuous disk report at two second intervals for the disk with the name hdisk1, enter:

```
iostat -d hdisk1 2
```

3. To display six reports at two second intervals for the disk with the logical name hdisk1, enter:

```
iostat -d hdisk1 2 6
```

4. To display six reports at two second intervals for all disks, enter:

```
iostat -d 2 6
```

5. To display six reports at two second intervals for three disks named disk1, disk2, disk3, enter:

```
iostat -d disk1 disk2 disk3 2 6
```

iostat report output

The **iostat** command generates two types of reports, the tty and CPU Utilization report and the Disk Utilization report. The meaning of the output parameters is shown in Table 12-4.

Table 12-4 iostat output parameters

Parameter	Description
TTY and CPU Utilization Report:	
The first report generated by the **iostat** command is the TTY and CPU Utilization Report. For multiprocessor systems, the CPU values are global averages among all processors. Also, the I/O wait state is defined system-wide and not per processor. This information is updated at regular intervals by the kernel (typically sixty times per second). The TTY report provides a collective account of characters per second received from all terminals on the system as well as the collective count of characters output per second to all terminals on the system. The report gives the following information:	
tin	Shows the total number of characters read by the system for all TTYs.
tout	Shows the total number of characters written by the system to all TTYs.
% user	Shows the percentage of CPU utilization that occurred while executing at the user level (application).
% sys	Shows the percentage of CPU utilization that occurred while executing at the system level (kernel).

Parameter	Description
% idle	Shows the percentage of time that the CPU or CPUs were idle, and the system did not have an outstanding disk I/O request.
% iowait	Shows the percentage of time that the CPU or CPUs were idle during which the system had an outstanding disk I/O request. This value may be slightly inflated if several processors are idling at the same time. This is an unusual occurance.

Disk Utilization Report:

The second report generated by the `iostat` command is the Disk Utilization Report. The disk report provides statistics on a per physical disk basis. The report has a format similar to the following:

% tm_act	Indicates the percentage of time the physical disk was active (bandwidth utilization for the drive).
Kbps	Indicates the amount of data transferred (read or written) to the drive in KB per second.
tps	Indicates the number of transfers per second that were issued to the physical disk. A transfer is an I/O request to the physical disk. Multiple logical requests can be combined into a single I/O request to the disk. A transfer is of indeterminate size.
Kb_read	The total number of KB read.
Kb_wrtn	The total number of KB written.

For large system configurations where a large number of disks are configured, the system can be configured to avoid collecting physical disk input/output statistics when the `iostat` command is not executing. If the system is configured in the above manner, the first Disk report displays the message Disk History Since Boot Not Available instead of the disk statistics. Subsequent interval reports generated by the `iostat` command contain disk statistics collected during the report interval. Any TTY and CPU statistics after boot are unaffected. If a system management command is used to re-enable disk statistics, the first `iostat` command report displays activity from the interval starting at the point that disk input/output statistics were enabled.

12.3.3 Using the netstat command

The **netstat** command syntax is as follows:

To display active sockets for each protocol or routing table information:

```
/bin/netstat [ -n ] [ { -A -a } | { -r -i -I Interface } ] [ -f AddressFamily ]
[ -p Protocol ] [ Interval ] [ System ]
```

To display the contents of a network data structure:

```
/bin/netstat [ -m | -s | -u | -v ] [ -f AddressFamily ] [ -p Protocol ]
[ Interval ] [ System ]
```

To display the packet counts throughout the communications subsystem:

```
/bin/netstat -D
```

The **netstat** command (Table 12-5) symbolically displays the contents of various network-related data structures for active connections. The Interval parameter, specified in seconds, continuously displays information regarding packet traffic on the configured network interfaces. The Interval parameter takes no flags. The System parameter specifies the memory used by the current kernel. Unless you are looking at a dump file, the System parameter should be /unix.

Table 12-5   Key flags for the netstat command

Flag	Description
-n	Shows network addresses as numbers. When this flag is not specified, the command interprets addresses where possible and displays them symbolically.
-r	Shows the routing tables. When used with the -s flag, the -r flag shows routing statistics.
-s	Shows statistics for each protocol.

Note: In the statistics output, a N/A displayed in a field value indicates the count is not applicable. For the NFS/RPC statistics, the number of incoming packets that pass through RPC are the same packets that pass through NFS; so, these numbers are not summed in the NFS/RPC Total field, thus, the N/A. NFS has no outgoing packet or outgoing packet drop counters specific to NFS and RPC. Therefore, individual counts have a field value of N/A, and the cumulative count is stored in the NFS/RPC Total field.

The collision count for Ethernet interfaces is not supported.

Examples

The following are examples of `netstat` command usage.

To display the routing table, use the command:

```
# netstat -r
Routing tables
Destination       Gateway            Flags   Refs      Use  If   PMTU Exp Groups

Route Tree for Protocol Family 2 (Internet):
default           itso240            UGc       0        0  tr0    -   -
9.3.240/24        server1            U        39   349098  tr0    -   -
127/8             localhost          U         4      696  lo0    -   -

Route Tree for Protocol Family 24 (Internet v6):
::1               ::1                UH        0        0  lo0 16896   -
#
```

To display the routing table with network addresses as numbers, use the command:

```
# netstat -rn
Routing tables
Destination       Gateway            Flags   Refs      Use  If   PMTU Exp Groups

Route Tree for Protocol Family 2 (Internet):
default           9.3.240.1          UGc       0        0  tr0    -   -
9.3.240/24        9.3.240.56         U        36   349117  tr0    -   -
127/8             127.0.0.1          U         4      696  lo0    -   -

Route Tree for Protocol Family 24 (Internet v6):
::1               ::1                UH        0        0  lo0 16896   -
#
```

To display the routing statistics use the command:

```
# netstat -r -s
routing:
        0 bad routing redirect
        0 dynamically created route
        0 new gateway due to redirects
        0 destination found unreachable
        0 use of a wildcard route
#
```

netstat output report

The default display for active sockets shows the following items:

► Local and remote addresses

- ▶ Send and receive queue sizes (in bytes)
- ▶ Protocol
- ▶ Internal state of the protocol

Internet address formats are of the form host.port or network.port if a socket's address specifies a network but no specific host address. The host address is displayed symbolically if the address can be resolved to a symbolic host name while network addresses are displayed symbolically according to the /etc/networks file.

NS addresses are 12-byte quantities consisting of a 4-byte network number, a 6-byte host number, and a 2-byte port number, all of which are stored in network standard format. For VAX architecture, these are word and byte reversed; for the Sun systems, they are not reversed.

If a symbolic name for a host is not known, or if the -n flag is used, the address is printed numerically according to the address family. Unspecified addresses and ports appear as an * (asterisk).

Interface Display (`netstat -i`)
The interface display format provides a table of cumulative statistics for the following items:

- ▶ Errors
- ▶ Collisions

  The collision count for Ethernet interfaces is not supported.

- ▶ Packets transferred

The interface display also provides the:

- ▶ interface name,
- ▶ number, and
- ▶ address, as well as
- ▶ the maximum transmission units (MTUs).

Routing Table Display (`netstat -r`)
The routing table display format indicates the available routes and their statuses. Each route consists of a destination host or network and a gateway to use in forwarding packets.

The flags field of the routing table shows the state of the route:

U   Up.

H   The route is to a host rather than to a network.

G   The route is to a gateway.

D   The route was created dynamically by a redirect.

M   The route has been modified by a redirect.

L   The link-level address is present in the route entry.

c   Access to this route creates a cloned route. This field only applies to AIX Version 4.2.1 or later.

W   The route is a cloned route. This field only applies to AIX Version 4.2.1 or later

Direct routes are created for each interface attached to the local host.

Gateway   The gateway field for these entries shows the address of the outgoing interface.

Refs   Gives the current number of active uses for the route. Connection-oriented protocols hold onto a single route for the duration of a connection, while connectionless protocols obtain a route while sending to the same destination.

Use   Provides a count of the number of packets sent using that route.

PMTU   Gives the Path Maximum Transfer Unit (PMTU). This field only applies to AIX Version 4.2.1 or later.

Interface   Indicates the network interfaces utilized for the route.

Exp   Displays the time (in minutes) remaining before the route expires. This field only applies to AIX Version 4.2.1 or later.

Groups   Provides a list of group IDs associated with that route. This field only applies to AIX Version 4.2.1 or later.

Netmasks   Lists the netmasks applied on the system.

12.3.4 Additional performance related commands

The following commands are used to examine specific system areas, either to complement the results from **vmstat**, **iostat** and **netstat**, or to provide more in depth information. Detailed descriptions of these tools is outside the scope of this chapter, but you should be aware of them.

The svmon command

The **svmon** command provides a more in-depth analysis of memory usage. It is more informative, but also more intrusive, than the **vmstat** commands.

The sar command

The **sar** command writes to standard output the contents of selected cumulative activity counters in the operating system. You can use flags to select information about specific system activities. Specifying no flags selects only system unit activity, specifying the -A flag selects all activities.

The tprof command

The **tprof** command can be used over a time period to trace the activity of the CPU. The CPU utilization is divided into kernel, user, shared, and other to show how many clock timer ticks were spent in each respective address space.

The schedtune command

The **schedtune** command allows you to modify the default behavior of the scheduling system for threads and processes, and should be used with extreme care by experienced administrators. Do not manipulate the scheduler without thorough knowledge of the scheduler mechanism.

12.4 Controlling resource usage

The following sections describe various methods to limit the consumption of system resources.

12.4.1 Using the nice and renice commands

The **nice** and **renice** commands are used to change the priority of a process. The **nice** command runs another command at a different priority, while the **renice** command changes the priority of an already running process. The root user can increase or decrease the priority of any process. Other users can only decrease the priority of processes they own.

The following example shows the **nice** command running the **cc** command at a lower priority:

```
# nice -n 15 cc -c *.c
```

The following example shows the **renice** command lowering the priority of process ID 16304 by 5:

```
# renice -n 5 16304
```

12.4.2 Workload Manager

The Workload Manager (WLM) allows the system administrator to divide resources between jobs. WLM provides isolation between user communities with very different system behaviors. This can prevent effective starvation of workloads with certain characteristics, such as interactive or low CPU usage jobs, by workloads with other characteristics, such as batch or high memory usage jobs. CPU time, memory, and I/O bandwidth are managed separately, therefore, different styles of applications can be managed.

AIX WLM delivers the basic ability to give system administrators more control over how scheduler, Virtual Memory Manager (VMM), and device driver calls allocate CPU, physical memory, and I/O bandwidth to classes-based user, group, application path, process type, or application tags.

The AIX WLM is an operating system feature introduced in AIX Version 4.3.3.

12.5 Performance analysis

In this section, system performance is analyzed to determine whether a system is CPU bound or memory bound. There is also a discussion on the idle time for Symmetric Multiprocessors (SMP) and Uniprocessor (UP) systems.

The following are some terms used during this discussion.

CPU bound A system is said to be CPU-bound if the total system (sy) and user (us) CPU usage is approaching 100 percent. This would imply that idle time and wait time for CPU are approaching zero.

Memory bound A system is memory-bound if some virtual memory is forced out to disk, meaning the system is waiting on a relatively slow disk instead of relatively fast RAM. This is indicated by a non-zero value in the page-in (pi) and page-out (po) values.

12.5.1 Determining CPU-bound and memory bound systems

In this section, you will look at the sy and us columns for the CPU usage to determine if the system was CPU-bound during the time the **vmstat** command was gathering system information.

You need to obtain a preliminary look at the performance of the system as shown in Figure 12-1.

```
# vmstat 5 5
kthr        memory             page                 faults           cpu
_____ _____  _____  _____  _____
 r  b    avm   fre  re  pi  po  fr   sr   cy   in    sy   cs us sy id wa
 0  0  22988   123   0   0   0   1    8    0  130   383   39  1  1 96  2
 2  0  23318   158   0   2   1  80  331    0  188  1945  339 66 31  0  3
 2  0  23213   332   0   0   0  11   98    0  224  1783  375 77 23  0  0
 4  0  23390   274   0   2   0  32  208    0  202  2247  366 60 40  0  0
 3  0  23449   157   0  11   0   0    0    0  270  5308 1078 88 12  0  0
#
```

Figure 12-1   vmstat report of cpu-bound system

Remember that a system is CPU-bound if the total system and user CPU usage approaches 100 percent.

For rows two through five, the system +user CPU usage are:

Row 2 =(66+31)%=97% and r = 2

Row 3 =(77+23)%=100% and r = 2

Row 4 =(60+40)%=100% and r = 4

Row 5 =(88+12)%=100% and r = 3

There are two indications that this system is CPU bound.

▶ The CPU usage values tend towards 100 percent, and

▶ The r values are nonzero indicating that the CPU has more work to perform. This is mentioned previously, as an indicator for CPU activity, in "vmstat report output" on page 338.

To determine if a system is memory bound, the pi and po columns are taken into consideration. As defined in Section 12.5, "Performance analysis" on page 348, a system is memory bound if the average page in rate (pi) for paging spaces and the average page out rate (po) for paging spaces were non-zero.

12.5.2 Idle time calculations

Idle time calculations on a Symmetric Multiprocessor (SMP) and an Uniprocessor system are the same. In an SMP environment, the output received from the **vmstat** and **iostat** commands are a summary of the system wait and idle time across all processors. You need only use the tools as laid out in the previous sections and calculate the system idle time based on the output received.

When calculating total system idle time over an interval, both the percentage of idle time (id), and the percentage of wait time (wa) are to be considered. Both fields are obtained from the `vmstat` command output.

Note: Total CPU Idle Time % = wait % + Idle Time %

To calculate the time that the system is idle using the output from the `vmstat` command, perform the following:

1. Calculate the average percentage idle time over the interval.

   Given the following output from an SMP system, calculate the system idle time from the command `vmstat 900 4`, that is, an output every 900 seconds or (15 minutes) four times.

```
kthr      memory                 page                  faults        cpu
-----  -----------  -----------------------  ------------  -----------
 r  b    avm    fre  re  pi  po  fr   sr  cy  in   sy  cs us sy id wa
 0  0 11015 205693   0   0   0   0    0   0 102   11   6  0  0 99  1
 0  1 13014 203638   0   0   0   0    0   0 513  202 233  0  0 97  2
 0  1 13903 202718   0   0   0   0    0   0 528  256 262  0  0 95  4
 0  1 13008 203613   0   0   0   0    0   0 509  178 225  0  0 99  1
```

   Average CPU Idle Time percentage = Sum (%Idle Times(id) + %wait)/ # readings, therefore, the Average CPU Idle Time percentage = ((99+1) + (97+2) + (95+4) + (99+1))/4 = 99.5%

2. Then calculate the Total CPU Idle Time in minutes.

   These readings were obtained over one hour, therefore, total CPU Idle Time for this system = 99.5% x 60 minutes = ~59 minutes

12.5.3 Calculating paging rate

Paging rate is the average number of page-ins and page-outs per CPU cycle.

If the pagein/pageout (pi/po) ratio is greater than one, it is indicating that for every pagein there is at least one pageout and, therefore, points to high paging activities. This system is, therefore, said to have a high paging rate.

12.6 Quiz

The following certification assessment questions help verify your understanding of the topics discussed in this chapter.

1. The finance department at the Widget Company needs a larger server. The current server has 40 GB of hard drive space, two processors and 2 GB of memory. The application is a fully multi-threaded process and is very I/O intensive. What configuration should the company purchase to fix current problems and plan for future expansion?

   A. One 60 GB SCSI hard disk, 4 processors, and 2 GB of memory.

   B. Two 20 GB SSA hard disks, 4 processors, and 4 GB of memory.

   C. Two 20 GB SCSI hard disks, 2 processors, and 8 GB of memory.

   D. Three 20 GB SSA hard disks, 4 processors, and 2 GB of memory.

2. The Widget Company is trying to implement disaster recovery procedures and techniques. They currently have two daily backups taken of all data. In the event that they need to restore data to another machine, what type of machine would be ideal?

   A. A slightly slower machine of the same type.

   B. An exact duplicate of the original machine.

   C. A slightly slower machine of the same type with less processors.

   D. An exact duplicate of the original machine with less processors.

The following are additional questions created by the authors to further test your understanding of the topics.

1. A system administrator is experiencing performance problems and runs the **vmstat** command. The output of **vmstat** is shown in the following exhibit.

```
procs    memory            page                  faults         cpu
-----  -----------  -----------------------   ------------  -----------
 r  b   avm   fre  re pi po  fr   sr cy  in   sy   cs us sy id wa
 2  0 22534  1465   0  0  0   0    0  0 238  903  239 77 23  0  0
 2  0 22534  1445   0  0  0   0    0  0 209 1142  205 72 28  0  0
 2  0 22534  1426   0  0  0   0    0  0 189 1220  212 74 26  0  0
 3  0 22534  1410   0  0  0   0    0  0 255 1704  268 70 30  0  0
 2  1 22557  1365   0  0  0   0    0  0 383  977  216 72 28  0  0
```

What can be concluded from this output?

A. The machine is CPU bound.

B. The machine needs memory optimized.

C. The machine needs a FDDI card installed.

D. A user program is causing unnecessary paging.

2. A system administrator runs the **vmstat** command. The output of **vmstat** is shown in the following exhibit (using a 15 minute interval).

```
kthr     memory            page                  faults         cpu
-----  -----------  -----------------------   ------------  -----------
 r  b   avm   fre  re pi po  fr   sr cy  in   sy   cs us sy id wa
 2  0 9200 11027    0  0  0   0    0  0 103   52  14 14 16  0 69
 2  1 9200 11027    0  0  0   0    0  0 207  251  29 12 11  0 67
 3  1 9200 11027    0  0  0   0    0  0 207  120  29  9 11  0 80
 5  1 9200 11027    0  0  0   0    0  0 206  120  29 13  5  0 79
 4  1 9200 11027    0  0  0   0    0  0 207  131  32  9  8  0 72
```

Based on this output, what is the average CPU idle time as a percentage?

A. 45.5

B. 75.3

C. 44.04

D. 73.4

12.6.1 Answers

The following answers are for the assessment quiz questions.

1. D
2. B

The following answers are for the additional quiz questions.

1. A
2. D

12.7 Exercises

The following exercises provide sample topics for self study. They will help ensure comprehension of this chapter.

1. Gather statistics using the **vmstat**, **iostat**, and **netstat** commands. Take a look at your system performance.

2. Calculate your systems idle time (in minutes) and the paging rate.

3. Determine if your system is CPU bound or memory bound.

13

User administration

This chapter discusses user administration that consists of creating and removing user accounts, defining and changing user attributes, and the important files referenced.

13.1 Overview

Users are the primary agents on the system. Each user is required to log in to the system. The user supplies the user name of an account and a password if the account has one (on a secure system, all accounts either have passwords or are invalidated). If the password is correct, the user is logged in to that account; the user acquires the access rights and privileges of the account. The /etc/passwd and /etc/security/passwd files maintain user passwords.

Groups are collections of users who can share access permissions for protected resources. A group has an ID, and a group is composed of members and administrators. The creator of the group is usually the first administrator. There are three types of groups:

User group
User groups should be made for people who need to share files on the system, such as people who work in the same department or people who are working on the same project. In general, create as few user groups as possible.

System administrator groups
System administrator groups correspond to the SYSTEM group. SYSTEM group membership allows an administrator to perform some system maintenance tasks without having to operate with root authority.

System-defined groups
There are several system-defined groups. The STAFF group is the default group for all nonadministrative users created in the system. You can change the default group by using the **chsec** command to edit the /usr/lib/security/mkuser.default file. The SECURITY group is a system-defined group having limited privileges for performing security administration.

An attribute is a characteristic of a user or a group that defines the type of functions that a user or a group can perform. These can be extraordinary privileges, restrictions, and processing environments assigned to a user. Their attributes control their access rights, environment, how they are authenticated, and how, when, and where their accounts can be accessed. These attributes are created from default values when a user is created through the **mkuser** command. They can be altered by using the **chuser** command.

Some users and groups can be defined as administrative. These users and groups can be created and modified only by the root user.

13.2 User administration related commands

The following are a few of the important commands used for user administration:

mkuser   Creates a new user.

passwd   Creates or changes the password of a user.

chuser   Changes user attributes (except password).

lsuser   Lists user attributes.

rmuser   Removes a user and its attributes.

chsec   Changes security related stanzas.

login   Initiates a user session.

who   Identifies the users currently logged in.

dtconfig   Enables or disables the desktop autostart feature.

13.3 User administration related files

The following files are referenced while doing user administration:

/etc/security/environ	Contains the environment attributes for users.
/etc/security/lastlog	Contains the last login attributes for users.
/etc/security/limits	Contains process resource limits for users.
/etc/security/user	Contains extended attributes for users.
/usr/lib/security/mkuser.default	Contains the default attributes for new users.
/usr/lib/security/mkuser.sys	Customizes new user accounts.
/etc/passwd	Contains the basic attributes of users.
/etc/security/passwd	Contains password information.
/etc/security/login.cfg	Contains configuration information for login and user authentication.
/etc/utmp	Contains the record of users logged into the system.
/var/adm/wtmp	Contains connect time accounting records.
/etc/security/failedlogin	Records all failed login attempts.
/etc/motd	Contains the message to be displayed every time a user logs in to the system.

/etc/environment	Specifies the basic environment for all processes.
/etc/profile	Specifies additional environment settings for all users.
$HOME/.profile	Specifies environment settings for specific user needs.
/etc/group	Contains the basic attributes of groups.
/etc/security/group	Contains the extended attributes of groups.

13.3.1 /etc/security/environ

The /etc/security/environ file is an ASCII file that contains stanzas with the environment attributes for users. Each stanza is identified by a user name and contains attributes in the Attribute=Value form with a comma separating the attributes. Each line is ended by a new-line character, and each stanza is ended by an additional new-line character. If environment attributes are not defined, the system uses default values.

The **mkuser** command creates a user stanza in this file. The initialization of the attributes depends upon their values in the /usr/lib/security/mkuser.default file. The **chuser** command can change these attributes, and the **lsuser** command can display them. The **rmuser** command removes the entire record for a user.

A basic /etc/security/environ file is shown in the following example, which has no environment attributes defined. Therefore, the system is using default values.

```
# pg /etc/security/environ
default:
root:
daemon:
bin:
sys:
adm:
uucp:
guest:
```

13.3.2 /etc/security/lastlog

The /etc/security/lastlog file is an ASCII file that contains stanzas with the last login attributes for users. Each stanza is identified by a user name and contains attributes in the Attribute=Value form. Each attribute is ended by a new-line character, and each stanza is ended by an additional new-line character. Two stanzas for users (root & john) are shown in Figure 13-1 on page 359.

The `mkuser` command creates a user stanza in the lastlog file. The attributes of this user stanza are initially empty. The field values are set by the `login` command as a result of logging in to the system. The `lsuser` command displays the values of these attributes; the `rmuser` command removes the user stanza from this file along with the user account.

```
root:
        time_last_login = 909674976
        tty_last_login = /dev/pts/7
        host_last_login = sv1166a.itsc.austin.ibm.com
        unsuccessful_login_count = 0
        time_last_unsuccessful_login = 909608576
        tty_last_unsuccessful_login = /dev/pts/2
        host_last_unsuccessful_login = sv1121c


john:
        time_last_unsuccessful_login = 909529946
        tty_last_unsuccessful_login = /dev/pts/2
        host_last_unsuccessful_login = sv1121c

        unsuccessful_login_count = 0
        time_last_login = 909529992
        tty_last_login = /dev/pts/2
        host_last_login = sv1121c

~
~
```

Figure 13-1   /etc/security/lastlog stanzas

13.3.3 /etc/security/limits

The /etc/security/limits file is an ASCII file that contains stanzas that specify the process resource limits for each user. These limits are set by individual attributes within a stanza.

Each stanza is identified by a user name followed by a colon and contains attributes in the Attribute=Value form. Each attribute is ended by a new-line character, and each stanza is ended by an additional new-line character. If you do not define an attribute for a user, the system applies default values.

The default attributes, and attributes for the user smith, are shown in Figure 13-2 on page 360.

When you create a user with the **mkuser** command, the system adds a stanza for the user to the /etc/security/limits file. Once the stanza exists, you can use the **chuser** command to change the user's limits. To display the current limits for a user, use the **lsuser** command. To remove users and their stanzas, use the **rmuser** command.

```
default:
        fsize = 2097151
        core = 2097151
        cpu = -1
        data = 262144
        rss = 65536
        stack = 65536
        nofiles = 2000

smith:
        fsize = 3007151
        data = 332144
        data_hard = 3400000

~
~
~
~
~
~
~
~
```

Figure 13-2   Contents of /etc/security/limits file

13.3.4 /etc/security/user

The /etc/security/user file contains extended user attributes. This is an ASCII file that contains attribute stanzas for users. The **mkuser** command creates a stanza in this file for each new user and initializes its attributes with the default attributes defined in the /usr/lib/security/mkuser.default file.

Each stanza in the /etc/security/user file is identified by a user name, followed by a colon (:), and contains comma-separated attributes in the Attribute=Value form. If an attribute is not defined for a user, either the default stanza or the default value for the attribute is used. You can have multiple default stanzas in the /etc/security/user file. A default stanza applies to all of the stanzas that follow, but does not apply to the stanzas preceding it.

Each attribute is ended by a new-line character, and each stanza is ended by an additional new-line character.

The mkuser command creates an entry for each new user in the /etc/security/user file and initializes its attributes with the attributes defined in the /usr/lib/security/mkuser.default file. To change attribute values, use the chuser command. To display the attributes and their values, use the lsuser command. To remove a user, use the rmuser command.

Password controls

The /etc/security/user file contains many attributes that allow you to control how users must manage their passwords. These attributes include:

histsize Defines the number of previous passwords a user cannot reuse. The value is a decimal integer string. The default is 0.

histexpire Defines the period of time (in weeks) that a user cannot reuse a password. The value is a decimal integer string. The default is 0, indicating that no time limit is set.

maxexpired Defines the maximum time (in weeks) beyond the maxage value that a user can change an expired password. After this defined time, only an administrative user can change the password. The value is a decimal integer string. The default is -1, indicating no restriction is set. If the maxexpired attribute is 0, the password expires when the maxage value is met. If the maxage attribute is 0, the maxexpired attribute is ignored.

maxage Defines the maximum age (in weeks) of a password. The password must be changed by this time. The value is a decimal integer string. The default is a value of 0, indicating no maximum age.

minage Defines the minimum age (in weeks) a password must be before it can be changed. The value is a decimal integer string. The default is a value of 0, indicating no minimum age.

minlen Defines the minimum length of a password. The value is a decimal integer string. The default is a value of 0, indicating no minimum length. The maximum value allowed is 8. The value of minlen is determined by the minalpha value added to the minother value. If the result of this addition is greater than the minlen attribute, the value is set to the result.

minalpha Defines the minimum number of alphabetic characters that must be in a new password. The value is a decimal integer string. The default is a value of 0, indicating no minimum number.

minother Defines the minimum number of non-alphabetic characters that must be in a new password. The value is a decimal integer string. The default is a value of 0, indicating no minimum number.

maxrepeats	Defines the maximum number of times a character can be repeated in a new password. Since a value of 0 is meaningless, the default value of 8 indicates that there is no maximum number. The value is a decimal integer string.
mindiff	Defines the minimum number of characters required in a new password that were not in the old password. The value is a decimal integer string. The default is a value of 0, indicating no minimum number.

13.3.5 /usr/lib/security/mkuser.default

The /usr/lib/security/mkuser.default file contains the default attributes for new users. This file is an ASCII file that contains user stanzas. These stanzas have attribute default values for users created by the `mkuser` command. Each attribute has the Attribute=Value form. If an attribute has a value of $USER, the `mkuser` command substitutes the name of the user. The end of each attribute pair and stanza is marked by a new-line character.

There are two stanzas, user and admin, that can contain all defined attributes except the ID and admin attributes. The `mkuser` command generates a unique ID attribute. The admin attribute depends on whether the -a flag is used with the `mkuser` command. The following example shows a typical stanza in /usr/lib/security/mkuser.default.

```
# pg /usr/lib/security/mkuser.default

user:
        pgrp = staff
        groups = staff
        shell = /usr/bin/ksh
        home = /home/$USER

admin:
        pgrp = system
        groups = system
        shell = /usr/bin/ksh
        home = /home/$USER
```

13.3.6 /usr/lib/security/mkuser.sys

The /usr/lib/security/mkuser.sys file is an ASCII file of runable commands that is called by the `mkuser` command. The /usr/lib/security/mkuser.sys file creates the new user's home directory with the correct owner and primary group, and creates the appropriate profile for the user's shell. This file can be customized to tailor the creation of new users.

13.3.7 /etc/passwd

The /etc/passwd file contains basic user attributes. This is an ASCII file that contains an entry for each user. Each entry defines the basic attributes applied to a user.

When you use the `mkuser` command to add a user to your system, the command updates the /etc/passwd file.

An entry in the /etc/passwd file has the following form with all attributes separated by a colon(:).

```
Name:Password: UserID:PrincipleGroup:Gecos: HomeDirectory:Shell
```

Password attributes can contain an asterisk (*) indicating an incorrect password or an exclamation point (!) indicating that the password is in the /etc/security/passwd file. Under normal conditions, the field contains an exclamation point (!). If the field has an asterisk (*) and a password is required for user authentication, the user cannot log in.

The shell attribute specifies the initial program or shell (login shell) that is started after a user invokes the `login` command or `su` command. The Korn shell is the standard operating system login shell and is backwardly compatible with the Bourne shell. If a user does not have a defined shell, /usr/bin/sh, the system default shell (Bourne shell) is used. The Bourne shell is a subset of the Korn shell.

The `mkuser` command adds new entries to the /etc/passwd file and fills in the attribute values as defined in the /usr/lib/security/mkuser.default file. The Password attribute is always initialized to an asterisk (*), which is an invalid password. You can set the password with the `passwd` or `pwdadm` commands. When the password is changed, an exclamation point (!) is added to the /etc/passwd file indicating that the encrypted password is in the /etc/security/passwd file.

Use the `chuser` command to change all user attributes except Password. The `chfn` command and the `chsh` command change the Gecos attribute and Shell attribute, respectively. To display all the attributes in this file, use the `lsuser` command. To remove a user and all the user's attributes, use the `rmuser` command.

The contents of /etc/passwd file in Figure 13-3 shows that the Password attributes for two users (john and bob) are ! and *, respectively, which implies that user bob cannot login, as it has an invalid password.

```
# pg /etc/passwd
root:!:0:0::/:/bin/ksh
daemon:!:1:1::/etc:
bin:!:2:2::/bin:
sys:!:3:3::/usr/sys:
adm:!:4:4::/var/adm:
uucp:!:5:5::/usr/lib/uucp:
guest:!:100:100::/home/guest:
nobody:!:4294967294:4294967294::/:
lpd:!:9:4294967294::/:
imnadm:*:200:200::/home/imnadm:/usr/bin/ksh
john:!:210:1::/home/john:/usr/bin/ksh
bob:*:213:1::/home/bob:/usr/bin/ksh
# 
```

Figure 13-3   Contents of /etc/passwd file

13.3.8 /etc/security/passwd

The /etc/security/passwd file is an ASCII file that contains stanzas with password information. Each stanza is identified by a user name followed by a colon (:) and contains attributes in the form Attribute=Value. Each attribute is ended with a new line character, and each stanza is ended with an additional new line character.

Although each user name must be in the /etc/passwd file, it is not necessary to have each user name listed in the /etc/security/passwd file. A typical file would have contents is similar to that shown in Figure 13-4.

```
root:
        password = .qKD2SmeIpoJo
        lastupdate = 904940604
        flags =

sys:
        password = *

adm:
        password = *

guest:
        password = *

lpd:
        password = *

john:
        password = 05.gOAdVORKB.
        lastupdate = 909529992
        flags =
```

Figure 13-4   Contents of /etc/security/passwd file

13.3.9 /etc/security/login.cfg

The /etc/security/login.cfg file (Figure 13-5 on page 366) is an ASCII file that contains stanzas of configuration information for login and user authentication. Each stanza has a name, followed by a : (colon). Attributes are in the form Attribute=Value. Each attribute ends with a new-line character, and each stanza ends with an additional new-line character. There are three types of stanzas.

port stanza   Defines the login characteristics of ports.

authentication stanza   Defines the authentication methods for users.

user configuration stanza Defines programs that change user attributes (usw).

```
default:
        sak_enabled = false
        logintimes =
        logindisable = 0
        logininterval = 0
        loginreenable = 0
        logindelay = 0

auth_method:
      ▌program =

usw:
        shells = /bin/sh,/bin/bsh,/bin/csh,/bin/ksh,/bin/tsh,/usr/bin/sh,/usr/bi
n/bsh,/usr/bin/csh,/usr/bin/ksh,/usr/bin/tsh,/usr/sbin/sliplogin
        maxlogins = 2
        logintimeout = 60

~
~
~
~
~
~
~
```

Figure 13-5   Contents of /etc/security/login.cfg file

13.3.10 /etc/utmp, /var/adm/wtmp, /etc/security/failedlogin

The utmp file, the wtmp file, and the failedlogin file contain records with user and accounting information. When a user successfully logs in, the login program writes entries in two files.

► The /etc/utmp file, which contains a record of users logged into the system. The command **who -a** processes the /etc/utmp file, and if this file is corrupted or missing, no output is generated from the **who** command.

► The /var/adm/wtmp file (if it exists), which contains connect-time accounting records.

On an invalid login attempt, due to an incorrect login name or password, the login program makes an entry in the /etc/security/failedlogin file, which contains a record of unsuccessful login attempts.

13.3.11 /etc/motd

The message of the day is displayed every time a user logs in to the system. It is a convenient way to communicate information to all users, such as installed software version numbers or current system news. The message of the day is contained in the /etc/motd file. To change the message of the day, simply edit that file.

A typical /etc/motd file would look like Figure 13-6.

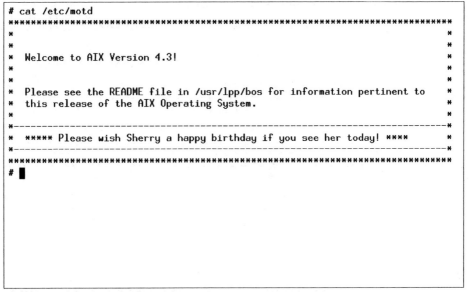

```
# cat /etc/motd
********************************************************************************
*                                                                              *
*                                                                              *
*   Welcome to AIX Version 4.3!                                                 *
*                                                                              *
*                                                                              *
*   Please see the README file in /usr/lpp/bos for information pertinent to     *
*   this release of the AIX Operating System.                                  *
*                                                                              *
*------------------------------------------------------------------------------*
*   ***** Please wish Sherry a happy birthday if you see her today! ****        *
*------------------------------------------------------------------------------*
********************************************************************************
# ▮
```

Figure 13-6   Sample /etc/motd file

13.3.12 /etc/environment

The /etc/environment file contains variables specifying the basic environment for all processes. When a new process begins, the exec subroutine makes an array of strings available that have the form Name=Value. This array of strings is called the environment. Each name defined by one of the strings is called an environment variable or shell variable. Environment variables are examined when a command starts running.

The /etc/environment file is *not* a shell script. It should only contain data in Name=Value format, and should not contain shell commands. Trying to run commands from this file may cause failure of the initialization process.

When you log in, the system sets environment variables from the environment file before reading your login profile, .profile. Following are a few variables that make up part of the basic environment.

HOME   The full path name of the user login or HOME directory. The login program sets this to the directory specified in the /etc/passwd file.

LANG   The locale name currently in effect. The LANG variable is set in the /etc/environment file at installation time.

NLSPATH   The full path name for message catalogs.

PATH   The sequence of directories that commands, such as `sh`, `time`, `nice`, and `nohup` search when looking for a command whose path name is incomplete. The directory names are separated by colons.

LPDEST   The printer to use when a print-related command does not specify a destination printer.

TERM   The terminal type.

EDITOR   The default editor to be used by various commands that perform editing functions, such as `crontab`.

TZ   The time zone information. The TZ environment variable is set by the /etc/environment file.

> **Attention:** Changing the time zone only affects processes that begin after the change is made. The init process only reads /etc/environment at startup, therefore init and its child processes will not be aware of a change to TZ until the system is rebooted.

13.3.13 /etc/profile and $HOME/.profile

The /etc/profile file contains further environment variables, as well as any commands to run, that apply to all users. Use the /etc/profile file to control variables such as:

► Export variables

► File creation mask (umask)

► Terminal types

► Mail messages to indicate when new mail has arrived

Commands to be included in /etc/profile should be appropriate for *all* users of the system. An example of a command that you may want all users to run when they log in is the **news** command.

The $HOME/.profile file enables you to customize your individual working environment. The .profile file also overrides commands and variables set in the /etc/profile file. Use the .profile file to control personal settings such as:

► Shells to open

► Default editor

► Default printer

► Prompt appearance

► Keyboard sound

13.4 User administration tasks

User administration creates users, defines or changes their attributes, and defines the security environment for the users. These topics are discussed in the following sections.

13.4.1 Adding a new user account

The `mkuser` command creates a new user account. The Name parameter must be a unique 8-byte or less string. By default, the `mkuser` command creates a standard user account. To create an administrative user account, specify the -a flag.

The `mkuser` command does not create password information for a user, therefore, the new accounts are disabled until the `passwd` command is used to add authentication information to the /etc/security/passwd file. The `mkuser` command only initializes the Password attribute of /etc/passwd file with an * (asterisk).

► To create the smith account with smith as an administrator, enter:

```
mkuser -a smith
```

You must be the root user to create smith as an administrative user.

► To create the smith user account and set the `su` attribute to a value of false enter:

```
mkuser su=false smith
```

► To create a user account, smith, with the default values in the /usr/lib/security/mkuser.default file, enter:

```
mkuser smith
```

Alternatively, you can use SMIT:

a. Run `smitty mkuser` to access the menu as shown in Figure 13-7 on page 370.

b. Type `smith` for the field User NAME.

c. Press the Enter key to create the user.

d. When SMIT returns an OK prompt, Press the F10 key to return to the command prompt

```
                              Add a User

Type or select values in entry fields.
Press Enter AFTER making all desired changes.

[TOP]                                              [Entry Fields]
* User NAME                                        [smith]
  User ID                                          []                      #
  ADMINISTRATIVE USER?                             false                   +
  Primary GROUP                                    []                      +
  Group SET                                        []                      +
  ADMINISTRATIVE GROUPS                            []                      +
  ROLES                                            []                      +
  Another user can SU TO USER?                     true                    +
  SU GROUPS                                        [ALL]                   +
  HOME directory                                   []
  Initial PROGRAM                                  []
  User INFORMATION                                 []
  EXPIRATION date (MMDDhhmmyy)                      [0]
[MORE...37]

F1=Help              F2=Refresh         F3=Cancel          F4=List
F5=Reset             F6=Command         F7=Edit            F8=Image
F9=Shell             F10=Exit           Enter=Do
```

Figure 13-7   Adding a user

13.4.2 Creating or changing user password

The **passwd** command will create an encrypted passwd entry in
/etc/security/passwd and change the Password attribute of /etc/passwd from * to
! (exclamation).

► To change your full name in the /etc/passwd file, enter:

```
passwd -f smith
```

The **passwd** command displays the name stored for your user ID. For
example, for login name smith, the **passwd** command could display the
message as shown in the following example.

```
# passwd -f smith
 smith's current gecos:
             "Mr J.Smith"
 Change (yes) or (no)? > n
 Gecos information not changed.
```

If you enter a Y for yes, the **passwd** command prompts you for the new name.
The **passwd** command records the name you enter in the /etc/passwd file.

► To change your password, enter:

```
passwd
```

The **passwd** command prompts you for your old password, if it exists and you are not the root user. After you enter the old password, the command prompts you twice for the new password.

Alternatively, you can use SMIT:

a. Running **smitty passwd** will prompt you to a menu as shown in Figure 13-8.

b. Type smith for the field User NAME.

c. Press Enter, and you will be prompted to enter the new password (twice) as shown in Figure 13-9 on page 372.

d. Enter the new password and press the Enter key.

e. When SMIT returns an OK prompt, press the F10 key to return to the command prompt.

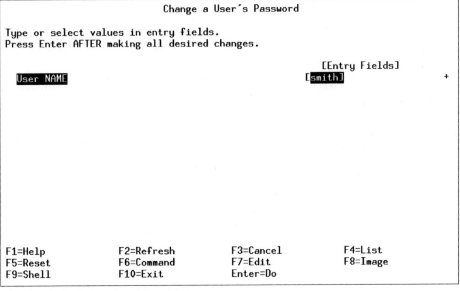

Figure 13-8 Changing a user password

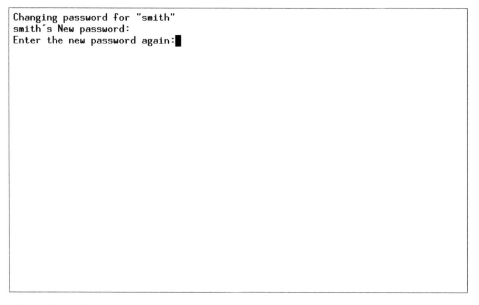

```
Changing password for "smith"
smith's New password:
Enter the new password again:█
```

Figure 13-9 Entering a user password

13.4.3 Changing user attributes

The **chuser** command changes attributes for the user identified by the Name parameter. The user name must already exist as an alphanumeric string of eight bytes or less.

> **Note:** Do not use the **chuser** command if you have a Network Information Service (NIS) database installed on your system.

Only the root user can use the **chuser** command to perform the following tasks:

► Make a user an administrative user by setting the admin attribute to true.

► Change any attributes of an administrative user.

► Add a user to an administrative group.

The following examples show the use of the **chuser** command with various flags.

► To enable user **smith** to access this system remotely, enter:

```
chuser rlogin=true smith
```

▶ To change the date that the smith user account will expire to 8 a.m., 1 December, 1998, enter:

```
chuser expires=1201080098 smith
```

▶ To add smith to the group programers, enter:

```
chuser groups=programers smith
```

Alternatively, you can go through the SMIT hierarchy by:

a. Running **smitty chuser** will prompt you to a menu as shown in Figure 13-10 on page 373.

b. Type smith for the field User NAME.

c. Use the Arrows key to highlight the Primary GROUP field and type programmer in it.

d. Press Enter.

e. When SMIT returns an OK prompt, press the F10 key to return to the command prompt.

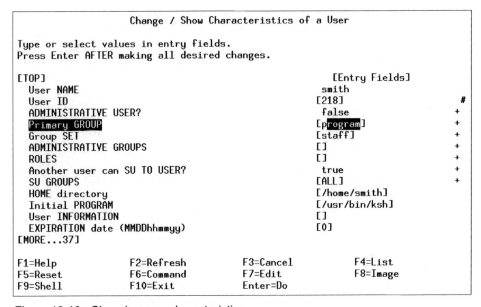

```
                    Change / Show Characteristics of a User

Type or select values in entry fields.
Press Enter AFTER making all desired changes.

[TOP]                                             [Entry Fields]
  User NAME                                       smith
  User ID                                         [218]                  #
  ADMINISTRATIVE USER?                            false                  +
  Primary GROUP                                   [program]              +
  Group SET                                       [staff]                +
  ADMINISTRATIVE GROUPS                           []                     +
  ROLES                                           []                     +
  Another user can SU TO USER?                    true                   +
  SU GROUPS                                       [ALL]                  +
  HOME directory                                  [/home/smith]
  Initial PROGRAM                                 [/usr/bin/ksh]
  User INFORMATION                                []
  EXPIRATION date (MMDDhhmmyy)                    [0]
[MORE...37]

F1=Help            F2=Refresh         F3=Cancel          F4=List
F5=Reset           F6=Command         F7=Edit            F8=Image
F9=Shell           F10=Exit           Enter=Do
```

Figure 13-10   Changing user characteristics

13.4.4 Displaying user attributes

The `lsuser` command displays the user account attributes. You can use this command to list all attributes of all the users or all the attributes of specific users except their passwords. Since there is no default parameter, you must enter the ALL keywords to see the attributes of all the users. By default, the `lsuser` command displays all user attributes. To view selected attributes, use the -a List flag. If one or more attributes cannot be read, the `lsuser` command lists as much information as possible.

> **Note:** If you have a Network Information Service (NIS) database installed on your system, some user information may not appear when you use the `lsuser` command.

By default, the `lsuser` command lists each user's attributes on one line. It displays attribute information as Attribute=Value definitions each separated by a blank space. To list the user attributes in stanza format, use the -f flag. To list the information as colon-separated records, use the -c flag.

The following examples shows the use of the `lsuser` command with various flags.

► To display the user ID and group-related information for the root account in stanza form, enter:

```
# lsuser -f -a id pgrp home root
root:
        id=0
        pgrp=system
        home=/
```

► To display the user ID, groups, and home directory of user smith in colon format, enter:

```
lsuser -c -a id home groups smith
```

► To display all the attributes of user smith in the default format, enter:

```
lsuser smith
```

All the attribute information appears with each attribute separated by a blank space.

► To display all the attributes of all the users, enter:

```
lsuser ALL
```

All the attribute information appears with each attribute separated by a blank space.

► Alternatively, you can use SMIT:

  a. Run **smitty lsuser**, which will prompt you to a menu as shown in Figure 13-11 on page 375.

  b. Type smith for the field User NAME and press Enter. This will display a screen as shown in Figure 13-12 on page 376.

  c. When SMIT returns an OK prompt, press the F10 key to return to the command prompt.

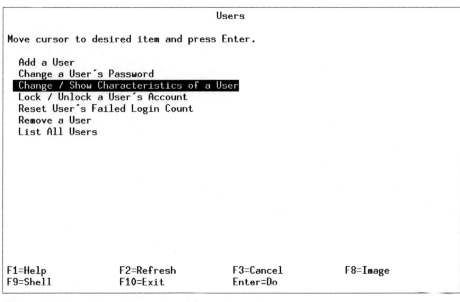

Figure 13-11 *smitty users command*

```
                  Change / Show Characteristics of a User

Type or select values in entry fields.
Press Enter AFTER making all desired changes.

[TOP]                                              [Entry Fields]
* User NAME                                        Smith
  User ID                                          [218]                    #
  ADMINISTRATIVE USER?                             false                    +
  Primary GROUP                                    [staff]                  +
  Group SET                                        [staff]                  +
  ADMINISTRATIVE GROUPS                            []                       +
  ROLES                                            []                       +
  Another user can SU TO USER?                     true                     +
  SU GROUPS                                        [ALL]                    +
  HOME directory                                   [/home/smith]
  Initial PROGRAM                                  [/usr/bin/ksh]
  User INFORMATION                                 []
  EXPIRATION date (MMDDhhmmyy)                      [0]
[MORE...37]

F1=Help               F2=Refresh          F3=Cancel          F4=List
F5=Reset              F6=Command          F7=Edit            F8=Image
F9=Shell              F10=Exit            Enter=Do
```

Figure 13-12   Listing user characteristics

13.4.5 Removing a user account

The **rmuser** command removes the user account identified by the Name
parameter. This command removes a user's attributes without removing the
user's home directory and files. The user name must already exist as a string of
eight bytes or less. If the -p flag is specified, the **rmuser** command also removes
passwords and other user authentication information from the
/etc/security/passwd file.

Only the root user can remove administrative users.

▶ The following example shows the use of the **rmuser** command to remove a
  user account smith and its attributes from the local system:

  rmuser smith

▶ To remove the user smith account and all its attributes, including passwords
  and other user authentication information in the /etc/security/passwd file, use
  the following command:

  rmuser -p smith

  Alternatively, you can go through the SMIT hierarchy by:

  a. Running **smitty rmuser** will prompt you to a menu as shown in
     Figure 13-13 on page 377.

b. Type `smith` for the field User NAME.

c. Press the Enter key.

d. When SMIT returns an OK prompt, Press the F10 key to return to the command prompt.

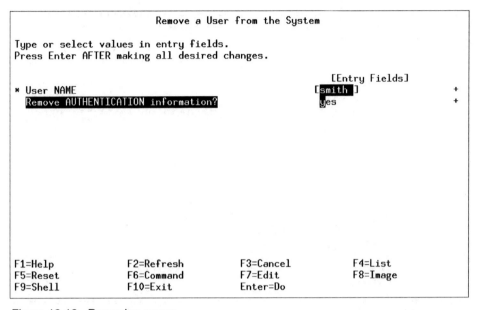

```
                    Remove a User from the System

Type or select values in entry fields.
Press Enter AFTER making all desired changes.

                                                   [Entry Fields]
* User NAME                                       [smith ]              +
  Remove AUTHENTICATION information?               yes                  +

F1=Help              F2=Refresh          F3=Cancel          F4=List
F5=Reset             F6=Command          F7=Edit            F8=Image
F9=Shell             F10=Exit            Enter=Do
```

Figure 13-13   Removing a user

13.4.6 Changing security attributes of user

The **chsec** command changes the attributes stored in the security configuration stanza files. The following security configuration stanza files have attributes that you can specify with the Attribute = Value parameter.

► /etc/security/environ

► /etc/security/group

► /etc/security/lastlog

► /etc/security/limits

► /etc/security/login.cfg

► /usr/lib/security/mkuser.default

► /etc/security/passwd

► /etc/security/portlog

► /etc/security/user

When modifying attributes in the /etc/security/environ, /etc/security/lastlog, /etc/security/limits, /etc/security/passwd, and /etc/security/user files, the stanza name specified by the Stanza parameter must either be a valid user name or default.

When modifying attributes in the /etc/security/group file, the stanza name specified by the Stanza parameter must either be a valid group name or default.

When modifying attributes in the /usr/lib/security/mkuser.default file, the Stanza parameter must be either admin or user.

When modifying attributes in the /etc/security/portlog file, the Stanza parameter must be a valid port name. When modifying attributes in the /etc/security/login.cfg file, the Stanza parameter must either be a valid port name, a method name, or the usw attribute.

When modifying attributes in the /etc/security/login.cfg or /etc/security/portlog files in a stanza that does not already exist, the stanza is automatically created by the **chsec** command.

> **Note:** You cannot modify the password attribute of the /etc/security/passwd file using the **chsec** command. Instead, use the **passwd** command.

The following examples show the usage of **chsec** command to change security stanzas in various files.

▶ To change the /dev/tty0 port to automatically lock if five unsuccessful login attempts occur within 60 seconds, enter:

```
chsec -f /etc/security/login.cfg -s /dev/tty0 -a logindisable=5 -a
logininterval=60
```

▶ To unlock the /dev/tty0 port after it has been locked by the system, enter:

```
chsec -f /etc/security/portlog -s /dev/tty0 -a locktime=0
```

▶ To allow logins from 8:00 a.m. until 5:00 p.m. for all users, enter:

```
chsec -f /etc/security/user -s default -a logintimes=:0800-1700
```

▶ To change the CPU time limit of user smith to one hour (3600 seconds), enter:

```
chsec -f /etc/security/limits -s smith -a cpu=3600
```

13.4.7 Displaying currently logged users

The **who** command displays information about all users currently on the local system. The following information is displayed: Login name, tty, and the date and time of login. Entering **who am i** or **who am I** displays your login name, tty, and the date and time you logged in. If the user is logged in from a remote machine, then the host name of that machine is displayed as well. The **who** command can also display the elapsed time since line activity occurred, the process ID of the command interpreter (shell), logins, logoffs, restarts, and changes to the system clock, as well as other processes generated by the initialization process.

> **Note:** The /etc/utmp file contains a record of users logged into the system. The command **who -a** processes the /etc/utmp file, and if this file is corrupted or missing, no output is generated from the **who** command.

The following examples show the usage of the **who** command with various flags.

▶ The following example shows the command to display information about all the users who are logged on to the system:

```
# who
root         pts/0      Nov 17 10:20    (sv1166a.itsc.aus)
root         pts/2      Nov 23 10:45    (sv1121c.itsc.aus)
root         pts/3      Nov 23 10:48    (sv1121c)
```

▶ The following example shows the command to display your user name:

```
# who am I
root         pts/3      Nov 23 10:48    (sv1121c)
```

▶ The following shows how to display the run-level of the local system:

```
# who -r
   .            run-level 2 Nov 17 10:19      2    0    S
```

▶ To display any active process that was spawned by init, run the following command:

```
# who -p
rc              .        Nov 17 10:19    4:12      2896 id=rc
fbcheck         .        Nov 17 10:19    4:12      2898 id=fbcheck
srcmstr         .        Nov 17 10:19    4:12      2900 id=srcmstr
rctcpip         .        Nov 17 10:19    4:12      4648 id=rctcpip
rcnfs           .        Nov 17 10:19    4:12      4650 id=rcnfs
cron            .        Nov 17 10:19    4:12      4652 id=cron
piobe           .        Nov 17 10:19    4:12      4984 id=piobe
qdaemon         .        Nov 17 10:19    4:12      4986 id=qdaemon
writesrv        .        Nov 17 10:19    4:12      4988 id=writesr
uprintfd        .        Nov 17 10:19    4:12      4990 id=uprintf
pmd             .        Nov 17 10:19    4:12      8772 id=pmd
dt              .        Nov 17 10:19    4:12      9034 id=dt
```

In the event that the /etc/utmp file becomes corrupt or lost, you can use the **ps** command to list processes and their associated users.

13.4.8 Preventing user logins

If the /etc/nologin file exists, the system accepts the user's name and password, prevents the user from logging in and displays the contents of the /etc/nologin file. The system does allow the root user to log in if this file exists. The /etc/nologin file is removed when you reboot the system. You can also allow users to log in again by deleting the file.

13.4.9 Changing a user's login shell

The **chsh** command changes a user's login shell attribute. The shell attribute defines the initial program that runs after a user logs in to the system. This attribute is specified in the /etc/passwd file. By default, the **chsh** command changes the login shell for the user who gives the command.

The **chsh** command is interactive. When you run the **chsh** command, the system displays a list of the available shells and the current value of the shell attribute, as shown in Figure 13-14. In addition to the default shells (/usr/bin/ksh, /usr/bin/sh, /usr/bin/bsh, /usr/bin/csh) your system manager may have defined more. Then, the system prompts you to change the shell. You must enter the full path name of an available shell.

If you have execute permission for the **chuser** command, you can change the login shell for another user.

```
# chsh
 Current available shells:
                /bin/sh
                /bin/bsh
                /bin/csh
                /bin/ksh
                /bin/tsh
                /usr/bin/sh
                /usr/bin/bsh
                /usr/bin/csh
                /usr/bin/ksh
                /usr/bin/tsh
                /usr/sbin/sliplogin
 root's current login shell:
                /bin/ksh
 Change (yes) or (no)? > yes
 To?>/bin/csh
#
```

Figure 13-14   chsh command

13.4.10 Changing the shell prompt

The shell uses the following three prompt variables.

PS1   Prompt used as the normal system prompt.

PS2   Prompt used when the shell expects more input.

PS3   Prompt used when you have root authority.

You can change any of your prompt characters by changing the value of its shell variable. The changes to your prompts last until you log off. To make your changes permanent, place them in your .env file.

The following command shows how to display the current value of the PS1 variable.

```
# echo "prompt is $PS1":
prompt is $
```

The following example shows the command to change the prompt to Ready>:

```
export PS1="Ready> "
```

The following example shows the command to change the continuation prompt to Enter more->:

```
export PS2="Enter more->"
```

The following example shows the command to change the root prompt to Root->:

```
export PS3="Root-> "
```

13.4.11 Starting AIX Common Desktop Environment

If the AIX Common Desktop Environment (CDE) is not set up to start automatically on a locally attached graphics display, you can use the following command to start the desktop from an AIX command line.

```
xinit /usr/dt/bin/Xsession
```

Using the **xinit** command starts the desktop without bringing up the whole desktop environment. You will bypass the login window when you start the desktop, and when you exit, you will return to a command line rather than an AIX CDE login window. You will, however, use the same desktop applications you would use had you started the desktop from the welcome window.

You can set up the system so that the AIX CDE comes up automatically when you start the system, or you can start AIX CDE manually. You must log in as root to perform each of these tasks.

Enabling and disabling desktop autostart

To enable the desktop autostart, use **smitty dtconfig** or **dtconfig -e.**

To disable the desktop autostart, use **smitty dtconfig** or **dtconfig -d.**

After enabling or disabling desktop autostart, reboot the system.

> **Note:** If the desktop autostart is enabled on a system with no graphics capability, it may make using the serial console difficult. To prevent problems, disable the desktop autostart and reboot.

Starting AIX Common Desktop Environment manually.

Use the following command to start the AIX CDE at the command line.

```
/usr/dt/bin/dtlogin -daemon
```

A Desktop Login window will display. When you log in, you will start a desktop session.

Stopping AIX Common Desktop Environment manually.

When you manually stop the login manager, all X servers and desktop sessions that the login manager started are stopped.

1. Open a terminal emulator window and log in as root.

2. Obtain the process ID of the Login Manager by entering the following:

   `cat /var/dt/Xpid`

3. Stop the Login Manager by entering:

   `kill -term` *process_id*

13.5 Common login errors

The following section summarizes a few of the Error Messages for Component ID 3004 (login errors) and their possible causes. Refer to the AIX product documentation for more information.

3004-004	`You must "exec" login from the lowest login shell.` You attempted to log off the system while processes are still running in another shell.
3004-007	`You entered an invalid login name or password.` You tried to log in to a system that does not recognize your login or password.
3004-008	`Failed setting credentials.` Login failed.
3004-009	`Failed running login shell.` You tried to log in to a system that has a damaged login shell. The login shell does not exist.
3004-030	`You logged in using all uppercase characters.` You attempted to log in with Caps Lock on.
3004-031	`Password read timed out--possible noise on port.` You logged in but did not enter your password within a specified amount of time. Your password was not validated within a specified amount of time due to a failed network connection.
3004-302	`Your account has expired. Please see the system administrator.` Your password has expired.
3004-312	`All available login sessions are in use.` You tried to log in to a system that had all present sessions in use.
3004-687	`User does not exist.` You specified an invalid user name with the **lsuser**, **chuser**, **rmuser**, or **passwd** command.

13.5.1 AIX Common Desktop Environment and full file systems

Users will not be able to log in using the AIX CDE when the /home file system is full. If /home is full, the AIX CDE welcome window will accept the user's name and password, the display will then go blank and appear to hang, then will return to the AIX CDE welcome window. To log in and investigate, press the Options button on the AIX CDE welcome window and select Command Line Login, or log in from a non graphics display.

13.6 Quiz

The following are questions created by the authors to further test your understanding of the topics.

1. A user is able to get a login prompt for the server but gets a failed login error message when trying to login with an ID. Which of the following is the most likely cause of this problem?

   A.   The hard drive is bad.

   B.   The /home file system is full.

   C.   The server is low on paging space.

   D.   The user has entered an invalid ID or password.

2. Which of the following files contains UID, home directory, and shell information?

   A.   /etc/passwd

   B.   /etc/security/user

   C.   /etc/security/environ

   D.   /etc/security/passwd

3. A customer has cloned a machine using **mksysb**. The source machine contained a graphics adaptor and display and was running Xwindows. The target machine has an IBM 3151 terminal and no graphics capability. The customer states that they are seeing the following message repeatedly scroll across the login screen.

```
*********************************************************
*   Starting Desktop Login on display :0÷
*
* Wait for the Desktop Login screen before logging in.
*
*********************************************************
```

To prevent this message from appearing, which of the following actions should be performed?

A. Run the **cdecfg -disable** command.

B. Run the **startx -no** command and reboot.

C. Run the **dtconfig -d** command and reboot.

D. Remove the X=start line from the /etc/security/login.cfg file and reboot.

4. After completing the installation of the Base Operating System on one of the servers, the system administrator would like for all users who **telnet** into this machine to see a specific message each time they successfully log in. Which file should be edited to provide this message?

A. /etc/motd

B. /etc/profile

C. /etc/environment

D. /etc/security/login.cfg

5. A marketing manager would like her shell prompt to reflect the directory she is in so that if she needs to remove a file, she will be sure to be in the proper directory. Which of the following environment variables can be set to accomplish this?

A. PS1

B. PATH

C. DISPLAY

D. LOCPATH

13.6.1 Answers

The following answers are for the quiz questions.

1. D
2. A
3. C
4. A
5. A

13.7 Exercises

The following exercises provide sample topics for self study. They will help ensure comprehension of this chapter.

1. Add a new user account (james) and try to log in to the new account. Can you log in without creating a password for this account?

2. Create a password for a newly created user account (james).

3. You want all the users to get the following message when they log in:

```
***************************************************************************

Please assemble in the meeting room at 13:00 hrs on Nov.20,2001

***************************************************************************
```

Which file needs to be edited to contain this message so that the message is displayed when a user logs in?

4. Move the file /etc/utmp to /etc/wtmp.org. Run the **who** command. What is the output?

5. Change the password of a user account who does not remember his old password.

6. How can you disable the desktop autostart?

7. Display the attributes of the user account.

8. Permanently change your shell prompt to display the current directory.

Printing

This chapter discusses the AIX print subsystem and does not cover the optional SRV4 print subsystem, which is available in AIX 5L Version 5.1.

The following defines terms commonly used when discussing UNIX printing.

► Print job

A print job is a unit of work to be run on a printer. A print job can consist of printing one or more files depending on how the print job is requested. The system assigns a unique job number to each job it runs.

► Queue

The queue is where you direct a print job. It is a stanza in the /etc/qconfig file whose name is the name of the queue and points to the associated queue device.

► Queue device

The queue device is the stanza in the /etc/qconfig file that normally follows the local queue stanza. It specifies the /dev file (printer device) that should be used.

> **Note:** There can be more than one queue device associated with a single queue.

▶ qdaemon

The qdaemon is a process that runs in the background and controls the queues. It is generally started during IPL with the `startsrc` command. See Section 9.1, "Starting the SRC" on page 244 for more information.

▶ Print spooler

A spooler is not specifically a print job spooler. Instead, it provides a generic spooling function that can be used for queuing various types of jobs including print jobs queued to a printer.

The spooler does not normally know what type of job it is queuing. When the system administrator defines a spooler queue, the purpose of the queue is defined by the spooler backend program that is specified for the queue. For example, if the spooler backend program is the `piobe` command (the printer I/O backend), the queue is a print queue. Likewise, if the spooler backend program is a compiler, the queue is for compile jobs. When the spooler's `qdaemon` command selects a job from a spooler queue, it runs the job by invoking the backend program specified by the system administrator when the queue was defined.

The main spooler command is the `enq` command. Although you can invoke this command directly to queue a print job, three front-end commands are defined for submitting a print job: The `lp`, `lpr`, and `qprt` commands. A print request issued by one of these commands is first passed to the `enq` command, which then places the information about the file in the queue for the qdaemon to process.

▶ Real printer

A real printer is the printer hardware attached to a serial or parallel port at a unique hardware device address. The printer device driver in the kernel communicates with the printer hardware and provides an interface between the printer hardware and a virtual printer, but it is not aware of the concept of virtual printers. Real printers sometimes run out of paper.

▶ Local and remote printers

When you attach a printer to a node or host, the printer is referred to as a local printer. A remote print system allows nodes that are not directly linked to a printer to have printer access.

To use remote printing facilities, the individual nodes must be connected to a network using Transmission Control Protocol/Internet Protocol (TCP/IP) and must support the required TCP/IP applications.

► Printer backend

The printer backend is a collection of programs called by the spooler's **qdaemon** command to manage a print job that is queued for printing. The printer backend performs the following functions:

- Receives a list of one or more files to be printed from the **qdaemon** command.

- Uses printer and formatting attribute values from the database; overridden by flags entered on the command line.

- Initializes the printer before printing a file.

- Runs filters as necessary to convert the print data stream to a format supported by the printer.

- Provides filters, for simple formatting of ASCII documents.

- Provides support for printing national language characters.

- Passes the filtered print data stream to the printer device driver.

- Generates header and trailer pages.

- Generates multiple copies.

- Reports paper out, intervention required, and printer error conditions.

- Reports problems detected by the filters.

- Cleans up after a print job is cancelled.

- Provides a print environment that a system administrator can customize to address specific printing needs.

Table 14-1 provides a list of commands that can perform the same function.

Table 14-1   Print commands and their equivalents

Submit print jobs	Status print jobs	Cancel print jobs
enq	enq -A	enq -x
qprt	qchk	qcan
lp	lpstat	lprm
lpr	lpq	

14.1 Creating a new print queue

The best way for you to create a new print queue is by using the SMIT interface. Here are the steps you need to follow.

Enter the following command:

`smitty`

Go to the System Management menu where you will select Print Spooling as shown in Figure 14-1 and press Enter.

```
                          System Management

Move cursor to desired item and press Enter.

   Software Installation and Maintenance
   Software License Management
   Devices
   System Storage Management (Physical & Logical Storage)
   Security & Users
   Communications Applications and Services
   Print Spooling
   Problem Determination
   Performance & Resource Scheduling
   System Environments
   Processes & Subsystems
   Applications
   Using SMIT (information only)




F1=Help              F2=Refresh          F3=Cancel          F8=Image
F9=Shell             F10=Exit            Enter=Do
```

Figure 14-1   System Management menu screen - Print Spooling option

Go into the Print Spooling menu where you will select Add a Print Queue as shown in Figure 14-2 and press Enter.

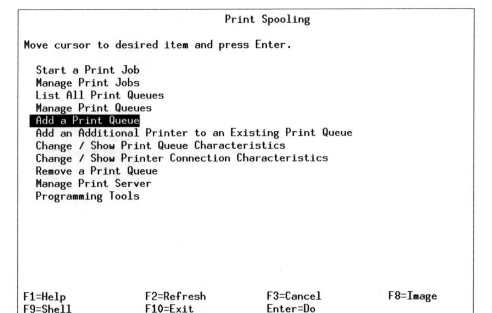

Figure 14-2   Print Spooling menu screen - Add a Print Queue option

Figure 14-3 shows the Print Spooling menu, in which an Add a Print Queue sub menu will appear. Select what the printer is connected to, in this case, local, and press Enter.

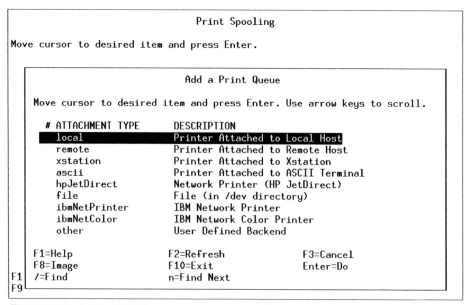

Figure 14-3   Add a Print Queue menu screen - print queue selection

Once you selected where the printer is connected to, select what kind of printer it is and press Enter. In Figure 14-4 on page 393, Other (select this if your printer type is not listed above) has been selected.

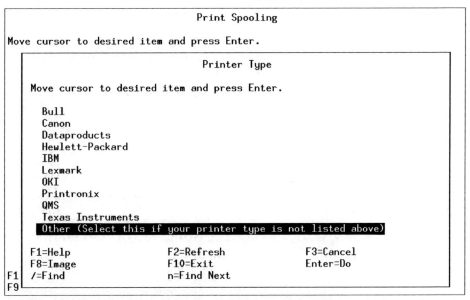

Figure 14-4   Print Spooling menu screen - Printer Type selection

Figure 14-5 shows where the Printer Type is selected. Here, select generic Generic Printer and press Enter.

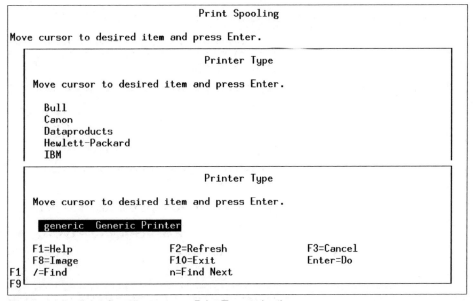

Figure 14-5   Print Spooling menu - Print Type selection

You now need to select the Printer Interface. As shown in Figure 14-6, select parallel as your choice and press Enter.

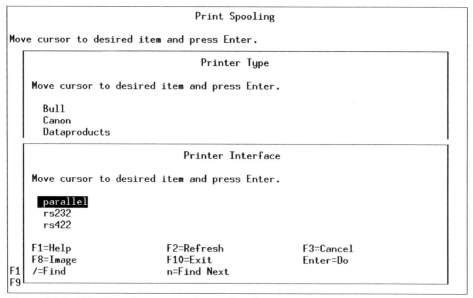

```
                          Print Spooling
Move cursor to desired item and press Enter.
 ┌──────────────────────────────────────────────────────────────┐
 │                       Printer Type                             │
 │                                                                │
 │  Move cursor to desired item and press Enter.                  │
 │                                                                │
 │      Bull                                                      │
 │      Canon                                                     │
 │      Dataproducts                                              │
 ┌────────────────────────────────────────────────────────────────┐
 │                      Printer Interface                           │
 │                                                                  │
 │   Move cursor to desired item and press Enter.                   │
 │                                                                  │
 │      ▉parallel▉                                                  │
 │       rs232                                                      │
 │       rs422                                                      │
 │                                                                  │
 │      F1=Help              F2=Refresh           F3=Cancel         │
 │      F8=Image             F10=Exit             Enter=Do          │
F1│     /=Find               n=Find Next                            │
F9└──────────────────────────────────────────────────────────────┘
```

Figure 14-6   Print Spooling menu - Printer Interface selection

Once your Printer Interface has been selected, you need to select the Parent Adapter (in Figure 14-7 on page 395, select ppa0 Available 01-D0 Standard I/O Parallel Port Adapter as your choice) and press Enter.

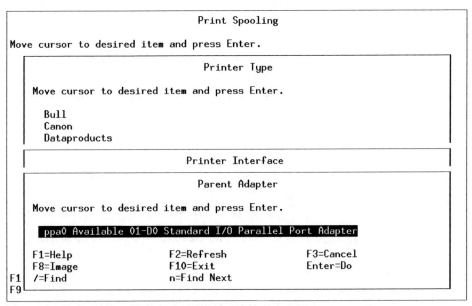

```
                        Print Spooling
Move cursor to desired item and press Enter.
┌─────────────────────────────────────────────────────────────────┐
│                        Printer Type                               │
│  Move cursor to desired item and press Enter.                     │
│                                                                   │
│     Bull                                                          │
│     Canon                                                         │
│     Dataproducts                                                  │
├─────────────────────────────────────────────────────────────────┤
│                     Printer Interface                             │
├─────────────────────────────────────────────────────────────────┤
│                       Parent Adapter                              │
│  Move cursor to desired item and press Enter.                     │
│                                                                   │
│    ▐ppa0 Available 01-D0 Standard I/O Parallel Port Adapter▌      │
│                                                                   │
│     F1=Help              F2=Refresh              F3=Cancel        │
│     F8=Image             F10=Exit                Enter=Do         │
│ F1│ /=Find               n=Find Next                              │
│ F9└                                                               │
└─────────────────────────────────────────────────────────────────┘
```

Figure 14-7   Print Spooling menu - Parent Adapter selection

Once this process is complete, you will Add a Print Queue, as shown in
Figure 14-8 on page 396. This is where you select what you want to call your
printer. In this case, the printer is called *lpforu*. You can change any of the
characteristics of the printer if you need; however, this is normally not needed.

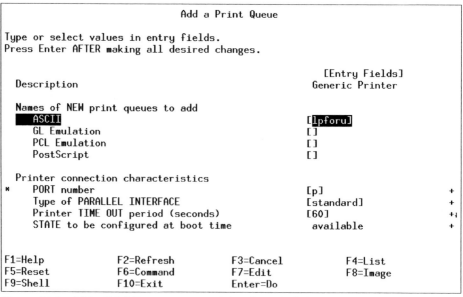

```
                      Add a Print Queue

Type or select values in entry fields.
Press Enter AFTER making all desired changes.

                                               [Entry Fields]
   Description                                Generic Printer

   Names of NEW print queues to add
       ASCII                                [lpforu]
       GL Emulation                         []
       PCL Emulation                        []
       PostScript                           []

   Printer connection characteristics
 *     PORT number                          [p]                  +
       Type of PARALLEL INTERFACE           [standard]           +
       Printer TIME OUT period (seconds)    [60]                 +i
       STATE to be configured at boot time   available           +


F1=Help             F2=Refresh         F3=Cancel          F4=List
F5=Reset            F6=Command         F7=Edit            F8=Image
F9=Shell            F10=Exit           Enter=Do
```

Figure 14-8   Add a Print Queue menu - printer characteristics

Once you have entered your characteristics, the COMMAND STATUS menu will appear informing you of the success of your action, as shown in Figure 14-9.

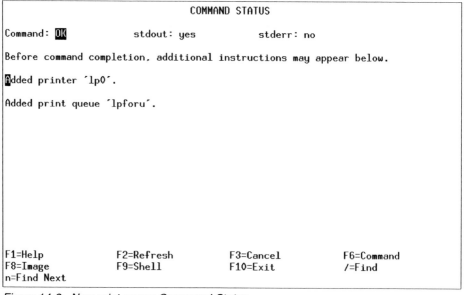

```
                      COMMAND STATUS

Command: OK              stdout: yes          stderr: no

Before command completion, additional instructions may appear below.

Added printer 'lp0'.

Added print queue 'lpforu'.




F1=Help             F2=Refresh         F3=Cancel          F6=Command
F8=Image            F9=Shell           F10=Exit           /=Find
n=Find Next
```

Figure 14-9   New print queue Command Status

Once complete, press F10 to exit.

You have now installed the print queue *lpforu* on the printer lp0.

14.2 The print configuration file

The file that holds the configuration for the printers that exist on the system is the /etc/qconfig file. It is the most important file in the spooler domain for these reasons:

▶ It contains the definition of every queue known to the spooler.

▶ A system administrator can read this file and discern the function of each queue.

▶ Although it is not recommended, this file can be edited to modify spooler queues without halting the spooler.

The /etc/qconfig file describes all of the queues defined in the AIX operating system. A queue is a named, ordered list of requests for a specific device. A device is something (either hardware or software) that can handle those requests one at a time. The queue provides serial access to the device. Each queue must be serviced by at least one device; often it can be handled by more than one device.

The following is an example of the contents of the /etc/qconfig file:

```
* @(#)33       1.6  src/bos/usr/bin/que/qconfig.sh, cmdque, bos430, 9737A_430
2/4/94 10:45:05
* IBM_PROLOG_BEGIN_TAG
..........
* IBM_PROLOG_END_TAG
*
* COMPONENT_NAME: cmdque configuration file for spooling
..........
* PRINTER QUEUEING SYSTEM CONFIGURATION
*
* This configuration file contains valid configurations for remote
* print queue rp0, local print queue lp0 and batch queue bsh.
* They may be deleted or changed as necessary.
*
* EXAMPLE of remote print queue configuration
* rp0:
*       host = hostname
*       s_statfilter = /usr/lib/lpd/aixshort
*       l_statfilter = /usr/lib/lpd/aixlong
*       rq = queuename
*       device = drp0
```

```
*
* drp0:
*         backend = /usr/lib/lpd/rembak
*
* EXAMPLE of local print queue configuration
*lp0:
*         discipline = fcfs
*         up = TRUE
*         device = dlp0
*
*dlp0:
*         backend = /usr/lib/lpd/piobe
*         file = FALSE
*         access = write
*         feed = never
*         header = never
*         trailer = never
*
* BATCH queue for running shell scripts
*
*bsh:
*         device = bshdev
*         discipline = fcfs
*bshdev:
*         backend = /usr/bin/bsh
lpforu:
device = lp0
lp0:
          file = /dev/lp0
          header = never
          trailer = never
          access = both
          backend = /usr/lib/lpd/piobe
```

The file /etc/qconfig is composed of text blocks referred to as stanzas. Each queue is represented by a pair of stanzas. The first stanza in a pair is referred to as the queue stanza; the second stanza in a pair is referred to as the device stanza. Stanzas are composed of parameters and parameter values that describe the queue's properties and functions.

14.3 Controlling the print queue

This section examines some of the commands that you would use with the print queue.

▶ The **lpstat** command displays information about the current status of the line printer.

The **lpstat** command syntax is as follows:

```
lpstat [ -aList ] [ -cList ] [ -d ] [ -oList ] [ -pList ] [ -r ] [ -s ]
[ -t ] [ -uList ] [ -vList ] [ -W ]
```

An example of the **lpstat** command, without any flags, is as follows:

```
# lpstat
Queue  Dev  Status  Job Files         User         PP% Blks Cp Rnk
------ ---- ------- --- ---------------- ------------ --- ---- -- ---
lpforu lp0  READY
```

▶ The **qchk** command displays the current status information regarding specified print jobs, print queues, or users.

The **qchk** command syntax is as follows:

```
qchk [ -A ] [ -L | -W ] [ -P Printer ] [ -# JobNumber ] [ -q ]
[ -u UserName ] [ -w Delay ]
```

An example of the **qchk** command, without any flags, is as follows:

```
# qchk
Queue  Dev  Status  Job Files         User         PP% Blks Cp Rnk
------ ---- ------- --- ---------------- ------------ --- ---- -- ---
lpforu lp0  READY
```

▶ The **lpq** command reports the status of the specified job or all jobs associated with the specified *UserName* and *JobNumber* variables.

The **lpq** command syntax is as follows:

```
lpq [ + [ Number ] ] [ -l | -W ] [-P Printer ] [JobNumber] [UserName]
```

The following is an example of the **lpq** command, without any flags:

```
# lpq
Queue  Dev  Status  Job Files         User         PP% Blks Cp Rnk
------ ---- ------- --- ---------------- ------------ --- ---- -- ---
lpforu lp0  READY
```

▶ The **lpr** command uses a spooling daemon to print the named File parameter when facilities become available.

The **lpr** command syntax is as follows:

```
lpr [ -f ] [ -g ] [ -h ] [ -j ] [ -l ] [ -m ] [ -n ] [ -p ] [ -r ] [ -s ]
[ -P Printer ] [ -# NumberCopies ] [ -C Class ] [ -J Job ] [ -T Title ]
[ -i [ NumberColumns ] ] [ -w Width ] [ File ... ]
```

The following is an example of using the **lpr** command to print the file /etc/passwd.

```
# lpr /etc/passwd
# lpstat
Queue  Dev  Status    Job  Files             User      PP %  Blks Cp Rnk
------ ---- --------- ---  ---------------- -------- ---- -- ---- -- ---
lpforu lp0  RUNNING    3   /etc/passwd       root       1 100  1  1   1
```

14.3.1 Editing /etc/qconfig

The /etc/qconfig file can be modified with your favorite text editor. This may be required if you are unable to remove a printer definition by any other means. There are unenforced rules concerning when you can and cannot edit /etc/qconfig without halting or corrupting the operation of the spooler. This is the topic of discussion in the next section.

14.3.2 Modifying /etc/qconfig while jobs are processing

The /etc/qconfig file should never be edited when jobs are processing. This is especially true when your system has a large number (greater than 25) of printers that are generally busy. When the qdaemon receives notification from **enq** that a new Job Description File (JDF) exists, the qdaemon examines the dates on both /etc/qconfig and /etc/qconfig.bin, the binary version of /etc/qconfig. If /etc/qconfig is younger than /etc/qconfig.bin, the qdaemon does not accept any new jobs, including the one that caused it to examine the aforementioned files, until all currently running jobs have finished processing. When the jobs have finished processing, the qdaemon creates a new version of /etc/qconfig.bin.

If you cause the qdaemon to go into this state while jobs are processing, it is possible for the spooler to hang.

14.4 Stopping the print queue

In the following scenario, you have a job printing on a print queue, but you need to stop the queue so that you can put more paper in the printer.

Check the print queue using the **lpstat** command, as shown in the following example. The reason for the -v flag is so that you do not get a listing of all the printers. See Table 14-4 on page 403 for a list of **lpstat** command flags.

```
# lpstat -vlpforu
Queue  Dev  Status    Job  Files             User      PP %  Blks Cp Rnk
------ ---- --------- ---  ---------------- -------- ---- -- ---- -- ---
lpforu lp0  RUNNING    3   /etc/passwd       root       1 100  1  1   1
```

Disable the print queue using the **enq** command, as shown in the following example. See Table 14-2 for a list of **enq** command flags.

```
# enq -D -P 'lpforu:lp0'
```

Check the printer queue using the **qchk** command, as shown in the following example. See Table 14-3 for some **qchk** command flags.

```
# qchk -P lpforu
Queue  Dev  Status    Job  Files            User      PP %  Blks Cp Rnk
------ ---- --------- ---  ---------------- --------  ---- -- ---- -- ---
lpforu lp0  DOWN        3  /etc/passwd      root         1 100   1  1   1
```

Table 14-2 Flags for the enq command

Flag	Description
-D	Device DOWN. Turns off the device associated with the queue. The qdaemon process no longer send jobs to the device.
-U	Brings UP the device associated with a queue. The qdaemon process sends jobs to it again.
-P *Queue*	Specifies the queue to which the job is sent. A particular device on a queue can be specified by typing -P *Queue:Device*.

Table 14-3 Flags for the qchk command

Flag	Description
-# *JobNumber*	Requests the status of the job number specified by the *JobNumber* variable. The **qchk** command looks for *JobNumber* on the default queue when the *-#JobNumber* flag is used alone. To search for *JobNumber* on all queues, the -# flag must be used with the -A flag. The -# flag may also be used in conjunction with the -P *Queue* flag.
-A	Requests the status of all queues.
-P *Printer*	Requests the status of the printer specified by the *Printer* variable.
-u *UserName*	Requests the status of all print jobs sent by the user specified by the *UserName* variable.
-w *Delay*	Updates requested status information at intervals, in seconds, as specified by the *Delay* variable until all print jobs are finished.

14.5 Starting the print queue

You have replaced the paper, and you now want to restart the print queue so that it will finish your print job. Here is how you would do this:

```
# lpstat -vlpforu
Queue  Dev  Status    Job  Files            User      PP %  Blks Cp Rnk
------ ---- --------- ---  ---------------- --------  ---- -- ---- -- ---
lpforu lp0  DOWN       3   /etc/passwd      root       1 100   1  1   1
# enq -U -P 'lpforu:lp0'
# qchk -P lpforu
Queue  Dev  Status    Job  Files            User      PP %  Blks Cp Rnk
------ ---- --------- ---  ---------------- --------  ---- -- ---- -- ---
lpforu lp0  RUNNING    3   /etc/passwd      root       1 100   1  1   1
```

The **enable** command can also be used to start the print queue. It takes the printer queue device as its only argument, as in the following example.

```
# enable lpforu:lp0
```

14.6 Flushing a print job

You discovered that the first job you printed was the incorrect one. You printed the correct one but now you want to delete the first job. This is how it would be done:

1. Check the status of the print queue.

```
# lpstat -vlpforu
Queue  Dev  Status    Job  Files            User      PP %  Blks Cp Rnk
------ ---- --------- ---  ---------------- --------  ---- -- ---- -- ---
lpforu lp0  RUNNING    3   /etc/passwd      root       1 100   1  1   1
```

2. Print the /etc/hosts file to the default printer.

```
# lpr -dlpforu /etc/hosts
```

3. Check the status of the print queue.

```
# lpstat -vlpforu
Queue  Dev  Status    Job  Files            User      PP %  Blks Cp Rnk
------ ---- --------- ---  ---------------- --------  ---- -- ---- -- ---
lpforu lp0  RUNNING    3   /etc/passwd      root       1 100   1  1   1
            QUEUED     4   /etc/hosts       root       1 100   2  1   2
```

4. Cancel the print job for /etc/passwd using one of the following commands:

```
# qcan -P lpforu -x 3
# cancel 3
# lprm -P lpforu 3
# enq -P lpforu -x 3
```

5. Check the print queue using the **qchk** command.

```
# qchk -P lpforu
Queue  Dev  Status    Job  Files            User        PP %  Blks Cp Rnk
------ ---- --------  ---  ---------------- --------  ---- -- ---- -- ---
lpforu lp0  RUNNING    4   /etc/hosts       root          1 100   2  1   2
```

14.7 How to check the print spooler

There are various commands to check a print spooler. This section covers the **lpstat** command and some of the flags you can use. The **enq** command has a similar function.

In Table 14-4 are some of the flags used by the **lpstat** command and, where available, an equivalent **enq** command.

Table 14-4   Flags for the lpstat command and enq command equivalents

Flag	enq Equivalent	Description
-a*List*	**enq -q -P**Queue1	Provides status and job information on queues.
-d	**enq -q**	Displays the status information for the system default destination for the **lp** command.
-o*List*		Displays the status of print requests or print queues.
-p*List*		Displays the status of printers.
-r	**enq -A**	Provides status and job information on queues.
-s	**enq -A**	Displays a status summary, including a list of printers and their associated devices.
-t	**enq -AL**	Displays all status information, including a list of printers and their associated devices.

Flag	enq Equivalent	Description
-u*List*	**enq -u**	Prints the status of all print requests for users specified in List. List is a list of login names.
-v*List*		Prints the status of printers. The List variable is a list of printer names.

The following is an example of using the **lpstat** command with different flag settings to get the status of the print queue *lpforu*:

```
# lpstat -plpforu
Queue   Dev Status     Job Files             User        PP %   Blks  Cp Rnk
------- --- ---------  --- ------------------ ----------  ----  --  ----- --- ---
lpforu  lp0 RUNNING     2 /etc/hosts          root                  2   1   1
# lpstat -u"root"
Queue   Dev Status     Job Files             User        PP %   Blks  Cp Rnk
------- --- ---------  --- ------------------ ----------  ----  --  ----- --- ---
lpforu  lp0  RUNNING    2 /etc/hosts          root                  2   1   1
```

The output for the **lpstat -t** command is the same as the output for the **lpstat -u** and **lpstat -p** commands, except that it gives the queue file, as well as the time stamp, for the file in the queue.

14.8 Setting the time out on a printer

Setting the time out on a printer specifies the amount of time, in seconds, the system waits for an operation to complete on a printer. The value must be greater than zero (0). The default value is calculated based on the device you select.

This option would be used in the following scenarios:

▶ A large network with many users utilizing the printers.

▶ A network with printers a long distance from the server or at another location.

The following example shows output from the **lpstat** command that indicates the printer time out should be increased.

```
# lpstat -plpforu
Queue   Dev   Status     Job Files             User        PP %   Blks  Cp Rnk
------- ----- ---------  --- ------------------ ----------  ----  --  ----- --- ---
lpforu  lp0   DEV_WAIT   17 smit.log           root                  50  1   1
```

To increase the printer time out, enter the following SMIT fast path:

```
smitty spooler
```

In the Print Spooling menu, select Change / Show Printer Connection Characteristics as in Figure 14-10.

```
                            Print Spooling

Move cursor to desired item and press Enter.

    Start a Print Job
    Manage Print Jobs
    List All Print Queues
    Manage Print Queues
    Add a Print Queue
    Add an Additional Printer to an Existing Print Queue
    Change / Show Print Queue Characteristics
    Change / Show Printer Connection Characteristics
    Remove a Print Queue
    Manage Print Server
    Programming Tools






F1=Help              F2=Refresh           F3=Cancel            F8=Image
F9=Shell             F10=Exit             Enter=Do
```

Figure 14-10   Print Spooling menu

In the Change/Show Printer Connection Characteristics sub window, select where the printer is connected to. In Figure 14-11, local is used.

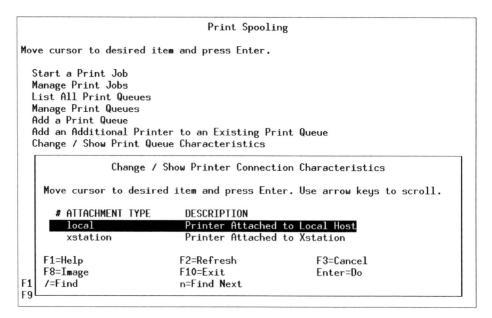

Figure 14-11   Print Spooling - Change/Show Printer Connection Characteristics

Shown in Figure 14-12 is the Local Printers selection sub-menu. Here you select lp0 Available 01-d0-00-00 Other parallel printer, and press Enter.

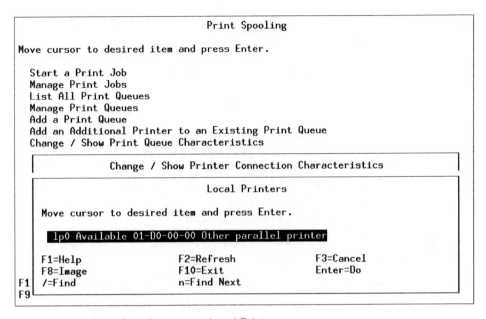

```
                          Print Spooling

Move cursor to desired item and press Enter.

  Start a Print Job
  Manage Print Jobs
  List All Print Queues
  Manage Print Queues
  Add a Print Queue
  Add an Additional Printer to an Existing Print Queue
  Change / Show Print Queue Characteristics
 ┌──────────────────────────────────────────────────────────────┐
 │        Change / Show Printer Connection Characteristics        │
 ┌──────────────────────────────────────────────────────────────┐
 │                        Local Printers                          │
 │                                                                │
 │   Move cursor to desired item and press Enter.                 │
 │                                                                │
 │   ▌lp0 Available 01-D0-00-00 Other parallel printer▐           │
 │                                                                │
 │   F1=Help            F2=Refresh            F3=Cancel           │
 │   F8=Image           F10=Exit             Enter=Do            │
 F1  /=Find             n=Find Next                               │
 F9 └──────────────────────────────────────────────────────────────┘
```

Figure 14-12   Print Spooling menu - Local Printers

Once everything is selected, you will go to the Change/Show Printer Connection Characteristics menu, as displayed in Figure 14-13. Here you select the Printer TIME OUT period (seconds) and change it, in this case, to 60 seconds.

```
                  Change / Show Printer Connection Characteristics

Type or select values in entry fields.
Press Enter AFTER making all desired changes.

                                                [Entry Fields]
        Printer name                           lp0
        Description                             Other parallel printer
        Interface                               parallel
        Status                                  Available
        Location                                01-D0-00-00
        Parent adapter                          ppa0

 *  PORT number                                 [p]                      +
        Type of PARALLEL INTERFACE              [standard]               +
        Printer TIME OUT period (seconds)       [60]                     +
        STATE to be configured at boot time     available                +
        Microseconds to delay between characters [0]                     +


    F1=Help              F2=Refresh          F3=Cancel           F4=List
    F5=Reset             F6=Command          F7=Edit             F8=Image
    F9=Shell             F10=Exit            Enter=Do
```

Figure 14-13   Change/Show Printer Connection Characteristics screen

Once the command has completed, you will get the COMMAND STAUS menu, as displayed in Figure 14-14, which shows the status of command completion.

```
                           COMMAND STATUS

   Command: OK              stdout: yes            stderr: no

   Before command completion, additional instructions may appear below.

   lp0 changed









   F1=Help          F2=Refresh        F3=Cancel         F6=Command
   F8=Image         F9=Shell          F10=Exit          /=Find
   n=Find Next
```

Figure 14-14   Changing printer connection characteristics results

14.9 Basic printer diagnostics checklist

In this section are some troubleshooting tips. This is not a comprehensive list, but it will assist you with resolving some of the more common problems you may encounter.

► Verify that the qdaemon is running. Make sure there are no forked processes running from the qdaemon.

► Make sure the system date is correct. The qdaemon automatically rebuilds the /etc/qconfig.bin file when the qconfig file changes. If the date on the qconfig file is earlier than the date on the /etc/qconfig.bin file, the qconfig file is not digested, even if it was just modified. Use the **enq -Y** command to redigest the qconfig file.

► If the dates on the /etc/qconfig.bin file and the /etc/qconfig file are correct, and changes to the qconfig file are correct, the /etc/qconfig file may no longer be linked to the /usr/lpd/qconfig file.

- Check that the /tmp directory is not full. The /tmp directory may be full if you receive a message, such as *No Virtual Printers Defined*, or if your are unable to print from InfoExplorer.

- If only the root user can print, check the permissions of the /tmp directory. Also, check the permissions of the print commands being used (including **enq**).

- Check for obsolete queue names in the /var/spool/lpd/qdir file. A problem with the installation of a new /etc/qconfig file occurs when a queue is removed from the new /etc/qconfig file and a print request is made using the obsolete queue name. In this case the qdaemon logs an error message. You must determine if the message refers to an old queue. If so, the problem will persist until you remove the obsolete queue entries from the /var/spool/lpd/qdir file.

- If operator-attention messages requested by remote print commands are not being received, make sure the socket is connected and the host name can be pinged.

14.10 Quiz

The following certification assessment question helps verify your understanding of the topics discussed in this chapter.

1. The Widget Company has installed a new laser printer on their network. The RS/6000 has been configured to print to that printer using the pcl queue. A print job was submitted to the pcl queue and was running until the printer ran out of paper. The printer was offline for 30 minutes before the paper was added. What needs to be done to continue the print job?

   A. `enable pcl`

   B. `startsrc -s lpd`

   C. `refresh -s lpd`

   D. resubmit the job

The following are additional questions created by the authors to further test your understanding of the topics.

1. To list the print job 120 on printer lineprinter, which command would you use?

   A. `qchk -P lineprinter`

   B. `qcan 120`

   C. `ps lineprinter`

   D. `lsdev lineprinter | grep 120`

2. To print the file /etc/host to the printer lineprinter, which command would you use?

A. `lpr /etc/hosts -P lineprinter`

B. `lpstat lineprinter`

C. `lprm /etc/hosts -P lineprinter`

D. `print /etc/hosts`

14.10.1 Answers

The following answer is for the assessment quiz questions.

1. A

The following answers are for the additional quiz questions.

1. A

2. A

14.11 Exercises

The following exercises provide sample topics for self study. They will help ensure comprehension of this chapter.

1. Create a new print queue called 3k120.

2. Explain the /etc/qconfig file.

3. Start the print queue 3k120.

4. Stop the print queue 3k120.

5. Change the Time Out on the printer to twice its original Time Out.

6. Check the print queue using four different print commands.

7. Flush a print job.

Sendmail and e-mail

The mail facility provides a method for exchanging electronic mail between the users on the same system or on multiple systems connected by a network. This chapter discusses mail configuration tasks, mail configuration files, mail aliases, and mail logs.

15.1 Overview of mail system

The mail system is an internetwork mail delivery facility that consists of a user interface, a message routing program, and a message delivery program (or mailer).

A mail user interface enables users to create, send, and receive messages from other users. The mail system provides two user interfaces, mail and mhmail. The `mail` command is the standard mail user interface available on all UNIX systems. The `mhmail` command is the Message Handler (MH) user interface, an enhanced mail user interface designed for experienced users.

A message routing program routes messages to their destinations. The mail system's message routing program is the `sendmail` command (a daemon). Depending on the type of route to the destination, the `sendmail` command uses different mailers to deliver messages as shown in Figure 15-1.

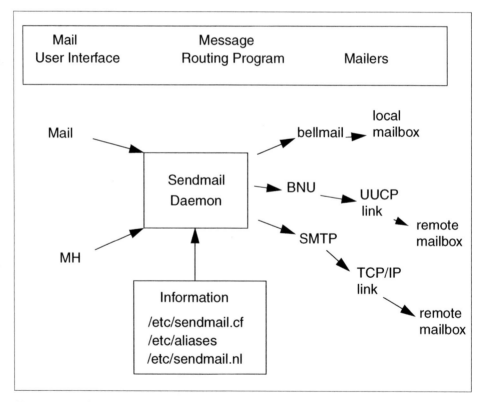

Figure 15-1   Overview of mail system

To deliver local mail, the sendmail program routes messages to the bellmail program. The bellmail program delivers all local mail by appending messages to the user's system mailbox, which is in the /var/spool/mail directory.

To deliver mail over a UNIX-to-UNIX Copy Program (UUCP) link, the sendmail program routes messages using Basic Network Utilities (BNU).

To deliver Transmission Control Protocol/Internet Protocol (TCP/IP)-routed mail, the `sendmail` command establishes a TCP/IP connection to the remote system then uses Simple Mail Transfer Protocol (SMTP) to transfer the message to the remote system.

Figure 15-2 shows the mail management tasks for a system administrator.

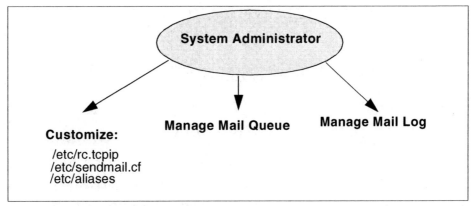

Figure 15-2   Mail management tasks

15.2 Mail daemons

The following is a description of the mail daemons:

Sendmail daemon A message routing program routes messages to their destinations. The mail system's message routing program is the `sendmail` command, which is part of the Base Operating System (BOS) and is installed with BOS. The `sendmail` command is a daemon that uses information in the /etc/sendmail.cf file, the /etc/aliases file, and the /etc/sendmail.nl file to perform the necessary routing.

Syslogd daemon The `sendmail` command logs mail system activity through the syslogd daemon. The syslogd daemon must be configured and running for logging to occur. Refer to section

15.4, "Mail logs" on page 420 for more information about the syslogd daemon.

15.2.1 Starting the sendmail daemon

To start the sendmail daemon, enter either of the following commands:

```
startsrc -s sendmail
```

or

```
/usr/lib/sendmail
```

If the sendmail daemon is already active when you enter one of these previous commands, you will see the following message on the screen:

```
The sendmail subsystem is already active. Multiple instances are not supported.
```

If the sendmail daemon is not already active, then a message indicating that the sendmail daemon has been started will be generated.

15.2.2 Stopping the sendmail daemon

To stop the sendmail daemon, execute the **stopsrc -s** command. If the sendmail daemon was not started with the **startsrc** command, find the sendmail PID and then kill the process issuing the following commands:

```
ps -ef |grep sendmail
kill -9 sendmail_pid
```

15.2.3 Refreshing the sendmail daemon

To refresh the sendmail daemon, issue the command:

```
refresh -s sendmail
```

15.2.4 Getting the status of sendmail daemon

The following example shows how to get the status of the sendmail daemon using **lssrc** command with the -s flag. The status can be active or inoperative.

```
# lssrc -s sendmail
Subsystem         Group         PID       Status
 sendmail         mail          5422      active
```

15.2.5 Autostart of the sendmail daemon (/etc/rc.tcpip)

To configure the /etc/rc.tcpip file so that the sendmail daemon will be started at system boot time:

1. Edit the /etc/rc.tcpip file.

2. Find the line that begins with start /usr/lib/sendmail. By default, this line should be uncommented, that is, there is no # (pound sign) at the beginning of the line. However, if it is commented, delete the pound sign.

15.2.6 Specifying time values in sendmail (in rc.tcpip)

The interval at which the sendmail daemon processes the mail queue is determined by the value of the -q flag when the daemon starts. The sendmail daemon is usually started by the /etc/rc.tcpip file at system startup. The /etc/rc.tcpip file contains a variable called the queue processing interval (QPI), which it uses to specify the value of the -q flag when it starts the sendmail daemon. By default, the value of QPI is 30 minutes. To specify a different queue processing interval:

1. Edit the /etc/rc.tcpip file.

2. Find the line that assigns a value to the qpi variable, such as: qpi=30m

3. Change the value assigned to the qpi variable to the time value you prefer.

These changes will take effect at the next system restart. For the changes to take effect immediately, stop and restart the sendmail daemon specifying the new -q flag value.

15.2.7 Specifying time values in sendmail (not in rc.tcpip)

To set the message time-out and queue processing interval, you must use a specific format for the time value. The format of a time value is:

-qNumberUnit, where Number is an integer value and Unit is the unit letter. Unit may have one of the following values:

s   Seconds

m   Minutes

h   Hours

d   Days

w   Weeks

If Unit is not specified, the sendmail daemon uses minutes (m) as the default. Here are three examples.

To process the queue every 15 days, issue the command:

```
/usr/sbin/sendmail -q15d
```

To process the queue every 15 hours, issue the command:

```
/usr/sbin/sendmail -q15h
```

To process the queue every 15 minutes, issue the command:

```
/usr/sbin/sendmail -q15
```

15.3 Mail queue directory: /var/spool/mqueue

The mail queue is a directory that stores data and controls files for mail messages that the **sendmail** command delivers. By default, the mail queue is /var/spool/mqueue. Mail messages may be queued for several reasons. First, the **sendmail** command can be configured to process the queue at certain intervals rather than immediately. If this is so, mail messages must be stored temporarily. Second, if a remote host does not answer a request for a mail connection, the mail system queues the message and tries again later.

15.3.1 Printing the mail queue

The contents of the queue can be printed using the **mailq** command (or by specifying the -bp flag with the **sendmail** command). This produces a listing of the queue IDs, the size of the message, the date the message entered the queue, and the sender and recipients.

15.3.2 Mail queue files

The mail queue directory /var/spool/mqueue contains four types of mail queue files:

- ▶ Data file
- ▶ Control file
- ▶ Temporary file
- ▶ Transcript file

Each message in the queue has a number of files associated with it. For example, if a message has a queue ID of AA00269, the following files are created and deleted in the mail queue directory while the **sendmail** command tries to deliver the message:

dfAA00269   Data file

qfAA00269	Control file
tfAA00269	Temporary file
xfAA00269	Transcript file

15.3.3 Forcing the mail queue to run

In some cases, the mail queue becomes unresponsive. To force a queue to run, use the **sendmail** command with a -q flag (with no value). You can also use the -v flag (verbose) to watch what happens.

```
/usr/sbin/sendmail -q -v
```

15.3.4 Moving the mail queue

When a host goes down for an extended period, many messages routed to (or through) that host may be stored in your mail queue. As a result, the **sendmail** command spends a long time sorting the queue, severely degrading your system's performance. If you move the queue to a temporary place and create a new queue, the old queue can be run later when the host returns to service. To move the queue to a temporary place and create a new queue:

1. Stop the sendmail daemon.
2. Move the entire queue directory by entering:

   ```
   cd /var/spool
   mv mqueue omqueue
   ```

3. Restart the sendmail daemon.
4. Process the old mail queue by entering:

   ```
   /usr/sbin/sendmail -oQ/var/spool/omqueue -q
   ```

   The -oQ flag specifies an alternate queue directory. The -q flag specifies to run every job in the queue. To get a report about the progress of the operation, use the -v flag. This operation can take a long time.

5. Remove the log files and the temporary directory when the queue is empty by entering:

   ```
   rm /var/spool/omqueue/*
   rmdir /var/spool/omqueue
   ```

15.4 Mail logs

The `sendmail` command logs mail system activity through the syslogd daemon. The syslogd daemon must be configured and running for logging to occur. Specifically, the /etc/syslog.conf file may contain the uncommented line:

```
mail.debug              /var/spool/mqueue/log
```

If it does not, use an editor to make this change; be certain that the path name is correct. If you change the /etc/syslog.conf file while the syslogd daemon is running, refresh the syslogd daemon by entering the command:

```
refresh -s syslogd
```

If the /var/spool/mqueue/log file does not exist, you must create it by entering the command:

```
touch /var/spool/mqueue/log
```

15.4.1 Managing the mail log files

Because information is continually appended to the end of the log file, it can become very large. Also, error conditions can cause unexpected entries to the mail queue. To keep the mail queue and log from growing too large, execute the /usr/lib/smdemon.cleanu shell script. This script forces the `sendmail` command to process the queue and maintains four progressively older copies of log files named log.0, log.1, log.2, and log.3. Each time the script runs, it moves:

1. log.2 to log.3

2. log.1 to log.2

3. log.0 to log.1

4. log to log.0

This allows logging to start over with a new file. Run this script either manually or at a specified interval with the cron daemon. A typical log file is shown in Figure 15-3 on page 421. The highlighted field, stat=Deferred refers to a message that could not get routed to the destination.

```
# pg /var/spool/mqueue/log
Nov  3 09:49:00 sv1051c sendmail[29038]: JAA29038: from user root: size is 43, c
lass is 0, priority is 30043, and nrcpts=1, message id is <199811031549.JAA29038
@sv1051c.itsc.austin.ibm.com>, relay=root@localhost
Nov  3 09:49:00 sv1051c sendmail[33716]: JAA29038: to=smith, ctladdr=root (0/0),
 delay=00:00:00, xdelay=00:00:00, mailer=local, stat=Sent
Nov  3 09:49:51 sv1051c sendmail[29042]: JAA29042: from user root: size is 57, c
lass is 0, priority is 30057, and nrcpts=1, message id is <199811031549.JAA29042
@sv1051c.itsc.austin.ibm.com>, relay=root@localhost
Nov  3 09:49:51 sv1051c sendmail[29330]: JAA29042: to=npsingh@in.ibm.com, ctladd
r=root (0/0), delay=00:00:00, xdelay=00:00:00, mailer=esmtp, relay=relay2.server
.ibm.com. [::ffff:9.14.2.99], stat=Deferred: Network is unreachable
#
```

Figure 15-3   /var/spool/mqueue/log file

15.4.2 Logging mailer statistics

The `sendmail` command tracks the volume of mail being handled by each of the mailer programs that interface with it (those mailers defined in the /etc/sendmail.cf file).

To start the accumulation of mailer statistics, create the /var/tmp/sendmail.st (refer to the sendmail.cf file for the exact path) file by entering:

`touch /var/tmp/sendmail.st`

The `sendmail` command updates the information in the file each time it processes mail. The size of the file does not grow, but the numbers in the file do. They represent the mail volume since the time you created or reset the /var/tmp/sendmail.st file.

15.4.3 Displaying mailer information

The statistics kept in the /var/tmp/sendmail.st file are in a database format that cannot be read as a text file. To display the mailer statistics, enter the command:

`/usr/sbin/mailstats`

This reads the information in the /etc/sendmail.st file, formats it, and writes it to standard output in the format shown in Figure 15-4 on page 422.

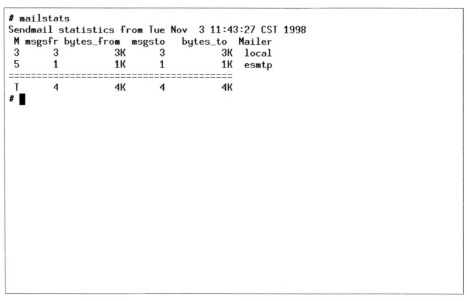

```
# mailstats
Sendmail statistics from Tue Nov  3 11:43:27 CST 1998
 M msgsfr bytes_from  msgsto   bytes_to  Mailer
 3      3        3K        3         3K  local
 5      1        1K        1         1K  esmtp
============================================
 T      4        4K        4         4K
#
```

Figure 15-4   Displaying mailer information

The fields in the report have the following meanings:

msgs_from   Contains the number of messages received by the local machine from the indicated mailer.

bytes_from   Contains the number of bytes in the messages received by the local machine from the indicated mailer.

msgs_to   Contains the number of messages sent from the local machine using the indicated mailer.

bytes_to   Contains the number of bytes in the messages sent from the local machine using the indicated mailer.

15.5 Mail aliasing and forwarding

Aliases map names to address lists. The aliases are defined in the /etc/aliases file by the user administrator. The /etc/aliases file consists of a series of entries in the following format:

```
Alias: Name1, Name2, ... NameX
```

where Alias can be any alphanumeric string that you choose (not including special characters, such as @ or !). Name1 through NameX is a series of one or more recipient names. The /etc/aliases file must contain the following three aliases (a sample file is shown in Figure 15-5):

▶ MAILER-DAEMON

▶ postmaster

▶ nobody

```
# Licensed Materials - Property of IBM
#
# US Government Users Restricted Rights - Use, duplication or
# disclosure restricted by GSA ADP Schedule Contract with IBM Corp.
#
##
#  Aliases in this file will NOT be expanded in the header from
#  Mail, but WILL be visible over networks or from /bin/bellmail.
#
#       >>>>>>>>>       The command "sendmail -bi" must be run after
#       >> NOTE >>      this file is updated for any changes to
#       >>>>>>>>>       affect sendmail operation.
##

# Alias for mailer daemon
MAILER-DAEMON:root

# Following alias is required by the new mail protocol, RFC 822
postmaster:root

# Aliases to handle mail to msgs and news
nobody: /dev/null

# ▮
```

Figure 15-5   /etc/aliases File

15.5.1 Creating or modifying local system aliases

To add the programer alias for four users working together in the same department (John, Smith, Mary, Bob), perform the following functions:

1. Edit the /etc/aliases file.

2. On a blank line, add an alias, followed by a colon (:), followed by a list of comma-separated recipients. For example, the following entry defines an alias named programer to be the names of the people in that group.

```
programer: john, smith, mary@sv1051c, bob@sv1051c
```

3. Create an owner for any distribution list aliases. If the **sendmail** command has trouble sending mail to the distribution list, it sends an error message to the owner of that list. For example, the owner of the above list is root of system sv1051a and is defined by the following entry in the /etc/aliases file:

```
owner-programer: root@sv1051a
```

4. Recompile the /etc/aliases file, as described in Section 15.5.2, "Building the alias database" on page 424.

15.5.2 Building the alias database

The **sendmail** command does not directly use the alias definitions in the local system /etc/aliases file. Instead, the **sendmail** command reads a processed database manager (dbm) version of the /etc/aliases file. You can compile the alias database using the following method.

Run the **/usr/sbin/sendmail** command using the -bi flag or run **newaliases**. This command causes the **sendmail** command to read the local system /etc/aliases file and creates two additional files containing the alias database information:

► /etc/aliases.dir

► /etc/aliases.pag

After you have completed building the alias database, you can use the alias (programer) to send mail to the users (smith and john) on the local system and the users (mary and bob) on system sv1051c by using the **mail** command as shown below:

```
mail programer
```

15.5.3 Forwarding mail with /etc/aliases

The /etc/aliases file also allows the automatic forwarding of mail to other systems or to other users on the system. This can be helpful, for example, if you are administering large amounts of systems and need a common address to place the mail for root from every system. To do this, place an entry in /etc/aliases in the following format:

```
User: Name1, Name2, ... NameX
```

where User is a user ID that exists on the system and Name1 through NameX is a list of names to which mail is to be forwarded.

For example, if the mail for root was to be forwarded to Smith and Bob, on a blank line in /etc/aliases, you would enter:

```
root: smith, bob@sv1051c
```

By doing this, however, root would no longer receive any mail. If you want to have a user retain a copy of its mail and still forward mail to other systems or users on the same system, place an entry in /etc/aliases in the following format:

```
User: \User, Name1, Name2, ... NameX
```

The backslash (\) instructs sendmail to keep a copy of mail for User, and send copies to Name1 through NameX. If the backslash were omitted, this would create an infinite forwarding loop and could lead to mail flooding for all the names in the list.

For example, if the mail for root was to be forwarded to Smith and Bob, and root was to retain a copy, in /etc/aliases you would enter:

```
root: \root, smith, bob@sv1051c
```

After /etc/aliases has been modified, the **/usr/sbin/sendmail -bi** or **newaliases** command must be run for the changes to take effect, as described in Section 15.5.2, "Building the alias database" on page 424.

15.5.4 Forwarding mail with $HOME/.forward

By creating a file named .forward in a user's home directory, mail can also be forwarded to other systems or other users on a system. This is a useful option for users on a system that cannot edit the /etc/aliases file. The .forward file uses the following format:

```
Name1, Name2, ... NameX
```

where Name1 through NameX is a list of names to which mail is to be forwarded.

For example, if John wants to forward his mail to Smith and Mary, he would do the following:

```
vi $HOME/.forward
```

This will allow him to create the .forward file in his home directory through vi. On a blank line he would enter:

```
smith, mary@sv1051c
```

Then, he would save and quit the file. If John wants to retain a copy of his mail, he would place a backslash (\) and his own user ID in the .forward file:

```
\john, smith, mary@sv1051c
```

The **sendmail -bi** or **newaliases** command does not have to be run for the changes to take effect.

Any modifications to the .forward file become effective as soon as the file is saved. To stop mail forwarding, delete the .forward file:

```
rm $HOME/.forward
```

15.5.5 Forwarding mail to /dev/null

To automatically delete mail for a particular user ID, mail can be forwarded to /dev/null in /etc/aliases or $HOME/.forward. This can be helpful, for example, for users who do not need to actively check their mail. To do this in /etc/aliases, you would enter:

```
User: /dev/null
```

where User is the user ID that will have its mail automatically deleted. Then you would run **sendmail -bi** or **newaliases** to have the changes take effect.

To do this in $HOME/.forward, you would enter:

```
/dev/null
```

15.6 Mail addressing

Mail is sent to a user's address. How you address mail to another user depends upon the user's location with respect to your system. The address would depend on whether you are sending the mail:

▶ To users on your local system.

▶ To users on your network.

▶ To users on a different network.

▶ Over a BNU or UUCP link.

15.6.1 To address mail to users on your local system

To send a message to a user on your local system (to someone whose login name is listed in your /etc/passwd file), use the login name for the address. At your system command line prompt, you can use the **mail** command in the way shown in the following example:

```
mail LoginName
```

If smith is on your system and has the login name smith, use the command:

```
mail smith
```

15.6.2 To address mail to users on your network

To send a message through a local network to a user on another system, at the command line enter:

```
mail LoginName@SystemName
```

For example, if john is on system sv1051c, use the following command to create and send a message to him:

```
mail john@sv1051c
```

15.6.3 To address mail to users on a different network

If your network is connected to other networks, you can send mail to users on the other networks. The address parameters differ depending on how your network and the other networks address each other and how they are connected.

Using a central database of names and addresses:

Use the **mail** command in the way shown in the following example:

```
mail LoginName@SystemName
```

Using domain name addressing

Use the **mail** command in the ways shown in the following examples:

```
mail LoginName@SystemName.DomainName
```

For example, to send mail to a user john, who resides in a remote network with a domain name in.ibm.com, use the following command:

```
mail john@in.ibm.com
```

15.6.4 To address mail over a BNU or UUCP link

To send a message to a user on another system connected to your system by the Basic Networking Utilities (BNU) or another version of UNIX-to-UNIX Copy Program (UUCP), you must know the login name, the name of the other system, and the physical route to that other system.

When your computer has a BNU or UUCP link, you can use the command as shown in the following.

```
mail UUCPRoute!LoginName
```

When the BNU or UUCP link is on another computer, use the **mail** command, as shown below:

```
mail @InternetSystem:UUCPSystem!username
```

Notice that, in this format, you are not sending mail to a user at any of the intermediate systems; , no login name precedes the @ in the domain address.

15.7 Storing mail

Mail is stored in different ways depending on the specific situation, as shown in Figure 15-6 on page 429. The mail program uses the following type of mailboxes or folders:

System mailbox This resides in /var/spool/mail directory and each system mailbox is named by the user ID associated with it. For example, if the user ID is smith, the system mailbox is /var/spool/mail/smith. When the mail arrives for any user ID, it is placed in the respective system mailbox. The shell checks for the new mail and issues the following message when the user logs in: YOU HAVE NEW MAIL

Personal mailbox Each user has a personal mailbox. When the mail is read using the `mail` command by the user, and if it is not saved in a file or deleted, it is written to user's personal mailbox, $HOME/mbox ($HOME is the default login directory). For user ID smith, the personal mailbox is /home/smith/mbox.

dead.letter file If the user interrupts the message being created to complete some other tasks, the system saves the incomplete message in the dead.letter file in the user's home directory ($HOME). For user ID smith, /home/smith/dead.letter is the dead.letter file.

Folders To save a message in an organized fashion, users can use folders. Messages can be put into a user's personal folder from the system mailbox or the personal mailbox as shown in Figure 15-6 on page 429.

The `mail` command can be used with various flags as shown below:

`mail`   Displays the system mailbox.

`mail -f`   Displays your personal mailbox (mbox).

`mail -f+folder` Displays a mail folder.

`mail user@address` Addresses a message to the specified user.

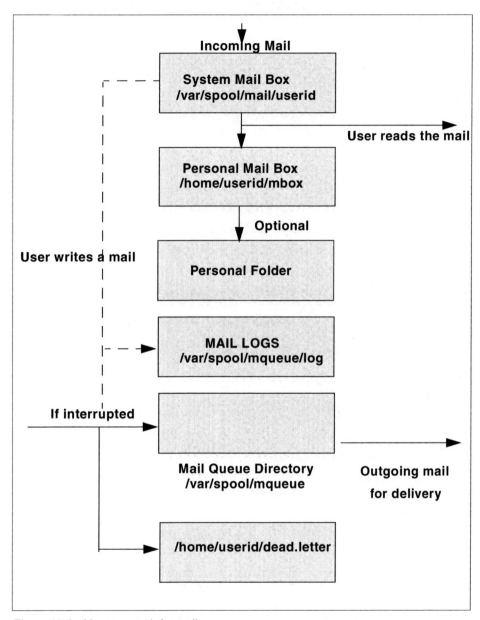

Figure 15-6   Message path for mail

15.8 Mail administrator's reference

This section provides a quick reference to the various mail commands, files, and directories.

15.8.1 List of mail commands

This list includes commands for using and managing the mail program.

`mailq`	Prints the contents of the mail queue.
`mailstats`	Displays statistics about mail traffic.
`newaliases`	Builds a new copy of the alias database from the /etc/aliases file.
`sendmail`	Routes mail for local or network delivery.
`smdemon.cleanu`	Cleans up the sendmail queue for periodic housekeeping.

15.8.2 List of mail files and directories

This list of files and directories is arranged by function.

Using the mail program

$HOME/.mailrc	Enables the user to change the local system defaults for the mail program.
$HOME/mbox	Stores processed mail for the individual user.
/usr/bin/Mail,	
/usr/bin/mail, and	
/usr/bin/mailx	Specifies three names linked to the same program. The mail program is one of the user interfaces to the mail system.
/var/spool/mail	Specifies the default mail drop directory. By default, all mail is delivered to the /var/spool/mail/UserName file.
/var/spool/mqueue	Contains the log file and temporary files associated with the messages in the mail queue.

Using the sendmail command

/usr/sbin/sendmail	The `sendmail` command.
/usr/ucb/mailq	Links to the /usr/sbin/sendmail. Using `mailq` is equivalent to using the `/usr/sbin/sendmail -bp` command.

/usr/ucb/newaliases	Links to the /usr/sbin/sendmail file. Using `newaliases` is equivalent to using the `/usr/sbin/sendmail -bi` command.
/usr/sbin/mailstats	Formats and prints the sendmail statistics as found in the /etc/sendmail.st file, if it exists. The /etc/sendmail.st file is the default, but you can specify an alternative file.
/etc/aliases	Describes a text version of the aliases file for the `sendmail` command. You can edit this file to create, modify, or delete aliases for your system.
/etc/sendmail.cf	Contains the sendmail configuration information in text form. Edit the file to change this information.
/etc/sendmail.cfDB	Contains the processed version of the /etc/sendmail.cf configuration file. This file is created from the /etc/sendmail.cf file when you run the `/usr/sbin/sendmail -bz` command.
/etc/sendmail.nl	Contains the sendmail National Language Support (NLS) configuration information in text form. Edit the file to change this information.
/usr/lib/smdemon.cleanu	Specifies a shell file that runs the mail queue and maintains the sendmail log files in the /var/spool/mqueue directory.
/var/tmp/sendmail.st	Collects statistics about mail traffic. This file does not grow. Use the `/usr/sbin/mailstats` command to display the contents of this file.
/var/spool/mqueue	Describes a directory containing the temporary files associated with each message in the queue. The directory can contain the log file.

15.9 Quiz

The following are questions created by the authors to further test your understanding of the topics.

1. A Company would like to create an e-mail alias on an AIX workstation that will forward e-mail to a user on another workstation for collection of data. The system administrator would like to add this entry to the /etc/aliases file. Which of the following actions should be performed in order for the change to take affect?

   A. Reboot the workstation.

   B. Run the `mailq` command.

   C. Stop and start TCP/IP.

   D. Use the `sendmail` command.

2. A system administrator wants to process a mail queue after every 45 minutes. Which of the following commands should be used if the change must take effect immediately and be permanent?

   A. `sendmail -q45d`

   B. `sendmail -q45h` and also edit /etc/rc.tcpip to change qpi=45h

   C. `sendmail -q45` and also edit /etc/rc.tcpip to change qpi=45m

   D. `sendmail -q45`

3. All mail sent to root on system mars needs to be redirected to user administrator on system earth. Prior to running the `newaliases` command, which command should be run to accomplish this goal?

   A. On system earth, run the command: `echo "mars: earth" >> /etc/hosts`

   B. On system mars, run the command: `echo "root:admin@earth" >> /etc/aliases`

   C. On system mars, run the command: `echo "root:admin@earth" >> /etc/sendmail.cf`

   D. On system earth, run the command: `echo "root:admin@earth" >> /etc/sendmail.cf`

15.9.1 Answers

The following answers are for the quiz questions.

1. D
2. C
3. B

15.10 Exercises

The following exercises provide sample topics for self study. They will help ensure comprehension of this chapter.

1. Display the status of the sendmail daemon on your system. If it is not active, start the sendmail daemon.

2. Locate the entry in the /etc/rc.tcpip file that starts the sendmail daemon at system boot time.

3. Customize the sendmail daemon to process the mail queue every 45 minutes. Make this change take effect immediately.

4. Create an alias for all the users in your department and compile the alias database. Compile the database.

5. Stop the sendmail daemon.

Online documentation

AIX Version 4.3, and later versions, provide an optionally installable component for Web based documentation, the Documentation Search Service. It allows you to search online HTML documents. It provides a search form that appears in your Web browser. When you type words into the search form, it searches for the words and then presents a search results page that contains links that lead to the documents that contain the target words.

You can set up one of your AIX systems in your organization to be the documentation server and all other systems as documentation clients. This will allow documentation to be installed on only one system, and all other systems can access this system without needing the documentation installed locally.

You need the following products and components installed for a complete set of services.

- ► For the client:
  - a. A Web browser
  - b. The bos.docsearch.client.* filesets (for AIX integration)
- ► For the documentation server (which may also act as a client)
  - a. The entire bos.docsearch package
  - b. The documentation libraries
  - c. A Web browser

d. A Web server

The browser must be a forms-capable browser, and the Web server must be CGI-compliant.

If you are planning on integrating your own documentation on the documentation server, you will also need to build the document's indexes.

Except for the end-user tasks described in Section 16.6, "Invoking Documentation Search Service" on page 441, you need root authority to perform the installation and configuration tasks.

There are a variety of ways to install the documentation, Web server, and Document Search Service. You can use the Configuration Assistant TaskGuide, Web-Based Systems Management, or SMIT.

The easiest way for a non-technical user to install and configure Documentation Search Services is by using the Configuration Assistant TaskGuide. To run the Configuration Assistant TaskGuide, use the `configassist` command, then select the item titled Configure Online Documentation and Search.

If you would rather install Documentation Search Services manually, you can use SMIT.

16.1 Installing the Web browser

Use **smitty install_latest** to install Netscape, supplied on the AIX Version 4.3 or later Bonus Pack CD-ROM. Use **smit list_installed** to check whether you have the following filesets installed as shown in Figure 16-1.

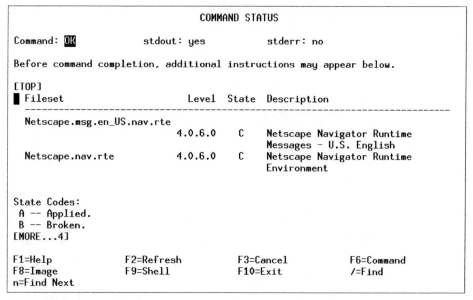

```
                            COMMAND STATUS

    Command: OK           stdout: yes            stderr: no

    Before command completion, additional instructions may appear below.

    [TOP]
    █ Fileset                    Level  State  Description
    --------------------------------------------------------------------------
      Netscape.msg.en_US.nav.rte
                                 4.0.6.0   C    Netscape Navigator Runtime
                                                Messages - U.S. English
      Netscape.nav.rte          4.0.6.0   C    Netscape Navigator Runtime
                                                Environment


    State Codes:
     A -- Applied.
     B -- Broken.
    [MORE...4]

    F1=Help              F2=Refresh           F3=Cancel            F6=Command
    F8=Image             F9=Shell             F10=Exit             /=Find
    n=Find Next
```

Figure 16-1   Netscape filesets

If you are installing the Netscape browser from other sources, or you are installing other Web browsers, follow the installation instructions that come with the software. Note that there will not be any records in the ODM if your product source is not in installp format.

16.2 Installing the Web server

You may install any CGI-compliant Web Server. The Lotus Domino Go Webserver is used here. It is supplied on one of the AIX Version 4.3 or later Bonus Pack CD-ROMs.

The Documentation Search Service uses its own search engine CGIs. Therefore, you do not need to install the NetQ fileset. Figure 16-2 shows the filesets installed.

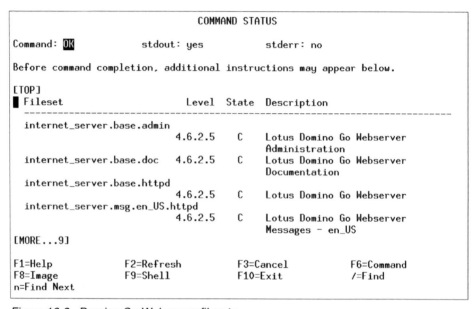

```
                            COMMAND STATUS

Command: OK              stdout: yes           stderr: no

Before command completion, additional instructions may appear below.

[TOP]
█ Fileset                  Level  State  Description
------------------------------------------------------------------------
  internet_server.base.admin
                          4.6.2.5   C      Lotus Domino Go Webserver
                                           Administration
  internet_server.base.doc  4.6.2.5   C    Lotus Domino Go Webserver
                                           Documentation
  internet_server.base.httpd
                          4.6.2.5   C      Lotus Domino Go Webserver
  internet_server.msg.en_US.httpd
                          4.6.2.5   C      Lotus Domino Go Webserver
                                           Messages - en_US
[MORE...9]

F1=Help          F2=Refresh        F3=Cancel         F6=Command
F8=Image         F9=Shell          F10=Exit          /=Find
n=Find Next
```

Figure 16-2   Domino Go Webserver filesets

If you are installing the Domino Go Webserver from other sources, or you are installing another Web server, follow the installation instructions that come with the software. Note that there will not be any records in the ODM if your product source is not in installp format.

16.3 Installing Documentation Search Service

The documentation search service is (at the time of writing) on the AIX Version 4.3 and later installation CD-ROMs. Install the client portions for a client AIX image or install the entire bos.docsearch package for a documentation server.

The following filesets are the prerequisite for other documentation search service filesets (such as IMNSearch):

▶ bos.docsearch.client.Dt

▶ bos.docsearch.client.com

▶ bos.docsearch.rte

For the documentation clients, you need only a Web browser. Installation of the bos.docsearch.client fileset will give you the CDE desktop icon and the **docsearch** command. Refer to Section 16.6, "Invoking Documentation Search Service" on page 441 for further details.

Use **smit list_installed** to check whether you have the following filesets installed, as shown in Figure 16-3.

```
                           COMMAND STATUS

Command: OK            stdout: yes           stderr: no

Before command completion, additional instructions may appear below.

[MORE...1]
■ ------------------------------------------------------------------
   IMNSearch.bld.DBCS          1.2.0.4    C    NetQuestion DBCS Buildtime
                                               Modules
   IMNSearch.bld.SBCS          1.2.1.3    C    NetQuestion SBCS Buildtime
                                               Modules
   IMNSearch.rte.DBCS          1.2.0.4    C    NetQuestion DBCS Search Engine
   IMNSearch.rte.SBCS          1.2.1.3    C    NetQuestion SBCS Search Engine
   IMNSearch.rte.httpdlite     1.1.1.1    C    NetQuestion Local HTTP Daemon
   bos.docsearch.client.Dt     4.3.2.0    C    DocSearch Client CDE Application
                                               Integration
   bos.docsearch.client.com    4.3.2.0    C    DocSearch Client Common Files
   bos.docsearch.rte           4.3.2.0    C    DocSearch Runtime
[MORE...9]

F1=Help            F2=Refresh         F3=Cancel          F6=Command
F8=Image           F9=Shell           F10=Exit           /=Find
n=Find Next
```

Figure 16-3 Documentation Search Service filesets

16.4 Configuring Documentation Search Service

Use either **wsm** or **smitty** to configure the documentation search service. If you used the Configuration Assistant TaskGuide to install and configure the Documentation Search Service, you will not need to perform any further configuration.

For **wsm**, double-click on the **Internet Environment** icon, or you can use `smit web_configure` to configure the following:

▶ Change / Show Default Browser

Type the command that launches the browser that you want to be the default browser for all users on this computer; for example, **/usr/prod/bin/netscape**. This will set the /etc/environment variable DEFAULT_BROWSER to the string you type in.

▶ Change Documentation and Search Server

You can define the documentation search server location to be:

– None - disabled

– Remote computer

Type the remote documentation server name. The default TCP/IP port address is 80. Change it to the port address used by the documentation server.

– Local - this computer

If you are using Lotus Domino Go Webserver or IBM Internet Connection Server in the default location, all the default settings of the cgi-bin directory and HTML directory will have been filled in for you. If you are using other Web servers, or you are not using the default location, you have to fill in your cgi-bin directory and HTML directory that the Web server requires. You may change the port address used by the server. If you change the port address, you have to use the same address for all your documentation clients.

16.5 Installing online manuals

You can either install the documentation information onto the hard disk or mount the documentation CD-ROM in the CD-ROM drive. Mounting the CD-ROM will save some amount of hard disk space, but it requires the CD-ROM to be kept in the CD-ROM drive at all times. Also, searching the documentation from the CD-ROM drive can be significantly slower (in some cases up to 10 times slower) than searching the information if it is installed on a hard disk. In addition, there are two documentation CD-ROMs:

▶ The AIX Base Documentation CD-ROM

▶ The AIX Extended Documentation CD-ROM

Use `smit install_latest` to install the online manuals onto the hard disk. The fileset bos.docregister is a prerequisite for all online manuals. It will be automatically installed the first time you install any online manuals even if you have not selected this fileset.

> **Note:** The installation images located on the AIX Version 4.3 or later Base Documentation and Extended Documentation CD-ROMs do not contain the HTML files. These files exist separately on the CD-ROM to allow access from non-AIX platforms. Installing the images from the CD-ROM will work correctly; however, copying the installation images by themselves to another location is not enough for a proper install.

16.6 Invoking Documentation Search Service

You must log out and log in again after the Documentation Search Service has been configured so that you will pick up the environment variables set up during the configuration.

If you are running the CDE desktop environment, double-click the Documentation Search Service icon in the Application Manager window.

Alternatively, you can use the command **docsearch** to invoke the documentation search service. Your Web browser will start, and you should see the Documentation Search Service page. Netscape is used as the default Web browser for this discussion.

You can invoke the Documentation Search Service without installing the docsearch client component. You do not even need to invoke the documentation search service from an AIX machine. You can do this by first invoking the browser and entering the following URL:

`http://`*server_name*`[:`*port_number*`]/cgi-bin/ds_form`

This URL points to a global search form on the document server where the name of the remote server is given in *server_name*. The *port_number* only needs to be entered if the port is different from 80.

If you have not run Netscape previously, a series of informational messages and windows will be shown while Netscape is setting up the environment in your home directory. This is standard behavior for the first use of Netscape. The messages will not be shown again the next time you start Netscape.

The top part of the Documentation Search Service page allows you to specify your search criteria, and the bottom part shows which online manuals have been installed. Figure 16-4 shows the documentation search service page with only the command reference manuals and the programming guide manuals installed.

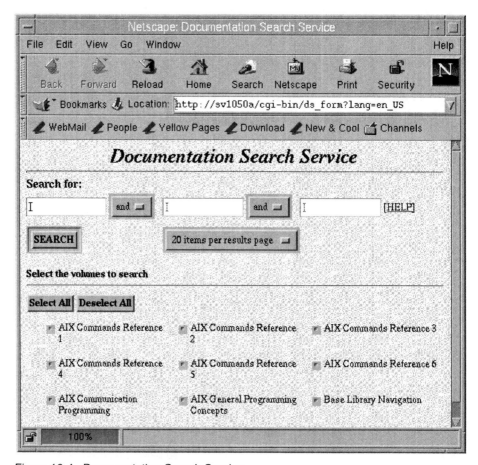

Figure 16-4   Documentation Search Service

If you have a problem starting the Documentation Search Service, check the following environment variables. These environment variables may be set, displayed, and changed using SMIT. Start SMIT, select System Environments, then select Internet and Documentation Services.

► On the client machine:

 a. Invoke the Web browser manually and enter the URL `http://`*server_name*`[:`*port_number*`]`/`cgi-bin/ds_form` to ensure that the server is up and running.

b. Ensure the DEFAULT_BROWSER variable is set to the command for starting your Web browser.

   Use the command **echo $DEFAULT_BROWSER** to find out the command used in starting the browser. Test whether that command can bring up the browser by manually entering it on the command line.

c. Ensure the DOCUMENT_SERVER_MACHINE_NAME variable is set to the document server's host name or IP address.

d. Ensure the DOCUMENT_SERVER_PORT variable is set to the port address used by the document server's port address.

► On the server machine:

a. Ensure the DEFAULT_BROWSER variable is set to the command for starting your Web browser.

   Use the command **echo $DEFAULT_BROWSER** to find out the command used in starting the browser. Test whether that command can bring up the browser by manually entering it on the command line.

b. Ensure the DOCUMENT_SERVER_MACHINE_NAME variable is set to the local host name.

c. Ensure the DOCUMENT_SERVER_PORT variable is set to the port address used by the local Web server.

d. Ensure that the CGI_DIRECTORY variable is set to the correct cgi-bin directory used by the local Web server.

e. Ensure that the DOCUMENT_DIRECTORY is set to the directory where the symbolic links doc_link and ds_images reside. If you have not changed the default, it should be in /usr/lpp/internet/server_root/pub for both IBM Internet Connection Server and Lotus Domino Go Web Server.

f. If you are not using the default directory, ensure that you have defined the necessary directory mapping in your Web server configuration file so that the directory can be resolved.

16.7 Quiz

The following are questions created by the authors to further test your understanding of the topics.

1. By installing the Documentation Search Services client fileset, the following will be made available to your AIX Version 4.3 system:

   A. CDE icon

   B. Web browser

   C. `docsearch` command and CDE icon

   D. `info` command and CDE icon

2. From a forms-capable Web browser, the URL used to access the online documentation server on an AIX Version 4.3 system is:

   A. `http://`*server_name*`[:`*port_number*`]/cgi-bin/ds_form`

   B. `http://`*server_name*`[:`*port_number*`]/cgi-bin/docsearch`

   C. `http://`*server_name*`[:`*port_number*`]/cgi-bin/info`

   D. `http://`*server_name*`[:`*port_number*`]/cgi-bin/man`

16.7.1 Answers

The following answers are for the quiz questions.

1. C

2. A

16.8 Exercise

The following exercises provide sample topics for self study. They will help ensure comprehension of this chapter.

1. Install a Web browser.

2. Install a Web server.

3. Install the Document Search Services fileset.

4. Install some online manuals.

5. Configure the document search service.

6. Access the online manuals using the `docsearch` command and from a Web browser on other systems.

The AIXwindows font server

XFS is the AIXwindows font server subsystem (prior to AIX Version 4.3, it was named fs) that supplies fonts to AIXwindows display servers. In the following sections, topics related to administration of the font server are discussed.

Note: To use the AIXwindows font server, the X11.fnt.fontserver fileset must be installed.

17.1 XFS server interrupts

The xfs server responds to the following signals:

SIGTERM   Causes the font server to exit cleanly.

SIGUSR1   Causes the server to re-read its configuration file.

SIGUSR2   Causes the server to flush any cached data it may have.

SIGHUP   Causes the server to reset, closing all active connections and re-reads the configuration file.

The server is usually run by a system administrator and started by way of boot files, such as /etc/rc.tcpip. Users may also wish to start private font servers for specific sets of fonts.

The configuration language is a list of keyword and value pairs. Each keyword is followed by an = (equal sign) and the desired value.

17.2 XFS keywords

Table 17-1 shows recognized keywords and the types and descriptions of valid values.

Table 17-1   XFS keywords

Keyword	Description
#	A comment character when located in the first column.
catalogue (List of string)	Ordered list of font path element names. The current implementation only supports a single catalogue ("all") containing all of the specified fonts.
alternate-servers (List of string)	List of alternate servers for this font server.
client-limit (Cardinal)	Number of clients that this font server will support before refusing service. This is useful for tuning the load on each individual font server.
clone-self (Boolean)	Whether this font server should attempt to clone itself when it reaches the client limit.
default-point-size (Cardinal)	The default point size (in decipoints) for fonts that do not specify.

Keyword	Description
default-resolutions (Series)	Resolutions the server supports by default. This information may be used as a hint for pre-rendering and substituted for scaled fonts that do not specify a resolution. A resolution is a comma-separated pair of x and y resolutions in pixels per inch. Multiple resolutions are separated by commas.
error-file (String)	File name of the error file. All warnings and errors are logged here.
port (Cardinal)	TCP port on which the server will listen for connections. The default is 7100.
use-syslog (Boolean)	Whether the syslog function (on supported systems) is to be used for errors.
deferglyphs (String)	Sets the mode for delayed fetching and caching of glyphs. *String* can be none, meaning deferred glyphs is disabled or all, meaning deferred glyphs is enabled for all fonts, and 16, meaning deferred glyphs is enabled only for 16-bit fonts.

17.3 XFS form conventions

One of the following forms can be used to name a font server that accepts TCP connections.

```
tcp/hostname:port
tcp/hostname:port/cataloguelist
```

The hostname specifies the name (or decimal numeric address) of the machine on which the font server is running. The port is the decimal TCP port on which the font server is listening for connections. The cataloguelist specifies a list of catalogue names with '+' as a separator. The following are some examples:

```
tcp/expo.lcs.mit.edu:7100, tcp/18.30.0.212:7101/all
```

One of the following forms can be used to name a font server that accepts DECnet connections.

```
decnet/nodename::font$objname
decnet/nodename::font$objname/cataloguelist
```

The nodename specifies the name (or decimal numeric address) of the machine on which the font server is running. The objname is a normal, case-insensitive DECnet object name. The cataloguelist specifies a list of catalogue names with '+' as a separator.

17.4 XFS command flags

Table 17-2 displays the flags used by the **xfs** command.

Table 17-2   Flags for the xfs command

Flag	Description
-cf *ConfigurationFile*	Specifies the configuration file the font server will use.
-ls *ListenSocket*	Specifies a file descriptor that is already set up to be used as the listen socket. This option is only intended to be used by the font server itself when automatically spawning another copy of itself to handle additional connections.
-port *Number*	Specifies the TCP port number on which the server will listen for connections.

17.5 Font server examples

The following is a sample of the /usr/lib/X11/fs/config file. Any changes made to the font server are done in this file.

```
# SCCSID_BEGIN_TAG
# @(#)99  1.2  src/gos/2d/XTOP/programs/xfs/config.cpp, xfontserver,
gos43D, 981
1A_43D 3/10/98 16:02:38
# SCCSID_END_TAG
# font server configuration file
# $XConsortium: config.cpp,v 1.7 91/08/22 11:39:59 rws Exp $

clone-self = on
use-syslog = off
catalogue = /usr/lib/X11/fonts/,/usr/lib/X11/fonts/misc/,/usr/lib/X11/fonts
/75dpi/,/usr/lib/X11/fonts/100dpi/,/usr/lib/X11/fonts/i18n/,/usr/lib/X11/fo
nts/ibm850/,/usr/lib/X11/fonts/TrueType/,/usr/lib/X11/fonts/Type1/
error-file = /usr/lib/X11/fs/fs-errors
# in decipoints
default-point-size = 120
default-resolutions = 75,75,100,100

# The fontserver will default to using port 7100 if not overridden.
# Historically in AIX (4.1 and 4.2) 7500 is used and specified here.
# To restore this default, simply uncomment the following line.
# port = 7500
```

Once you have made your changes to the /usr/lib/X11/fs/config file you then run the following:

```
xfsconf
```

When this script is run, you can start the fontserver sub process by entering the following:

```
startsrc -s xfs
0513-059 The xfs Subsystem has been started. Subsystem PID is 19746.
```

In this case, the system has given the font server subsystem a PID of 19746.

17.6 Quiz

The following certification assessment question helps verify your understanding of the topics discussed in this chapter.

1. A system administrator uses the **startsrc** command to start the font server and gets the following message:

   ```
   subsystem not on file
   ```

   Which of the following is the proper way to make this subsystem available?

   A. Run the **definesrc -s xfs** command.

   B. Run the **fsconf** script and then run **startsrc -s xfs** command.

   C. The font server can not be controlled by the system resource //controller.

   D. Run the **startsrc -s xfs** command and then **refresh -s inetd** command.

17.6.1 Answers

The following answer is for the assessment quiz questions.

1. B

17.7 Exercises

The following exercises provide sample topics for self study. They will help ensure comprehension of this chapter.

1. Configure and start the font server.

2. Understand the various locations the fonts are located

3. Install a double-byte code page and try to use.

Related publications

The publications listed in this section are considered particularly suitable for a more detailed discussion of the topics covered in this redbook.

IBM Redbooks

For information on ordering these publications, see "How to get IBM Redbooks" on page 452.

- *Communication Solutions Guide for RS/6000 and AIX V4*, SG24-4899
- *IP Network Design Guide*, SG24-2580
- *IBM @server Certification Study Guide - pServer AIX System Support*, SG24-6199
- *Understanding IBM @server pSeries Performance and Sizing*, SG24-4810
- *AIX 5L Differences Guide, SG24-5765*
- *IBM Certification Study Guide: AIX Installation and System Recovery*, SG24-6183
- *IBM Certification Study Guide: AIX Performance and System Tuning*, SG24-6184
- *IBM Certification Study Guide: AIX Problem Determination Tools and Techniques*, SG24-6185
- *IBM Certification Study Guide: AIX Communications*, SG24-6186
- *IBM @server Certification Study Guide - pSeries HACMP for AIX*, SG24-6187
- *IBM Certification Study Guide RS/6000 SP*, SG24-5348
- *AIX Logical Volume Manager, From A to Z: Introduction and Concepts*, SG24-5432
- *AIX 5L AIX Workload Manager (WLM)*, SG24-5977

Other resources

These publications are also relevant as further information sources:

- *AIX 5L Version 5.1 Installation Guide*, SC23-4374
- *AIX Version 4.3 Messages Guide and Reference*, SC23-4129

▶ You can access all of the AIX documentation through the Internet at the following URL:

`http://www.ibm.com/servers/aix/library`

The following types of documentation are located on the documentation CD-ROM that ships with the AIX operating system:

- User guides
- System management guides
- Application programmer guides
- All commands reference volumes
- Files reference
- Technical reference volumes used by application programmers

Referenced Web sites

These Web sites are also relevant as further information sources:

▶ Main IBM certification URL.

`http://www.ibm.com/certify`

▶ AIX Essentials CD-ROM.

`http://www.ibm.com/services/learning/spotlight/pseries/cdrom.html`

▶ Downloadable AIX fixes.

`http://service.software.ibm.com`

How to get IBM Redbooks

Search for additional Redbooks or Redpieces, view, download, or order hardcopy from the Redbooks Web site:

`ibm.com/redbooks`

Also download additional materials (code samples or diskette/CD-ROM images) from this Redbooks site.

Redpieces are Redbooks in progress; not all Redbooks become Redpieces and sometimes just a few chapters will be published this way. The intent is to get the information out much quicker than the formal publishing process allows.

IBM Redbooks collections

Redbooks are also available on CD-ROMs. Click the CD-ROMs button on the Redbooks Web site for information about all the CD-ROMs offered, as well as updates and formats.

Special notices

References in this publication to IBM products, programs or services do not imply that IBM intends to make these available in all countries in which IBM operates. Any reference to an IBM product, program, or service is not intended to state or imply that only IBM's product, program, or service may be used. Any functionally equivalent program that does not infringe any of IBM's intellectual property rights may be used instead of the IBM product, program or service.

Information in this book was developed in conjunction with use of the equipment specified, and is limited in application to those specific hardware and software products and levels.

IBM may have patents or pending patent applications covering subject matter in this document. The furnishing of this document does not give you any license to these patents. You can send license inquiries, in writing, to the IBM Director of Licensing, IBM Corporation, North Castle Drive, Armonk, NY 10504-1785.

Licensees of this program who wish to have information about it for the purpose of enabling: (i) the exchange of information between independently created programs and other programs (including this one) and (ii) the mutual use of the information which has been exchanged, should contact IBM Corporation, Dept. 600A, Mail Drop 1329, Somers, NY 10589 USA.

Such information may be available, subject to appropriate terms and conditions, including in some cases, payment of a fee.

The information contained in this document has not been submitted to any formal IBM test and is distributed AS IS. The information about non-IBM ("vendor") products in this manual has been supplied by the vendor and IBM assumes no responsibility for its accuracy or completeness. The use of this information or the implementation of any of these techniques is a customer responsibility and depends on the customer's ability to evaluate and integrate them into the customer's operational environment. While each item may have been reviewed by IBM for accuracy in a specific situation, there is no guarantee that the same or similar results will be obtained elsewhere. Customers attempting to adapt these techniques to their own environments do so at their own risk.

Any pointers in this publication to external Web sites are provided for convenience only and do not in any manner serve as an endorsement of these Web sites.

Any performance data contained in this document was determined in a controlled environment, and therefore, the results that may be obtained in other operating environments may vary significantly. Users of this document should verify the applicable data for their specific environment.

This document contains examples of data and reports used in daily business operations. To illustrate them as completely as possible, the examples contain the names of individuals, companies, brands, and products. All of these names are fictitious and any similarity to the names and addresses used by an actual business enterprise is entirely coincidental.

Reference to PTF numbers that have not been released through the normal distribution process does not imply general availability. The purpose of including these reference numbers is to alert IBM customers to specific information relative to the implementation of the PTF when it becomes available to each customer according to the normal IBM PTF distribution process.

The following terms are trademarks of other companies:

Tivoli, Manage. Anything. Anywhere.,The Power To Manage., Anything. Anywhere.,TME, NetView, Cross-Site, Tivoli Ready, Tivoli Certified, Planet Tivoli, and Tivoli Enterprise are trademarks or registered trademarks of Tivoli Systems Inc., an IBM company, in the United States, other countries, or both. In Denmark, Tivoli is a trademark licensed from Kjøbenhavns Sommer - Tivoli A/S.

C-bus is a trademark of Corollary, Inc. in the United States and/or other countries.

Java and all Java-based trademarks and logos are trademarks or registered trademarks of Sun Microsystems, Inc. in the United States and/or other countries.

Microsoft, Windows, Windows NT, and the Windows logo are trademarks of Microsoft Corporation in the United States and/or other countries.

PC Direct is a trademark of Ziff Communications Company in the United States and/or other countries and is used by IBM Corporation under license.

ActionMedia, LANDesk, MMX, Pentium and ProShare are trademarks of Intel Corporation in the United States and/or other countries.

UNIX is a registered trademark in the United States and other countries licensed exclusively through The Open Group.

SET, SET Secure Electronic Transaction, and the SET Logo are trademarks owned by SET Secure Electronic Transaction LLC.

Other company, product, and service names may be trademarks or service marks of others

Abbreviations and acronyms

ABI	Application Binary Interface	**BOS**	Base Operating System
AC	Alternating Current	**BSC**	Binary Synchronous Communications
ACL	Access Control List		
AFPA	Adaptive Fast Path Architecture	**CAD**	Computer-Aided Design
		CAE	Computer-Aided Engineering
AH	Authentication Header	**CAM**	Computer-Aided Manufacturing
AIX	Advanced Interactive Executive	**CATIA**	Computer-Graphics Aided Three-Dimensional Interactive Application
ANSI	American National Standards Institute		
APAR	Authorized Program Analysis Report	**CCM**	Common Character Mode
		CD	Compact Disk
API	Application Programming Interface	**CDE**	Common Desktop Environment
ARP	Address Resolution Protocol	**CDLI**	Common Data Link Interface
ASCI	Accelerated Strategic Computing Initiative	**CD-R**	CD Recordable
		CD-ROM	Compact Disk-Read Only Memory
ASCII	American National Standards Code for Information Interchange	**CE**	Customer Engineer
		CEC	Central Electronics Complex
ASR	Address Space Register	**CFD**	Computational Fluid Dynamics
ATM	Asynchronous Transfer Mode		
AuditRM	Audit Log Resource Manager	**CGE**	Common Graphics Environment
AUI	Attached Unit Interface		
AWT	Abstract Window Toolkit	**CHRP**	Common Hardware Reference Platform
BCT	Branch on CounT		
BFF	Backup File Format	**CISPR**	International Special Committee on Radio Interference
BI	Business Intelligence		
BIND	Berkeley Internet Name Daemon	**CLIO/S**	Client Input/Output Sockets
		CLVM	Concurrent LVM
BIST	Built-In Self-Test	**CMOS**	Complimentary Metal-Oxide Semiconductor
BLAS	Basic Linear Algebra Subprograms		
		CMP	Certificate Management Protocol
BLOB	Binary Large Object		

COFF	Common Object File Format	DMA	Direct Memory Access
COLD	Computer Output to Laser Disk	DMT	Directory Management Tool
		DN	Distinguished Name
CORBA	Common Object Request Broker Architecture	DNS	Domain Naming System
		DOE	Department of Energy
CPU	Central Processing Unit	DOI	Domain of Interpretation
CRC	Cyclic Redundancy Check	DOS	Disk Operating System
CSID	Character Set ID	DPCL	Dynamic Probe Class Library
CSR	Customer Service Representative	DRAM	Dynamic Random Access Memory
CSS	Communication Subsystems Support	DS	Differentiated Service
CSU	Customer Set-Up	DSA	Dynamic Segment Allocation
CWS	Control Workstation	DSE	Diagnostic System Exerciser
DAD	Duplicate Address Detection	DSMIT	Distributed SMIT
DAS	Dual Attach Station	DSU	Data Service Unit
DASD	Direct Access Storage Device	DTE	Data Terminating Equipment
DAT	Digital Audio Tape	DW	Data Warehouse
DBCS	Double Byte Character Set	EA	Effective Address
DBE	Double Buffer Extension	EC	Engineering Change
DC	Direct Current	ECC	Error Checking and Correcting
DCE	Distributed Computing Environment	EEPROM	Electrically Erasable Programmable Read Only Memory
DDC	Display Data Channel		
DDS	Digital Data Storage	EFI	Extensible Firmware Interface
DE	Dual-Ended	EHD	Extended Hardware Drivers
DES	Data Encryption Standard	EIA	Electronic Industries Association
DFL	Divide Float		
DFP	Dynamic Feedback Protocol	EISA	Extended Industry Standard Architecture
DFS	Distributed File System		
DHCP	Dynamic Host Configuration Protocol	ELA	Error Log Analysis
		ELF	Executable and Linking Format
DIMM	Dual In-Line Memory Module		
DIP	Direct Insertion Probe	EMU	European Monetary Union
DIT	Directory Information Tree	EOF	End of File
DIVA	Digital Inquiry Voice Answer	EPOW	Environmental and Power Warning
DLT	Digital Linear Tape		

ERRM	Event Response resource manager	GAMESS	General Atomic and Molecular Electronic Structure System
ESID	Effective Segment ID		
ESP	Encapsulating Security Payload	GPFS	General Parallel File System
		GPR	General-Purpose Register
ESSL	Engineering and Scientific Subroutine Library	GUI	Graphical User Interface
		GUID	Globally Unique Identifier
ETML	Extract, Transformation, Movement, and Loading	HACMP	High Availability Cluster Multi Processing
F/C	Feature Code	HACWS	High Availability Control Workstation
F/W	Fast and Wide		
FC	Fibre Channel	HCON	IBM AIX Host Connection Program/6000
FCAL	Fibre Channel Arbitrated Loop		
FCC	Federal Communication Commission	HDX	Half Duplex
		HFT	High Function Terminal
FCP	Fibre Channel Protocol	HIPPI	High Performance Parallel Interface
FDDI	Fiber Distributed Data Interface	HiPS	High Performance Switch
FDPR	Feedback Directed Program Restructuring	HiPS LC-8	Low-Cost Eight-Port High Performance Switch
FDX	Full Duplex	HostRM	Host Resource Manager
FIFO	First In/First Out	HPF	High Performance FORTRAN
FLASH EPROM	Flash Erasable Programmable Read-Only Memory	HPSSDL	High Performance Supercomputer Systems Development Laboratory
FLIH	First Level Interrupt Handler	HTTP	Hypertext Transfer Protocol
FMA	Floating point Multiply Add operation	Hz	Hertz
		I/O	Input/Output
FPR	Floating Point Register	I^2C	Inter Integrated-Circuit Communications
FPU	Floating Point Unit		
FRCA	Fast Response Cache Architecture	IAR	Instruction Address Register
		IBM	International Business Machines
FRU	Field Replaceable Unit		
FSRM	File System Resource Manager	ICCCM	Inter-Client Communications Conventions Manual
FTP	File Transfer Protocol	ICE	Inter-Client Exchange
GAI	Graphic Adapter Interface	ICElib	Inter-Client Exchange library
		ICMP	Internet Control Message Protocol

ID	Identification	**ISO**	International Organization for Standardization
IDE	Integrated Device Electronics	**ISV**	Independent Software Vendor
IDS	Intelligent Decision Server	**ITSO**	International Technical Support Organization
IEEE	Institute of Electrical and Electronics Engineers	**JBOD**	Just a Bunch of Disks
IETF	Internet Engineering Task Force	**JDBC**	Java Database Connectivity
IHV	Independent Hardware Vendor	**JFC**	Java Foundation Classes
IIOP	Internet Inter-ORB Protocol	**JFS**	Journaled File System
IJG	Independent JPEG Group	**JTAG**	Joint Test Action Group
IKE	Internet Key Exchange	**KDC**	Key Distribution Center
ILS	International Language Support	**L1**	Level 1
		L2	Level 2
IM	Input Method	**L3**	Level 3
INRIA	Institut National de Recherche en Informatique et en Automatique	**LAN**	Local Area Network
		LANE	Local Area Network Emulation
IP	Internetwork Protocol (OSI)	**LAPI**	Low-Level Application Programming Interface
IPL	Initial Program Load	**LDAP**	Lightweight Directory Access Protocol
IPSec	IP Security		
IrDA	Infrared Data Association (which sets standards for infrared support including protocols for data interchange)	**LDIF**	LDAP Directory Interchange Format
		LED	Light Emitting Diode
		LFD	Load Float Double
IRQ	Interrupt Request	**LFT**	Low Function Terminal
IS	Integrated Service	**LID**	Load ID
ISA	Industry Standard Architecture, Instruction Set Architecture	**LLNL**	Lawrence Livermore National Laboratory
		LP	Logical Partition
ISAKMP	Internet Security Association Management Protocol	**LP64**	Long-Pointer 64
		LPI	Lines Per Inch
ISB	Intermediate Switch Board	**LPP**	Licensed Program Product
ISDN	Integrated-Services Digital Network	**LPR/LPD**	Line Printer/Line Printer Daemon
ISMP	InstallSheild Multi-Platform	**LRU**	Least Recently Used
ISNO	Interface Specific Network Options	**LTG**	Logical Track Group
		LV	Logical Volume

LVCB	Logical Volume Control Block	NBC	Network Buffer Cache
LVD	Low Voltage Differential	NCP	Network Control Point
LVM	Logical Volume Manager	ND	Neighbor Discovery
MAP	Maintenance Analysis Procedure	NDP	Neighbor Discovery Protocol
		NFB	No Frame Buffer
MASS	Mathematical Acceleration Subsystem	NFS	Network File System
MAU	Multiple Access Unit	NHRP	Next Hop Resolution Protocol
MBCS	Multi-Byte Character Support	NIM	Network Installation Management
Mbps	Megabits Per Second	NIS	Network Information System
MBps	Megabytes Per Second	NL	National Language
MCA	Micro Channel Architecture	NLS	National Language Support
MCAD	Mechanical Computer-Aided Design	NT-1	Network Terminator-1
		NTF	No Trouble Found
MDI	Media Dependent Interface	NTP	Network Time Protocol
MES	Miscellaneous Equipment Specification	NUMA	Non-Uniform Memory Access
MFLOPS	Million of FLoating point Operations Per Second	NUS	Numerical Aerodynamic Simulation
MII	Media Independent Interface	NVRAM	Non-Volatile Random Access Memory
MIP	Mixed-Integer Programming	NWP	Numerical Weather Prediction
MLR1	Multi-Channel Linear Recording 1	OACK	Option Acknowledgment
MMF	Multi-Mode Fibre	OCS	Online Customer Support
MODS	Memory Overlay Detection Subsystem	ODBC	Open DataBase Connectivity
		ODM	Object Data Manager
MP	Multiprocessor	OEM	Original Equipment Manufacturer
MPC-3	Multimedia PC-3		
MPI	Message Passing Interface	OLAP	Online Analytical Processing
MPOA	Multiprotocol over ATM	OLTP	Online Transaction Processing
MPP	Massively Parallel Processing		
MPS	Mathematical Programming System	ONC+	Open Network Computing
		OOUI	Object-Oriented User Interface
MST	Machine State	OSF	Open Software Foundation, Inc.
MTU	Maximum Transmission Unit		
MWCC	Mirror Write Consistency Check	OSL	Optimization Subroutine Library
MX	Mezzanine Bus		

OSLp	Parallel Optimization Subroutine Library	PPP	Point-to-Point Protocol
P2SC	POWER2 Single/Super Chip	PREP	PowerPC Reference Platform
PAM	Pluggable Authentication Mechanism	PSE	Portable Streams Environment
PAP	Privileged Access Password	PSSP	Parallel System Support Program
PBLAS	Parallel Basic Linear Algebra Subprograms	PTF	Program Temporary Fix
PCI	Peripheral Component Interconnect	PTPE	Performance Toolbox Parallel Extensions
PDT	Paging Device Table	PV	Physical Volume
PDU	Power Distribution Unit	PVC	Permanent Virtual Circuit
PE	Parallel Environment	QoS	Quality of Service
PEDB	Parallel Environment Debugging	QP	Quadratic Programming
PEX	PHIGS Extension to X	RAID	Redundant Array of Independent Disks
PFS	Perfect Forward Security	RAM	Random Access Memory
PGID	Process Group ID	RAN	Remote Asynchronous Node
PHB	Processor Host Bridges	RAS	Reliability, Availability, and Serviceability
PHY	Physical Layer	RDB	Relational DataBase
PID	Process ID	RDBMS	Relational Database Management System
PII	Program Integrated Information	RDISC	ICMP Router Discovery
PIOFS	Parallel Input Output File System	RDN	Relative Distinguished Name
PKR	Protection Key Registers	RDP	Router Discovery Protocol
PMTU	Path MTU	RFC	Request for Comments
POE	Parallel Operating Environment	RIO	Remote I/O
POP	Power-On Password	RIP	Routing Information Protocol
POSIX	Portable Operating Interface for Computing Environments	RIPL	Remote Initial Program Load
POST	Power-On Self-test	RISC	Reduced Instruction-Set Computer
POWER	Performance Optimization with Enhanced Risc (Architecture)	RMC	Resource Monitoring and Control
PPC	PowerPC	ROLTP	Relative Online Transaction Processing
PPM	Piecewise Parabolic Method	RPA	RS/6000 Platform Architecture

RPA	RS/6000 Platform Architecture	**SHLAP**	Shared Library Assistant Process
RPC	Remote Procedure Call	**SID**	Segment ID
RPL	Remote Program Loader	**SIT**	Simple Internet Transition
RPM	Red Hat Package Manager	**SKIP**	Simple Key Management for IP
RSC	RISC Single Chip		
RSCT	Reliable Scalable Cluster Technology	**SLB**	Segment Lookaside Buffer
		SLIH	Second Level Interrupt Handler
RSE	Register Stack Engine		
RSVP	Resource Reservation Protocol	**SLIP**	Serial Line Internet Protocol
		SLR1	Single-Channel Linear Recording 1
RTC	Real-Time Clock		
RVSD	Recoverable Virtual Shared Disk	**SM**	Session Management
		SMB	Server Message Block
SA	Secure Association	**SMIT**	System Management Interface Tool
SACK	Selective Acknowledgments		
SAN	Storage Area Network	**SMP**	Symmetric Multiprocessor
SAR	Solutions Assurance Review	**SMS**	System Management Services
SAS	Single Attach Station		
SBCS	Single-Byte Character Support	**SNG**	Secured Network Gateway
		SOI	Silicon-on-Insulator
ScaLAPACK	Scalable Linear Algebra Package	**SP**	IBM RS/6000 Scalable POWER parallel Systems
SCB	Segment Control Block	**SPCN**	System Power Control Network
SCO	Santa Cruz Operations		
SCSI	Small Computer System Interface	**SPEC**	System Performance Evaluation Cooperative
		SPI	Security Parameter Index
SCSI-SE	SCSI-Single Ended	**SPM**	System Performance Measurement
SDLC	Synchronous Data Link Control		
		SPOT	Shared Product Object Tree
SDR	System Data Repository	**SPS**	SP Switch
SDRAM	Synchronous Dynamic Random Access Memory	**SPS-8**	Eight-Port SP Switch
		SRC	System Resource Controller
SE	Single Ended	**SRN**	Service Request Number
SEPBU	Scalable Electrical Power Base Unit	**SSA**	Serial Storage Architecture
SGI	Silicon Graphics Incorporated	**SSC**	System Support Controller
SGID	Set Group ID	**SSL**	Secure Socket Layer

STFDU	Store Float Double with Update	**VESA**	Video Electronics Standards Association
STP	Shielded Twisted Pair	**VFB**	Virtual Frame Buffer
SUID	Set User ID	**VG**	Volume Group
SUP	Software Update Protocol	**VGDA**	Volume Group Descriptor Area
SVC	Switch Virtual Circuit		
SVC	Supervisor or System Call	**VGSA**	Volume Group Status Area
SWVPD	Software Vital Product Data	**VHDCI**	Very High Density Cable Interconnect
SYNC	Synchronization		
TCE	Translate Control Entry	**VLAN**	Virtual Local Area Network
Tcl	Tool Command Language	**VMM**	Virtual Memory Manager
TCP/IP	Transmission Control Protocol/Internet Protocol	**VP**	Virtual Processor
		VPD	Vital Product Data
TCQ	Tagged Command Queuing	**VPN**	Virtual Private Network
TGT	Ticket Granting Ticket	**VSD**	Virtual Shared Disk
TLB	Translation Lookaside Buffer	**VT**	Visualization Tool
TOS	Type Of Service	**WAN**	Wide Area Network
TPC	Transaction Processing Council	**WLM**	Workload Manager
		WTE	Web Traffic Express
TPP	Toward Peak Performance	**XCOFF**	Extended Common Object File Format
TSE	Text Search Engine		
TTL	Time To Live	**XIE**	X Image Extension
UCS	Universal Coded Character Set	**XIM**	X Input Method
		XKB	X Keyboard Extension
UDB EEE	Universal Database and Enterprise Extended Edition	**XLF**	XL Fortran
		XOM	X Output Method
UDI	Uniform Device Interface	**XPM**	X Pixmap
UIL	User Interface Language	**XSSO**	Open Single Sign-on Service
ULS	Universal Language Support	**XTF**	Extended Distance Feature
UP	Uniprocessor	**XVFB**	X Virtual Frame Buffer
USB	Universal Serial Bus		
USLA	User-Space Loader Assistant		
UTF	UCS Transformation Format		
UTM	Uniform Transfer Model		
UTP	Unshielded Twisted Pair		
UUCP	UNIX-to-UNIX Communication Protocol		

Index